The LAST EXPEDITION

DANIEL LIEBOWITZ IS THE AUTHOR OF

The Physician and the Slave Trade:
John Kirk, the Livingstone Expeditions, and
the Crusade against Slavery in East Africa

The LAST EXPEDITION

DANIEL LIEBOWITZ *and* CHARLIE PEARSON

Stanley's
fatal journey
through
the Congo

PORTRAIT

Visit the Portrait website!

· ·

PORTRAIT

Portrait publishes a wide range of non-fiction, including biography, history, science, music, popular culture and sport.

Visit our website to:
- read descriptions of our popular titles
- buy our books over the internet
- take advantage of our special offers
- enter our monthly competition
- learn more about your favourite Portrait authors

VISIT OUR WEBSITE AT: www.portraitbooks.com

First published in the USA in 2005 by W.W. Norton & Company, Inc.

First published in Great Britain in 2005 by
Piatkus Books Ltd
5 Windmill Street
London W1T 2JA
e-mail: info@piatkus.co.uk

The moral right of the author has been asserted

*A catalogue record for this book is
available from the British Library*

ISBN 0 7499 5063 3 hb
ISBN 0 7499 5086 2 pb

Book design by Charlotte Staub

Data manipulation by Phoenix Photosetting, Chatham, Kent
Printed and bound in Great Britain by
MPG Books, Bodmin, Cornwall

DEDICATIONS

To Florence—DL

To Lynette, of course—CP

Contents

A Note on Quotations

WHENEVER POSSIBLE, we have reproduced quotations from journals, diaries, books, and other accounts by the participants in the Emin Pasha Relief Expedition exactly as they appeared when originally published, leaving misspellings, grammatical errors, and tortured syntax as we found them. Hence the occasional odd phrasing, missing word, or archaic terminology, as well as variations in the spelling of names of people and places.

Who's Who

Muhammad Ahmed— Sudanese boat builder who, in 1883, declared himself the Mahdi, or Expected One. Leader of the Sudanese rebellion and jihad that effectively ended Egypt's sovereignty over Sudan, isolated Emin Pasha, and ultimately provoked the Emin Pasha Relief Expedition.

Muhammad Ali —Egyptian khedive (viceroy) from 1805 to 1848. During his reign, Egypt annexed Sudan (1820).

Sir Samuel Baker—British explorer and adventurer. His expedition in 1869, commissioned by Ismail, Muhammad Ali's grandson, expanded the territory of Sudan to include the new province of Equatoria.

Barghash —Sultan of Zanzibar when Baker's expedition began.

Major Edmund Musgrave Barttelot—Regular Army, 7th Fusiliers, Stanley's second in command for the Emin Pasha Relief Expedition.

Selim Bey—Commander of Emin's garrison at Laboré, an Emin loyalist.

William Bonny—Sergeant, Army Medical Corps, member of the Emin Psha Relief Expedition.

Bula Matari—Stanley's African nickname.

Gaetano Casati—Italian traveler in Africa, companion, occasional envoy, and chronicler of Emin Pasha.

Farida—Emin's daughter, whose Abyssinian mother died from complications of a subsequent childbirth when Farida was only two.

Robert Felkin—Scottish physician, African explorer and abolitionist, friend and correspondent of Emin Pasha.

William Gladstone—Prime Minister of England at the time of the Mahdist uprising.

Charles Gordon—British solider and diplomat, Governor of Equatoria, Governor-General of Sudan, martyr of Khartoum

James Grant and John Speke—British explorers of Africa, discoverers of the source of the White Nile. Grant was also a member of the Emin Pasha Relief Committee.

Hamad Aga—an officer in Equatoria's rebellious First Battalion who remained an Emin loyalist.

Vita Hassan—a Tunisian apothecary who was part of Emin Pasha's retinue.

Hawash Effendi—station chief at Dufilé, Commander of Emin's Second Battalion, loyal to Emin and trusted by him, but despised by many of his other officers.

Frederick Holmwood—acting British Consul-General in Zanzibar in 1887, when the Emin Pasha Relief Expedition was launched.

Ismaili, Khamisi, and Sangarameni—Kilonga-longa's Manyuema sub-chiefs at Ipoto; tormentors of Parke, Nelson, and other members of the expedition left behind by Stanley.

James Sligo Jameson—gentleman volunteer to the Emin Pasha Relief Expedition.

Arthur Jeremy Mounteney Jephson—gentleman volunteer to the Emin Pasha Relief Expedition.

Wilhelm Junker—Russo-German explorer and scientist, friend and colleague of Emin Pasha. He brought news of Emin's predicament to the outside world in 1886.

Kabba Rega—ruler of Unyoro, the territory immediately southeast of Equatoria, often in conflict with both Emin and with neighboring Uganda.

Kavalli—chief of the settlement where Stanley made camp while awaiting the return of Jephson and Emin prior to the final evacuation of Equatoria.

John Kirk—British physician and explorer, Consul-General to the Sultanate of Zanzibar, architect of the abolition of slavery in east Africa.

Kodi Aga—Emin's station chief at his headquarters at Wadelai.

Karamallah Kurquwasi—the Mahdi's second-in-command and successor as leader of the Mahdist rebellion.

Kilonga-longa—Arab slaver and ivory hunter in whose jungle camp at Ipoto Stanley was forced to leave Nelson, Parke, and other members of the expedition.

King Leopold II—Monarch of Belgium, sovereign of the Congo Free State, employer of Henry Stanley and Tippu Tib, relentless imperialist, exploiter of Africa and Africans.

Alexander Mackay—Scottish missionary in Uganda, friend to Emin Pasha, host to the expedition, staunch Imperialist.

William Mackinnon—Scottish shipping magnate, founder and chair of the Emin Pasha Relief Committee, President of the Imperial British East Africa Company (IBEAC).

Achmet Mahmoud—Egyptian clerk, co-conspirator in the rebellion against Emin Pasha.

Mazamboni—African chieftain whose hospitality greatly aided the expedition.

Fadl el Mulla—a leader of the rebellion against Emin.

Mutesa—King of Uganda, archrival of Kabba Rega.

Mwanga—Mutesa's son and successor on the Ugandan throne.

Captain Rupert Nelson—Regular Army, Metheun's Horse, third officer of the Emin Pasha Relief Expedition.

Thomas Heazle Parke—Major, Army Medical Corps, expedition medical officer.

Carl Peters—German explorer of Africa and ardent imperialist. Often called "the German Stanley."

John Rowlands—Henry Stanley's given name.

Robert Salisbury—British Prime Minister, William Gladstone's successor.

Sanga—the Manyuema porter who shot Major Barttelot.

Lieutenant Rochas Schmidt—ranking officer at the German military installation at Mpwapwa, who hosted the expedition as it neared the end of its trek.

Eduard Schnitzer—Emin Pasha's given name.

George Schweinfurth—German scientist and explorer of Africa, who corresponded extensively with Emin Pasha.

Shukri Aga—Commander of M'swa, southernmost of Emin's stations on Lake Albert, an Emin loyalist.

Muni Somai—Arab "headman" hired by Barttelot to command the Manyuema porters when the Rear Column left Yambuya.

Lieutenant William G. Stairs—Regular Army, Royal Engineers, the first man selected by Stanley for the Emin Pasha Relief Expedition.

Henry Hope Stanley—New Orleans cotton broker who took John Rowlands under his wing and from whom Stanley borrowed his name.

Henry Morton Stanley—leader of the Emin Pasha Relief Expedition.

Suleiman Aga—Commander of Emin's station at Tunguru, on Lake Albert.

Tippu Tib—the most notorious slaver and ivory hunter in central Africa, appointed by King Leopold II to be governor of the Stanley Falls district of the Congo Free State; nemesis of Henry Stanley.

John Rose Troup—member of the Emin Pasha Relief Expedition.

Ugarrowa—Arab slaver and ivory hunter whose settlement in the Ituri forest provided a temporary haven for the expedition.

Uledi—Zanzibari porter, coxswain of the *Advance*, veteran of previous Stanley expeditions.

Adbul Wahab—Egyptian officer, co-conspirator with Achmet Mahmoud, a primary instigator of the rebellion against Emin Pasha.

John Walker—engineer taken on in Cape Town to assist with the Congo River fleet that transported the expedition to Yambuya.

Herbert Ward—English adventurer who joined the expedition after it reached the Congo.

Sir Francis de Winton—successor to Stanley as chief administrator of the Congo Free State, member of the Emin Pasha Relief Committee.

Herr Von Wissman—Commander of the German garrison at Bagamoyo.

Prologue

THE FOREST

"Avisibba," the woman said. They thought she was telling them the name of the village, but they couldn't be sure. None of the interpreters or porters could decipher her language. They had captured her during a foraging expedition two days earlier and kept her with them in hopes that she could show them a shortcut around the next set of rapids.

Avisibba turned out to be a collection of small settlements perched at the river's edge. Stanley arrived first in the *Advance,* the 28-foot steel boat he'd had built especially for the expedition, followed by a flotilla of fourteen dugout canoes. The rest of the men were on foot, more than three hundred of them, hacking their way slowly through the forest. They straggled in throughout the afternoon, Captain Nelson and Major Parke, the expedition's surgeon, bringing in the last of the line around four. The temperature still hovered near ninety degrees, with humidity to match.

The natives waited until everyone was in camp before they attacked.

It was hard to say how many there were, perhaps a hundred, perhaps twice that many, darting in and out of the shadows and bushes on the opposite bank, loosing fusillades of tiny arrows across the river. Most of the arrows fell harmlessly to the ground, but not all. Before they could return fire, half a dozen men were hit, including Lieutenant Stairs, who was shot in the left breast, just below the heart. Surgeon Parke reached him quickly, but he was already very pale, though he didn't seem to be bleeding very much. The young Canadian, usually so stoic, was screaming in pain and gasping for breath.

The arrow, no more than two feet long, had broken off, the tip lodged beneath his ribs. Parke probed and dug, but the needle-like point was in too deep to be retrieved. Then he noticed the foul odor coming from the wound. Poison. The Zanzibari porters said the stuff was strong enough to kill an elephant. Parke had no choice. He held his breath and began sucking around the edges of the wound, which was no bigger than the point of a knitting needle, filling his mouth with blood and a sickening, tarry paste, then spitting and rinsing his mouth with a solution of carbolic acid. He kept at it until his mouth was filled only with blood. By the time he finished dressing the wound, Stairs was close to going into shock. Parke gave him an injection of morphine and had him carried back to camp.

AUGUST 14

Stanley announced that they would rest for one day. A scouting party crossed the river and retrieved an enemy corpse and weapons. The corpse confirmed what Stanley had suspected from the size of the arrows. Pygmies. The dead man was scarcely four feet tall. He wore a necklace made of human teeth and was utterly naked. The arrows in his quiver were only eighteen inches long, with leaves instead of feathers to guide the flight. The bow was barely two feet long, but its power was remarkable. Stanley fired an arrow that went clean through a saddle flap from twenty yards. The points had been fire hardened, then coated with a thick black tar and notched a few inches from the tips so that the points would break off easily inside a victim, as poor Stairs had discovered, ensuring that the poison could do its lethal work.

Stairs's night was sleepless and painful, with every breath a struggle. At first light, Major Parke was moderately encouraged when Stairs's temperature was only 100 degrees. It soon started climbing, however, and his pain got worse.

Stanley sent out a foraging party of two hundred men, but when they returned after several hours, they brought only plantains, and not nearly enough of them to feed everyone. Amid all their other problems, finding enough to eat was rapidly becoming the most urgent.

AUGUST 15

Stanley ordered everyone back to the river and the trail, though the trail would exist only after they created it with their axes and bill-hooks. Stairs was loaded into the *Advance*. Remarkably, his tempera-ture had returned to normal, and he even insisted on walking from his tent to the boat, but Parke feared that the worst might be yet to come. Unless the poisoned arrow point was spontaneously expelled—and soon—he couldn't be very optimistic.

Jephson led the overland contingent, followed by Parke and then Captain Nelson. No sooner had they moved out than the rain came, heavy and relentless. It would last all day.

The river contingent, with Stanley in command, consisted of thirty-nine canoe men and boatmen. They ferried the wounded, who now numbered nine, after two more brief skirmishes with the pygmies the preceding day, and twenty-nine porters who were too sick to walk, let alone carry their loads. They were suffering from dysentery, pleurisy, and various other debilities, not the least of which were exhaustion and starvation.

The plan was for the river group to row upstream until it encoun-tered the next rapids. Jephson and the land contingent were to cut through the forest and rendezvous with them at the foot of the rapids. They would then make a portage around the rapids and continue on. The native woman captured below Avisibba was to be Jephson's guide.

The rain reduced visibility to a matter of meters, so Jephson had no idea how far the overland column stretched out; it could be more than three miles from the point man to the rear guard. He soon realized they wouldn't make the river rendezvous with Stanley before nightfall. As the light began to fail, his forward company encountered a series of camouflaged traps, cavernous pits, some as deep as twelve feet, their bottoms lined with sharpened stakes to impale whatever or whoever fell in. They were almost undetectable from even a few feet away. That night Jephson, using torches improvised from dried stalks, made his way back along the trail to warn Nelson and Parke of the danger.

Despite the driving rain, Stanley reached the foot of the rapids by midafternoon. Rain or not, he still expected the land contingent before nightfall. At dusk, with no sign of them, Stanley ordered shots fired, the standard signal when elements of the expedition became separated. There was no answer.

AUGUST 16

The land party stumbled on, crossing streams and small rivers, some so deep and swift that temporary bridges had to be improvised. The treacherous footing made the porters slip and fall, spilling their loads, slowing them even more. At one point, Jephson became convinced that their guide was leading them in a huge circle, whether by accident or by design. Major Parke grew increasingly worried about the sick and wounded men, who had been without care for more than twenty-four hours. Stanley, for all his skills and experience, wasn't much of a medic.

Still at the base of the rapids and now genuinely alarmed, Stanley sent out search parties in three directions. They returned after dark, having found no trace of the missing column.

AUGUST 17

From Parke's journal: "Things now look very serious; we are simply lost in the forest, with the great bulk of the Expedition and *there is no food whatsoever*."

AUGUST 18

The land column marched for twelve hours, most of it in the rain. Before noon, six men collapsed on the trail and had to be carried, their loads apportioned out, amid much grumbling, to their colleagues. Parke noted in his journal that the Zanzibaris were particularly unsuited to the rain and cold, because they had never experienced such harsh conditions on their native island. That afternoon, one of the men who had collapsed died. Parke listed the cause as "exposure." He could as easily have written "starvation."

In his river camp, after yet another day of rain and waiting, Stanley confided to his diary, "One is almost tempted to think that the end is approaching. The very 'flood gates of heaven' seem opened, and nature is dissolving."

After forty-eight hours of agony, Maruf, one of the Zanzibaris wounded in the same skirmish as Stairs, died of tetanus-like symptoms. Another of the wounded men was showing similar symptoms— stiff neck, headaches, throat constrictions, and spasms. Stairs was terrified. Where was Major Parke?

On February 24, 1887, the day before he left Zanzibar, Henry Stanley, commander of the Emin Pasha Relief Expedition, had written a letter to the man he was going to rescue. In it, he announced, among other things, his expected schedule. After journeying up the Congo River to a base camp at Yambuya, which would take, at most four months, he anticipated the crossing of the Ituri forest to take fifty days, maximum. That would bring the expedition to Lake Albert and its rendezvous with Emin Pasha no later than the end of August 1887.

On August 18, 1887, with more than two-thirds of the forest still in front of him, Stanley wrote in his diary, "A few days ago I was chief of 370 men, rich in goods, munitions of war, medicines, and contented with such poor comforts as we had, and today, I have actually only eighteen men left fit for a day's march. The rest have vanished."

The rain continued for three more days.

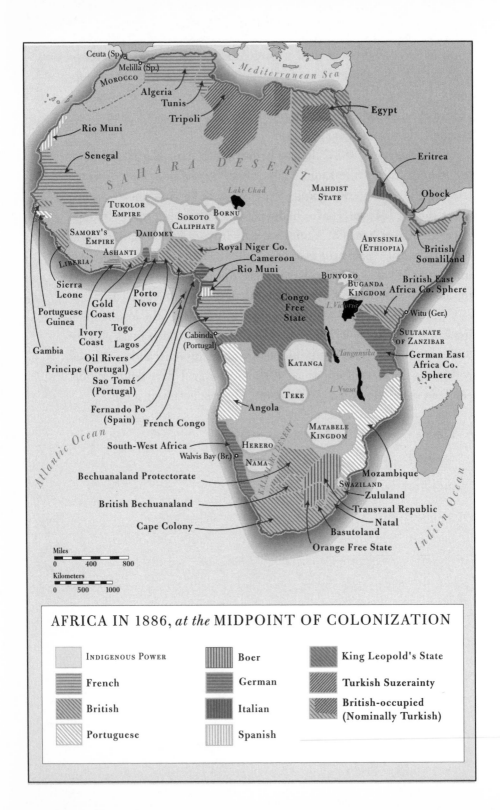

Ceuta (Sp.)
Melilla (Sp.)
MOROCCO
Algeria
Tunis
Tripoli
Rio Muni
Senegal

Mediterranean Sea

Egypt

Eritrea

Obock

SAHARA DESERT

Lake Chad

MAHDIST STATE

TUKOLOR EMPIRE
SOKOTO CALIPHATE
BORNU
BURNU

SAMORY'S EMPIRE
DAHOMEY
ASHANTI
LIBERIA
Sierra Leone
Portuguese Guinea
Gambia
Gold Coast
Ivory Coast
Togo
Porto Novo
Lagos
Oil Rivers
Principe (Portugal)
Sao Tomé (Portugal)
Fernando Po (Spain)
French Congo

Royal Niger Co.
Cameroon
Rio Muni
Cabinda (Portugal)

Congo Free State

ABYSSINIA (ETHIOPIA)

British Somaliland

BUNYORO
BUGANDA KINGDOM
L. Victoria

British East Africa Co. Sphere

Witu (Ger.)

SULTANATE OF ZANZIBAR

German East Africa Co. Sphere

Tanganyika

KATANGA

TEKE
L. Nyasa

Angola

MATABELE KINGDOM

South-West Africa
Walvis Bay (Br.)
HERERO
NAMA

Bechuanaland Protectorate

British Bechuanaland

Cape Colony

KALAHARI DESERT

Mozambique
SWAZILAND
Zululand
Transvaal Republic
Natal
Basutoland
Orange Free State

Atlantic Ocean

Indian Ocean

Miles
0   400   800

Kilometers
0   500   1000

AFRICA IN 1886, *at the* MIDPOINT OF COLONIZATION

INDIGENOUS POWER	Boer	King Leopold's State
French	German	Turkish Suzerainty
British	Italian	British-occupied (Nominally Turkish)
Portuguese	Spanish	

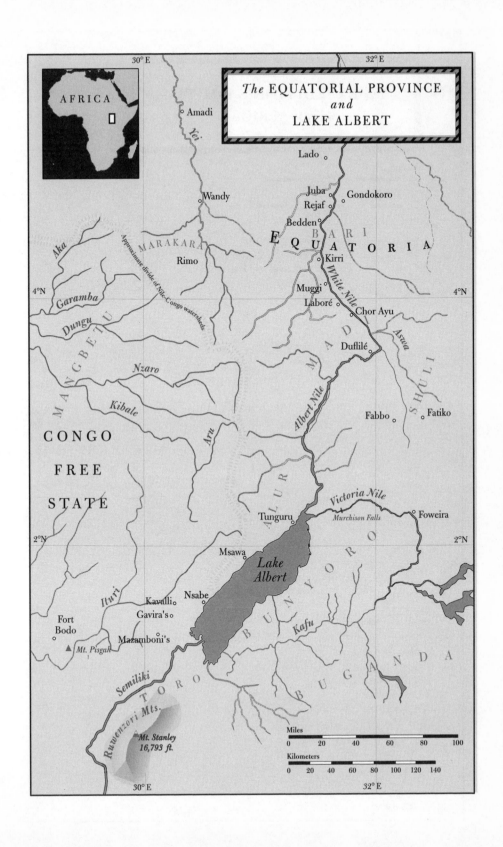

AFRICA

The EQUATORIAL PROVINCE
and
LAKE ALBERT

30° E
32° E

Amadi
Yei
Lado
Wandy
Juba
Gondokoro
Rejaf
Bedden
E Q U A T O R I A
B A R I
MARAKARA
Aka
Rimo
Kirri
Garamba
4°N
Muggi
Laboré
Chor Ayu
White Nile
Dungu
M A D
Duflilé
Aswa
Approximate divide of Nile-Congo watershed
Nzaro
S H U L I
Kibale
M A N G B E T U
Fabbo
Fatiko
Albert Nile
Aru
CONGO
A L U R
FREE
Victoria Nile
STATE
Tunguru
Murchison Falls
Foweira
2°N
Msawa
Lake
Albert
B U N Y O R O
Kavalli
Nsabe
Gavira's
Ituri
Kafu
Fort
Bodo
Mazamboni's
Mt. Pisgah
Semiliki
T O R O
B U G A N D A
Ruwenzori Mts.
Mt. Stanley
16,793 ft.

Miles
0   20   40   60   80   100

Kilometers
0   20   40   60   80   100   120   140

30° E
32° E

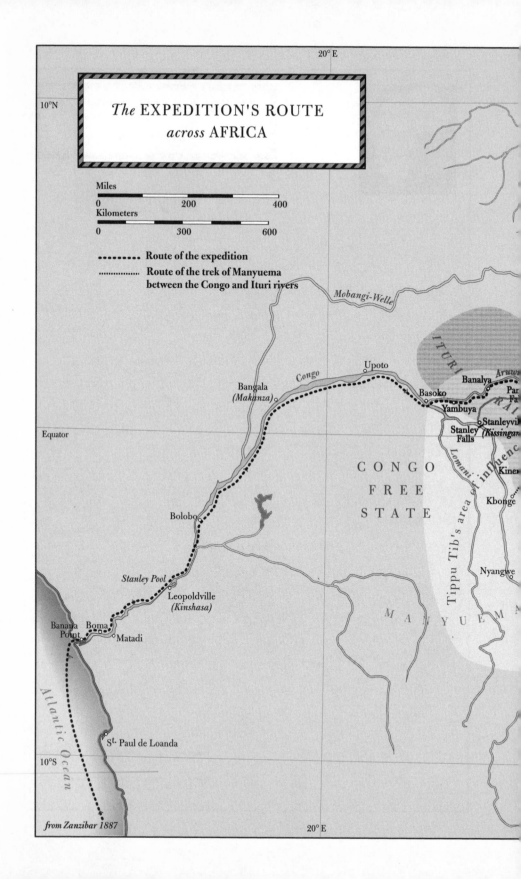

20° E

10°N

The EXPEDITION'S ROUTE
across AFRICA

Miles

0   200   400

Kilometers

0   300   600

••••••••• Route of the expedition

·············· Route of the trek of Manyuema
between the Congo and Ituri rivers

Mobangi-Welle

Upoto

Congo

Bangala
(Makanza)

Basoko   Banalya   *Aruwi*

Yambuya   Par
                       Fa

Stanleyvi
Stanley   *(Kissingan*
Falls

Equator

C O N G O   Kine

F R E E

S T A T E   Kbonge

Bolobo   Nyangwe

Stanley Pool

Leopoldville
(Kinshasa)   M A N Y U E M A

Banana Boma
Point
        Matadi

Atlantic Ocean

St. Paul de Loanda

10°S

from Zanzibar 1887   20° E

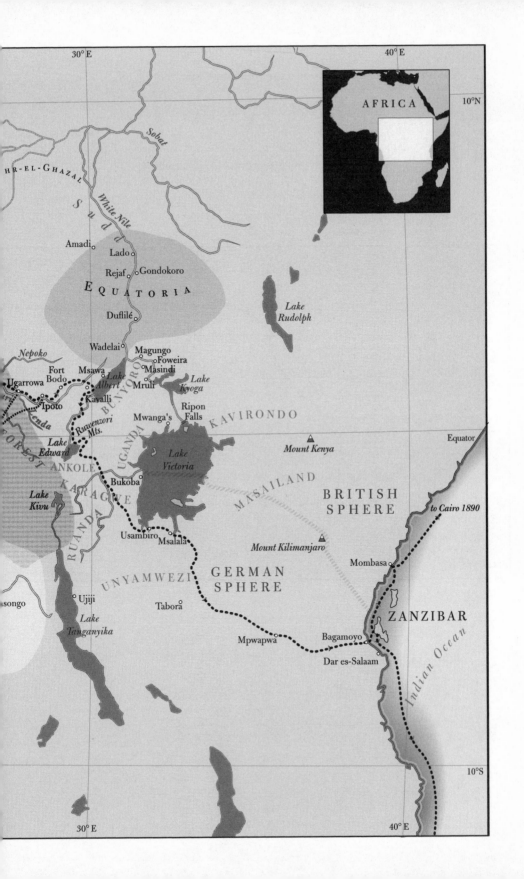

30° E

40° E

10°N

AFRICA

Sobat

HR-EL-GHAZAL

White Nile

S   u   d   d

Amadi

Lado

Rejaf   Gondokoro

E Q U A T O R I A

*Lake
Rudolph*

Duflilé

Nepoko

Wadelai

Magungo

Foweira

Masindi

Fort
Bodo

Msawa

*Lake
Albert*

Ugarrowa

Kavalli

Mruli

*Lake
Kyoga*

Ipoto

Ripon
Falls

*Ruwenzori
Mts.*

Mwanga's

KAVIRONDO

*Lake
Edward*

*Lake
Victoria*

Mount Kenya

Equator

ANKOLE

*Lake
Kivu*

Bukoba

BRITISH
SPHERE

to Cairo 1890

Usambiro

Msalala

Mount Kilimanjaro

Mombasa

UNYAMWEZI

GERMAN
SPHERE

ZANZIBAR

asongo

Ujiji

Tabora

*Lake
Tanganyika*

Mpwapwa

Bagamoyo

Indian Ocean

Dar es-Salaam

10°S

30° E

40° E

BUNYORO

UGANDA

KARAGWE

RUANDA

MASAILAND

FOREST

enda

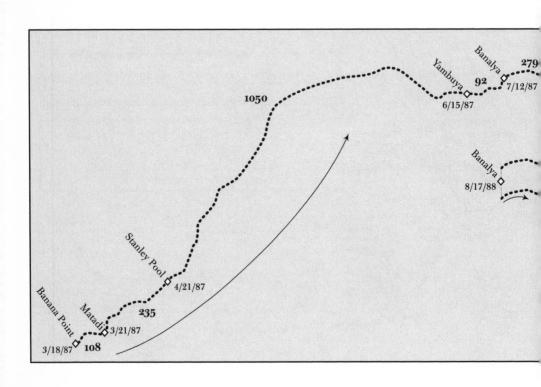

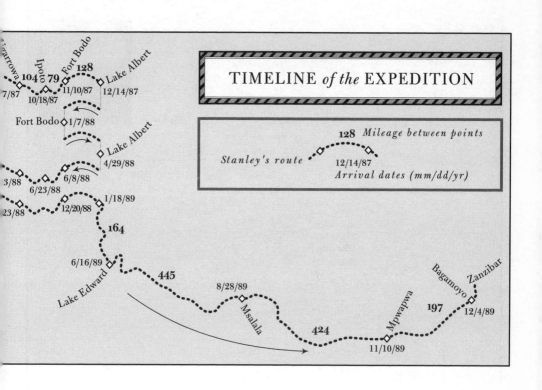

TIMELINE *of the* EXPEDITION

128 *Mileage between points*

Stanley's route ....◇......◇
12/14/87
Arrival dates (mm/dd/yr)

Yarrowa ...◇ 104 ◇ Ipoto 79 ◇ Fort Bodo 128 ◇ Lake Albert
7/87   10/18/87   11/10/87   12/14/87

Fort Bodo ◇ 1/7/88

◇ Lake Albert
4/29/88

3/88 ◇   6/23/88 ◇   6/8/88 ◇
23/88 ◇   12/20/88 ◇   1/18/89 ◇

164

6/16/89 ◇
Lake Edward   445

8/28/89 ◇
Msalala

424
11/10/89 ◇

Mpwapwa ◇   197   Bagamoyo ◇ Zanzibar ◇
                              12/4/89

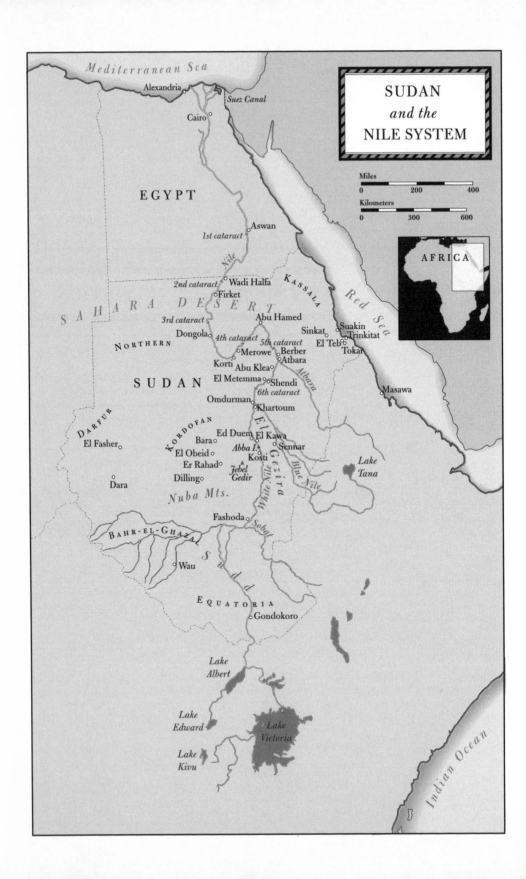

SUDAN
and the
NILE SYSTEM

Miles
0   200   400

Kilometers
0   300   600

AFRICA

Mediterranean Sea

Alexandria
Suez Canal
Cairo

EGYPT

Aswan
1st cataract

Nile

2nd cataract Wadi Halfa
Firket

KASSALA

Red Sea

S A H A R A   D E S E R T

3rd cataract
Dongola   Abu Hamed
4th cataract   *5th cataract*   Sinkat   Suakin
NORTHERN   Merowe   Berber   El Teb   Trinkitat
Korti   Abu Klea   Atbara   Tokar
El Metemma   Shendi

S U D A N   *6th cataract*

Masawa

Omdurman   Khartoum

DARFUR

KORDOFAN   Ed Duem El Kawa
El Fasher   Bara   *Abba I.*   Sennar
El Obeid   Kosti
Er Rahad   *Jebel   Lake
Dara   Dilling   Gedir*   *Tana*

Gezira
White Nile
Blue Nile
Atbara

Nuba Mts.

Fashoda
Sobat

BAHR-EL-GHAZAL
Sudd

Wau

E Q U A T O R I A
Gondokoro

*Lake
Albert*

*Lake
Edward*   *Lake
Victoria*

*Lake
Kivu*

Indian Ocean

Part

ONE

Chapter One

GORDON'S LAST
LIEUTENANT

ON DECEMBER 10, 1886, a letter appeared in *The Times* of London in which Robert Felkin, a prominent Scottish physician who had traveled extensively in Africa, implored the people of Britain to rally to the cause of a man with a distinctly un-British name, Dr. Mehemet Emin. He was the governor of Equatoria, the southernmost province of Egyptian Sudan, in the heart of Africa. In the restrained, yet elegant, prose of the day, Felkin concluded his letter by commenting, "Emin Pasha is the noblest of Gordon's lieutenants. To remove [him] would be to deliver his province once more to barbarism and the slaver; to maintain him where he is and give him adequate support would be to plant a broad area of civilization in the very heart of Africa." It was the phrase "the noblest of Gordon's lieutenants" that stirred every patriotic heart in England and set in motion the most ambitious, most expensive, and, ultimately, most disastrous expedition in Anglo-African history.

It could be argued that this story starts way back in 1801, the year that a combined British and Turkish force managed to drive Napoleon out of Egypt. Thus began a period of British involvement in Egypt's political and economic affairs that persisted well into the twentieth century.

In the first half of the nineteenth century, however, Egypt was still nominally a part of the Ottoman Empire, though it operated largely as a sovereign state. Its autonomy was due, in large part, to the extraordinary abilities of a common soldier named Muhammad Ali, who was appointed Egypt's ruler, or khedive, in 1805. Muhammad Ali did many things during his forty-year reign, including undertaking massive political, educational, and social reforms, but he also had visions of a new Egyptian empire. To that end, in 1820 he successfully invaded and annexed Sudan, Egypt's southern neighbor. The Egyptians established a capital at Khartoum, where the Blue Nile and the White Nile are joined, and settled into the business of collecting usurious taxes from their Sudanese subjects and profiting handsomely by trading in the country's two most valuable commodities, ivory and slaves.

Unfortunately for Egypt, Muhammad Ali's successors, his sons Abbas and Said and grandson Ismail, lacked his abilities, if not his ambition. In 1856, Said granted the concession for the construction of the Suez Canal to a Frenchman named Ferdinand de Lesseps. By the time the canal was completed, in 1869, Ismail was on the throne. Like his grandfather, Ismail had visions, if not delusions of grandeur for his country, but his vision was to make Egypt a modern, European-style nation. However, the building of the canal and other expenditures* ordered by Ismail plunged the country deeply into debt, which was held largely by England and France.

Egypt's mounting fiscal troubles were the main reason for Ismail's appointment, also in 1869, of the British explorer, sportsman, and adventurer Sir Samuel Baker to head an expedition to expand the borders of Egyptian Sudan to the south and east. Ismail had two objec-

*This included the building of a beautiful new opera house and the commissioning of Giuseppe Verdi to write *Aïda,* to be premiered in the opera house to celebrate the canal's opening.

tives in sending Baker to the Sudan. The first was to bring the entire 3,000-mile length of the Nile under Egyptian control, something not even the greatest pharaohs had accomplished. The second was to increase the number of Sudanese subjects from whom he could collect taxes.

Baker was not a stranger to the Sudan, having explored the region in 1863, at the same time the famous expedition of James Grant and John Speke was establishing Lake Victoria as the source of the White Nile. Baker made a significant discovery of his own, finding a large lake some two hundred miles to the northwest of Lake Victoria. He named it Lake Albert.

To reach their destination, Baker and his force of one thousand Sudanese and Egyptian troops had first to negotiate the Sudd. To call the Sudd a swamp fails to do justice to a 30,000-square-mile thicket of free-floating vegetation, principally papyrus, so dense and impenetrable that it constitutes a semipermanent blockage of the mighty Nile. Baker attacked the Sudd with a fleet of small steamers and portable metal whaleboats. After three attempts and fifteen months, he finally got through.

Once free of the Sudd, Baker and his force, including a handpicked corps of shock troops he called the Forty Thieves, spent the next three years working their way south along the Upper Nile, using brute force to subdue the local tribes, doing battle with the Arab* slavers who were already well entrenched in the area in a largely futile attempt to suppress their thriving trade, and establishing a shaky sort of Egyptian sovereignty over the territory from Gondokoro to Lake Albert. But Lake Victoria and the headwaters of the Nile would remain beyond Baker's grasp, because between Lake Albert and Lake Victoria was the kingdom of Unyoro. Here Baker and his forces met such fierce resistance from the armies of the king, Kabba Rega, that they ultimately had to retreat.

---

*In this account, the term "Arab" refers to a group of Swahili-speaking people, often of mixed Arab and African blood, who lived in eastern and central Africa. Many, though not all of them, traced their origins to Zanzibar. In the areas where this story takes place, Arabs were the principal traders in ivory and slaves.

Nevertheless, when Baker left Africa in 1873, he had added a significant amount of territory to Egyptian Sudan and established three fortified stations along the Nile from which Ismail's authority over the new territory was to be maintained. He also gave the new province a name—Equatoria.

To consolidate the gains made by Baker, Ismail turned to Colonel Charles Gordon, the charismatic British military hero whose name would become more closely linked to the Sudan than that of any other European. During his three years as Equatoria's governor, Gordon dramatically expanded Egyptian authority. He tripled the number of government stations along the Nile, extending them to the northern edge of Lake Albert, spacing them so that they were within a day's march or steamer ride of each other, thereby vastly improving communication within the province. He encouraged each station to be self-sufficient, had all of them plant grains and other crops to sustain themselves, and thereby curtailed the practice of raids against local tribes for food and supplies. Not surprisingly, this policy improved relations with the natives. Like Baker, however, Gordon was frustrated in his attempts to extend the boundaries of Equatoria to Lake Victoria. In fact, it was in conjunction with a failed attempt to establish a station closer to Lake Victoria that he first made the acquaintance of an eccentric physician named Dr. Mehemet Emin.

Mehemet Emin arrived in Khartoum in December 1875. Though he affected the dress and manner of a Turkish Muslim and presented a résumé that included service on the staff of the Ottoman governor of northern Albania, he was, in fact, a German who was Jewish by birth though raised as a Protestant. His given name was Eduard Schnitzer.

He was born in Oppeln, in the Prussian province of Silesia (now Poland), on March 28, 1840 (making him ten months older than Stanley). His father, Ludwig, was a merchant. When Emin (for the purposes of the account, we will refer to him by the name by which the world came to know him) was two, his father died and his mother remarried shortly thereafter. Emin's stepfather, a man named Schweitzer, was a Protestant, and when Emin was six, he was baptized and then raised in that faith. The family moved to Neisse, where Emin lived until he went to the university at Breslau to begin his medical studies. He also studied at the universities of Königsberg and Berlin, where he received his degree in 1864.

While still a student, Emin began publishing in various scientific journals, exhibiting the same scrupulous scholarship and attention to detail that would characterize his scientific work for the rest of his life. At the same time, he began to exhibit a tendency to "fluctuate between extremes," as his principal biographer (also his cousin), George Schweitzer, noted. "What one day he looked upon as highly promising, he would reject the next day as completely hopeless. In all things he inclined to exaggeration."

Upon finishing his studies, either through his own negligence or through bureaucratic error, Emin failed to register in time for his state examination, which he had to pass in order to practice medicine in Germany. Rather than wait to take the examination at a later date, he abruptly left, traveling to Vienna.*

While in Vienna, he applied for a post with Maximilian's expeditionary force to Mexico, but was rejected. He went to the Turkish embassy to apply for a post in the Ottoman Imperial Service, and though he was initially rejected there, too, he was told that his chances might be better if he applied in person in Constantinople. With this in mind, he went to Trieste, where he hoped to get a ship to the Ottoman capital. Unfortunately, he ran out of money, managing to get only as far as Antivari, on the Adriatic coast, in Albania, which was then a Turkish province. (Antivari is now called Bar, and is in Yugoslavia.) After scuffling for a time, he managed to secure a position as a district medical officer and port quarantine officer, posts that he continued to occupy for almost six years.

It was during this period that Emin shed his European identity and took on the appearance and manners of a Turk,† With a naturally dark

---

*Before he left for Vienna, Emin applied to the British Foreign Office for a post in Africa, an early indication of the continent's attraction for him. He was turned down.

†Although he took on the appearance, manners, and even name of a Turk, it is not clear whether Emin ever truly converted to Islam. In his correspondence with his family, he insisted that he had not, yet in Africa he sometimes maintained that he had. In all likelihood, Emin said he was Muslim when he thought it was advantageous, but it is impossible to know from his accounts whether he ever genuinely embraced the faith.

complexion, augmented by a dense black mustache, when he began dressing in the local style, including a fez, he easily passed for a local. In addition, thanks to his facility with languages, he was soon fluent in Turkish, Albanian, and Modern Greek, all useful in his adopted country.

In 1871, he took a position on the staff of the governor of northern Albania, Ismail Hakki Pasha. As the governor's personal physician, Emin traveled extensively throughout the Near East, including Anatolia, Armenia, Persia, and Syria. Not long after joining the governor's staff, he completed his transformation by taking a Turkish name, calling himself Hairoullah Effendi. He was also often seen smoking the long Turkish pipe called a chibouk.

Ismail Hakki Pasha had a beautiful young wife who was from Transylvania. During his three years' service on the governor's staff, Emin apparently fell in love with her, and she with him, though their liaison had to remain completely secret. Even in his correspondence with his family, he was circumspect, but he did say, "I should never have dreamt of finding my life ideal in a Turkish harem!" Of Madame Ismail, he wrote only that she was "very kind and amiable."

Nevertheless, when the pasha died, in 1873, Emin was helped with the settlement of his estate, a task that would likely have deepened his connection with the newly widowed Madame Ismail. The primary evidence was that in 1875 he turned up again at his family's home in Neisse, accompanied by Madame Ismail, whom he introduced as his wife, her four children, and her personal servants, a group of Circassian slave girls. The conscientious German medical student who had left a decade earlier now returned as a Turkish official, complete with his own harem!

There is no evidence that Emin and Madame Ismail were actually married. He may have created this fiction simply to ease the shock to his family caused by his unexpected return. In any event, Emin quickly discovered that the maintenance of a woman who had wanted for nothing when she was married to the pasha, to say nothing of her retinue of eleven people, was driving him to the poorhouse. On the pretext of visiting old friends in Breslau, Emin took his leave of Neisse—and never returned. Just as he had fled after the snafu with his

state medical examination, Emin fled his newfound family responsibilities. Six weeks later, he surfaced in Cairo, staying only briefly before
continuing on to Khartoum. A few weeks after his disappearance,
Madame Ismail and her entourage returned to Turkey.

Fastidious, gracious, and charming, Emin quickly ingratiated himself with the small European community in the Sudanese capital. A
true polymath, he not only established a modest medical practice but
also proved himself adept at a variety of endeavors, ranging from
botany and ornithology to chess and the piano, on which he played
polished renditions of Chopin and Mendelssohn.

Charles Gordon was constantly scrambling to find competent
Europeans to assist him with the thorny administrative problems of
Equatoria, so when word of this talented newcomer reached him, he
promptly recruited him by offering him a position as Equatoria's
provincial medical officer. Not long after Emin arrived in Equatoria,
however, Gordon asked him to take on an assignment that had nothing
to do with medicine. It was a delicate diplomatic mission involving the
king of Uganda, the formidable Mutesa.

In January 1876, Gordon had dispatched a company of 160 troops,
under an Egyptian commander named Nuer Agha, to Mutesa's capital
at Mengo. Their mission was to obtain permission from Mutesa to
build another station only a few miles from Lake Victoria. Mutesa
promptly took all of them prisoner. It was Mehemet Emin's job to
negotiate their release.

He succeeded brilliantly, impressing the wily king, in part, because
he quickly acquired a working knowledge of the local dialect. In addition, his manner marked a refreshing change from the usual arrogance
and condescension exhibited by most of the "Turks" Mutesa had met
previously.* Emin was respectful and solicitous, and Mutesa not only
agreed to free the soldiers but even sent a letter to Gordon asking him
to appoint this charming newcomer as his permanent representative at
Mutesa's court.

Emin stayed on in Equatoria, traveling extensively and returning to

---

*In Mutesa's parlance, all Egyptians and their Europeans agents who came from the
north were Turks.

visit Mutesa in Uganda as well as establishing a friendship with Mutesa's archrival, Kabba Rega, in neighboring Unyoro. As he traveled, he pursued his passion for collecting native flora and fauna, making meticulous notes, sending specimens to museums in England and Germany, and publishing articles in various European scientific journals.

In October 1876, an exhausted Gordon resigned his post as governor of Equatoria. He returned to London to explore his options, only to be offered the position as governor-general of all of Egyptian Sudan. He accepted and by February 1877 was back in Khartoum. Emin remained in Equatoria, assuming the duties of inspector of stores, while a series of ineffectual governors moved in and out of Gordon's old post. Finally, dismayed by the deterioration of his old province, Gordon, in July 1878, appointed Mehemet Emin governor of Equatoria.

For the next several years, Dr. Emin governed peacefully and productively, and Equatoria flourished. He oversaw the expansion of the ivory trade and initiated a program of economic development that was as innovative as it was ambitious. He introduced the growing of rice, tobacco, indigo, coffee, and nutmeg, as well as the harvesting of local rubber. He experimented with making soap for possible export, did research into medicines that could be extracted from indigenous plants and trees, and designed a simple loom and taught his subjects (as he thought of them) to weave locally grown cotton into a loose-knit, but strong, fabric that became a successful trade and export commodity. Somehow, he also found time to pursue his passions for botany, ornithology, and zoology.

Because Emin's provincial capital at Lado was a thousand miles from Khartoum, with the ever-present obstacle of the Sudd in between the two, his successes went largely unnoticed by his superiors. With only an occasional steamer bringing mail and a few supplies from the north, Emin had little contact with Khartoum and virtually none with Cairo. For the most part, Emin and his subjects existed in splendid isolation. He didn't seem to mind.

While Emin and Gordon labored in the Sudan, Ismail, their employer, was flailing desperately in Cairo as his country drowned in a sea of debt. In 1875, he had been forced to sell Egypt's interest in the Suez Canal to Britain. As a further insult, the European powers had established a commission to oversee Egypt's financial affairs, with Britain and France sending agents to Cairo to that end.

Predictably, this humiliating arrangement led to considerable dissatisfaction, particularly in the Egyptian army and civil service. Finally, in 1882, an Egyptian army colonel named Ahmed Arabi led a rebellion against Ismail, but the real target was Europe's continuing control of Egyptian affairs. The British and French perceived the rebellion as an attempted military coup, and the British gave a military answer. They first assaulted Alexandria with a massive naval bombardment and then attacked with an expeditionary force. When the dust had settled, an occupying force of 25,000 British troops remained, and the last pretense that Egypt was anything but a European satellite state was gone. Though Ismail was allowed to remain on the throne, and Egypt was still nominally a part of the nearly toothless Ottoman Empire, Egypt's de facto ruler became the queen's representative in Cairo, Sir Evelyn Baring.

Ironically, Britain's prime minister, William Gladstone, had always been a reluctant imperialist and had, for some time, been looking for a politically acceptable means of extricating Britain from its involvement in Egypt's affairs. In this case, "politically acceptable" meant that he would be able to keep the French from filling any vacuum a British withdrawal might create, and that unfettered access to the Suez Canal could be maintained. As a result of the Arabi rebellion, however, Gladstone found his government more deeply embroiled in Egypt than ever before, including a new problem that was brewing in the Sudan.

On an island called Abbas, in the middle of the Nile opposite Khartoum, a young boatbuilder had dug himself a cave and was living the life of a pious Muslim ascetic. His name was Muhammad Ahmed, and at about the time the British were obliterating the seafront in Alexandria, Muhammad Ahmed was declaring himself to be the Mahdi, or Expected One, anointed by the Prophet Muhammad himself to restore the true Muslim faith and punish the infidels.

After sixty years of Egyptian exploitation, Sudan proved ripe for rebellion. The charismatic Mahdi's message of liberation and ven-

geance attracted more and more adherents. By the time Britain started
paying attention, the Mahdi's movement had attained critical mass.
His militant followers were ready to embark on a holy war, a jihad, to
rid their land of unbelievers. Over the next two years, a succession of
military victories, including the annihilation of an Egyptian-Sudanese
force of ten thousand troops under the command of the British
colonel William Hicks, brought most of Sudan's territory under the
Mahdi's control.

In London, Gladstone and his cabinet, urged on by Sir Evelyn Baring in Cairo, decided that enough was enough. The decision was
made to abandon the Sudan once and for all. Charles Gordon, who
had resigned as governor-general in 1880, was once again summoned.
He was to return to Khartoum one last time to supervise the withdrawal of Egyptian personnel from the capital and from any other surviving garrisons he could reach. Gordon reached Khartoum in
February 1884. Three weeks after his arrival, the Mahdi attacked the
capital, and the siege of Khartoum was on. At the same time, the
Mahdi ordered one of his most trusted generals, Emir Keramallah
Kurqusawi, to take a force of several thousand troops and begin an
assault on Sudan's southernmost provinces, Bahr al-Ghazal and
Equatoria.

The siege at Khartoum lasted almost a year, with Gordon valiantly
leading the city's defense. Bowing to public pressure at home, the
British belatedly sent a force to relieve him, but in January 1885, with
the advance column of the relief force only a few miles away, Khartoum
fell and Gordon was killed. The relief force promptly retreated.

After Gordon was killed, his body was hung in a public square,
to be pelted with stones and mutilated by swords and spears. Then
his head was severed, wrapped in linen, and taken to the Mahdi in
his headquarters outside the city. When the Mahdi stood before his
troops and held aloft the severed head as a symbol of triumph, Gordon became more than a hero; he became a martyr in Britain.

Ironically, only a few months after his victory at Khartoum, the
Mahdi was also dead, a victim of typhoid, but the movement he had
spawned lived on. In fact, in April 1884, well before the fall of Khartoum, Keramallah's army had taken Bahr al-Ghazal, the province

immediately north of Equatoria. Mehmet Emin's province became the last prize for the jihad.

WITH THE FALL OF KHARTOUM, Mehmet Emin and his subjects were effectively cut off from the outside world. With Bahr al-Ghazal already in Mahdist hands, it seemed only a matter of time before Equatoria would be attacked, but Keramallah took his time, waiting until November 1884 to attack Emin's northernmost station at Amadi. The station held out for several months, but in March 1885 Amadi fell. The Mahdi's army was less than 125 miles from Emin's capital at Lado.

Emin decided to fall back to the south, taking mostly women and children with him to his southernmost station at Wadelai, just north of Lake Albert, leaving the majority of his troops at Lado to defend it against the anticipated onslaught. Remarkably, it didn't come. Keramallah was forced to turn his attention to a disruption in the north, but Emin remained convinced that it was only a matter of time before the Mahdi's army would come back.

As he waited in Wadelai, Emin began to focus on the only feasible route of escape left open to him and his people, which was to the southeast. Here, however, he faced another problem. As was often the case, Unyoro and Uganda were at war. Passage through their territories had become extremely hazardous, even for individual travelers, though with his long personal history of diplomacy and friendship with the two kingdoms, Emin might have been able to negotiate a safe passage for himself. To his credit, he never seemed to consider doing so. He would not abandon his post or his people. To the contrary, he was exploring the possibilities for leaving Equatoria and *taking all of his people with him,* an exodus of as many as ten thousand, the majority of them women and children.

In addition to the logistical problems such an undertaking could entail, Emin's friend King Mutesa of Uganda had died, and his son and successor, Mwanga, had proved to be quite a different kind of monarch. Whereas Mutesa had resorted to violence and even brutality when he thought the situation demanded it, Mwanga had shown himself to be a bloodthirsty pederast, unstable, unreliable, and, at the moment, out to make life extremely difficult for almost any European he could get his hands on. He had already murdered an English bishop named William Hannington and was slaughtering his own subjects, mostly young men, who had been converted to Christianity by the English and French missionaries, whom his father had welcomed to the kingdom some twenty years before. The missionaries who had not already fled the kingdom were terrified.

Still, Emin believed that his best chances for withdrawal, if that became his only option, would be to the southeast, so he set about strengthening communications, via letter and messenger, with contacts in Unyoro and Uganda, and with the acting British consul in Zanzibar, Frederick Holmwood.

His most important correspondent was a Scottish missionary named Alexander Mackay, who had been in Uganda almost as long as Emin had been in Equatoria. His missionary zeal was exceeded only by his enthusiasm for British colonialism in Africa, and despite his current problems with Mwanga, Mackay saw an opportunity in Emin's situation.

In an exchange of letters, Mackay tried to convince Emin that, properly wooed, the English could be enticed into providing the support needed to maintain him in Equatoria. Mackay wrote,

> The old government at Khartoum no longer exists, but you can deliver over a large territory into English hands, if you wish to do so. . . . A good governor such as you are should take over the whole territory of the Nile sources. I know quite well that you could bring all this about if you took it in hand. You must, however, be supported and England will without doubt help you if you say so.

Emin replied,

> To your question, am I prepared to aid in the annexation of this country by England, I answer frankly "Yes." If England intends to occupy these lands and to civilize them, I am ready to hand over the government into the hands of England, and I believe that thereby I should be doing a service to mankind and lending an advance to civilization.

Mackay encouraged him to write letters explicitly stating his readiness to annex Equatoria to England to Frederick Holmwood, to Robert Felkin, the Scottish physician who was Mackay's friend and advocate in England (and who had met Emin while traveling in Africa), and to Charles Allen, the secretary of the prestigious and influential Anti-Slavery Society in London. Emin wrote the letters and gave them to his friend Wilhelm Junker, a fellow scientist and explorer who had been marooned with him in Wadelai for several months, awaiting an opportunity to make his way back to Zanzibar. Junker left Wadelai in January 1886 on what would prove to be a perilous journey through Unyoro and Uganda to the coast.

At this point, though Emin knew of the fall of Khartoum and Gordon's death, he did not yet know that the Egyptian government had, at Britain's insistence, decided to abandon all of Sudan. Then, in February 1886, the first mail dispatch to reach him in almost three years arrived in Wadelai. It contained a letter from the Egyptian prime minister, Nubar Pasha, giving him formal notice of Egypt's decision. The letter advised Emin that he was, in effect, a free agent. He could stay or leave Equatoria as he chose, but under no circumstances was he to expect any further assistance in any form from the government in whose service he had labored for a decade.

It was a cruel blow to a proud and sensitive man, but it served, at least for the moment, to crystallize his thinking. In defiance of Egypt's abandonment, he vowed that he would not leave his people or his province. Somehow, he would stay in Equatoria.

Junker, meanwhile, was struggling eastward with Emin's letters. When he reached Uganda in July, he got word to Holmwood in Zanzibar about Emin's plight as well as about the dire straits of the missionaries in Uganda. Holmwood promptly cabled London,

News from Uganda, 12 July. Terrible persecution broken out, all native Christians being put to death. Missionaries in extreme danger; urgently requests our demanding from King their being allowed to withdraw. Emin at Wadelai holds province, but urgently needs ammunition and stores. Objects, if he can avoid it, deserting the 4,000 loyal Egyptian subjects there. No time to be lost if assistance decided on.

Assistance was not decided upon, at least not at that point. The British Foreign Office proved largely indifferent to Emin's predicament. Adopting a policy of benign neglect, it hoped that Emin, having been notified of Egypt's decision to abandon Sudan, would simply withdraw on his own. Its policy did not reckon with the determined Junker and the effect that his appearance in Zanzibar would have.

As he made his way out of Uganda, traveling along established Arab trade routes toward the east coast of Africa, Junker was finally able to send a packet of letters, his own and Emin's, via courier to Zanzibar. The letters were then forwarded to their recipients in Britain and on the Continent, providing the first reliable news of Emin's situation in over three years. When, in turn, the recipients, especially Robert Felkin and the Anti-Slavery Society's Charles Allen, arranged to have Emin's letters published in the newspapers, the effect was immediate and dramatic. In one passage, Emin wrote, "I remain here the last and only representative of Gordon's staff. It therefore falls to me, and is my bounden duty, to follow up the road he showed us. Sooner or later a bright future must dawn for these countries; sooner or later these people will be drawn into the circle of the ever-advancing civilized world."

Such noble sentiments, combined with the reference to the martyred Gordon touched nerves that were still very raw. Though more than a year had passed since the tragedy at Khartoum, many Englishmen believed that Gordon's death, and those of thousands of others in the doomed city, were directly attributable to Britain's failure to recognize and react to the Mahdist threat. In the popular imagination, the martyred Gordon embodied the Victorian ideal of a soldier-statesman, a pious, courageous, charismatic servant of queen and country who had distinguished himself throughout the empire and beyond. His loss was seen as a black mark on the honor of the nation. Now, however, in the person of Gordon's last lieutenant, there was an opportunity to erase that mark, to avenge the fallen hero, to prove that the martyr had not died in vain. In saving Mehemet Emin, the ledger would be righted and the nation's honor restored. Such was the fervor that began to build for an initiative to save the beleaguered governor from the savage Muhammadan horde.

There was only one problem. The British government wanted nothing to do with rescuing Dr. Mehemet Emin Pasha, as he was called in the newspapers. (Technically, Emin's rank was still that of bey, a step below pasha, but the press awarded the higher honorific title anyway.) As far as Gladstone's successor, Prime Minister Robert Salisbury, was concerned, Mehemet Emin was a German citizen and should therefore be Germany's problem. Failing that, if any mission to relieve or rescue him were to be mounted in Britain, it would have to come from the private sector.

The situation presented a perfect opportunity for a Scotsman named William Mackinnon. He had made a fortune as one of the proprietors of the British East India Steam Navigation Company. Starting with a single vessel, his fleet eventually grew to more than one hundred cargo ships, steamers, and troop carriers, plying the world's oceans from England to India to Africa. He was a pillar of the Church of Scotland, a committed abolitionist, a shrewd and ambitious entrepreneur, and a staunch imperialist. He now became the chairman of the Emin Pasha Relief Committee.

William Mackinnon was no stranger to Africa. His ships had been calling at the island of Zanzibar for many years, and he had long pursued a variety of business ventures on both sides of the continent. He was enthusiastic about the continent's commercial potential, and he packed the relief committee with like-minded colleagues and business associates.

By the time the committee was formally announced, Mackinnon had already spoken privately with the only man he thought qualified to lead any sort of expedition to relieve Emin Pasha, the legendary Henry Morton Stanley. Though Stanley was about to embark on a lecture tour in the United States, he assured Mackinnon that, if asked, he would serve and would return to England immediately.

Mackinnon had known Stanley for several years, and admired the work he had done for King Leopold II of Belgium, as the king's principal agent in the development of the Congo Free State, a vast portion of the Congo River basin that was, in effect, Leopold's privately owned country. The Congo Free State was an inspiration to Mackinnon.* For several years, he and his cronies had talked of securing a similar territory in East Africa, a corridor stretching all the way from the Indian Ocean to the Great Lakes† that would be controlled through a private trading company, similar to the Association Internationale du Congo (AIC), which Leopold had created to run the Congo Free State. Mackinnon already knew that England had no interest in Emin's offer to turn Equatoria into a British protectorate. As far as he was concerned, that simply cleared the way for a private initiative.

Specifically, Mackinnon planned to petition Her Majesty's Government to charter a new trading company, the Imperial British East Africa Company (IBEAC), to develop the East African corridor. Then Stanley, while leading the Emin Pasha Relief Expedition, could simultaneously function as the IBEAC's agent, negotiating treaties and trading agreements on behalf of the company with the kings and chiefs through whose territories the expedition passed on its way to Equatoria. He had already performed the same function for King Leopold in his development of the Congo Free State. The pièce de résistance in Mackinnon's plan, or so he thought, was the offer he would authorize Stanley to make to Emin Pasha himself. Mackinnon was sure that a prominent, well-salaried position with the IBEAC would prove irresistible to the newly unemployed governor of Equatoria, especially if the position would also provide him with the means to retain his soldiers as a private army to safeguard the IBEAC's activities and assets. It seemed such a perfect fit. Emin Pasha would be saved, which everyone wanted. What's more, he would get to stay in Equatoria, which Emin wanted. A grateful government would grant a charter to the IBEAC, which Mackinnon wanted. And the IBEAC would gain the knowledge, skills, and reputation of the most experienced administra-

---

*In late 1886, Mackinnon, like virtually everyone else in Europe, was unaware of the atrocities being committed against Africans by Leopold's agents and employees in the Congo. He was inspired by Leopold's apparent success in private colonization.
†"Great Lakes of Africa" refers principally to Lake Victoria and Lake Tanganyika, the two largest bodies of water on the continent, along with several smaller lakes, including Lake Albert in Equatoria.

tor in central Africa. Hence the enthusiasm with which William Mackinnon began to raise funds for the Emin Pasha Relief Expedition.

Because this scenario was so highly speculative, it was deemed inappropriate for public disclosure. Officially, the objective of the Emin Pasha Relief Expedition had nothing to do with charters or trading companies or private armies. Rather, the stated objective of the expedition was to provide relief to Emin Pasha and his subjects in the form of guns, ammunition, and supplies with which they might once and for all repel the Mahdist forces and maintain their position in the province. In the alternative, the expedition would also be prepared to escort to the east coast of Africa those of Emin Pasha's noncombatant subjects who wished to leave. So said Henry M. Stanley, who, true to his word, had now returned from America to accept command of the expedition.*

However, just as William Mackinnon had his own agenda for the expedition, so did Henry Stanley. He had little interest in being a mere delivery boy to the beleaguered governor. Though he kept his own counsel in the matter, as far as Stanley was concerned, the mission was not to relieve Emin but to rescue him from the Muhammadan savages and deliver him safely back to civilization. In doing so, Stanley would at last be fulfilling a dream deferred, a dream that had begun with his first and most famous African exploit, the rescue of David Livingstone in 1872.

When Stanley had gone looking for Livingstone, his plan, indeed his expectation, was that he would bring the legendary explorer home to England. He envisioned a lecture tour, in which the two of them would appear before adoring audiences throughout Britain, then perhaps on to the Continent and even the United States. The rescuer and the rescued, equally celebrated, would recall their adventures together on a triumphal world tour. The only problem was that, after finding Livingstone, traveling with him for several months, and becoming so close to him that Stanley came to regard Livingstone as the father he

---

*To his credit, accepting the position meant walking away from a lecture tour in the United States and Australia that would have earned him as much as $80,000. His agent was not pleased.

never had, Livingstone decided to stay in Africa. Despite Stanley's pleadings, the great missionary-physician-explorer would not be swayed. Stanley had to return to England alone, where he faced the humiliation of a disbelieving public that nearly turned his triumph into a farce. It took him weeks to convince the bluebloods of the establishment that he had really done what he said he did. Even though his book about the rescue, *How I Found Livingstone*, eventually became a best seller, the sting of the initial disbelief, the arrogant dismissal of his accomplishment, had never left him.

Now, in the person of Emin Pasha, Stanley finally had the opportunity to claim the trophy that had eluded him so many years before. He would not only rescue Emin Pasha; he would bring him back to England to testify to Stanley's heroism. He would take the grateful governor with him on an international lecture tour that would cement his reputation, once and for all, as the greatest explorer ever to set foot on the Dark Continent. But just as Mackinnon said nothing in public about *his* plans for what might happen after the rescue of Emin Pasha, neither did Stanley.

Chapter Two

BULA MATARI

STANLEY HAD TAKEN a suite of rooms in Bond Street. As he prepared to interview prospective candidates for the expedition, he was full of his usual hard-nosed confidence. After all, the Emin Pasha Relief Expedition was shaping up as the best-financed, best-equipped expedition ever undertaken on the continent. And, after almost three years away, in a matter of weeks, Stanley would once again hear the African nickname he loved so well, Bula Matari. It meant "Breaker of Stones" and, in Stanley's mind, bespoke both the fear and the respect he inspired across the continent. At five feet five inches tall and 180 pounds, he was a diminutive bulldog of a man, long on fortitude, short on patience, a relentless and seemingly fearless leader of men who was generally considered the most successful explorer of his day. Not bad for a man who had started life as an unwanted bastard, banished to an orphans' workhouse in a poverty-stricken village in northern Wales.

Henry Stanley's origins had been a source of profound, lifelong shame for him, the soft underbelly of his cocksure persona. Born on January 28, 1841, to an unmarried eighteen-year-old domestic servant named Elizabeth Parry in the village of Denbigh, he was named after his father, a village drunk named John Rowlands, though even this dubious lineage was questioned by some. Rumors abounded that John Rowlands had agreed to say he was the father only because the real father, a married man named John Vaughn Horne, who was a local solicitor as well as the town clerk, had paid him to do so. In any case, as soon as Elizabeth Parry was well enough to travel, she went back to domestic service in London, leaving her infant son in the care of her father and her two brothers. There he remained until the age of five, when one of the brothers married. His new wife decreed that she had no need of her absent sister-in-law's bastard child in her household, so the youngster was summarily boarded out to a local family named Price. After a few months, however, it was decided that the weekly charge of two shillings, sixpence being paid to the Prices was an unnecessary expense. Young John would be sent to St. Asaph's work-house. Barely seven, the boy had already been rejected by his mother, her family, and a foster family.

The pain of the last rejection was no doubt deepened by the man-ner in which it was carried out. The Prices told their young boarder that he was going back to live with his *real* family, specifically at his aunt Mary's farm, outside the village. The Price's son Richard was elected to deliver the unsuspecting boy to his destination. It was a long, tiring trek, with Richard cajoling his young charge with stories about the delights of the life he'd soon be leading on the farm, so when they arrived at the forbidding iron gates of St. Asaph's, the local dumping ground for the unwanted, incompetent, and insolvent of all ages, John had no idea what was about to happen to him. In a final act of betrayal, Richard told him that his aunt Mary would be coming shortly to take him the rest of the way. With that, he handed him over to the staff of St. Asaph's, and left. Several hours passed before John began to understand that Aunt Mary wasn't coming. And then, as he would write with understated poignancy in his autobiography, "It took me some time to learn the unimportance of tears in a workhouse."

John Rowlands spent more than nine years at St. Asaph's. Without doubt, they were filled with experiences no child should be made to endure. Prostitution, both male and female, was rampant; sexual and physical abuse was commonplace; flogging was the standard form of punishment (a practice Stanley would resort to throughout his career in Africa). In what must have been a particularly excruciating episode, Elizabeth Parry, the mother who had abandoned him, was briefly committed to St. Asaph's, along with two more illegitimate children, a girl and a boy. (She would have five in all by four different men.) When she was pointed out to Rowlands, she returned his shy glance "with a look of cool, critical scrutiny." "I had expected to feel a gush of tenderness towards her," he would write in his autobiography, "but her expression was so chilling that the valves of my heart closed as with a snap."

Despite the horrors and heartbreaks of the workhouse, John Rowlands managed to derive a few hard-won benefits at St. Asaph's, including a rudimentary education. He particularly excelled in geography and arithmetic and was repeatedly praised for his penmanship. Near the end of his stay, he was appointed "head boy" and would be placed in charge of the classroom when the teacher was absent. The honor was both a reward for his conscientiousness as a student and recognition of his emerging leadership qualities. The head boy quickly gained a reputation as a strict disciplinarian.

In later years (and in his autobiography), Stanley was fond of relating the dramatic story of his "escape" from St. Asaph's. In his version, he and the other boys were about to receive yet another beating from their supervisor for some minor infraction when something in him snapped. Instead of taking the beating, he administered it, snatching away the supervisor's switch and beating him senseless with it, then fleeing over the wall with a boy named Moses. The story's Dickensian overtones (very similar to an episode in *Nicholas Nickleby*) are perhaps more than coincidental because, in fact, it never occurred. Instead, in May 1856, at the age of fifteen, John Rowlands was routinely discharged from St. Asaph's to the care of his cousin, a schoolmaster named Moses (!) Owen.

Stanley's melodramatic and fictitious account of his departure from the workhouse fit into a pattern of exaggeration, deception, and outright fantasy that would characterize the story of his life as he presented it both in person and in print. Deeply shamed and scarred by the true story of his early life, he did what many have done in similar circumstances; he invented a new one, a story that had enough basis in truth to be plausible, yet was ever so much more dramatic, romantic, and impressive. Indeed, within a year of his departure from St. Asaph's, John Rowlands, Welsh bastard, would disappear. In his place would appear Henry Stanley, the adopted son of adoring (and wealthy) parents in far-off America. This, too, while containing a grain of truth, would be a lie.

After leaving the workhouse, Rowlands spent roughly a year living with various relatives, none of whom were the least bit welcoming. In Liverpool, he was offered a position as a cabin boy aboard an American merchant vessel, the *Windermere.* He jumped at it and three days later found himself on the high seas.

Life aboard the *Windermere* proved to be a seaborne version of his worst days at St. Asaph's, with wretched living conditions, abominable food, backbreaking work, and the constant predations of his fellow sailors, so upon arriving in New Orleans in February 1859, Rowlands promptly jumped ship. Looking for work near the waterfront, he introduced himself to a prosperous-looking cotton broker who arranged for him to get a week's trial as a clerk in a warehouse. The broker's name was Henry Hope Stanley.

An Englishman by birth, *this* Stanley had come to America twenty years earlier to seek his fortune, and he had found it. He owned a fine house in New Orleans and a large plantation called Jefferson Hall in the country near Arcola, Louisiana. Over the next few months, Rowlands ingratiated himself with Henry Hope and his young wife, Frances. They started inviting him for Sunday breakfasts, and gradually Henry Hope Stanley began to groom the young man for a career in business, taking a paternal interest in everything from his wardrobe to his reading material. Rowlands began to feel that perhaps he'd finally found the loving family he'd never had. By the end of the year, with Henry Hope Stanley's blessing, Rowlands took his benefactor's name. But then, for reasons that have never become completely clear, it all went terribly wrong.

The cause may have been a quarrel or perhaps a misinterpretation on young Stanley's part about the extent of the elder Stanley's affection for him. In either case, a distinct cooling of familial feeling led the elder Stanley to send his namesake to a godforsaken backwater called Cypress Bend, Arkansas. The excuse was that he was to be tutored in the retail trade by a business associate named Altschul, but it was, in effect, an exile.

Years later, in his autobiography, Stanley fabricated another dramatic story to account for his departure from his "adoptive" family, this one even more outrageous than the tale of his departure from St. Asaph's. He wrote that, in 1859, Frances Stanley died suddenly during a yellow fever epidemic in New Orleans and that her husband was so overcome by grief that he fled the city on a ship bound for Havana. There, only a few weeks after his wife's untimely demise, he too succumbed to a heart attack. This touching and tragic story was an utter fiction. In truth, Henry Hope Stanley and his wife both lived another twenty years, but in the younger Stanley's mind, even several decades later, their perceived betrayal, whatever the cause, could be avenged by nothing less than death.

In Cypress Bend, young Henry Stanley quickly discovered the differences between the cosmopolitan diversity of New Orleans and the backcountry provincialism of Arkansas. He found the locals to be suspicious of outsiders, small-minded, and class-conscious—not all that different from the parochial attitudes in Denbigh he had fled. In addition, the area was plagued by swamp fever,* and, soon after arriving, Stanley became violently ill. He was also subjected to the endless talk among the citizenry of secession and war, which he found tedious. By the end of 1860, however, more and more local lads were ready to enlist in the Confederate cause, and pressure began to mount. The Southern code of honor and chivalry was so pervasive that when a local lass, in whom Stanley had exhibited some passing interest, sent him a parcel containing a lady's petticoat, the Southern equivalent of the Victorian white feather as a symbol of cowardice, Stanley buckled.

*A term of the times used to describe malaria.

Against his better judgment, he enlisted in the Dixie Greys, as the local regiment was called.

For ten months, the Dixie Greys did nothing but drill and wait. Then, in the spring, they were marched 350 miles to a place called Pittsburgh Landing, on the Tennessee River. There, on April 6, 1862, Henry Stanley got his first taste of combat at the bloody battle of Shiloh. The next day, in what may have been an oddly fortunate turn of events, given the appalling carnage of Shiloh, Private Stanley was captured by federal troops and shipped north to a prison camp on the outskirts of Chicago.

Camp Douglas, a converted cattle yard, was a hellhole. Rife with vermin and disease, it had a mortality rate not much better than that of the battlefield. Stanley, who already knew a thing or two about survival, befriended the camp commissary, who suggested that he and several of his fellow prisoners consider changing sides and joining the Union cause. Though Stanley later wrote that he agonized over the decision, in fact he seized the opportunity immediately. Within days, he found himself a member of the Illinois Light Artillery, bound for Harpers Ferry, West Virginia, in anticipation of immediate combat. Upon reaching Harpers Ferry, however, Stanley suffered an attack of dysentery and landed in the hospital. A few days later, he was pronounced unfit for active duty and summarily mustered out of the Union Army, less than three weeks after he'd joined. Now what?

In his weakened condition, it took him two weeks to stagger twelve miles to Hagerstown, Maryland, where he collapsed at a farm on the outskirts of town. Luckily, the family took him in and nursed him back to health. When he was strong enough, they even paid his train fare to Baltimore, where he eventually signed on to a schooner bound for Liverpool. His three-year stay in the New World, despite its initial promise, had proven to be as full of rejection and disappointment as the life he had fled.

When he arrived in Liverpool, Stanley learned that his mother was now married to a respectable innkeeper and living near his home village of Denbigh, so he sought her out, hoping for a reconciliation and, perhaps, a place to make a new start. Instead, he suffered another brutal rejection. His mother sent him away, telling him not to return until he had a proper vocation and some decent clothes, which she doubted would ever happen! Devastated, he could think of nothing to do but return to New York.

For the next several years, Stanley led a vagabond life. For a while, he was a merchant seaman, and then he actually reenlisted in the military, this time joining the Union Navy, but he deserted after only a few months. He traveled west, spending time in the mining towns of Colorado, trying his hand at various trades, living by his wits, concocting schemes and scams, and having occasional run-ins with the law.

With two acquaintances, he devised a scheme to travel the breadth of Asia, from Turkey to China, with the vague idea they would support themselves by selling stories about their adventures to newspapers and magazines. Within a few days of their arrival in Turkey, they quarreled with a band of Turkish tribesmen and were briefly taken prisoner. When they were released, Stanley abandoned both his trans-Asia travel plans and his traveling companions, heading instead to England. Before he left Istanbul, however, he had a local tailor make him a jacket and vest in the style of a naval officer's uniform, complete with brass buttons and gold braid, though it was unclear in whose navy Stanley was supposed to be serving. In this uniform he appeared once again in his native Denbigh, hiring a coach and horses for the occasion. He even returned to St. Asaph's, where he treated the children to tea and cakes and exhorted them to follow his example of diligence and application so that they, too, might make a success of themselves one day! He signed the register, "John Rowlands, formerly of this parish, now ensign in the United States Navy in North America, belonging to the US ship Ticonderoga, now at Constantinople, Turkey; absent on furlough." This bold fiction was arguably the last time he ever used his birth name. He then set sail, yet again, for America.

Throughout his adventures and misadventures, Stanley kept notes and diaries, including several highly doctored and/or patently false accounts of his "exploits" under fire in the Civil War. Back in the States, he used these Civil War stories to land a job as a correspondent with the *Missouri Democrat*, a St. Louis newspaper.

He was initially assigned to cover the state legislature, which bored him to tears, but then he was sent west to cover General Hancock's military campaign against the Cheyenne Indians. Stanley's lively accounts were so well received that several eastern newspapers requested reprint rights, including the New York *Herald*. Stanley saw his chance. He went to New York and camped out in the *Herald*'s offices until he got an interview with the paper's flamboyant publisher, James Gordon Bennett. When the meeting was over, he had an agreement to cover a story that would not only change his life in ways that he could not possibly have foreseen but also influence the course of history in both Europe and Africa.

The story he proposed to Bennett was an impending British military campaign against the "mad king" of Abyssinia, Theodore I. It seemed that this eccentric monarch had taken umbrage at an imagined slight from Queen Victoria and retaliated by taking hostage several British diplomats and their families. After protracted negotiations failed to secure their release, Britain decided to launch a punitive military campaign. Stanley proposed to join the force—13,000 troops and 55,000 pack animals—at Annesley Bay, near the tip of the Horn of Africa, and then report on the ensuing campaign against Theodore in his mountain stronghold at Magdala.

What attracted Stanley to this relatively obscure story in a very remote corner of Africa? Perhaps it was the most exotic locale he could imagine. Perhaps he thought the proposal to cover a war would show courage and initiative, traits he thought would impress Bennett. Whatever his reasons, the Abyssinian campaign was the story he proposed. Bennett was unconvinced that the story would interest his American readers, so Stanley agreed to a compromise. He would pay his own way in exchange for a higher than normal freelance rate if his dispatches were published. More important, he secured a promise from Bennett that, if he acquitted himself well, he would be given a full-time position as a roving foreign correspondent.

Stanley did well indeed, in part because he bribed the telegrapher in Suez, the end point of the telegraph line to London, to send his dispatches before any of those written by his English colleagues, virtually guaranteeing him an international scoop. The gambit worked. His stories in the *Herald* beat his British counterparts to press by a full week. In addition, Stanley's prose was vivid and compelling in the melodramatic style of journalism circa 1868, and the story that Bennett doubted would interest his readers became a sensation. When Stanley made his way back to Alexandria, Egypt, a cable was waiting informing him of his appointment as a foreign correspondent at a salary of $2,000 a year. At twenty-seven, his transformation from bastard outcast to man of the world seemed complete. He felt himself to be on the brink of a splendid career. The last piece of his metamorphosis was the selection of a proper middle name to give his byline the desired gravitas. He toyed with Morley, Morelake, and Moreland before deciding finally to become Henry *Morton* Stanley.

Twenty years later, Henry Morton Stanley was much more than a foreign correspondent, more even than a best-selling author, though he was that several times over. Henry Morton Stanley had become the most famous explorer in the world. He had led three death-defying, globe-altering expeditions into the heart of Africa; he had traversed the continent from east to west; he had become the first European to navigate the length of the mighty Congo River; he had paved the way for the economic development of an enormous portion of central Africa; and, perhaps most famously, he had found the legendary missionary-explorer David Livingstone and uttered the immortal words (which he came to despise) "Dr. Livingstone, I presume."

The Livingstone expedition had been the brainchild of Stanley's publisher, James Gordon Bennett. After Stanley's brilliant performance in Abyssinia, Bennett sent his intrepid reporter into the African jungle to search for a man many believed was already dead. Not only did Stanley find Livingstone; he found him in only seven months, an astonishing feat for someone who had no experience in the African bush, let alone leading an expedition. And, to Bennett's delight, he scooped the British press once again. The feat was so astonishing that, when Stanley returned to London, he found that his dispatches had been flatly disbelieved by the English establishment, especially by the esteemed Royal Geographical Society, of which Livingstone was a decorated member. When he produced Livingstone's diaries as proof of his claims, he was accused of forging them. When the diaries were authenticated by Livingstone's son, he was accused of stealing them. Only after Queen Victoria herself took the extraordinary step of pub-

licly expressing her "high appreciation" for his service to the crown
and for "relieving her anxiety over Dr. Livingstone" were his claims
accepted and his accomplishments reluctantly acknowledged. Only
then could he get his book about the expedition, *How I Found Livingstone,* published. That it became a runaway best seller eased the sting
just a little.

Stanley followed up the Livingstone expedition with the most
ambitious exploration of the continent undertaken up to that time.
Cosponsored by Bennett's *Herald* and the London *Telegraph*, the
expedition had two principal objectives: to determine, once and for
all, the true source of the Nile, a question that had obsessed Britain for
decades, if not centuries (Grant and Speke's 1863 claim that the Nile
originated at Ripon Falls, at the northern end of Lake Victoria, was not
yet universally accepted); and to traverse the continent east to west by
way of the Congo River basin, something never before done by a white
man.

Over the course of a thousand days, Stanley's original party of 347
shrank to 88, his three European crewmen perished, Stanley himself
suffered near-fatal bouts of malaria, fever, and dysentery, and the expedition was constantly harassed by hostile natives, including cannibals.
Still, the expedition was considered a stunning success. Stanley
became the first man to circumnavigate both Lake Tanganyika and
Lake Victoria, establishing the latter beyond doubt as the source of the
White Nile. His navigation of the Congo River from the heart of central Africa to the Atlantic Ocean opened European eyes to the possibilities of development in a vast new region of the continent. And his
stories of encounters with man-eating crocodiles, natives shooting
poisoned arrows, and perilous journeys through thundering cataracts
where a forty-foot dugout canoe could disappear without a trace,
became the fodder for his second international best seller, *Through the
Dark Continent.* When he returned to London from the Congo, the
skepticism that had greeted him after the Livingstone search was
replaced by unbridled adulation. Praise came from every quarter.
Stanley found himself in the exclusive fraternity of celebrated African
explorers that included Burton, Baker, Grant, Speke, and Livingstone
himself. In short, he had become a national hero.

Even as a hero, though, Stanley soon began to chafe under the constraints and obligations of civilization. He'd never been very good at the social whirl. He was too blunt, too impatient, too much a commoner. He wanted to go back to Africa, and he hoped to do it as the head of an official English expedition whose purpose would be to annex the territory he'd traversed on his epic journey down the Congo. He had begun lobbying for such an undertaking as soon as he'd returned to London, but neither the prime minister nor the Foreign Office demonstrated much enthusiasm for his proposal. As far as Her Majesty's Government was concerned, Britain's African holdings were deemed sufficient, at least for the moment.

Stanley's case was further damaged by a report submitted to the Foreign Office by John Kirk,* longtime British consul in Zanzibar, concerning the explorer's conduct on the Congo expedition. The report asserted that, without provocation, Stanley had repeatedly attacked unarmed natives, that he had physically abused his porters, even beating at least one of them to death, that he had captured natives and then bartered them for food with other tribes, in effect selling them into slavery, if not making them into human sacrifices, and that he had taken a native woman as a concubine. Kirk had an excellent reputation at the Foreign Office, and his report was taken seriously. If Stanley's proposal to lead an official English expedition had been a tough sell to begin with, Kirk's report made it impossible.

There was, however, another patron-in-waiting who had no qualms about Stanley's alleged conduct in Africa. King Leopold II of Belgium had been lusting after a colony of some sort throughout his decade on the throne. At first, he did not seem to care particularly where on the globe the colony was, but thanks in part to Stanley's most recent exploits, Leopold became increasingly interested in Africa. In June 1878, less than a year after Stanley's triumphant return from the Congo, Leopold invited him to Brussels.

The king, who was as devious and cunning as Stanley was impolitic and abrasive, had already been developing his African strategy for

---

*See Daniel Liebowitz, *The Physician and the Slave Trade* (New York: W. H. Freeman, 1999).

some time. His first step had been to convene an international geographical conference on Africa, out of which emerged an affiliation of
governments and national geographical societies called the International African Association, or AIA, for short. The AIA became, in
effect, Leopold's cover. Under its auspices (and with Leopold as its
chairman), a plan was agreed upon to create a series of outposts across
the African continent dedicated, first and foremost, to the suppression
of the slave trade (opposition to this trade was a political constant
throughout Europe at the time); second, to serve as bases from which
to conduct scientific and geographical research; and, finally, to foster
commerce and economic development, which was, in fact, all that
Leopold was really interested in.

The AIA led, in turn, to the creation of the Comité d'Etudes du
Haut-Congo, through which Leopold raised $100,000 for what he
called "a purely exploratory" expedition. It was at that point that he
summoned Stanley to Brussels.

When the negotiations were concluded, Stanley had a five-year
contract, at $5,000 per year, to lead an expedition that would establish
a series of stations along a 1,500-mile stretch of the Congo River. In
addition, he was to pursue a more personal agenda on Leopold's
behalf. He was to negotiate treaties between the Association Internationale du Congo, or AIC, which had quietly supplanted the Comité
d'Etudes du Haut-Congo, and the chieftains and kings who controlled
the territories adjacent to the Congo River and its major tributaries.
The AIC was, in effect, a private trading company controlled by
Leopold, and the instrument through which he pulled off one of the
most astonishing land grabs in history.

At the end of his five-year contract, in a feat of endurance, improvi-
sation, bravado, and sheer, unbreakable will, Stanley had built twenty-
two stations along the Congo River, stretching from the Atlantic
Ocean to the center of the continent. He had also obtained the signa-
tures or marks of more than three hundred kings and chiefs whose
combined territories totaled more than 900,000 square miles, an area
larger than France. In exchange for the AIC's pledge to "protect its
inhabitants from all oppression or foreign intrusion" and "to promote
to its utmost the prosperity of . . . said country," the chiefs and kings

ceded their "sovereignty and all sovereign rights to their territory . . . for ever." Leopold had turned most of the Congo River basin into his personal fiefdom, and Stanley had been his realtor.

With surpassing irony, Leopold named his personal colony the Congo Free State. Even more remarkably, at the Berlin Conference of 1885, he succeeded in having his dominion over this vast territory recognized by the great powers of Europe and by the United States.

AS STANLEY PREPARED to interview the short list of candidates chosen from more than four hundred applicants eager to join the Emin Pasha Relief Expedition, he already knew the kind of men he wanted: military men. The expedition would be run as a military undertaking, so he was looking for men who were already trained to fight, to follow orders, and to withstand uncommon hardship without complaint. If they had previous experience in Africa, so much the better. He told all prospective recruits that his word would be law and that any infractions would be dealt with swiftly and severely.

The first man he hired fit the criteria perfectly. Lieutenant William Stairs, a twenty-nine-year-old officer in the Royal Engineers, originally from Nova Scotia, had served with distinction in the regiment of Lord Wolseley, the commander of the force that put down the Arabi rebellion. Wolseley recommended him highly. Young, fit, disciplined, and looking for a challenge, he was also single, another of Stanley's preferences. As he explained to all interviewees, he wanted no widows on his hands.

For his second in command, Stanley chose Major Edmund Musgrave Barttelot, twenty-seven, a florid-faced, red-haired veteran of the Seventh Fusiliers who had a reputation as a strong disciplinarian with more than a bit of a temper. He had already served in both Afghanistan and Sudan.

Captain Rupert Nelson was also a veteran of Africa, having seen action in the Zulu wars with Methuen's Horse.* Stanley hired him to be in charge of drilling the African soldiers they would be recruiting.

---

*A British Army unit in the Boer War.

Then there was William Bonny, a sergeant recently resigned from the Army Medical Service, who wanted to prove that he was as good a soldier as any officer. Stanley liked his attitude and needed his medical skills.

John Rose Troup had three years' experience in the Congo Free State, having only recently returned. His primary responsibility would be to take charge of the donkeys the officers would ride when the terrain permitted.

For the final two positions, Stanley chose two gentlemen volunteers. Both were Englishmen of good social background and education, but they brought only tangentially relevant skills to the undertaking. The first was James Jameson, who had spent time in South Africa shooting game and collecting wild birds. He was also a talented artist whose drawings impressed Stanley, though he cautioned him that there might not be much time to sketch on the expedition. Jameson was also married, though it is not clear whether Stanley was aware of that when he took him on.

The other volunteer was a tall, slender, fair-haired twenty-eight-year-old named Arthur Jeremy Mounteney Jephson, who appeared to be a bit of a dandy. Though he came from a good family and had received a first-rate education, Jephson had yet to decide on a career. He had occupied himself primarily as a companion to his wealthy, socially prominent cousin, the countess de Noailles, helping with her various charities and social obligations and wintering with her in the south of France. His only relevant experience was a brief stint in the merchant marine that had given him a perfunctory knowledge of boats. Still, Stanley liked his honesty and directness, so he took him on, telling him he would be in charge of his pride and joy, the *Advance*, a steel boat of Stanley's design that could be broken down into twenty-two sections, each of which could be transported by two porters overland. Since much of the expedition's route was to be river based, Stanley was convinced that the *Advance* would prove indispensable.

Unquestionably, part of Stanley's attraction to his two gentlemen-volunteers was their willingness not only to serve without pay but also to contribute £1,000 each to the Emin Pasha Relief Committee. In addition, all expedition members were required to sign an agreement stipulating that they would make no attempt to publish any account of the journey until at least six months after Stanley had published his, the title of which he had already selected—"In Darkest Africa."

Jephson had to turn to his cousin, the countess, for the money. When she gave it to him, she also handed him a tiny pearl-handled Bulldog revolver, telling him she would feel better about his upcoming travels if he had a weapon small enough to conceal on his person. He didn't bother to remind her that the primary cargo of the expedition was guns and ammunition, but he did tell her that he would be home for Christmas. Luckily, he didn't specify the year.

Chapter Three

THE LONG WAY
HOME

WHEN MOUNTENEY JEPHSON received his Bulldog revolver from the countess, he was likely unaware of the debate raging between his new commander and the members of the Emin Pasha Relief Committee about the best route for the expedition to take. Thanks to the Mahdi's forces, the most direct route, from the north via the Nile, was no longer available. Most of the committee members thought the best alternative was from the east. Porters could be hired in Zanzibar.* Then the expedition would travel some nine hundred miles inland to Equatoria, following one of several proposed routes. Two of the routes would go around Lake Victoria to the south, one would skirt the lake to the

---

*The Zanzibaris were to nineteenth-century East African exploration what sherpas are to Mount Everest—the default standard. No matter the route or destination, Zanzibari porters were a given.

north, and a fourth would go directly across it. Stanley didn't like any of them. The southern routes would take them through territory that was either unknown or hostile, or perhaps both; the northern routes went through Masailand, whose fabled warriors were hostile to all outsiders; and Stanley thought the water route across the lake was impractical for such a large expedition. He further argued that any eastern route increased the likelihood of desertions by the Zanzibaris because, when the going got rough, they would still be relatively close to home. With their Arab kinsmen scattered across the areas through which the proposed routes would pass, they would have little trouble finding refuge. No, Stanley argued, the best route was not from the east but from the west, starting on the other side of the continent! The best route was through the Congo.

His argument began with the Congo River itself. The expedition could travel on the main river and then on its tributary, the Aruwimi, to a point that Stanley calculated was only 320 miles from Lake Albert, where they expected to rendezvous with Emin Pasha.* After reaching the end of the river route, he estimated, it would take no more than six weeks to reach his man. Most important (perhaps) from Stanley's point of view, a western route would greatly reduce Zanzibari desertions because, instead of heading away from their home, they would be heading toward it and, because of Stanley's knowledge of the Congo, staying with him would give them their best chance of getting home, which would increase their loyalty and obedience.

Stanley also maintained that there were political considerations. Taking any of the eastern routes might arouse the suspicions of the Germans, with whom the British had recently concluded an East African territorial agreement, creating "spheres of influence" along a line that roughly corresponded to the border of modern Kenya and Tanzania. In addition, he cited Junker's reports about the dangers posed to English and French missionaries by Uganda's unpredictable young king, Mwanga. A large expedition attempting to travel through

*As it turned out, he misjudged the distance by almost exactly half. As he later admitted, it was closer to 650 miles. He also predicted that food and water would be plentiful all along the route, another disastrous miscalculation.

his lands would no doubt antagonize him further, thereby putting the clerics at even greater risk. All in all, Stanley concluded, the western route was clearly preferable.

He didn't bother to address the problem (and expense) of transporting several hundred people from one side of the continent to the other. Nor did he dwell on the fact that the last 320 (or 650) miles to Lake Albert would require traversing the vast Ituri forest, the largest remaining unexplored territory in all of Africa. As for reducing Zanzibari desertions, Stanley knew as well as anyone that there were Swahili-speaking Arab traders throughout the Congo region who would likely welcome any disgruntled porters, but he didn't mention this, either. The argument went back and forth, but finally it appeared that the committee would have its way. Stanley seemed resigned to taking an eastern route. Then, at the last moment, King Leopold entered the conversation, and everything changed.

Leopold's communication was uncharacteristically direct. In a letter to Stanley, he reminded him (and the committee) that the expedition leader was still under contract to Leopold, and that the king expected to have an important assignment for him in the near term, certainly before the Emin Pasha Relief Expedition would be concluded.* Therefore, the king regretfully concluded, it would be impossible for him to release Mr. Stanley from his contract *unless* the committee were willing to consider the Congo route for the expedition. As a gesture of good faith, the king offered to make the entire river fleet of the Congo Free State available for the expedition's use.†

Leopold's letter was a thunderbolt. As far as the committee members were concerned, if they wished to retain Stanley's services, which they most certainly did, Leopold's ultimatum left them no choice. They reversed their decision. The expedition would go from west to east.

---

*This "important assignment" was ironic at best, cruel at worst. Stanley had spent two frustrating years since his last Congo expedition pestering King Leopold for another assignment, *any* assignment, without success.

†Just as Stanley omitted several key pieces of information in his arguments for the Congo route, Leopold neglected to mention that his "entire river fleet" consisted of exactly one vessel that was large enough, and in adequate repair, to be of use.

Publicly, Stanley expressed surprise at Leopold's intervention, as though it had come unexpectedly. In truth, he had most likely engineered it. His first meeting with the Emin Pasha Relief Committee had taken place December 29, 1886. That night, he had slipped away to Brussels to confer with the king.

Leopold had long been aware of the situation in Equatoria and of the opportunity that Emin Pasha's difficulties created to feed his insatiable appetite for territory. As early as 1884, he had talked with none other than Charles Gordon about annexing Equatoria and Bahr al-Ghazal into the Congo Free State, with Gordon serving as administrator of the new territory. Now, he thought, he might be able to use the Emin Pasha Relief Expedition to accomplish the same objective, simply substituting Emin for Gordon, with the added benefit that someone else would be paying Stanley to facilitate the transaction! At their meeting, Leopold instructed Stanley to make the same offer to Emin Pasha that he'd discussed with Gordon: the Congo Free State would annex Equatoria; Emin would continue as governor at a salary of £1,500 a year, with an administrative budget of £12,000 to £15,000 a year in exchange for a "reasonable yield" of ivory and other commodities; Emin's troops would be absorbed into the forces of the Congo Free State, and he would be given the rank of general. Like Mackinnon, Leopold thought his scheme was a perfect fit for all concerned: Emin would get to stay in his beloved province; the king would get the benefit of his administrative skills and experience, not to mention his army; and Leopold's personal fiefdom would stretch all the way to the banks of the Nile, a crucial step in the fulfillment of his ultimate megalomaniacal dream—to become, in effect, a modern pharaoh.

Before Leopold could start designing his pyramid, however, he had another, more pressing problem, which he hoped the Emin Pasha Relief Expedition could help him solve. In the preceding two years, lack of funds and manpower had forced the abandonment of some of the Congo Free State's river stations that Stanley had so laboriously carved out during his epic five-year expedition. Then, in August 1886, the station at Stanley Falls, the easternmost outpost in the colony, had been overrun and occupied by Arab ivory hunters and slavers. The next closest station, at Banalya, was almost four hundred

miles downriver, putting much of the eastern half of the colony's territory at risk for further Arab encroachment. Leopold desperately
needed to recapture Stanley Falls, but he didn't have the resources for
an armed confrontation with the Arabs. So, he reasoned, if he couldn't
beat them, perhaps he could persuade them to join him by making a
deal. He would co-opt the most powerful Arab in the entire Congo,
the legendary Arab slaver Tippu Tib. Leopold would offer Tippu Tib
a job.

Tippu Tib, whose real name was Hamed bin Muhammad, was the
son of an Arab trader from the island of Muscat and an African
mother. Literate, shrewd, and ruthless, he had first gone to the interior
of East Africa with his father, who tutored him in the ivory and slave
trades. He learned his lessons well, and within a few years he had
eclipsed his father in both wealth and influence. Like other Arabs,
Tippu Tib used a combination of strategies to insinuate himself into
the affairs of the tribes of the interior. Though certainly not opposed
to using violence, he preferred to begin by establishing trade relationships, often asserting some kinship with the locals. He would then pay
the chiefs and headmen to assist in the gathering of ivory. After ivory
came slaves. As his foothold grew more secure, he would bring in
more and more Arabs, or other Africans already under his control,
armed with guns rather than with the bows and arrows and spears carried by the natives. Before long, their numbers would be sufficient for
him to take control of a tribal area, either by pitting one tribe against
another as part of his slave-gathering operations or by launching a
campaign of intimidation that included brutal raids on native villages
in which the men were slaughtered, the women and children taken as
slaves, and the dwellings and crops burned to the ground.

Tippu Tib's particular claim to fame was that he had succeeded in
establishing control over the dreaded Manyuema tribe, a group of cannibals whose ferocity made them especially adept at slave raids. It was
said that he rewarded them with 10 percent of their catch, some of
whom they turned into their own slaves but most of whom were only
staying for dinner.

With the Manyuemas as his henchmen, Tippu Tib rapidly
expanded his territory until it reached north from Lake Tanganyika to

the Aruwimi River and west to the Lomami River. He was, in effect, the sovereign of an undeclared state that encompassed some 200,000 square miles, an area considerably larger than Equatoria.

Leopold's stroke of genius, or so he thought, was to appoint Tippu Tib the governor of the Stanley Falls district of the Congo Free State. He would pay him a monthly salary of thirty pounds and let him bring his considerable retinue of wives, concubines, slaves, and attendants with him to his new post. All that Leopold asked in return was the Arab's promise that he would refrain from taking slaves or letting others take slaves in his district. What Tippu Tib did outside the Stanley Falls district remained his own business. It is doubtful that Leopold believed or even cared that Tippu Tib would actually lift a finger against the trade that had contributed so much to his wealth and power. The promise was strictly a sop to Leopold's powerful European neighbors to show them that he, too, was striving to stamp out the scourge that still plagued the Dark Continent.

Leopold reasoned that with Tippu Tib in charge at Stanley Falls, the danger of further Arab encroachment in the Congo Free State would be blunted, because no other Arab would dare challenge the new governor. In addition, Leopold knew that Stanley would need Tippu Tib to arrange for additional porters to supplement the Zanzibaris when the expedition reached the end of the navigable river route.* This time, Stanley might need as many as six hundred porters, a significant piece of business for Tippu Tib, which Leopold hoped would make him more favorably disposed to his proposition.

For a man who said he hated politics, Stanley had maneuvered himself into an interesting position as he made his final preparations before leaving London. In Mackinnon and Leopold, he had two employers for whom he would be delivering two competing proposals to Emin Pasha (though it appears that neither Mackinnon nor Leopold knew about the other's offer, because Stanley didn't tell them). He was also responsible for wooing Tippu Tib to Leopold's scheme for recapturing the Stanley Falls district. Most important, there was Stanley's own agenda

*Stanley and Tippu Tib already knew each other; Tippu Tib had supplied porters to Stanley during his first Congo expedition a decade earlier.

to bring Emin Pasha back with him to England. That agenda, if successful, would effectively thwart the aims of both of his employers. With all the intrigue building up around the expedition before it had even gotten underway, it was easy to forget that all Emin Pasha really wanted was some bullets and some guns, and then to be left alone.

ON TOP OF THE political maneuvering, Stanley was also in charge of all the practical arrangements for what was shaping up as the largest, most lavishly equipped expedition ever mounted in Africa. Generous contributions were received from various British merchants and manufacturers. Mssrs. Fortnum and Mason contributed forty cases of foodstuffs for the officers, including champagne, brandy, coffee, tea, jam, and meat extract. Burroughs and Wellcome, the pharmaceutical company, contributed nine fully provisioned medical cases, and the firm of Benjamin Edgington contributed officers' tents treated with copper sulfate to make them waterproof. (Remarkably, the tents held up for the entire expedition.) Hiram Maxim, an inventor, presented the expedition with his latest brainstorm, a machine gun capable of firing 330 rounds a minute.* The War Office was persuaded to provide the bullets.

The most important items in the expedition's inventory were, of course, the guns and ammunition it would be carrying to Emin Pasha. These consisted of 510 Remington rifles, 100,000 rounds of ammunition, two tons of gunpowder, 350,000 percussion caps, 35,000 special Remington cartridges, 50 Winchester repeating rifles, and 50,000 rounds of Winchester ammunition.

Because of weight and worries about spoilage in the African heat and humidity, it was considered impractical to try to carry enough food for such a large contingent of men. Instead, the usual expedition practice was to carry goods that the natives valued in trade. These could not only be exchanged for food but also be used as gifts to secure the friendship and goodwill of kings, chiefs, and headmen whose territory they would be traversing. The most common trade goods were cheap

---

*Maxim, an American, had first offered his invention to the U.S. War Department, which turned him down.

cotton cloth, beads of various shapes, sizes, and colors, and copper, brass, and iron wire cut into one foot lengths or wound into coils. The Africans called the wire pieces *matokos*, and in some areas these were highly prized. Before he left London, Stanley sent an order ahead to Zanzibar for a ton of wire, 27,000 yards of cloth, and 3,600 pounds of assorted beads. In addition, he ordered 100 shovels, 100 hoes, 100 axes, and 100 billhooks. He also requested forty pack donkeys and ten riding donkeys with saddles. Finally, he ordered the *Advance*, the steel boat for which he furnished the designs.

While Stanley was busy provisioning the expedition, Mackinnon and his committee were busy raising the money to pay for it. A public subscription was suggested by Mackinnon's business partner, J. F. Hutton, but Mackinnon vetoed the idea, in part because he had already been assured through his contacts in the Foreign Office that the Egyptian government would contribute £10,000 in support of the expedition, as well as most of the rifles and ammunition. Stanley had estimated the total expedition costs at £20,000,* so the Egyptian contribution got them halfway to the goal. Mackinnon himself pledged £3,000, Jameson and Jephson had already paid £1,000 each for the privilege of joining the expedition, and the remaining £5,000 were quickly raised from among the other members of the committee and their friends.

The fund-raising effort was no doubt aided by persistent rumors that Emin Pasha had amassed an enormous cache of ivory that was hidden somewhere in Equatoria. It was said that there was as much as seventy-five tons, worth a staggering £60,000. Mackinnon made it clear that, if the rumors were true, he expected the committee to receive a "just proportion" of the ivory to compensate for its outlay.

For Stanley's part, he not only agreed to serve without pay; he further offered to donate his anticipated fees from the newspaper dispatches he expected to send on the expedition's progress (once a journalist . . .). Remarkably, it took Stanley and the committee less than a month to raise the necessary funds and provision an expedition of unprecedented scale.

---

*In 1887, the British pound was worth approximately five U.S. dollars, meaning the expedition's budget was about $100,000. Adjusted for inflation, the figure would be approximately $2,000,000 today.

Stanley had arrived in London on Christmas Eve 1886; he left for Africa on January 21, 1887. Before he departed, he made a number of speeches outlining his expected timeline, now fine-tuned since he (and King Leopold) had persuaded the committee to use the Congo route. He would reach the mouth of the Congo by the end of March 1887. Using steamers to speed up the Congo, he would establish a base camp at the confluence of the Congo and the Aruwimi rivers by early June. Then he would lead an advance column into the Ituri forest, the unknown territory between the Aruwimi and Lake Albert, a march he expected to take approximately thirty-five days, leading to an expected meeting with Emin Pasha no later than the end of July. His return plans contemplated two different routes. The women and children* of Emin's Egyptian officers and civil servants who wished to return to their country would follow the trail just blazed by Stanley's advance column back to the base camp on the Aruwimi, then down the Congo by steamer to the ocean, around the Cape of Good Hope to Zanzibar, and then home to Egypt. In addition, the intention was to transport a substantial portion of Emin's cache of ivory along the same route.

Stanley would then lead a second party, including Emin Pasha himself, if he chose to leave his province, that would take a southeastern route through Unyoro and Uganda, and on to the east coast opposite Zanzibar. This route would require a sufficient force of Emin's troops to provide security for their passage through what was expected to be hostile territory. The entire expedition would be finished by December 1887. The cost would not exceed £20,000. For Stanley, whose most recent African adventure had lasted five years, it must have seemed like little more than a long weekend in the country.

---

*Stanley and the committee anticipated that the number would not exceed one hundred, though it is hard to know on what they based their calculations.

Chapter Four

ASSEMBLING
THE TROOPS

STANLEY WAS ACTUALLY the last to leave London. Major Barttelot had departed a week earlier, bound for Aden, where he was to recruit a group of crack Somali troops to serve as a security force for Stanley and the forward company of the expedition; Jameson traveled on his own toward a rendezvous at Suez with Stanley; John Rose Troup, the donkey wrangler, had been dispatched directly to the Congo, where he was to make arrangements for river transport and additional porters to supplement those who would be brought from Zanzibar; and Stairs, Jephson, and Nelson traveled together aboard one of Mackinnon's ships, the *Navarino*, bound for Egypt. Since Her Majesty's Government had declined to provide any transportation for the expedition, Mackinnon had been forced to provide ships from his own fleet to get everyone first to Zanzibar and then around the Cape of Good Hope to the mouth of the Congo—a considerable expense.

William Bonny, the medical assistant, was to have sailed on the *Navarino* as well, but he missed the boat—literally. It seemed that Stanley had given Bonny responsibility for his "boy," a fifteen-year-old African lad named Baruti. Baruti had been "given" to Stanley by a member of the Emin Pasha Relief Committee, Sir Francis de Winton, who, in turn, had been "given" the boy as a gift by Tippu Tib several years earlier, when de Winton succeeded Stanley as administrator of the Congo Free State. De Winton's rationale for accepting such a gift, let alone passing it (him) on to Stanley can only be speculated upon. In any event, Bonny was to collect Baruti at Stanley's rooms in Bond Street at 8:00 a.m. and then go to London's Fenchurch Street Station, where they would catch the train to Tilbury to board the *Navarino*. When they got to the station, Bonny, for reasons known only to him, abandoned the boy and went to visit the Tower of London. When he returned, around 2:00 p.m., he discovered not only that he had missed the train but that there was no sign of Baruti. As it turned out, the boy had been found wandering the station, cold and hungry, by none other than Colonel J. A. Grant (of the Grant and Speke expedition), also a member of the committee, who took Baruti back to Stanley at Bond Street. Remarkably, Bonny wasn't fired, perhaps because he was the only Expedition member with any medical training. Instead, the next day, he and Baruti were sent to Plymouth, where they boarded a vessel bound for India that would get them to Suez.

The *Navarino* turned out to be a rust bucket; both Stairs and Jephson complained about its poor accommodations and slow progress. They spent their time reading Stanley's accounts of his previous African adventures, smoking (though there wasn't a separate smoking room, which irked Stairs), chatting with the other passengers, most of whom were soldiers and civil servants bound for India, and on occasion walking Barttelot's dog, a Manchester terrier named Satan, and Stanley's donkey, about which Jephson commented, "a fine looking beast, a good deal larger than the ordinary English donkey."

The *Navarino* proceeded at a cruise-like pace, putting in for a few hours at the island of Malta, where the young officers went ashore to stock up on tobacco and oranges and scan the most recent English newspapers for coverage of the expedition. On February 4, they

arrived in Port Said—"the filthiest place I ever was in," wrote Jephson
—where they still managed to find a decent French meal at the city's
main hotel, drop a few pounds at a local casino, and visit a music hall,
where Stairs reported that they "heard a choice collection of French
songs and saw some very bad comic acting." Two days later, their
cruise came to an end as they put in at Ismailia, at the head of the Suez
Canal, where Stanley awaited them.

While his junior officers had been sightseeing, Stanley had been his
usual hyperactive self. Traveling by train and boat, he reached Alexandria in six days, where he was greeted with the news, delivered by Sir
Evelyn Baring, the queen's representative in Egypt, that "there was a
hitch somewhere." The hitch was that the Egyptian khedive (viceroy),
Tewfik, and his prime minister, Nubar Pasha, were dismayed over the
choice of the Congo route, fearing that it would take much longer to
reach Emin than an eastern route, in part because Stanley might be
tempted to do some exploring and mapping while on his way to
relieve the governor. The Egyptians were so exercised that they threatened to withdraw their contribution of £10,000.

Stanley went on the attack. He reminded his doubters that the
Emin Pasha Relief Committee included in its membership such distinguished veterans of African exploration as Colonel Grant (Baruti's
savior), de Winton, Sir John Kirk, the esteemed former consul-general
at Zanzibar, Sir Lewis Pelly, former political agent at Zanzibar, and the
Honorable Guy Dawnay of the War Office, not to mention Mr. Stanley
himself. All of them had agreed on the selection of the Congo route. In
addition, Stanley asserted, "nothing has been settled without the con-
currence and assent of the Foreign Office." He then proceeded
through his well-rehearsed recitation of the advantages and disadvan-
tages of the eastern and western routes. When he was through, Baring
reported to London that the Egyptians were "thoroughly satisfied of
the wisdom of Mr. Stanley's choice in adopting the Congo route in
preference to that from Zanzibar." It was agreed, too, that the expedition would travel under the Egyptian flag and that Emin should be
encouraged to bring as much ivory with him as possible, if and when
he chose to return to Cairo. Stanley was also given official letters to
present to Emin, letters that reiterated the government's official posi-

tion regarding the abandonment of Equatoria, its governor, and its garrisons. Though they contained no new information, these letters proved to be problematical in the extreme when they were finally delivered almost two years later.

There were two other men whom Stanley needed to see in Cairo, men who had information that no one else of Stanley's acquaintance could provide, because they actually knew Emin Pasha. Georg Schweinfurth, a German, and Wilhelm Junker, a German whose family lived in Russia, both belonged to that breed of European scientists-cum-explorers whose scientific curiosity and wanderlust had brought them to central Africa in the late 1860s. Both had spent time exploring the Nile and Congo watersheds, and Schweinfurth had provided one of the first authoritative reports about the pygmies of the Congo region. Like Emin Pasha, they were keen collectors and catalogers of native flora and fauna and had published their scientific and ethnographic observations of Africa in various learned European journals. Though Schweinfurth and Emin had never actually met face to face, they had corresponded extensively for a decade, and Emin considered him a friend. Wilhelm Junker not only knew Emin Pasha personally, having spent more than a year with him at Lado and Wadelai, but was the last European to have laid eyes on him. It was Junker who had brought news of Emin's plight to the outside world and, along with Schweinfurth, had been instrumental in securing Egypt's contribution of money and arms to the expedition.

As it turned out, Schweinfurth and Junker, like the khedive and his prime minister, were initially skeptical about the choice of the Congo route, but Stanley argued that Junker's recent difficulties in securing safe passage through Unyoro and Uganda only strengthened the case for the Congo route. (Evidently, he chose not to mention that his return route would be the same one that Junker had just followed.) Stanley was nothing if not persuasive, and Schweinfurth and Junker soon dropped their objections. Junker even presented Stanley with his most recently completed maps of the northern Congo region.

He was also able to tell Stanley more than he'd heard before about the man he was going to rescue. Given the extraordinary effort being made to save him, it was remarkable how little was actually known about Emin Pasha. His status as "Gordon's last lieutenant" had auto-matically cast him in the martyred general's image. Like Gordon, Emin was seen as a hero, a charismatic, inspiring leader rallying his people in their brave, desperate fight to hold out against the Mahdist hordes. Junker painted a somewhat different picture. After their conversa-tions, Stanley came away with an impression of Emin as "tall, thin [and] short-sighted. . . . As an administrator, he is sagacious, tactful and prudent." His fighting abilities, however, did not impress anyone. He was also told that Emin had only 250 troops with him at Wadelai, and no more than 1,800 altogether, spread among eight stations, and that his authority over some of his garrisons was tenuous at best. Fur-thermore, in Junker's opinion, most of Emin's men would not choose to return to Egypt, and Emin would not abandon them.

Stanley was unfazed. If Emin wasn't quite the gallant hero everyone wanted him to be, he still needed help, and Stanley's would bring it to him. As for his reluctance to leave his province, that remained to be seen. After all, he had yet to feel the full force of Stanley's considerable powers of persuasion. With objections overcome, political niceties observed, weapons and ammunition secured, and intelligence gath-ered, Stanley was ready to go. He turned his attention to his only remaining task in Egypt; the expedition still needed a doctor.

The position had first been offered to a Dr. Leslie, who had previ-ous experience in the Congo, but he had balked at Stanley's clause that no expedition member could publish any account of his travels until six months after Stanley published his. After that, it appeared that Stanley was prepared to head into the jungle with only William Bonny, the army medical assistant, to tend to the health of the men. Then, in Alexandria, Major Barttelot, Stanley's second in command, who was traveling in advance of Stanley, had run into an old friend, a physician named Thomas Heazle Parke, who was a major in the Army Medical Service. Barttelot urged Parke to apply for the position, offer-ing to write a letter of introduction and arrange an interview.

Parke was enthusiastic. He found life in Alexandria boring, "with its sleepy, apathetic, one-eyed inhabitants, and its engrossing native industry of '*backsheesh*' [bribery]." A veteran of several Egyptian cam-paigns, including the mission that had arrived too late to save Gordon,

Parke craved a return to action. His only immediate concern seems to have been finding someone to assume his position as master of hounds for the Alexandrian Hunt Club, Parke having introduced fox hunting to Egypt the preceding year.

Barttelot made the appropriate arrangements, and when Stanley arrived in Alexandria, Parke had his interview. To his surprise, Stanley explained that he already had a sufficient number of officers and could take on no one else. Disappointed and somewhat confused, Parke gave Stanley his card and left.

The next evening, he received a telegram from Stanley in Cairo: "If allowed [to] accompany Expedition, what terms required?" Parke wired back, "Coming to Cairo tonight."

Evidently, Stanley thought better of taking several hundred men into unexplored territory in the heart of the Congo without a trained physician in his party. Within twenty-four hours of his arrival in Cairo, Parke had been released from his duties with the Army Medical Service and had signed the expedition's standard contract to serve as medical officer for the Emin Pasha Relief Expedition. Unlike Dr. Leslie, Parke had no problem with Stanley's rules about publications. He was given fifteen pounds to buy surgical instruments and forty pounds to buy his "outfit," the clothing and other personal items he would need for the trip. The expedition's cadre was finally complete.

On February 12, 1887, at the port of Aden, on the Red Sea, the entire officer corps of the Emin Pasha Relief Expedition boarded another Mackinnon ship, the *Oriental*, for the ten-day voyage to Zanzibar. They were joined by sixty-two Sudanese soldiers, regulars in the Egyptian army who had been made available to the expedition by Baring, Britain's consul in Cairo. Baring reasoned that, since many of Emin Pasha's troops were also Sudanese, it would add to Stanley's credibility, as well as expedite communications, if he arrived with a Sudanese contingent of his own. Stanley concurred. In his diary, Parke provided a description of the Sudanese, whom he called "Nubians," that reflected a rather common Victorian attitude toward black Africans:

> It has been said that the typical Negro is essentially a being of the moment, who enjoys his immediate surroundings without care or fore-

thought for future contingencies, and is aroused to a direct sense of his wants only by the pressure of hunger or pain; that he is a born communist, with an open heart and an open hand, and shares whatever he happens to possess at the moment with all his friends and well-wishers, on the supposition that they will do the same upon like occasion.

Jephson chimed in, "They are of the regular thick-lipped, flat-nosed type of negroes. They have the thinnest legs I ever saw, but what they lack in calf they make up for in feet. I never saw such enormous shapeless feet as they have."

Stairs, the regular army officer, liked the size of the Sudanese, "tall, well-knit, and deep chested," and their sharp khaki uniforms, well-maintained rifles, and gleaming bayonets. It fell to him to handle their daily instruction in military drill,* a task made considerably more difficult by the fact that the Sudanese spoke no English and Stairs no Arabic. For several hours each day, he would bark his commands and then wait as an interpreter relayed them. Sometimes the results were more or less what he expected; sometimes the Sudanese would listen to the interpreter, look at one another for a moment, and then dissolve into hysterical laughter. To his credit, Stairs realized it would be easier for him to try to learn the commands in Arabic than for sixty-two African soldiers to learn them in English.

The Sudanese were joined on board by the thirteen Somalis recruited by Barttelot to serve as Stanley's bodyguards and provide additional security for his company. Parke liked them better than the Sudanese, finding their "Asiatic" features and lighter skin more pleasing as well as judging them "quicker and more intelligent."

The second day aboard the *Oriental*, Parke diagnosed one of the Sudanese with smallpox and immediately embarked on a vaccination program for the Africans and Europeans alike. Some of the Sudanese were afraid of the procedure, so Stairs volunteered to go first to show them there was nothing to worry about. Jephson, to the surprise of the other officers, pronounced himself "an anti-vaccinationist" and declined immunization.

*Stanley had decided that Stairs was better suited to the task than Nelson.

As they steamed south toward the equator, the temperature and humidity rose in tandem. The officers took to sleeping on the decks to escape the heat of their cramped cabins. Jephson wrote that the ship looked like "a bazaar" and smelled "horribly of natives, sheep, and indifferently cured fish." Parke was moved to post a memo detailing his "Rules for the Preservation of Health in the Tropics." Among his recommendations were these:

> *"All drinking-water—no matter how sparkling and pure—should be invariably boiled. . . ."*
> *"Water should always be drawn from the centre of the stream."*
> *"No precaution is too great for protecting the head from the direct rays of the sun."*
> *"Loosely fitting woollen clothes are preferable."*
> *"Sleep as far as possible off the ground."*
> *"Avoid camping under trees."*

The *Oriental* arrived in Zanzibar on February 22. Stairs noted, "Zanzibar appears to be a very pretty place from the sea, but the illusion is dispelled on landing and moving up into the town." From the harbor, Jephson was impressed by the Sultan's new palace, nearly completed, and by the nearby harem that housed the sultan's 170 wives. Upon closer inspection, though, he decided the royal quarters "are fitted up in a trumpery sort of way. [The sultan] seems to spend his money in a childish sort of fashion; on bad electric lights, lighthouses which are never regularly lighted, clocks which do not go, and bells which ring cracked and untuneful peals."

Amid the darkened lighthouses and broken clocks, there was an enormous amount of work to do. Stairs, Jephson, Nelson, and Jameson were detailed to supervise the loading of the two tons of gunpowder destined for Emin Pasha into 45-pound magazines. The task took them to the sultan's powder storage facility, where they found a trio of elderly Zanzibaris in residence who "cook[ed] their food with a delightful disregard of the danger of lighting a fire with several tons of powder lying within a few yards of them."

Barttelot and Parke were charged with the loading of goods and personnel aboard the *Madura,* yet another Mackinnon vessel, which would take them on the final leg of their journey around the Cape of Good Hope to the mouth of the Congo. The goods included all the matériel ordered in advance by Stanley, including tools, the cotton cloth and wire to be used as trade goods, food for the voyage, and livestock. The latter included several dozen goats and sheep, a good-sized flock of chickens, and twenty donkeys.

After the supplies came the men. In addition to the Sudanese and Somalis, Frederick Holmwood, the acting British consul in Zanzibar, had, at Stanley's request, recruited 620 Zanzibari porters for the expedition. The Zanzibaris were brought to the *Madura* aboard launches in groups of fifty. Jephson decribed the scene: "There must have been two thousand, or more of their friends and relations on the beach to see them off and there were dozens of canoes full of men and women paddling backwards and forwards to and from the ship shouting to their friends on board—the ship was a sort of pandemonium." Stairs remarked that "the scene on the decks defied description: donkeys goats, fowls, sheep, and seven hundred men all strewn over the deck in every direction."

For his part, Surgeon Parke, the resident ethnographer, commented that the Zanzibaris were "rather well-built men, strong and muscular; average height, about 5 ft. 9 in. The native Zanzibaris have some Arab blood in their veins; but a large proportion of our men were captured as slaves when young. They accordingly include representatives of nearly every tribe in Equatorial Africa. They seem to be jolly, good-humoured creatures. . . ." It was Stairs who observed, "The Soudanese look with disdain on the Zanzibaris but will have to knuckle down to them." He had no idea how prescient he was.

While his officers were busy turning the *Madura* into "Henry's Ark," Stanley was engaged in a whirlwind series of meetings and negotiations, some out of obligation, others by choice. One of the most important was with the sultan of Zanzibar, the aging, ailing Barghash. Although his authority on the mainland had been substantially undermined by the Anglo-German agreement, the sultan was still the sovereign to whom the Arab traders of eastern and central Africa gave nominal allegiance, including the notorious Tippu Tib. It behooved Stanley to seek his blessing for the expedition. In addition, he carried with him a letter to the sultan from William Mackinnon. The Scotsman hoped that the letter, along with Stanley's talent for persuasion, would bolster Mackinnon's efforts to secure a charter for a trading company to do business in East Africa. Though the charter would come from Her Majesty's Government, it, too, would need the sultan's ratification.

Of the several European powers trying to encroach on his territories and undermine his authority, including France and Portugal as well as England and, most aggressively, Germany, the sultan had the most faith in the British, thanks principally to his long relationship with Holmwood's immediate predecessor, the gifted John Kirk. Now, at the urging of Holmwood and Stanley, the sultan agreed that he would sign the charter for the Imperial British East Africa Company, if and when Her Majesty's Government saw fit to grant it. With that concession, Stanley was certain that the IBEAC would be chartered soon (he was right—Her Majesty's Government granted the charter three months later), and that meant that, between the competing proposals of Mackinnon and King Leopold to Emin Pasha for his services, Mackinnon now clearly had the upper hand. Of course, if things worked out as Stanley hoped, Emin would begin providing those services *after* an interlude at Stanley's side on the English lecture circuit.

Stanley's other meetings, which took up most of rest of his time on the island, were with Tippu Tib. Jephson had already heard so much about Tippu Tib that he refereed to him as "the king, prince and emperor of slave dealers." He was actually disappointed to discover that Tippu Tib was "only" six feet tall and that "there was nothing particular in his appearance to indicate in any way his being a remarkable man." Parke, on the other hand, found him

> a very remarkable man, both physically and morally. His presence is very impressive, standing as he does nearly six feet, with bright intelligent black eyes, and displaying manners of imperial dignity and courtesy. His career has been a most romantic one: first a slave, then an adventurer from Zanzibar to trade in ivory and slaves, he has now succeeded in establishing himself as an uncrowned king on the banks of the Mid-Congo. His personality is altogether an extremely interesting one.

(Where Parke got the notion that Tippu Tib had once been a slave is anyone's guess.)

For his part, Stanley commented, "Tippu-Tib is a much greater man to-day that he was in the year 1877 when he escorted my caravan, preliminary to my descent of the Congo." Tippu Tib had, in fact, increased his influence by following the trail blazed by Stanley in the Congo and adding considerable territory to his empire. Though Stanley would assert in his account of the expedition that he had been prepared to give Tippu Tib a wide berth if he perceived "hostile intentions" on the part of the Arab, the truth was that he needed him to achieve the expedition's goals, both public and private.

Stanley began the conversation by presenting King Leopold's proposition to make Tippu Tib the governor of the Stanley Falls district. If he accepted, Stanley would be killing several birds with one ploy: he'd please one of his employers by returning control of the lost station at Stanley Falls to the Congo Free State; he would convert a potential adversary into an ally for both the Congo Free State and himself, and that, in turn, would reduce the likelihood of trouble with the roving bands of Arab mercenaries whom he thought (incorrectly, as it turned out) Tippu Tib could control.

Tippu Tib could easily have argued that he was being offered something that he already had, but he didn't. He was savvy enough to realize that, sooner rather than later, the Congo's future would be determined by Europeans, not Arabs. Between the French, the Belgians, the English, the Portuguese, and the Germans, not to mention the Italians and perhaps even the Russians, there was simply too much wealth and power to resist. If the powers of Europe judged the rewards in central Africa to be great enough, there would be nothing Tippu Tib and his Arab brethren could do to stop them. Tippu Tib's sense of the future worked to Stanley's benefit because it disposed him to a strategy of cooperation rather than confrontation. Though the salary of thirty pounds a month was pocket change to him, and though he knew the decision would not sit well with some of the other Arab traders operating in the Congo, Tippu Tib accepted Leopold's offer. He would take over at Stanley Falls; he would fly the flag of the Congo Free State; and he would do all in his power to put an end to slave taking in the district (ahem!). He and his retinue would travel with Stanley's expedition to his new post. The agreement also stipulated that Tippu Tib would have a European secretary to assist him, and, most important from his point of view, outside the Stanley Falls district he would remain "at full liberty" to carry on his "legitimate private trade in any direction, and to send his caravans to and from any places he may desire." In other words, it was business as usual.

With Leopold's offer accepted, Stanley turned to his second major concern—the need for additional porters in the interior. In Stanley's mind, the Congo route could be divided into three sections. The first leg, from Banana Point at the river's mouth to Stanley Pool (clearly Stanley had no problem with eponymity), would move on both land and water. John Rose Troup would be in the Congo shortly to make arrangements for both boats and additional carriers for the first segment. The second leg, from Stanley Pool to the confluence with the Aruwimi, would move primarily on the river and require no additional carriers, since the loads would be transported by steamer. It was the third leg, from the Aruwimi to Lake Albert, where they hoped to find Emin Pasha, that would require more porters—hundreds more.

The porters were needed to carry the relief supplies and ammunition they were bringing to Emin Pasha; of equal interest to all parties concerned, they would also be needed to bring back Emin Pasha's enormous cache of ivory by retracing their footsteps to Stanley Falls. It could then be transported back down the river by steamer. In Cairo, Junker had confirmed that there could be enough ivory not only to pay all the expenses of the expedition but also to allow everyone to realize a handsome profit. That was music to Tippu Tib's ears, for though his notoriety was based on his reputation as a slave dealer, in truth, his main business was ivory, and he was already well aware of Emin Pasha's alleged cache.

After the obligatory period of wrangling, the new governor of the Stanley Falls district agreed that he would also provide the needed porters. Stanley would later insist that he specified six hundred carriers, just as Tippu Tib would insist that the number was to be determined. Each carrier would be paid thirty pounds plus food. Tippu Tib would supply each man with a weapon; Stanley would provide the ammunition. Tippu Tib would be paid a fee of one thousand pounds for his troubles. More important, he would receive a liberal (though also unspecified) share of Emin's ivory.

When Stanley announced the results of his negotiations with Tippu Tib to his officers, he was clearly very pleased with himself. Jephson enthused, "It is a wonderful piece of policy Stanley's getting him to come with us," though he acknowledged that the governor's appointment would be controversial at home. "The philanthropists of Exeter Hall [home of the Anti-Slavery Society] will be loud in their reproaches of Stanley's disgraceful conduct and will be dubbing him a fiend incarnate!!" Nevertheless, the agreements with Tippu Tib, he said, "will be of the greatest use to Stanley with his enormous knowledge of the country and I expect the prestige of his name will help us in many a difficulty and enable us to march unmolested through districts through which otherwise we should have to fight our way—it will therefore in many ways save great loss of lives and time."

Jephson was dead right about the reception in Europe; the agreement was roundly condemned both in England and on the continent as "open encouragement of the slave-trade." But, as several hundred men would learn the hard way, he was dead wrong about the imagined benefits the arrangement would bring to the expedition.

With less than twenty-four hours before departure, Stanley made final arrangements to have letters sent to Emin Pasha, to be carried overland by couriers through Uganda and Unyoro, announcing the expedition's expected arrival within five to six months. He also arranged with Holmwood for two hundred additional loads of supplies to be taken to the south end of Lake Victoria in anticipation of his arrival there in March 1888, in approximately one year. The loads would be taken overland from the east coast, along the routes used by Arab traders, presumably to be carried by Zanzibaris under the command of an English officer, to be appointed at a later date. After a farewell dinner at the consulate, Stanley took a launch out to the *Madura,* which had been moved farther offshore to discourage any of the Zanzibaris from changing their minds about going, especially since they'd been paid four months' wages in advance. Waiting for him aboard the *Madura* were 600 Zanzibari men and 23 boys; Tippu Tib and his party, which totaled 97, including his 35 wives; 62 Sudanese;

13 Somalis; 9 Europeans—the cadre hired by Stanley plus his German valet, William Hoffmann; 2 interpreters; and, last but not least, Baruti.

At daybreak on February 25, 1887, the *Madura* weighed anchor and "the most perfectly organized expedition that has hitherto entered tropical Africa," as Holmwood called it, steamed into the Indian Ocean. The first fight broke out in less than two hours.

Chapter Five

HENRY'S ARK

"IT SEEMED AS IF hell itself was let loose," wrote Jephson in his diary. "Sticks, iron bars, coal and every sort of moveable thing were flying through the air, an indescribable scene of confusion and noise was going on—our men seemed transformed into devils and many were bleeding in their heads and arms." The fight was between the Sudanese soldiers and the Zanzibaris. Each side, of course, blamed the other.

Stanley reported the casualties as "ten broken arms, fifteen serious gashes with spears on the face and head, and contusions on shoulders and backs not worth remark, and several abrasions of the lower limbs." He may have been indulging in his penchant for overstatement. Surgeon Parke mentioned only, "One Nubian had his left middle finger broken; and a Zanzibari was disabled, by having both bones of his fore-arm badly smashed. The other injuries were less considerable." Barttelot, the senior military man on the expedition, seemed almost pleased by the fight, observing, "The Soudanese got a jolly good licking, which has done them a power of good." As for his own involvement, he reported regretfully, "I was in my bath at the time."

As far as Stanley was concerned, the most important aspect of the fracas wasn't the casualty list but the comportment of his officers, especially Jephson. "There is a great deal in Mounteney Jephson, though he is supposed to be effeminate. He is actually fierce when roused, and his face becomes dangerously set and fixed. I noted him during the late battle aboard, and I came near crying out, 'Bravo, Jephson!'" In a cryptic postscript, he added, "He will be either made or marred if he is with this Expedition long enough."

The fight was perhaps inevitable, given that the Emin Pasha Relief Expedition had crammed 803 people onto a ship designed to carry only 700. The Zanzibaris and the Sudanese were simply thrown too close together. Sensing the need to impose order and discipline as quickly as possible on the crowded vessel, Stanley divided the men into companies, each with an English officer. Barttelot got all of the Sudanese soldiers and the 13 Somalis he'd recruited in Aden. The other companies, all Zanzibaris, consisted of approximately 115 men each, with 6 chiefs and 6 subchiefs. Each officer was also allowed to pick 2 boys to act as body servants and gun bearers.

Stanley also issued a set of general orders, making it clear, once again, that the expedition was to be run as a military campaign: "Each officer is personally responsible for the good behaviour of his company, and for the good condition of arms and accoutrements after distribution." In addition, "Officers will inspect frequently, when on shore, cartridge pouches of their men to see that the cartridges are not lost, or sold to natives or Arabs *en route*. For an intentional loss of one cartridge a fine of one dollar will be imposed; two cartridges, two dollars and a corporal punishment of five strokes with a rod."

Ironically, given his reputation for heavy reliance on the rod and the whip on his earlier expeditions, Stanley admonished his officers to resort to such measures only in moderation:

> For trivial offences, a slight corporal punishment only can be
> inflicted, and this as seldom as possible. Officers will exercise a proper

discretion in this matter, and endeavour to avoid irritating their men by being too exacting or unnecessarily fussy; it has been usual with me to be greatly forbearing, allowing three pardons for one punishment. Officers should endeavour to remember that the men's labour is severe; their burdens are heavy, the climate hot, the marches fatiguing, and the rations poor and scanty. Under such conditions, human nature becomes soon irritable, therefore, punishments should be judicious, to prevent straining the patience of the men; nevertheless, discipline must be taught, and, when necessary, enforced for the general well-being of the Expedition.

He also set up a rotation in which each officer would take a turn as "officer of the day," and that said officer should carry or wear a sword and "be distinguished by a sash." The officer of the day was responsible for the distribution of rations, the cleaning of the men's quarters, guard postings, including "Soudanese guards on either side of the deck, to prevent Zanzibaris crowding on the Soudanese quarters," care of the animals, and, in general, "to see that every duty, great and small, that ought to be done for the general health and well-being of the Expedition is performed."

Surgeon Parke was perhaps the busiest man on board. Sick call was at 5:30 a.m., and the lines got longer every day. The most common complaint was seasickness, the victims including Tippu Tib and almost all of his wives. (Jephson observed, "Either Tippu Tib is not a good judge of beauty, or the Arab standard of beauty differs widely from the English." He found the Arab's wives "all perfectly hideous.") After seasickness came respiratory ailments that Parke began to suspect were due to the difference in temperature between the lower deck, where the Zanzibaris slept, which was usually in the mid-nineties, and the outside temperature, which could be as much as twenty-five degrees cooler. He reasoned that the porters were emerging from their stifling quarters drenched in sweat and then catching a chill in the cooler air.

Parke also continued with his smallpox vaccination program, though many of the Zanzibaris exhibited the scars that told him they had already had the disease and were therefore immune. The Somalis had been vaccinated when they joined the army, but Parke still wor-

ried that "Central Africa is the true home of small-pox, just as Bengal
notoriously is of cholera," so unless a man could convince Parke that
he'd been successfully vaccinated recently, he was treated again.

Not long after the voyage began, Jephson fell into a long and revealing conversation with Stanley, an exchange he labeled "an argument"
in his diary:

> [Stanley] seemed to think that the only thing worth doing was to
> succeed, no matter how, in anything you undertook and that success
> was everything, whilst I contended that failure was sometimes a nobler
> thing than success—circumstances made it so. I think the argument
> started on the subject of Gordon's failure at Khartoum. Stanley seems
> to have no sort of patience with anything which does not succeed. Of
> course such a feeling is splendid, how could great things be done with-
> out a good deal of that feeling, still if one has *only* that feeling it leads to
> a great deal of injustice and intolerance towards other people who have
> not been so lucky in succeeding as he has done. He spoke very nicely
> about religion and how he envied people who still retained their child-
> ish faith and belief, how he wished he could have the same implicit
> faith that he had as a child, but that it was impossible.

A week into the voyage, the ship had cleared the punishing tropical
heat of Zanzibar, but as it headed south, the milder weather brought
rougher seas and then storms. Everyone got seasick. Slings had to be
improvised in which the donkeys were suspended to keep them from
breaking their legs. The stormy seas necessitated the closing of port-
holes and hatches, which made the pungent smells of the ship even
worse. Jephson found the stench in his cabin "perfectly unbearable."
The ship smelled of salted fish, sweat, human and animal waste, coal
smoke, cooking fires, and several varieties of incense, courtesy of
Tippu Tib's contingent, but the aroma that Surgeon Parke found the
worst came from the disinfectants that were used throughout the ship
twice a day. As he delicately phrased it, "The odours of our various
disinfectants fill the place, and they are not all of the variety which pro-
motes sensuous gratification. . . ."

After two weeks at sea, the *Madura* rounded the Cape of Good
Hope and put in at Cape Town. The officers took the opportunity to

collect mail, go shopping, and, in the case of Stanley, Jephson, and Jameson, look for dogs to accompany them on the expedition. Stanley took a fancy to a pair of fox terriers, one of which he decided would become a present for Tippu Tib. He kept the other one for himself, naming it Randy. Jameson and Jephson found a pair of bull terriers, a brindle and a white, which Jameson described as "the two most ruffianly-looking dogs" he had ever seen. They flipped a coin to determine ownership; Jameson got the brindle, and the "horribly low" white one went to Jephson.*

When they returned to the ship, they found that a crowd had gathered to wish them well and to meet the great Stanley, but, most of all, to get a glimpse of the famous Tippu Tib and his wives. The lady visitors, in particular, insisted on being taken aboard so that they could see the Arab's harem for themselves.

While in Cape Town, they also added another crew member. John Walker, an engineer, was charged with maintaining the fleet of steamers and barges that would take them up the Congo River. He would stay with the expedition only to the end of the navigable river.

When they returned to sea, there was a palpable air of anticipation aboard the *Madura*. The mouth of the Congo River was only a few days away. The expedition was about to begin in earnest. The officers were ordered to weigh their baggage again to be sure they were under the 180-pound limit Stanley had imposed. To their dismay, Jephson, Jameson, and Parke all discovered that they were over the limit. Jameson had to choose between keeping his hunting rifle and equipment for collecting bird and animal specimens and taking along all of the items in his personal "kit." He chose to keep the gun and the collecting equipment, noting, "I have reduced myself to one spare coat besides the one on my back, one pair of boots on and one pair packed, one blanket, and all the rest on the same scale." He voiced the greatest regret over having to leave behind all his tobacco.

Parke had to choose between taking all the medicine and medical

*One week later, according to Jameson's diary, "Jephson, disgusted with the low habits and appearance of his dog, flung him overboard in the dead of the night, with a furnace-bar attached to him. Alas! Poor Bill, his life on board was a short and anything but a merry one."

supplies he could and taking personal belongings. He chose the medicine. Jephson hadn't realized that his camp gear, including his bed
and campstool, counted against the 180-pound allowance. He, too,
had to leave behind personal items to compensate. He was also
annoyed to discover that his personal saddle had been left on the dock
at Tilbury and that he would have to make do with the one issued to
him by Stanley. He did manage to hang on to his mahogany writing
desk.

On March 11, the beginning of their third week, the expedition suffered its first casualty—a donkey. Parke also had a patient with a serious case of dysentery as well as one whose respiratory ailment had
turned into pneumonia. He was exasperated by the seeming indifference of the Africans to the sufferings of their comrades who were ill or
injured. "I experience great difficulty in getting the sick men properly
looked after: the attendants always walk away when my back is turned.
. . . All our coloured friends seem to be very negligent of their disabled
comrades. . . ."

Whether because of negligence or not, on March 13, the dysentery
patient died and was buried at sea; two days later, the pneumonia victim succumbed as well. Parke reported to Stanley that there were at
least three or four other men in such weakened condition that he felt
they would be unable to march after landing. "I thought it would be
well to leave them behind," he said. How these unfortunates were supposed to get back to Zanzibar was, evidently, not considered the expedition's problem.

Shortly after leaving Zanzibar, Parke had noted in his journal the
daily rations for each man:

Meat – 1/2 lb. (3 times per week)
Rice – 1 lb, 8 oz.
Sugar – 1 oz.
Biscuit – 8 oz.
Ghee [clarified butter] *– 2 oz.*
Potatoes – 4 oz.
Fish – 4 oz.
Dahl [a vegetable paste similar to hummus] *– 2 oz.*
Tea – 1 oz.

Curry stuff [made from onions, chilies, turmeric, garlic and black pepper]
Salt – 1 oz.

Parke judged, "The above represents a very substantial bill of fare, and there is no reason to be discontented with it. We can only hope that the supply will last till we find the unknown stranger of whom we are in search." As he would learn all too soon, it wouldn't even come close.

AT THE MOUTH OF the Congo River, a sand spit with the whimsical name Banana Point juts out into the river, separating it from the Atlantic Ocean. It was there that the *Madura* dropped anchor and, in many respects, that the Emin Pasha Relief Expedition truly began. It was also at Banana Point that Stanley had to confront his first crisis.

He had cabled ahead (as had King Leopold) requesting that steamers be waiting at Banana Point to take the expedition upriver some one hundred miles to a settlement called Matadi. Unfortunately, the cable near Banana Point was broken, so neither request got through and no preparations had been made. In fact, the expedition's arrival seemed to come as something of a surprise to the locals.

While Stanley scrambled to patch together a fleet large enough to carry eight hundred men and one thousand loads to Matadi, Parke couldn't help noticing that "the cemetery is the first object of interest which the enterprising adventurer sees when he lands at the Congo's mouth—a cheery introduction to one of the most unhealthy parts of Africa." The expedition had need of the cemetery because there was another casualty, a Zanzibari named Sarboko Makatubu.* The cause, according to Parke, was "heat apoplexy."

A number of European trading companies had offices at Banana Point, and Stanley managed to scrounge one boat from the Portuguese, one from the Dutch, one from the English, and one from the

---

*Parke was the only European who consistently noted the names of the Africans he wrote about. The other officers, for the most part, distinguished only between "Zanzibaris," "Soudanese," and "Somalis."

Congo Free State. Since they were already behind schedule, loads and men were distributed quickly and somewhat haphazardly among the boats. The result, predictably enough, was that some of the officers got separated from both their men and their personal gear. Nevertheless, after only three days, the expedition steamed upriver toward Matadi.

Barttelot and Jephson were the last to leave Banana Point, Jephson managing to commandeer another boat from the Portuguese, thanks to a letter of introduction to the local consul he'd been given. The two officers spent their first night in a settlement called Boma, some sixty miles upstream. There, wrote Barttelot, the Belgian major in charge of the station gave him "such a bad account of the probabilities of obtaining food up to the [Stanley] Falls Station that [he] wrote a letter to the captain of the *Madura* to land all the rice we had left on board." It seemed that much of the Congo region was in the grip of a famine, not news one wanted to hear when hoping to feed eight hundred men by trading cheap cloth and beads with the locals.

When the expedition reached Matadi on March 21, 1887, John Rose Troup, who had been sent ahead from England by Stanley, was waiting for them with 150 additional carriers. It took three more days to sort out all the stores and supplies and pack them up into sixty-pound loads. Despite having already eliminated excess gear after the weigh-in aboard the *Madura,* the officers were told, once again, that they would have to jettison some of their personal items in order to make the weight limits. Major Parke wrote in his diary, "Accordingly many hundreds of pounds' worth of valuables of various kinds were rejected, or left in store. I loaded my donkey as well as I could, still I was obliged to throw away a number of things—among others, some of 'Jameson's oldest,' which he had kindly given me." (Jameson's family made the famous Irish whiskey.)

The trip from Matadi to Leopoldville would be an overland trek of 235 miles, made necessary because steamers were unable to navigate the endless rapids that punctuated that stretch of the Congo River. Only small boats were of any use, so Stanley's pride and joy, the *Advance,* was assembled. It would be used to carry supplies as well as any men who were too sick to travel on foot. It would also be used to ferry the expedition across the larger streams and tributaries encountered along the way. To Jephson's delight, since he was to be in charge of it, the *Advance* was relatively easy to assemble and proved a sturdy, watertight river craft, capable of carrying as many as sixty men at a time.

They also tested one other piece of equipment while at Matadi. Under Lieutenant Stairs's direction, the Maxim gun was assembled and fired for the first time. It took just over one minute to fire 400 rounds. Tippu Tib and his wives seemed particularly impressed.

The first march, on March 25, is described in Stanley's book *In Darkest Africa*:

> On the 25th the trumpets sounded in the Soudanese camp at 5:15 a.m. By 6 o'clock tents were folded, the companies were ranged by their respective captains, and near each company's stack of goods, and by 6.15 a.m. I marched out with the vanguard behind which streamed the Expedition, according to their company, in single file. . . . The setting out was admirable, but after the first hour of the march the mountains were so steep and stony, the sunshine was so hot, the loads so heavy, the men so new to the work after the glorious plenty on board the *Madura*, and we ourselves were in such an overfed condition, that the Expedition straggled in a most disheartening manner to those not prepared for such a sight.

On the third day out from Matadi, the expedition encountered another caravan, moving in the opposite direction. It consisted of some three hundred porters under the command of a young adventurer named Herbert Ward. Ward had heard about the Emin Pasha Relief Expedition from John Rose Troup, Stanley's advance man on the Congo, and Charles Ingham, the missionary who was helping Troup find extra porters for the first phase of the journey. Ward had been in the Congo for three years; he already knew Troup and Stanley from their work for the Congo Free State, and he thought joining Stanley's latest expedition "promised new experiences, unthought of adventures, and all those things which from [his] early days had appeared to [his] sporting mind to make life worth the living." After meeting Troup and Ingham and hearing what they were doing, Ward had taken the initiative and "gathered some three hundred of the required porters together and . . . set out with them to meet Stanley and his company." He added, "With the much-desired supply of porters as an outward and visible argument in my favour, I felt pretty confident that my request for permission to join the Expedition as a volunteer would not be refused."

Ward's account of his first meeting with Stanley contains a vivid description of the expedition's appearance on the trail:

I had broken camp early one morning and was marching rapidly along ahead of my caravan, when in the distance coming over the brow of a hill I saw a tall Soudanese soldier bearing [James] Gordon Bennett's yacht flag.* Behind him, astride a fine henna stained mule, whose silver-plated strappings shone in the morning sun, was Mr. Henry M. Stanley, attired in his famous African costume. Following immediately in his rear were his personal servants, Somalis with their curious braided waistcoats and white robes. Then came Zanzibaris with their blankets, water-bottles, ammunition belts and guns. Stalwart Soudanese soldiers with dark-hooded coats, their rifles on their backs, and innumerable straps and leather belts around their bodies; and Zanzibari porters bearing iron-bound boxes of ammunition, to which were fastened axes and shovels as well as their little bundles of clothing, which were rolled up in coarse sandy-coloured blankets. . . . A steel whale-boat was being carried in sections, suspended from poles which were each borne by four men; donkeys heavily laden with sacks of rice were next met with, and a little further on the women of Tippoo-Tib's harem, their faces partly concealed, and their bodies draped in gaudily-covered cloths; then at intervals along the line of march an Engish officer with whom, of course, I exchanged friendly salutations; then several large-horned African goats, driven by saucy little Zanzibari boys. A short distance further on, an abrupt turn of the narrow footpath brought into view the dignified form of the renowned Tippoo-Tib, as he strolled along majestically in his flowing Arab robes of dazzling whiteness, and carrying over his left shoulder a richly-

*The publisher Bennett was also a commodore of the New York Yacht Club, so he had given the club's flag to Stanley when he went looking for Livingstone. Whether out of loyalty, superstition, or simply because Bennett asked him to, Stanley flew the yacht club flag on all his subsequent expeditions. On the Emin Pasha Relief Expedition, he also flew the Egyptian flag and the Ottoman flag, depending on the occasion.

decorated sabre . . . Behind him at a respectful distance followed several Arab sheiks, whose bearing was quiet and dignified. . . . In that way I passed along the line of 700 men, in whose ranks were represented various types from all parts of eastern equatorial Africa, each wearing the distinguishing garb of his own country. . . . As the procession filed along the narrow, rugged path, it produced an effect no less brilliant than striking. Its unbroken line extended over a distance of probably four miles.

Stanley wasted little time in agreeing to take Ward on and promptly dispatched him with his porters down to Matadi to fetch some of the loads left behind. Ward recalled, "If I could manage to clear out the 1,000 loads from Matadi and be up at the [Stanley] Pool by the end of April, he would 'take me along.' "

As Ward and his men headed down the trail, the expedition continued up, "up" being the operative word. Jameson wrote in his diary, "Marched . . . over one of the worst roads I have ever seen . . . my donkey fell three times . . . lucky I did not attempt to ride him; I very nearly shot him in simple disgust." Barttelot spent his twenty-eighth birthday (March 28), trudging on "a bad road, very much up and down hill, and greatly fatiguing to the men." At day's end, he bathed in a muddy stream.

The expedition was so large that, in the mornings, it could take several hours just to get everyone on the move. Inevitably, the line became fragmented on the trail, and the days would end with the various companies separated from one another, making camp wherever they could. The officers kept getting separated from their gear, including tents and extra clothes, an inconvenience at first, but one that soon turned into a genuine deprivation when it rained.

A typical day, if there was such a thing, began early, with reveille at 5:00 a.m. in anticipation of a 6:00 a.m. march. The objective was to reach the next camp by 2:00 p.m. so that the men wouldn't have to march in the worst heat of the day. The officers' assignments rotated each day. When the track was poor, the advance party had responsibility for clearing the path, an exhausting task. Nevertheless, the officers came to prefer leading to being assigned to "bring up the rear," because it meant meting out a steady stream of physical punishment to

keep recalcitrant porters on the move. Before the first week of marching had ended, a disgusted Jameson wrote, "The work we are doing is
not fit for any white man, but ought to be given to slave-drivers. It is all
very nice for Mr. Stanley, who rides ahead straight on to the next
camp, where we arrive hours afterwards, having done nothing all day
but kick lazy carriers, and put the loads on to the heads of those who
choose to fling them down." After a long day in which the entire march
seemed to be uphill, Barttelot wrote, "I felt like a brute flogging the
men to get them on."

The optimism and high spirits exhibited by the young officers during the voyage to Zanzibar and then around the Cape of Good Hope
quickly gave way to a kind of despondency that some of them attrib-
uted to their leader. Jameson wrote, "It is all so serious, a sort of gloom
hangs over it all." Barttelot observed that he'd never been "on such a
mournful, cheerless trip as this one. The harder we worked, the glum-
mer Stanley looked."

Part of the problem may have been that Stanley simply didn't
believe in praise (the stifled "Bravo, Jephson" after the fight aboard
the *Madura*). "I never permitted myself in Africa to indulge in lauda-
tion of any act however well done," he later wrote. "To faithful performance of imperative duties I considered myself entitled. . . . [I]t was
what they each and all had pledged to do." It seemed he still carried
the harshness of St. Asaph's with him.

It fell to Surgeon Parke, as Stanley referred to him, to try to keep
everyone healthy enough to do his job. It wasn't easy. On the day of
the first march, he recorded the temperature in the shade at ninety-
eight degrees. Four more men had died at Matadi, and eleven others
were left behind, too sick from fever to be able to march. Once they
were underway, the trail was so rocky and treacherous that it tore the
men's feet to shreds (most of the Zanzibaris marched barefoot or in
thin leather sandals). Their cuts and scratches usually became
infected; as a result, within a few days, many of the porters had ugly
ulcerations on their feet and lower legs. The sores would often eat
through the skin all the way to the bone.

The English officers proved vulnerable to fevers, with nearly all of
them feeling "seedy," as they put it, within the first week. Even the

indomitable Stanley was felled by an attack of dysentery that he said was brought on by "an overindulgence in guavas." His illness brought out his temper, something the young officers had not seen much before, but soon found to be a regular feature of life on the trail. Jephson, perhaps the most naïve of the group, wrote in his diary, "One has seen today when he is put out what a temper Stanley has & it is trying at the time & yet I know him to be one of the kindest hearted men possible & I like him extremely."

At the end of the first week, the rain began. These were no gentle showers, but ferocious thunderstorms unleashing downpours that sometimes lasted for hours. Streams became rivers; rivers became raging torrents. Getting the men and animals across them could take a day or more, with loads inevitably being swept away in the strong currents. Stairs's donkey slipped, broke a leg, and had to be shot. One evening, Parke pitched a hammock between two trees on the edge of a stream, only to discover, after it started raining during the night, that he was stranded in the middle of a river. Howling winds were strong enough not only to blow down tents but to topple stacks of ammunition boxes. Everyone's clothes were soaked, but the loads were soaked as well, so there was nothing dry to change into.

The weather was also making more people sick. Fevers, respiratory infections, and exhaustion took a daily toll. In addition, the weather fragmented the expedition even more. On more than one occasion, Parke found himself separated from his medical supplies and could do little to treat his patients.

On April 2, Jephson was sent ahead with the *Advance* to take a small contingent of men and several dozen loads up the main river. He liked being on his own but soon found the river itself to be oppressive.

It was peculiar what a feeling of hatred the river inspires one with. One hates it as if it were a living thing—it is so treacherous & crafty, so overpowering and relentless in its force & overwhelming strength. No two yards of its face are alike—here are whirlpools rushing round with horrid gurgles & there the water eddies up—whilst the river seethes & boils all around you—it is a bad river to navigate. The banks too have a dreary ghostly appearance, black jagged rocks stand out from the banks as if ready to devour anything that came near them & the very

Kites & cranes seem to add to the inexpressible dreariness of the scene—it is all like a bad night mare.... The Congo river god is an evil one, I am persuaded.

APRIL 10 WAS Easter Sunday. As they were preparing to move out, Jameson reported to Stanley that one of his Zanzibari chiefs was too sick to march. Stanley exploded, "Don't bring me such reports, I will not listen to them. My orders were for all the sick to go on and you are to see that they do." Jameson described in his journal what ensued:

> I behaved very cruelly in making the man get up, amidst the mur-murs of all the chiefs, and then driving him on. In a few yards he fell down and could not get up. Mr. Stanley, on passing, recognized him, and went up to see how he was. He called to Dr. Parke to come to him, and told him that, as he was a good man, we must not lose him; gave him medicine then, and left more with him, at the same time telling one of the officers of the [Congo Free] State to look after him, get him into a hut, and do everything he could for him. Of course all the men now look on me as a brute and Mr. Stanley as a sort of guardian-angel....

Episodes like this made it clear that, deliberately or not, Stanley was distancing himself from his junior officers. He generally took his meals alone, though his tent was large enough to have easily accommodated all of his officers (it took forty porters to carry its component parts). He rarely consulted with them or even announced his plans in advance. Perhaps he was only trying to establish his authority; per-haps he wanted to see how the younger men would handle the stress of the march. Whatever his motives, his command style vexed the younger men, even the army veterans. Barttelot, in particular, clashed with his commander.

Stanley decided quickly that his second in command was head-strong and impetuous and therefore a problem. At the same time, he decided that the Sudanese contingent seconded to the expedition by Evelyn Baring in Cairo was also a problem. So he lumped them together, holding Barttelot responsible for the behavior of the Sudanese, even though he'd had nothing to do with the decision to bring them. In fact, most of the officers had already come to dislike the Sudanese. Stairs had written,

> They are poor material for an expedition such as this. At making themselves comfortable in camp and in foraging for food they are not a patch on the Zanzibaris. Why, when we draw up to the shore at nights to camp, the Zanzibari's in fifteen minutes have their fires going, their shelters made and pots boiling, whereas one sees these Soudanese wandering aimlessly about, bemoaning their fate and cursing themselves for coming.

The irony of Stanley's association of Barttelot with the Sudanese was that the major disliked them more than anyone. He found their sloth and rudeness appalling, their behavior toward the Zanzibaris inexcusable, and their lack of pride or discipline utterly unacceptable from men who called themselves soldiers. Yet Stanley had placed him in the impossible position of being responsible for the very men he hated, and who, of course, hated him in return. It was a recipe for failure, which may have been exactly what Stanley had in mind.

When the expedition left Matadi, the Sudanese had been given three weeks' rations, intended to sustain them until they reached Leopoldville. After two weeks, they announced to Barttelot that their rations were finished and that they would not go a step farther unless they got more. Barttelot said he would go to Stanley, but the Sudanese demanded to see Stanley themselves to present their demands. In a heated exchange, their spokesman berated Stanley, saying they had been brought on the expedition under false pretenses; if they'd known how they were to be treated, they never would have come. Stanley flew into a rage, threatening to shoot them all if they came one step closer. He even turned on the interpreter who had translated the Sudanese diatribe, threatening to fire him on the spot. Later, when Barttelot went to him to apologize for the problems the Sudanese were causing, Stanley said it was Barttelot's fault. His anger seemed to feed on itself until he was screaming that he would ruin Barttelot's career, that news of his failures "would be in every paper, that General Brackenbury would hear of it, and he had the ear of Wolseley [the British commander in Egypt]." Barttelot, who had a short fuse of his own, blasted back. "An empty threat," he said, and told Stanley that he didn't have the power to ruin him or anyone else.

The next morning, Stanley called a general muster. In front of the entire company, he picked out seventy men, mostly Sudanese, supplemented by a few Zanzibaris. It was clear that his primary criteria were laziness and unwillingness to follow orders, selecting the worst laggards in the entire expedition. He then announced that they would become a new company under Barttelot's command. They were to march ahead of the rest of the expedition, with orders to stay well clear of the main group. He warned Barttelot that if his new company lost a single load getting to Leopoldville, he was through.

Remarkably, in Stanley's account, the creation of Barttelot's company of malcontents is presented as a pragmatic management decision. There is no mention of his animus toward his second in command: "Thinking that there would be less chance of the Soudanese storming so furiously against the Zanzibaris on the road, I requested Major Barttelot to keep his Soudanese a day's march ahead of the Zanzibaris."

Nevertheless, Stanley's antipathy toward Barttelot was now out in the open for all to see. Eventually, that prejudice had consequences that neither man, in his wildest imaginings, could have conjured, consequences so profound that they ultimately changed the world's opinion of Henry M. Stanley.

As the expedition made its slow, soggy way toward Leopoldville, another problem became apparent; Stanley's assumption that the natives they encoutered along their way would be able to trade trinkets for food was seriously off the mark. For one thing, many of the villages they found were empty. Jameson's diary noted, "Marched to the deserted native village of Congo da Lemba, which, until burnt by the Congo Free State, was a flourishing native town. The Congo Free State people have burnt the huts and driven away the natives from nearly every village on the road, consequently there is not a scrap of food to be obtained for love or money. They [the CFS agents] say that the natives interfered with their carriers on the road." The carriers were hauling ivory and India rubber to the coast.

When they did encounter populated villages, a different problem arose, thanks to the behavior of the Zanzibaris. Jameson again: "We passed through two small villages, one of which our men looted, taking all the manioca roots and driving off the poor frightened natives like so many sheep. I sailed in at last with a big stick and drove them off, but not before they had filled their blankets with *chakula*."* Unfortunately, some of the Zanzibari chiefs and subchiefs were as prone to thievery as their men, so the English officers had to try to maintain order by themselves. Once the Zanzibaris bolted toward a village, there was little they could do.

Before long, their reputation began to precede them, and the natives started to retaliate. One of Stairs's subchiefs, Khamis bin Athman, was shot dead while raiding a village, but his death had little, if any, impact on the Zanzibaris. They kept behaving like hooligans in every village they encountered. A week after Khamis's death, three more Zanzibaris were shot by natives determined to defend their turf.

Stealing from the natives wasn't the only problem the officers were having with their porters; they were also stealing from the expedition itself. Rifles and ammunition were disappearing; so were food and tools. The officers were expected to take inventory of their company's loads each night. When loads were missing, men were sent back on the trail to look for them. Sometimes, they'd find them discarded near the trail, but usually they found nothing.

On such occasions, the officer was expected to report the loss to Stanley immediately. One evening, Jameson reported that his company was short one box of ammunition. He had already sent two of his chiefs back along the trail to look for it, but they had returned empty-handed. Stanley ordered the company to fall in and began interrogating the chiefs as to which men had carried which loads during that day's march. The chiefs became confused; the men sometimes switched loads and many of the loads looked virtually identical. After several minutes of this charade, in desperation, one of the chiefs cast suspicion on one of the porters, even though Jameson later recorded in his diary that the man was one of his best carriers and undoubtedly *not* the culprit. Stanley ordered the three chiefs stripped to the waist

---

* *Chakula* means food in Swahili.

and held on the ground. He then instructed the Somalis to give each of them fifty lashes. The unfortunate porter got one hundred lashes, and, as he was being beaten, Stanley stood over him, demanding that he tell him where he had hidden the box. The man, screaming in pain, continued to protest his innocence. Stanley wasn't through. He ordered the chiefs put in chains and padlocked together. The next day, they were to remain that way and would also to be made to carry a load.* He concluded this performance by telling Jameson how lucky he was; had the incident occurred on his expedition of 1877, he would have had him shot.

As was often the case with Stanley, it was hard to tell whether he had behaved so brutally out of genuine rage or for effect. Perhaps, in this instance at least, it was the latter. He had become increasingly exasperated with the pilferage problem, so he decided that an example needed to be made. To reinforce his dissatisfaction, Stanley started bringing up the rear himself to show the proper way to deal with laggards. The effect was dramatic. Surgeon Parke noted that Stanley's presence at the back of the line

> made a very happy difference in our day's progress—after a few examples had been made by whipping in the incorrigible loiterers. Whatever may be said or thought at home by members of philanthropic African societies, who are so anxious about the extension of the rights of humanity, there is no getting an expedition of Zanzibari carriers across this country without the use of a fair amount of physical persuasion.

If harsher methods helped to quicken the expedition's pace, the gain was offset by continuing sickness. Parke worried especially about the Somalis, of whom he had already become very fond. They constantly ran fevers and seemed more susceptible to the symptoms of "marsh-miasm" (malaria).†

---

*Ironically, after two days of this brutality, Tippu Tib, the most notorious slaver in Africa, whose henchmen were reportedly the most brutal in a brutal business, intervened on the chiefs' behalf, and Stanley relented.

† It was not yet known that malaria is an insect-borne disease. Rather, it was thought that "marsh-miasm" was caused by air infected with a noxious substance, especially an unhealthy exhalation from marshy soils. While Parke knew that the malarial parasite had

The Zanzibaris brought some of their health problems on them-selves. Despite repeated warnings from the officers, they continued to drink unsafe water and eat raw manioc. This tuber, a staple in the diet of most of the local tribes, required careful preparation to leech away toxins that could cause severe cramping and nausea. Correct prepara-tion, however, took time. After an arduous day on the trail, many of the Zanzibaris were too hungry to wait. They ate their manioc raw—and paid the price.

Though they had been on the trail less than a month, it was already apparent that finding enough food was going to be a problem. Jame-son, who had expected to be able to supplement the expedition's food supply by shooting game, noted that while they saw plentiful tracks of elephants, hippopotami, and antelope, they almost never saw the ani-mals themselves. Evidently, the sound of eight hundred men tromping through the jungle was something of a warning signal. Stairs noted dryly, "We killed a large venomous centipede in our tent this evening, quite enough to do for us all if he had got a chance." As for their rations, he put it plainly, "Our grub on this expedition is very bad. In fact much worse then bushmen or surveyors in New Zealand or Canada get," presumably a harsh standard of comparison.

Just in case the officers weren't feeling sorry enough for themselves, they would occasionally come across officers from the Congo Free State who, according to Stairs, all seemed "to travel from place to place like lords: they have the very best of tinned goods of all sorts—jams, bacon, oatmeal, tea, coffee, condensed milk, tinned fish, besides fruits and whatever else the country yields. They generally have three or four native boys as servants, carry swell tents and beds, and gener-ally do themselves up well. In fact, I know of one or two officers of the CFS [who] get carried about by porters wherever they go."

Jephson, who spent most of the first month with his small contin-gent of porters navigating the river in the *Advance,* ran into an English-

---

been seen in human red blood cells under a microscope, the mode of transmission was not known. The discovery that the disease is carried by the female *Anopheles* mosquito happened in 1888, while Parke and the expedition were deep in Africa. At the end of the expedition, Parke estimated the surviving Europeans had each suffered "at least 150 attacks of African fever [malaria] during the march."

man named Roger Casement, who worked for an American trading company called the Sanford Exploring Expedition, which operated on the upper Congo. Casement invited Jephson to join him for dinner at his camp one evening. Like the Belgians, Casement lived well despite his circumstances with "a large tent and plenty of servants," noted Jephson. "It was delightful sitting down to a *real* dinner at a *real* table with a table cloth & dinner napkins & plenty to eat with Burgundy to drink & cocoa and cigarettes after dinner." He added ruefully, "It will be a long time before I pass such a pleasant evening again." Meanwhile, the expedition was dining on bouillon, biscuits, and half rations of rice.

Despite the harsh conditions and difficulties with the men, at least some of the young officers managed to find moments of enjoyment and appreciation of their surroundings. For one thing, everyone liked Tippu Tib, who proved to be an affable and entertaining traveling companion. In addition, Jameson found parts of the countryside so beautiful that he continually wanted to stop to capture the scenery in sketches. He was enthralled by the variety of exotic birds and butterflies he saw, and was delighted when he managed to capture a few specimens.

Jephson waxed rhapsodic about the plant life he found on his river journey, including "quite the most beautiful Lycopodium moss [he'd] ever seen—what wouldn't people give for it at home in the green houses." Jephson also seemed to be discovering things about himself, about his resourcefulness, stamina, and leadership ability that pleased and perhaps surprised him. As the expedition neared Leopoldville, the end of the first major segment of the trip, he wrote in his diary, "I like this life, I like the hard work & the constant moving & pushing forward, & I would not change it's hardships & unpleasantness for the ease of civilization."

Still, by the time the expedition reached Stanley Pool, where the Congo River widened to the proportions of a medium-sized lake, certain facts were unavoidable. In less than a month, by Stanley's reckoning, they had lost fifty-seven men to death or desertion, with one hundred more "useless as soldiers or carriers" because of illness or injury. Thirty-eight rifles were missing, along with over half of the axes, shovels, billhooks, and canteens they had started with. They had consumed 27,000 pounds of rice and had scoured the famine-plagued countryside of just about every other edible morsel. As Stairs put it, "Food is absolutely unobtainable here for the men; our rice is finished; we can get no manioca for the men; there is no meat; what are we to do?"

The answer, Stanley hoped, was to get back on the river and head east for Yambuya. There was only one problem. Just as King Leopold's "magnificent fleet of steamers" had failed to materialize at Matadi, it was nowhere to be found at Leopoldville, either. There was only one boat, a steamer named, as so many things in the Congo Free State were, for Stanley. But *Stanley* the steamer could hold only two hundred men, and despite their losses, the Emin Pasha Relief Expedition still numbered well over seven hundred.

Chapter Six

THE RIVER

LEOPOLDVILLE, the settlement next to Stanley Pool, had been one of Stanley's finer achievements during his tenure as the primary builder of the Congo Free State. Of the twenty-two stations he carved out of the jungle, Leopoldville was one of the most extensive, with officers' quarters, storehouses, wharf facilities, and fields of bananas, rice, and maize under cultivation. He could not have been pleased by what he saw as the expedition made camp. Jephson noted in his diary,

> Leopoldville must in Stanley's time have been a pretty place & a great amount of labour must have been expended in making it. . . . Today Leopoldville is a different place. It is a mere collection of tumbledown huts—grass grows on the once tidy terraces & chokes up the groves of plantain & pine apple, the blacksmith's forge is roofless, the paths are furrowed by the rain water, rotten doors hang creaking on their rusty hinges, all is neglect & decay.

Nevertheless, the locals were thrilled to see Bula Matari again. Jephson noted with amazement, "Until night Stanleys tent was thronged with neighbouring chiefs, all of whom brought some present—they crowded to pay their respects to the great white chief & to see him after his long absence. It gave one an idea of the power he was & is in the country, his name acts like magic & to be one of Bula Mataris 'sons' means that you will always be treated with consideration by the natives."

Unfortunately, the warm welcome did little to help Stanley solve his immediate problems—food and boats. The visiting chiefs brought a few chickens and goats, but like much of the rest of the Congo Free State, Leopoldville was in the grip of a near-famine. There wasn't enough food for the people who were already there, let alone for several hundred more. Stanley immediately dispatched Jameson upriver to hunt hippopotami while he focused on his transportation problem, which Jephson described succinctly in his diary, albeit with uncharacteristic sarcasm:

> It looked very well in the newspapers, the paragraph "His Majesty the King of the Belgians has placed his whole flotilla of steamers at the disposal of Mr Stanley, thus the Expedition will be conveyed up river to a point only a few hundred miles from Wadelai." On our arrival the "flotilla" was found to consist of one steamer "The Stanley" capable of holding two hundred men & 500 loads, a whale boat holding 50, & a small steamer, the En Avant, which has no engines & no paddles, capable of holding 85 men. Such a "flotilla" is but of little use to an Expedition consisting of 800 men & 1000 loads.

The situation didn't come as a complete surprise to Stanley. As soon as the expedition reached the Congo, he had started making inquiries about the availability of boats upriver; the news had not been encouraging, and he suspected that he would have to improvise when he reached Leopoldville.

He'd even gotten a hint of the trouble that awaited him before leaving London. During his frenetic preparations in January, he had approached Mr. Robert Arthington, a wealthy industrialist who was a major supporter of English missionary work in the Congo, about borrowing or renting a small steamer called the *Peace*, which belonged to the English mission at Leopoldville. Not only had Arthington given him an emphatic no; he'd lectured him about his behavior on previous expeditions and warned him to "repent and believe the Gospel" lest his soul be lost forever! With this unpleasant history in mind, Stanley had arranged with Congo Free State authorities to have any mail to the Leopoldville mission from headquarters in London intercepted and held until the Expedition had come and gone, in case Arthington's objections were forwarded to the mission. It turned out to be an astute precaution.

With so many men and loads, Stanley needed to get his hands on just about everything in Leopoldville that floated, whether the owners wanted him to have it or not. In addition to the *Peace*, there was another small steamer, the *Henry Reed*, which belonged to the settlement's American Baptist mission. Though both boats were small, they shared one feature that made them particularly desirable; they had engines.

Thanks to Stanley's precaution with the mail, Mssrs. Bentley and Whitley, the English missionaries at Leopoldville, had received no instructions from London regarding letting Stanley use the *Peace*. They protested that the boat was in need of significant repairs, but Stanley would not be dissuaded. After some minor waffling, and Stanley's agreeing to assist in the cost and labor of the repairs, they agreed to make the *Peace* available to the expedition.

The Americans, on the other hand, turned out to pose a real problem. Their first objection was that the Reverend Billington, head of the mission, was to be married shortly to a woman missionary who lived near the coast, so he needed the *Henry Reed* to get to his wedding. Stanley sent Barttelot and Jephson to plead with him, telling them to cite the urgency of the expedition's mission and to offer "liberal terms" to charter the *Henry Reed* for two months. Billington and his colleague Dr. Sims didn't budge.* Stanley then enlisted Lieutenant

---

*Stanley wrote that Dr. Sims had applied for a position with the expedition but had been passed over, implying that the real reason for the withholding of the *Henry Reed* was simple spite.

Liebrechts, the Congo Free State officer in charge of the Stanley Pool district, to impress upon Billington, "the irrationality of his position, and of his obstinacy in declining to assist us out of our difficulties." According to Stanley's version of the events, after twelve hours of "demanding, explaining, and expostulating" by Liebrechts, Billington agreed to charter the *Henry Reed* for £100 a month.

According to Jephson, Barttelot, Parke, and the others, the *Henry Reed* was acquired in a manner somewhat less diplomatic than the one Stanley described. After Billington's initial refusal, Stanley sent Jephson with an armed contingent of Sudanese to put the *Henry Reed* under guard. Then he sent Barttelot with another armed contingent to demand the surrender of several engine parts that Billington had removed to render the steamer inoperable. When those tactics failed, Stanley had Liebrechts declare the situation to be a state of emergency threatening the Congo Free State. The lieutenant then requisitioned the *Henry Reed* on behalf of the Congo Free State and promptly turned it over to Stanley, though Stanley did eventually pay £100 to the Americans for its use.

As these "negotiations" proceeded, Jameson was upriver, hunting hippos. To assist him, he hired a gang of natives from Bangala, a settlement farther to the east. According to Jameson, the men were cannibals, as evidenced by their teeth, which had been filed into points. In a letter to his wife, Jameson wrote, "They told me that one of their chiefs, who was very rich, is now quite poor from buying nice, fat, young women to eat; this I know to be a fact. . . . They eat all those whom they kill in battle. They remove the inside, stuff them with bananas, and roast them whole over a big fire." It's hard to tell from his tone whether Jameson was appalled or excited, or both.

With the Bangalas paddling an enormous canoe, and using a rifle he had borrowed from Bartellot, Jameson managed to get several kills but discovered, to his dismay, that the dead hippos sank rapidly to the bottom of the river, where they remained for several hours. Eventually, the carcasses floated to the surface again, at which point they could be hauled to the shore to be butchered. The problem was that the river current tended to carry the submerged animals downstream, sometimes *well* downstream, so that by the time they surfaced, they could be long gone. Jameson lost more than half of his kills in just this way. Then, to add insult to injury, much of the freshly butchered meat that he sent downriver to the expedition spoiled in the blazing sun. Still, he managed to get enough edible meat to the men to avoid outright starvation.

While Jameson waited for his dead hippos to surface, Stanley was filling out his "fleet" as best he could. He reasoned that he could use the three steamers now at his disposal to pull along several other, engineless craft, employing them as barges. To that end, he arranged for the use of a partially built steamer, the *Florida*, which could carry upwards of 150 men and loads, and he rounded up a few more whale boats, similar in capacity to the *Advance*. His navy now consisted of three steamers and five other vessels—every river-worthy craft in Leopoldville. It wasn't enough; Stanley still couldn't move all the men and loads at the same time. He would have to make multiple trips, which would cause unacceptable delays. The alternative was to leave some of the loads behind and to make some of the men walk, which was exactly what he did.

The next morning, he sent Barttelot, Parke, and 153 men, including all the Sudanese, upriver on the *Stanley*. After two days, they were to disembark in an area where it was thought food might be more available. They were then to march overland to a rendezvous point some one hundred miles farther upriver. Then, when the *Stanley* returned to Leopoldville, it would have just enough capacity to take all the remaining men upriver at the same time.

The Barttelot/Parke contingent left on the morning of April 25. The *Stanley* got back to Leopoldville on the twenty-eighth. On the thirtieth, Herbert Ward and John Rose Troup, who had been left at Matadi to make arrangements to have the loads that had been left there brought up to Leopoldville, arrived in a canoe. Poor Troup, one of the first men hired by Stanley back in London, had spent all of his time handling logistics in the Congo; he had yet to spend a single day on the trail with the expedition, let alone wrangling the donkeys, the job he thought he'd been hired for. No sooner had he arrived in Leopoldville than he was told he would be left behind again. He was to wait for the arrival of the matériel from Matadi and keep an eye on an additional cache of nonessential supplies for which there was no room in the flotilla. Then, when the expedition reached the end of the navigable river at Yambuya, where a permanent camp was to be built, Stanley would send the steamers back to retrieve Troup and the additional loads. He assured the disappointed Troup that he would still get the opportunity to march with the expedition to Lake Albert.

On May 1, Stanley's ungainly navy was ready to begin its voyage upriver. Jephson described the scene:

> Stanley & Ward in the Peace, carrying 50 men, & having in tow a lighter belonging to the State, carrying 50 men, & the missionary boat Plymouth carrying 35 men. The Henry Reed having Tippu Tib's men numbering 50 & towing the En Avant (a hull) with 50 men, & our boat, the Advance with 35. The Stanley with 168 men, with Stairs, Nelson, Jameson & myself on board, towing the Florida with 168 men & 9 donkeys. There were also 594 loads distributed amongst the steamers.

Jephson's reference to lighters and hulls "being towed" was somewhat misleading, since the engineless boats couldn't really be towed behind the steamers, because the *Stanley* and the *Henry Reed* were stern-wheelers. Instead, the other boats had to be lashed to the sides of the steamers in order to avoid their churning paddle wheels and considerable wakes. These jury-rigged craft, riding three abreast, proved just as unwieldy as one might imagine. In fact, the *Peace,* which was carrying Stanley, and was the last boat to pull away from the docks, had no sooner eased into the current than her steering gear snapped. Stanley watched helplessly as the rest of his navy chugged upstream and out of sight.

Still, in all, Stanley must have been pleased with himself. He had surmounted—or so it seemed—an obstacle that could have proven a disastrous setback for the Expedition. He had not only kept his force intact (the Parke/Barttelot contingent notwithstanding) and more or less on schedule; he had improvised the means by which he could move everyone upriver more than one thousand miles in less than sixty days. His Congo strategy was working. Bula Matari was proving to be as formidable as ever.

———

INDEED, THE RIVER TRIP from Leopoldville to Yambuya unfolded as smoothly as any phase of the entire expedition, which is not to say there were no problems. The *Peace* proved to be a continuing source of aggravation, because of an "asthmatic" boiler (Stanley's word) that often failed to produce enough pressure to create forward progress. All of the steamers had engine troubles from time to time, but the greater problem was running aground on the numerous sandbars that dotted the river, necessitating laborious operations to move the ponderous vessels back into navigable river channels. The *Stanley* hit a submerged reef, tearing several large holes in her hull. John Walker, the engineer brought on at Cape Town specifically for the river voyage, devised patches from flattened oil drums, and the Somalis did the treacherous work of attaching the plates below the water line.

Each steamer, with its various attached barges, proceeded at a different speed up the river; as a result, just as had been the case on land, the expedition was rarely all together at night. In addition, when the boats tied up at the end of the day, every available hand was ordered ashore for several hours of wood cutting. The steamers had voracious appetites for fuel, with the *Stanley* requiring twelve thousand pounds of wood a day. In all, the trio of steamers consumed well over twenty thousand pounds of wood per day, all of which had to be cut as they went. The exhausting, mind-numbing work often lasted well into the night.

While the bulk of the expedition cruised up the river, Barttelot and Parke found themselves back on the trail with 150 disgruntled Sudanese and Zanzibaris. None of their men understood why they were being forced to walk while everyone else got to spend lazy days on the boats, shooting at hippos, and leering at Tippu Tib's wives. To make matters worse, both Barttelot and Parke were sick. Parke, in fact, had been unwell since before their arrival at Leopoldville, and he continued to feel "seedy" almost every day.

Stanley had devised a plan that called for the Barttelot/Parke contingent to march most of the way to a large settlement upriver called Bolobo, where they would reunite with the rest of the expedition. There Stanley would choose some 125 men who would be left behind while the rest of the expedition made its way to Yambuya, on a Congo tributary called the Aruwimi, the easternmost village in the Congo Free

State that was reachable by river. The steamers would then go all the way back downriver to retrieve Troup and the loads left at Leopold-ville, then back to Bolobo to pick up the contingent left there, and finally back to Yambuya, where the rear column (as Stanley was calling it) would remain in a fortified camp. There they would either await Stanley's return after he reached Emin Pasha at Lake Albert or follow him to the lake, provided that Tippu Tib came through with the additional porters needed to carry all the ammunition and supplies.

The plan to split the expedition in two was not a new development. Stanley had announced his intent to build a fortified camp at Yambuya even before he left London. What wasn't clear was who would have to stay at Yambuya and who would get to go on with Stanley to Lake Albert and the anticipated rendezvous with Emin Pasha. Barttelot, however, was already convinced that he would be one of the unlucky ones, and he was right. During an overnight rendezvous with the main expedition, five days out of Leopoldville, Stanley gave him the news. Surprisingly, in view of his antipathy toward the major, Stanley tried to present his decision as a vote of confidence in Barttelot. "Had there been a person of equal rank with him, I should certainly have dele-gated this charge to another, . . . [but] I informed the Major that I could not really undertake the responsibility of appointing youthful lieutenants to fill a post that devolved on him by rank, experience and reputation."

Barttelot didn't buy the sugar coating for a moment. In his journal, he wrote, "His object at present is personal dislike to me and hatred of the Soudanese. . . ." He added, "Unless I obtain a distinct assurance of aid from Tippu-Tib, and promise of proceeding to Wadelai [Emin Pasha's headquarters on Lake Albert], I would go home."

Barttelot knew the sort of men Stanley would leave with him; he would get the sick and injured. In addition, he would get the trouble-makers, the lazy ones, the thieves and looters, the ones who followed orders only when the stick was applied. In short, he would get the dregs, while Stanley took the fittest, most capable carriers for himself on the sprint to the lake. To a man who had volunteered for the expe-dition in part to further his military career, it was a bitter blow. Instead of a chance to distinguish himself on a high-profile mission, he would be stuck commanding a garrison full of invalids, misfits, and malcontents. Nevertheless, Barttelot's threat that he would go home if not permitted to continue on to Lake Albert was probably an empty one; his sense of duty as an officer and a gentleman was too strong. He would follow his orders.

THE EXPEDITION CONTINUED upriver, the steamers leapfrogging past one another, depending on which one was having the best luck avoiding the sandbars and/or engine trouble. The officers' diaries sounded almost like travelogues. Jephson and Jameson commented on sightings of new species of butterflies and birds (Jameson also did a fair amount of sketching); Parke and Stairs took a more anthropological bent, commenting on styles of native body paint, dress, and coiffure. They continued to have problems with the Zanzibaris behaving badly in native villages, though there were no more shootings, and they were actually managing some successful trading encounters, with *matokos*, the lengths of brass, iron, and copper wire, being exchanged for goats, chickens, fish, corn, and manioc. Unfortunately, the officers still took turns getting sick with fever and dysentery, and Jephson suffered an episode of blood poisoning that rendered his right arm virtually useless for almost two weeks and caused him a great deal of pain. Nonetheless, when they steamed into Bolobo on May 14, the expedition was in relatively good shape, well fed, and peaceful.

Bolobo was actually a series of settlements arrayed along the river. Jephson estimated the total native population at close to twenty thousand. In contrast to that around Leopoldville, the area around Bolobo offered plenty to eat. The villages were surrounded by fields of manioc and shaded by plaintain trees. Each village seemed to have a healthy herd of goats and large flocks of chickens, and the river was full of fish.

The plentiful food supply was the primary reason Stanley chose Bolobo as the place to leave 125 of the weakest men behind; they would be able to regain their health and strength for the long walk home. Though Stanley had originally intended to leave Barttelot at Bolobo, the other officers protested that since he had been with the expedition from the start, he should be allowed to continue at least to Yambuya. Stanley acquiesced and named the recently arrived Ward to stay with William Bonny, the former army medical assistant, at Bolobo instead.

After only a day at Bolobo, the flotilla was back on the river, minus 127 men. Those left behind were suffering from one or more of the usual maladies that had afflicted the expedition since leaving Zanzibar—fevers, dysentery, malarial symptoms, and respiratory problems—and all of them were malnourished. It would be up to Bonny to care for them. Parke left him with medicines and supplies, along with two books, one to help him with diagnoses, the other containing instructions on how to perform various surgeries.

For several days after departing Bolobo, the steamers continued slowly upriver, the Congo spreading as wide as eleven miles in some places, its banks lined with hippos and crocodiles. At night, they usually docked near native villages, the men going ashore to cut wood and trade for food with the villagers, unless they decided to save their *matokos* and cowries, and simply help themselves to whatever they cared to steal. It was just such an incident that precipitated perhaps the ugliest internal confrontation the expedition had yet seen.

On the night of May 17, Stairs and Jephson and a contingent of Zanzibaris and Sudanese were put ashore near a small village to cut wood. Jephson's diary entry reports the ensuing fiasco:

> Stairs was ahead with the axemen when some of the Zanzibaris came running back saying the natives were unfriendly & meant to fight them. Stairs therefore thought it advisable to return on board & take some ammunition with him before going off into the bush to cut wood. Meantime the Zanzibaris & Soudanese made a rush into the village looting everything & setting a house on fire. It was all a hoax, the villagers were not unfriendly but were only afraid at seeing so large a force landing, it was however impossible to stop the looting altogether, though we did our best. . . . Next morning every man had an enormous bundle of loot consisting of food spears chickens etc. Stairs & I stopped each man as he came on board & made him leave what he had stolen—first because the men were packed as closely as possible on board & there would not have been room for it . . . & secondly we thought if they saw they did not benefit from stealing in a friendly country it would be a lesson to them that it would be useless to do so in

the future. On arriving at Lukolela . . . some of the men went & complained to Stanley about what Stairs & I had done or rather to put it more exactly—what they said we had done, for of course they denied the stealing & said the food we took away from them was what they had bought.

Jameson's diary picked up the story at this point:

This morning, I am sorry to say that the most disgraceful row I have ever heard of happened between Mr. Stanley and Jephson and Stairs. It appears that early this morning a number of the men and chiefs went to Mr. Stanley, and complained that the officers had flung away their rations for one day. Mr. Stanley sent for Stairs. The men swore they had bought the food from the natives last Saturday at the village they looted. . . . Stairs told Mr. Stanley this, assuring him that only stolen stuff was taken away from them, and sent for Jephson, who gave the same testimony. It is still quite evident that Mr. Stanley takes the word of the Zanzibaris on every occasion before that of the white men, and when he saw that he had hold of rather the wrong end of this stick, he attacked them about their tyranny to the men. He attacked them in a frantic state, stamping up and down the deck of the *Peace*. He called Jephson all sorts of names, a "G——d d——n son of a sea-cook, you d——d ass, you're tired of me, of the Expedition, and of my men. Go into the bush, get, I've done with you. And you too, Lieutenant Stairs, you and I will part to-day; you're tired of me, Sir, I can see. Get away into the bush." Then he turned round to the men (about 150) sitting down, and spoke Swahili to the effect that the men were to obey us no more, and that if Lieutenant Stairs or Jephson issued any orders to them, or dared to lift a hand, they were to tie them up to trees. He had already told Stairs that he had only to lift his hand for the men to throw him into the sea. He lastly offered to fight Jephson, "If you want to fight, G——d d——n you, I'll give you a bellyful. If I were only where you are, I'd go for you. It's luck for you I'm where I am." Mr. Stanley was on the deck of the *Peace,* Jephson on shore. All this was said before the missionaries, Tippu-Tib, and every one. As for Stairs or Jephson being tired of the Expedition, no men could work harder or have their hearts more in it. I should think a repetition of this kind of thing would make them both pretty sick of Mr. Stanley and the Expedition.

Stanley wasn't through. He summoned Parke onto the *Peace* to deliver himself of the opinion that all the officers were "talking about him" and "had formed a compact against him and were tired of the Expedition, and had only made a row to get sent back." Parke "assured him of our loyalty, and earnest wishes to carry on the work."*

After Parke departed, it was Barttelot's turn. (Despite his disappointment about the assignment to Yambuya, Barttelot's sense of duty seemed never to falter.) He gave Stanley some time to calm down and then approached him to see whether he really wanted to dismiss Jephson and Stairs. Stanley said he did, and again mentioned his conspiracy theory, barking at Barttelot that "he could carry on the Expedition without any of us." Barttelot noted, "I asked him whether I was to tell Jephson and Stairs that his decision was irrevocable. He hesitated, and then said, 'As regards myself, it is.' By that alone I knew he was blustering. I went away, and Jephson and Stairs came over, at my advice, and saw him and squared it."

"Squared it" may have overstated the result. In his diary, Stairs wrote, "I have stood more swearing at, heard more degrading things and swallowed more intemperate language from another man today than I have ever before," and he fretted that, because the confrontation had taken place in public view, "discipline must suffer and the men [will] think less of us and become incited to mutiny. I am awfully sorry this has happened as it destroys all harmony among us." As for Stanley's reaction, we shall never know; *In Darkest Africa* never mentions the incident.

Stanley's corrosive performance notwithstanding, the expedition was now having a relatively easy time of it. They had entered a stretch of the river where the natives were cautiously friendly, willing to trade foodstuffs for *matokos*, cowrie shells, and beads. They would row out to the steamers in their canoes, hold chickens and manioc bread aloft, and exhort the flotilla to stop and do business.

At Equator Station, the principal commodity offered by the natives

---

*Startlingly, Parke dismissed the entire affair, writing, "After further explanation and apology the affair was smoothed over, and never once thought of again by either black or white."

was ivory. Parke noted that they would take payment in the form of spoons, forks, and plates, in addition to the usual beads, cloth, and *matokos*. He reckoned that their usual buyers, mainly Arabs and Congo Free State agents, were making at least a 200 percent profit when they resold the ivory for eight to ten shillings per pound. Parke himself bought a handsome tusk in exchange for a teaspoon of salt.

After more than four months away, telltale signs of homesickness were creeping into the officers' diaries. Stairs noted the queen's birthday; Jameson remarked on Cup Day at Ascot: "I wonder if, amongst the number of one's friends there, any of them will give a thought to those who are absent like myself." Parke even found a reminder of home in the costumes of the native women. "They wear picturesque fringes of brown bark-fibre cloth, pretty nearly identical in shape and make with a Highland kilt. I could not help thinking at the moment what an attractive ballet costume it would make for our theatres at home." All the officers were writing letters at every opportunity in anticipation of the day when the steamers would leave them at Yambuya and head back to Leopoldville, marking their last contact with civilization for many months.

On May 30, the expedition arrived at Bangala, the last CFS station they would see on the Congo. The next day, Barttelot, Walker, the engineer, and a contingent of forty Sudanese (no Zanzibaris) were dispatched on the *Henry Reed* to deliver Tippu Tib and his retinue to the station at Stanley Falls. In his journal Jameson noted, "The reason that Stanley is sending the Soudanese instead of the Zanzibaris, is that he fears that if they saw Tippu's place and people, the discontented ones would come back to the camp, and persuade the others to desert us; as, should they once get to Tippu-Tib's camp, it would be a simple matter for them to get out to Zanzibar with one of his caravans, or find employment in some of his towns." An interesting observation, given that one of Stanley's most persuasive arguments for the Congo route versus a route from the east had been the reduced chance of desertion by the Zanzibaris.

There was also some concern about the reception Tippu Tib might receive. Stanley warned Barttelot that such a large contingent might be mistaken for a CFS raiding party sent to retake the station from the

Arabs who had overrun it some ten months before. There was no way of knowing whether word of Tippu Tib's appointment as the new governor of the district under King Leopold had reached Stanley Falls. Barttelot and the Sudanese were told to be ready for trouble.

As the last CFS outpost on the river, Bangala not only represented the officers' last contact with civilization (meaning white people); it also moved several of them to deliver opinions about what Stanley and King Leopold had created in the heart of Africa. Stairs spoke for the group when he wrote, "We have now seen the whole of the working of the Congo Independent State. We have seen how it treats the different trading houses under its jurisdiction. We have also seen a fair portion of the country it governs and the natives under its charge. Our unanimous opinion is that the state, as now constructed, is one huge mistake." Jameson noted drily, "I notice that one of the chief occupations of the Belgian officers at the different stations is to civilize the country by adding to the population specimens of half-breeds, as they are all more or less married to native women. This mode of civilization seems to be adopted by all the white men here, whether officers of the State or not."

Throughout their journey upriver, the officers had commented on the sad state of most of the CFS stations. Inevitably, there were only vestiges of the considerable work done by Stanley and his crews when the settlements had first been built. Rather than expanding on those impressive initial efforts, the Belgian agents had allowed the stations to deteriorate, largely surrendering to the jungle's efforts to reclaim what Stanley had developed. Fields went untended, buildings were abandoned, and roads and paths were allowed to become so overgrown that they ceased to exist. From the outset, Stanley had maintained that to succeed, the Congo Free State must establish an efficient system of communications, principally through the construction of a railroad paralleling the river, but not a single section of track had been laid since his departure. Leopold's "river navy" had proved a poor substitute. The chief means of communication between villages remained what it had been since prehistory—the native drum. Though Stanley made few comments in his own account about revisiting the territory he had labored so mightily to subdue, and though he continued to drink to the health of King Leopold when dining with the various CFS agents he encountered, the deterioration he saw at every turn must have represented a major disappointment.

The day after Barttelot departed with Tippu Tib and his entourage for Stanley Falls, the rest of the expedition was back on the river as well. Steaming away from Bangala, the officers experienced an almost palpable shift in mood. Their senses seemed sharpened as they went where few white men had been before. Jameson, the naturalist, commented on the increasingly exotic birds and butterflies he saw, as well as the appearance of large monkeys in the treetops. The natives in the villages they passed now covered their bodies in war paint. They would rush to the riverbanks with spears and shields, gesticulating wildly at the passing steamers, making obscene gestures, apparently uninterested in making contact, let alone trading. There were, however, exceptions.

On June 6, in the middle of the afternoon, the *Stanley* was running out of fuel. As the captain approached a village in hopes of sending men ashore to cut wood, the natives appeared on the riverbank, seemingly ready to fight. An expedition interpreter established contact, attempting to assure them that the expedition had no hostile intentions, but after an hour of "palaver" (the default term for conversations with the natives), the tribal chief made it clear that they would be allowed to come ashore only if one of the expedition's "chiefs" made blood brotherhood with him. Stairs was elected. Jameson described the ensuing ceremony:

> Stairs and the Captain of the steamer landed, and the ceremony was performed with much pomp. Stairs' arm was slightly cut until blood came, and the chief's also, then the bleeding parts were rubbed together, each man swearing to be a "true brother" to the other. All this time a wild song was kept up by the natives, beer was drunk, and the chief sent us a present of a goat. The fierce natives of half an hour ago were in one moment transformed into the sharpest and most eager traders, ready to sell everything they possessed.

Jameson also noted another trend spotted by several of the officers as they made their way farther into the jungle: the disappearance of clothing on the female natives. "What little modesty one has left, after seeing daily so many naked forms, here received rather a shock, for the women are as Eve was before she went to Madame Figuier* for her costumes. . . . The people here are the genuine savage, without a vestige of civilization."

With his gentlemanly reserve, Parke's fashion commentary was as follows: "An interesting gradation in the arrangement of the female costume has been observable as we ascended the Congo. The higher up the river we found ourselves, the higher the dress reached, till it has now, at last, culminated in absolute nudity." The natives did, however, still wear "accessories," and these gave the young officers more than a moment's pause. Parke's diary: "The natives offer for sale necklaces, and other ornaments, made from the teeth, dried fingers, etc., of their victims." The expedition had unquestionably entered the land of the cannibals.

On June 12, the expedition finally reached the mouth of the Aruwimi River, the Congo tributary that continued almost due east while the main river turned south. The confluence was the site of the principal villages of the Basoko tribe and also the place where Stanley's "boy," Baruti, had lived as a child. As the steamers approached the village, Stanley told Baruti to hail his fellow tribesmen and invite them to visit. The offer wasn't as altruistic as it might have seemed, for Stanley had been to Basoko before and, as he put it, his "previous attempts at winning the confidence of these forest natives had been failures." Stanley was anxious to trade with the Basokos to lay in a store of provisions for the expedition to use while the camp was being built for the rear column, a few miles upriver at Yambuya.

Baruti talked with the natives who approached the *Peace* in canoes. He told them who he was and asked to speak to his older brother. After much yelling back and forth, the brother appeared in another canoe, but he was skeptical that the young man in Western attire on the deck of a steamboat could be his brother. (Baruti had been gone for six years.) Even after Baruti gave the names of their parents and siblings, the brother remained unconvinced. Then Baruti showed him a scar on his arm left from an encounter with a crocodile. That did the

Figuier is French for "fig tree."

trick. As Stanley put it, "The young, broad-chested native gave a shout of joy, and roared out the discovery to his countrymen on the further bank, and Baruti for the first time shed tears."

That night, Stanley gave Baruti the option of leaving to rejoin his family, but the boy chose to stay with the expedition. Parke thought Baruti had made the right choice: "Baruti's reason for not staying with his relatives we were strongly disposed to attribute to a suspicion that he would be cooked and eaten by them."

Unfortunately, Baruti's family connections cut little mustard with the Basokos. Even after Stanley had a long "palaver" with the chief, who may or may not have been Baruti's father, the natives refused to let the expedition come ashore. Instead, it had to tie up on the opposite bank to make camp and cut wood. The next day, the expedition waited until early afternoon, hoping that the natives would come in their canoes to trade, but none appeared. Disappointed, Stanley ordered the flotilla to proceed upstream.

The Aruwimi proved to be a beautiful river, wider at its mouth than the Nile at Cairo, according to Parke, but it quickly narrowed to only four hundred yards across, giving the expedition a good look at the natives in the villages that lined the banks. Once again, they were greeted by tribesmen in full war paint, shaking their spears and shields, making gestures either threatening or obscene. They also displayed new body markings and mutilations unlike those seen on the Congo—ears deliberately enlarged to two or even three times normal size, noses pierced straight through with pieces of bone.

The native villages were composed of conical huts made of palm leaves. Occasionally, a few brave inhabitants interested in trading would paddle out to the steamers, impressing the Englishmen with their skill as boatmen. They maneuvered their canoes from a standing position and were capable of both remarkable speed and great precision, using long, beautifully crafted paddles with ivory knobs on the end. Still, most of the natives seemed frightened at best, hostile at worst. As the expedition approached its final destination on the river, at Yambuya, Stanley appeared resigned to another less than welcoming reception. He wrote, "We were now over 1300 miles from the sea. Opposite to us were the villages which we hoped, with the goodwill of the natives, to occupy temporarily as a depot for the men and stores left at Bolobo and Leopoldville, 125 men and about 600 porter-loads of impedimenta; if not with the natives' goodwill by fair purchase of the privilege, then by force."

On the first morning after their arrival, Stanley steamed across the river in the *Peace* to have a "palaver" with the chief of the village. Before he did, he left orders with his junior officers, as described by Jameson:

> We were to steam out into the middle of the river, and just keep headway against the stream. No whistle would be blown except by the *Peace*, and that would be a signal that negotiations had failed. We were then to cross over to her, when Jephson would land his company, Stanley having already landed his; they were to ascend the bank, and spread in skirmishing order through the village. Whilst the others were landing, Stairs, if necessary, was to work the Maxim gun from the top deck of the *Stanley*.... No shots were to be fired, and no damage done to the village unless the natives showed active resistance.

Stanley, in his version of the morning, said that the palaver lasted for three hours without reaching an agreement. "It was now nine o'clock, my throat was dry, the sun was getting hot, and I signalled to the steamer *Stanley* to come across and join us ... the Zanzibaris and Soudanese scrambled up the steep sides of the bluff like monkeys, and when the summit was gained not a villager was in sight."

It never seemed to occur to anyone, or at least not to any of the officers, that routing several hundred peaceful natives from their village and then occupying it was anything other than simple logistics. Jameson casually noted, "We put up our tents, and destroyed the huts which were not required for our men." Jephson, sounding a bit peevish, wrote, "The natives had taken every bit of food with them & we only found pots & tools etc. in the houses. We pitched our tents & Stanley pitched his on the highest bit of ground in the village which he at once decided should be the site of the entrenched camp."

Before nightfall, a switchback had been cut down to the river, poles had been cut to begin construction of a fortified palisade, the bush had been cleared to a distance of fifty yards around the village "to prevent the natives from creeping up close to the village & surprising" the newcomers, and crews were already cutting wood for the steamers' return trip to Leopoldville. Less than twelve hours after they'd arrived, Yambuya belonged to the expedition.

Baruti chose the first night after the taking of Yambuya to change his mind about staying with the expedition. Jephson wrote, "Baruti, Stanley's boy, & a man & boy from the *Stanley* ran away last night . . . Baruti took Stanley's revolver & hunting belt & the *Stanley's'* men stole guns from the steamer. It is most ungrateful of Baruti for when Stanley bought him years ago from Tippu Tib he was a bag of bones & he has trained him & been good to him ever since." For his part, Stanley, was remarkably calm—at least in print:

> [Baruti] came into my tent in the dead of night, armed himself with my Winchester rifle and a brace of Smith and Wesson revolvers, a sup-ply of rifle and revolver cartridges, took possession of a silver road-watch, a silver pedometer, a handsome belt with fitted pouches, a small sum of money, and, possessing himself of a canoe, disappeared down river to some parts unknown, most probably to his tribe. At any rate, we have never seen or heard of him since. Peace be with him!

For the next ten days, Stanley supervised the building of the camp that would house the rear column. The crews worked from before dawn until after dark, digging a deep trench around the camp into which nine-foot poles were set side by side to form a palisade. In addition, at strategic points, raised platforms were built to accom-modate several riflemen in case the natives attempted to storm the camp.

As far as they could tell, most of the natives who had been rousted from the village were now reconvened on the opposite shore of the river. Wanting to demonstrate the expedition's honorable intentions, Stanley embarked on a bizarre campaign, encouraging his men to cap-ture natives and forcibly bring them into camp so that they could see the benign nature of the expedition's presence! "Several captures were made in the woods, and after being shown everything, the natives were supplied with handfuls of beads to convey the assurance that no fear ought to be entertained of us and no harm done to them." Not surprisingly, Stanley's version of public relations proved unsuccessful. The Yambuyans continued to stay away.

Parke was detailed to survey the extensive manioc fields adjoining the camp. He reported that they were "capable of sustaining the garrison of Yambuya for years, if necessary." That was the good news, but Parke went on, "There is, however, little or no prospect of obtaining any other provisions, as game is scarce—on account of the fact that the river bank is very high in this neighbourhood, which does not afford animals the convenience of coming down to drink. . . . The hippo also seems scarce." Like Stanley, Parke expressed the hope that the natives would change their minds about trading with the rear column, "when they have had an opportunity of seeing that they will be honestly paid for their goods, and not plundered." He might have added that he hoped they would change their minds soon because, once again, the expedition had run out of meat, as well as sugar and salt. The same day these observations were written, the *Stanley,* her decks laden with a ten-day supply of wood hewn out of the Yambuyan jungle, headed back down the river to Leopoldville. "We all stood on the bank and saw the last of her," wrote Stairs. "Nelson and I have spent some pleasant days on the old *Stanley.* . . .One feels a pang at losing her."

By the end of their first week at Yambuya, Stanley was becoming anxious about Barttelot. By his calculations, the major should have rejoined them on or before June 19. When June 22 dawned with no sign of his second in command, he decided to send Stairs out to look for him. He had already imagined several scenarios that might have arisen, none of them good. In the tamest scenario, he reasoned that the mission had been delayed by the usual hang-ups on sandbars and perhaps by harassment from hostile natives. He also worried that the Sudanese had been unable or unwilling to cut sufficient wood to keep the *Henry Reed* moving, and they were simply stranded. More ominously, he thought that Tippu Tib might have seized the steamer and taken Barttelot, Walker, and the steamer captain prisoner. This bit of melodrama struck Jameson as "rather a curious fact, since he [Stanley] stated to us that he considered Tippu's word as good as any white man's." Finally, and most dramatically, Stanley feared that the Sudanese might have mutinied and perhaps even murdered Barttelot.

Stanley wrote out an elaborate set of orders for Stairs and told him to prepare to embark with thirty Zanzibaris on the *Peace*. (It was a measure of Stanley's concern, if not panic, that he was willing to risk the same Zanzibaris he'd pulled back from the mission to deliver Tippu Tib in the first place.) Stairs was to go as far as Stanley Falls, if necessary, and take whatever action he saw fit to recover the *Henry Reed* and its men. Happily, as Stairs was making his final preparations to leave, the *Henry Reed* rounded the bend with two fat goats and a cow tethered to its decks, along with Barttelot, Walker, and their men.

As it turned out, Barttelot and company had indeed run into trouble with the natives along the river; they had been hung up on sandbars; they had had difficulty getting enough wood to keep steam up; and Tippu Tib's arrival at Stanley Falls had initially provoked a hostile reaction. In other words, Barttelot's voyage had differed little from the rest of the expedition's river-borne journey. In the end, however, Tippu Tib had been embraced by his Arab comrades at Stanley Falls, and while there had been a few injuries from hostilities with the natives, there were no fatalities. Overall, Barttelot reckoned the mission a success. After all, hadn't he returned with two fat goats, a cow,* and generous bunches of bananas and plantains? What more could Stanley want?

With Barttelot back in the fold, the expedition turned its attention to its imminent separation. The juggernaut that had begun in Zanzibar with more than eight hundred men was about to be split in two. Shortly after Barttelot's departure to Stanley Falls, Stanley had called the other officers together for a briefing. Afterward, each man seemed to take away a different impression of what was about to happen.

Parke wrote,

> Mr. Stanley ... informed us that he intended marching to the Albert Nyanza [Lake Albert], relieving Emin Pasha by handing him over the ammunition, and returning to Yambuya about October or November. He would leave the entrenched camp here in charge of Barttelot and

---

*Unfortunately, the cow was not for Yambuya. It was a gift from Tippu Tib to the native chief at Leopoldville. Jameson was especially disappointed: "I do not see a chance of our getting any meat after he is gone."

Jameson. He went on to say that Barttelot was not sufficiently forbearing, but that Jameson's experience of Africa would, he thought, correct
his impetuosity. Also, that Tippu-Tib with 600 men were coming
here, to assist in carrying the ammunition to Emin Pasha.

Jephson wrote, "In the evening Stanley called us together & told us
what work we were to do tomorrow & gave us an idea of his plans. We
shall remain here seven days to wait for Tippu Tib's men to come up
& to make the entrenched camp."

Jameson, who, as it turned out, would be remaining at Yambuya
with Barttelot, also recorded his impressions:

> After dinner Mr. Stanley called us all to his tent, and had a long talk
> with us. . . . He told us that Tippu-Tib was coming with as many men
> as he could get together, seven days after our landing, and going on
> with him to the Lake. He would also send enough men to enable us to
> follow after him with all the stores left here, and those brought up by
> the *Stanley* on her return journey. He also said that where there was
> enough food for so many natives, there must be far more than enough
> for us. He dwelt a long time on the great importance of Barttelot's and
> my position, being left in charge of the fort to guard all the stores, as, if
> anything should happen to them, the Expedition would be at an end.
> . . . He also told us of his intention of returning from Lake Albert
> Nyanza on the route which he will take from here, in case we had not
> enough men to come on with the ammunition and stores; in any case
> we would meet on the road.

Ironically, on the same night that the officers were forming such var-
ied impressions from Stanley's briefing, Barttelot was having his own
briefing with Tippu Tib at Stanley Falls. The Arab was annoyed with
Stanley because the arrangement they had made in Zanzibar called for
Tippu Tib to supply six hundred armed porters to assist the expedition once they reached the farthest extent of the Aruwimi, *provided
that Stanley furnished them with ammunition*. Now, as everyone
knew, Stanley had left most of the ammunition back in Leopoldville.
As far as Tippu Tib was concerned, that constituted a breach of contract, and he was no longer obligated to supply any porters to the

expedition at all. This was a terrifying prospect to Barttelot, whose only chance of getting out of Yambuya and following Stanley to Lake Albert rested with Tippu Tib and his promised porters. The best the major could do was to cut his own deal with Tippu Tib, an agreement that was as flimsy as it was desperate. "I effected a sort of compromise," he wrote in his diary, "by making him half promise to supply, at any rate, 200 men with ammunition, to be repaid. This will suit me admirably, because then, directly Ward and Troup come up, [with the ammunition stores from Leopoldville] I can cut on, unless Stanley changes his mind."

The day after he returned from Stanley Falls, Barttelot wrote, "I had a long talk with Stanley in the afternoon and he gave me permission to move on eastward directly Ward and Troup, etc., were up." Either Stanley had an overnight change of heart about this "permission," or it was a case of wishful hearing on Barttelot's part, because the next day Stanley delivered a long letter of instructions to Barttelot with a copy to Jameson, who was to be his second in command. The letter keenly disappointed Barttelot.

After reading his instructions, and also after learning about Stanley's panicky plan to send Stairs to "rescue" him when he was two days late returning from Stanley Falls, Barttelot had yet another conversation with Stanley, which quickly became a heated argument. What seemed to gall Barttelot the most was that after Stanley's earlier words of praise for Tippu Tib, it was becoming apparent that Stanley didn't really trust the Arab at all, and that boded poorly for the prospects of the rear column. Barttelot wrote, "He [Stanley] thought Tippu Tib had captured us, or the Soudanese had mutinied. The former I told him was absurd, and I could not understand how he could have entertained it, especially after what he had told me, viz., *that he would as soon trust Tippu-Tib as a white man.*" Stanley's reply: "Yes; but I would only trust a white man to a certain point, and no further. . . ."

At that point Barttelot, whose temper was already up, made the mistake of telling Stanley that Tippu Tib felt that his contract with the expedition had already been breached and that he was no longer obligated to provide *any* porters to the expedition. Stanley became enraged. He screamed that he didn't care what Tippu Tib said or

HENRY M. STANLEY at age twenty.

STANLEY in 1895, the year he was elected to Parliament.

MAJOR EDMUND MUSGRAVE BARTTELOT,
the doomed commandant at Yambuya.

JAMES S. JAMESON.
"I asked him just now if he was in any pain.
'No, old chap, no pain, only tired—Oh! So tired.'"
—Herbert Ward describing Jameson's last hours.

LIEUTANANT WILLIAM G. STAIRS,
who longed for Canada.

A. J. MOUNTENEY JEPHSON.
Naïve, resilient, steadfast, he reminded
Stanley of himself as a younger man.

CAPTAIN ROBERT H. NELSON.
He suffered the most and said the least.

MAJOR THOMAS HEAZLE PARKE.
Stanley said of him, "Skilled as a physician,
tender as a nurse, gifted with remarkable
consideration and sweet patience."

HAMED BIN MUHAMMAD, aka TIPPU TIB,
slaver, ivory hunter, and governor of the
Stanley Falls district of the Congo Free State.

WILLIAM BONNY,
Army medical specialist, the only
European survivor of Yambuya.

HERBERT WARD.
His appetite for adventure very nearly killed him.

JOHN ROSE TROUP.
All he ever wanted was to march with Stanley.

EMIN PASHA in the uniform of a German officer.

THE SURVIVORS AT ZANZIBAR.
Parke was in the hospital, close to death, when the photo was taken.
Typically, none of the Zanzibaris was identified.

thought or did, because he no longer even wanted his help. It was a telling moment, since in his petulance and anger Stanley revealed not only his feelings about Tippu Tib but also his true expectations about the rear column.

It is important to remember that the decision to split the expedition at Yambuya had been made before Stanley left London, let alone Zanzibar. Speed had been his overriding objective from the beginning. When he told Barttelot that he didn't need Tippu Tib, he was admitting, in effect, that "relieving" Emin Pasha, in the sense of bringing him ammunition and supplies that would enable him to remain in Equatoria to fight the Mahdi's army, was never his real objective He had paid lip service to the concept of "relief" while he needed to, but once he was deep in the jungle, with no political niceties to be observed, and no one to answer to, he no longer had to maintain that pretense.

In addition, Stanley still believed he could reach Emin at Lake Albert in a matter of weeks—two months at most. He then anticipated spending no more than two weeks with Emin Pasha before beginning the return march to Yambuya, which presumably would go even faster than the outbound trip. Two months going, two weeks at the Lake, two months back—even with an allowance of two more weeks for delays, he was looking at five months—tops.

Even if Tippu Tib wasn't upset, and therefore likely to drag his heels, if he cooperated at all, it could easily have taken him at least half that time to just to find 600 porters who were willing to brave the Ituri. Then they would have to be transported to Yambuya, where Barttelot and Jameson would have to organize them, and then undoubtedly reorganize and repack the loads, before being ready to move out. The rear column would then number well over 850 men and loads, larger than the entire expedition when it left Zanzibar. Without Stanley to lead them, with new porters to be broken in, plunging into the unknown terrors of the Ituri forest under the command of a man whose competence Stanley openly questioned . . . Clearly, he never expected it to happen. What he expected was that Barttelot and Jameson would sit tight in their camp, to be joined by Troup, Ward, and Bonny and the additional men and loads from Leopoldville and Bolobo, and then everyone would recover his health and strength until the advance guard returned.

Stanley's obsession with speed may have been informed, in part, by his reporter's instincts. He still made his living as a journalist; his books (and the lectures that followed them) were his livelihood. Stanley, the journalist, knew that the story of this expedition had at least as much to do with Charles Gordon as with Emin Pasha. It could be argued that the ultimate purpose of the Emin Pasha Relief Expedition, at any rate in the public mind, was catharsis. In this regard, the expedition was about avenging Gordon's death at Khartoum, a tragedy that most Britons believed had occurred for only one reason; Britain had been too slow to act. On the day that Gordon's head was literally delivered on a plate to the Mahdi, the British force sent for *his* relief had been less than ten miles away from Khartoum. One day had made all the difference. One day! Henry Morton Stanley was not about to let that happen again. If he had to leave the expedition's ammunition and supplies behind, so be it. What mattered above all was reaching Emin Pasha while he was still alive. Dead men don't need bullets. And, in this case, they wouldn't sell books.

Still, as Stanley got ready to march out of Yambuya, he prepared for Barttelot a set of instructions whose elaborateness was exceeded only by their ambiguity. Regardless of his real intentions, he still needed to maintain the pretense that the rear column would eventually be following him to the lake, since the stated objective of the expedition was to bring ammunition to Emin Pasha, and almost all of the ammunition would be with the rear column. In typical Stanley fashion, he sketched out several scenarios. He began by stating the gravity of the responsibility he was entrusting to his second in command:

> The interests now entrusted to you are of vital importance to this Expedition. The men you will eventually have under your command consist of more than an entire third of the whole Expedition. The

goods that will be brought up are the currency needed for transit through the regions beyond the lakes; there will be a vast store of ammunition and provisions, which are of equal importance to us. The loss of these goods and the men there would be certain ruin to us, and the advance force would in its turn need to solicit relief. Therefore, weighing all these matters well, I hope you will spare no pains to maintain order and discipline in your camp and make your defences complete. . . .

These do not seem to be the words of a commander who anticipated being followed. Rather, they are an admonition to take no chances. Stanley then continued with the first scenario, though his tone was cautionary and speculative rather than directive:

It *may happen* [italics added], should Tippu Tib have sent the full number of adults promised by him to me—viz., 600 men able to carry loads—and the *Stanley* has arrived in safety with the 125 men left by me at Bolobo, that you will feel yourself sufficiently competent to march the column, with all the goods brought by the *Stanley* and those left by me at Yambuya, along the road pursued by me. In that event, which would be desirable, you will follow closely our route, and before many days we should most assuredly meet.

He continued with a second possibility:

It may happen also that, though Tippu Tib has sent some men, he has not sent enough to carry the goods with your own force. In that case you will, of course, use your discretion as to what goods you can dispense with to enable you to march. For this purpose, you should study your list attentively—viz.:
  1st. Ammunition, especially fixed, is important.
  2nd. Beads, brass wire, and cowries rank next.
  3rd. Private baggage.
  4th. Powder and caps.
  5th. European provisions.
  6th. Brass rods, as used in the Congo.
  7th. Provisions (rice, beans, peas, matamas, biscuit.)

He cautions, however, "it would be better to make marches of six miles twice over, *if you prefer marching to staying for our arrival* [italics added], than throw too many things away."

If Stanley was serious (and humor was never his long suit), the logistics of double marches, even over decent roads and through hospitable terrain, would have been staggering, but he was suggesting double marches through utterly unknown and presumably forbidding terrain. The idea was absurd, and even the redoubtable Bula Matari must have known it.

There was a third, very real possibility: that Tippu Tib would never send any porters at all. What was Barttelot to do in that event? On this possibility, Stanley was silent. Presumably, he thought that even the impetuous Barttelot wouldn't be foolish enough to try to follow him under those conditions.

Of all the decisions Stanley made in the course of the expedition—indeed, of all the decisions he made in his entire career in Africa—his decision to leave almost half his men and more than half his supplies at Yambuya had, arguably, the most profound consequences. Not only did the fates of more than 250 men hang in the balance, but what happened at Yambuya would eventually change the way the world viewed Henry Stanley, both during his lifetime and in the later judgment of history.

THE WORK WAS nearly finished on the camp's defenses, the trenches dug, the palisades erected, the rifle platforms built. The *Stanley*, the *Peace*, and the *Henry Reed* had all been sent back down the river. When the last of them disappeared, Stairs observed, "Thus we have seen the last white man till we reach Emin Pasha!" The officers who were going with the advance column all sent packets of letters on the steamers, their last communications with Europe for an indefinite period, along with various souvenirs they'd collected. Parke's cache included an elephant tusk, several spears and shields, a canoe paddle, and one of the native skirts that had reminded him of a Highland kilt.

The natives across the river were still proving to be reluctant trading partners, so when one of their chiefs asked to make blood brotherhood with his white counterpart, Stanley took it as a good sign. Perhaps relations would begin to warm up. Since Barttelot would be the senior man at Yambuya, the task fell to him. Of all the officers, Barttelot was arguably the most antipathetic toward Africans, so, of course, this particular ceremony proved to be the most elaborate ritual the expedition had yet seen. Jephson's account was the most vivid: "This time an incision was made in the arms of each, & each sucked the blood of the other & then rubbed some blood on each others neck, a chicken was then killed & the blood strewed about & amid the chanting of the few assembled men the bond was complete." He failed to mention that a pinch of dirty salt was rubbed into the incisions before the licking took place. Barttelot pronounced the experience "exceedingly nasty." Jameson, however, looked at the practical side: "Let us hope that it will induce them to bring us something to eat."

If Barttelot was angry about being left behind, Jameson was aggrieved. "Alas for all my bright dreams about the march from the Falls to Wadelai," he wrote to his wife. Later, trying to put the best face on it, he added, "I shall have time to draw, paint, and write all sorts of things for you. I like to linger over my letters to you for hours, for then the Expedition and all it surroundings seem to fade far away. . . ." But as the date of the advance column's departure drew closer, reality—and resentment—began to close in. "There is not a pound of game-meat, either bird or animal, in the whole country round. Had Mr. Stanley only used three of his many men to carry tinned meat, the Major and I might have had 1/2 lb. a day each of good meat for the whole six months, far more than we should ever have used." (This reference to "the whole six months" indicates that Jameson, at least, didn't expect to be following Stanley; he expected to stay at Yambuya.)

On the last day before departure, when Stanley announced which Africans would be staying with the rear column, Jameson sounded as though he had moved from resentment to resignation:

> All morning and forenoon were taken up in arranging the men who are going on, into companies, and sorting out those who are to be left behind. Seventy-six of the very worst were left, and only one chief

called Munichandi, a man who is utterly worthless, as the men do not care one rush for what he says. Had Mr. Stanley tried, he could not have left a worse man as chief over the class of men left behind. It was the greatest mistake not to leave us at least one good man whom the men would respect and obey, but I suppose beggars must not be choosers.

Barttelot filled in the details: "Such a lot of wretched men as were left behind you never saw. . . . The worst Muniapara (head-man), called Munichandi, is left, who has no authority with the men, and is laziness personified. . . . I have with me here 45 Soudanese, (41 fit for duty), 1 interpreter, 4 Somalis (all more or less sick), 76 Zanzibaris, (40 sick), my 3 boys and Jameson's 2, myself and Jameson—133 persons." Clearly, Barttelot was already anticipating that he was about to assume the command from hell. It would turn out to be considerably worse than that.

Chapter Seven

FOREST PRIMEVAL

LOOKING AT THAT black wall of forest . . . each of us probably had his own thoughts far hidden in the recesses of the mind. Mine were of that ideal Governor in the midst of his garrisons, cheering and encouraging his valiant soldiers, pointing with hand outstretched to the direction whence the expected relief would surely approach if it were the will of God, and in the distance beyond I saw in my imagination of the Mahdist hordes advancing with frantic cries . . . and between them and us was this huge area of the unknown without a track or a path.

Stanley's melodramatic characterization of the challenge that lay before them might have been crafted for effect, but the fact was that 389 men and boys were going where no men, or at least no European men, had ever gone before. Indeed, it was possible that no one, not even Africans and Arabs, had ever traversed the entire breadth of the Ituri forest. No one even knew exactly how large it was, though Stanley had estimated the distance at 320 miles across. That was as the crow flies. The advance column might have to cover twice that distance before reaching the other side.

As they prepared to leave Yambuya, Stanley announced the breakdown and march order. There would be four companies, with Company no. 1—Stanley's, of course—being the largest with 113 men, all armed. It would include fifty "pioneers" equipped not only with rifles but with billhooks and axes to cut the path for the rest of the column. The other companies, with 90 men each, would follow the pioneers by fifteen minutes and include all the carriers as well as "all men sick or well who are not detailed for rear guard." At the end of the procession came the all-important rear guard. Its job was to protect the column from attacks and to make sure no one fell behind. "No member of the Expedition must be passed by the rear guard. All stragglers must be driven on at all costs, because the person left behind is irretrievably lost." Each company would have a bugler attached to it to facilitate communication up and down the line. At the end of each day's march, a camp with a diameter of 250 feet would be cleared, to be surrounded by a "boma or bushfence," a defensive perimeter built of trees, bushes, and brush, preferably with thorns or other impediments to discourage interlopers. All tents, equipment, loads, and personnel would spend the night inside the boma.

In addition to the 389 men of the advance column, Stanley did an accounting of the rest of the expedition: at Yambuya, 129 men, including 44 Sudanese and 71 Zanzibaris, equipped with 87 rifles; at Bolobo and Leopoldville, 131 men and 52 rifles, which, when they arrived at Yambuya, would bring the rear column's strength up to 260. Stanley calculated the losses from Zanzibar to Yambuya at 57 men and 28 rifles, leaving the expedition with 706 men and 524 rifles—completely acceptable, as far as Stanley was concerned. On the basis of the rates of travel of his previous expeditions, Stanley expected to make six miles a day. At that rate, they "should reach Lake Albert about the last day of September."

The expedition members were in high spirits as they left Yambuya on the morning of June 28, 1887. Jephson was particularly delighted with one of his Zanzibari chiefs, Murabo, who had fashioned a special outfit for the occasion consisting of a turban made from handkerchiefs of various colors, to complement an orange-and-green jacket, red shirt, and blue loincloth. By this time, Jephson had a crew of regular boatmen who manned the *Advance,* all of whom had painted their faces bright red for the occasion. With bugles blaring and flags flying, the advance column moved out around 7:00 a.m., having said their good-byes to a dejected Barttelot and Jameson. At least, they were dejected according to the diaries of Jephson, Barttelot, and Stairs. According to Stanley, with his typical journalistic embroidery, the parting exchange went as follows: "Now Major, my dear fellow, we are in for it. Necks or nothing! Remember your promise and we shall meet before many months." To which Barttelot supposedly replied, "I vow to goodness. I shall be after you sharp. Let me once get those fellows from Bolobo and nothing shall stop me." According to Barttelot, their parting exchange was considerably different. Stanley simply said, "Good-bye, Major; I shall find you here in October, when I return."*

It rained hard the night before they left Yambuya, so the trail was slippery, especially for the dozen men assigned to carry Lieutenant Stairs. He'd become ill at Yambuya, running a persistent fever and growing weaker by the day. Parke had recommended leaving him behind, and Stanley had told Jameson to be ready for a last-minute change. But Stairs had been adamant that he could rally, and Stanley, despite their earlier dustup, valued his engineering skills and persistence. Besides, as he pointed out, "if death is the issue, it comes as easy in the jungle as in the camp."

They were slowed not only by Stairs's carriers but also by the unwieldy sections of the *Advance*, each of which required four carriers rather than the two Stanley had hoped for. In addition, the Zanzibaris, who carried their loads balanced on their heads, constantly became entangled in the vines hanging low overhead. Parke noted that the natives of the region carried their provisions on their backs, no doubt to avoid such interference, but the Zanzibaris knew no other way than

---

*The difference in the two versions of their parting words is significant. Barttelot's were recorded in his diary; Stanley's in *In Darkest Africa*, written well after the fact, and when, as will become clear, there was considerably more at stake.

their traditional method. They would sooner keep their loads on their heads and crawl on all fours than change their technique.

The column was soon spread out over several miles, so when gunshots rang out around four-thirty in the afternoon, Jephson, at the back of the column with the *Advance*, didn't know at first whether it was a signal or a skirmish. It turned out to be the latter. According to Stanley's report that evening, the inhabitants of the first substantial village they came to had at first appeared friendly, but then had suddenly turned hostile, shooting poisoned arrows and throwing spears at the first company, wounding two men. Naturally, the expedition returned fire, routing the attackers and inflicting substantial casualties; Stanley put the number at around thirty killed and dozens more wounded.

With the natives dispersed, Stanley decided to commandeer their village for the first night's camp. As the carriers entered, they discovered that the natives had booby-trapped the entrance paths with tiny barbed sticks, buried in the ground and canted at the perfect angle to penetrate deep into their bare feet. There were hundreds of them, all camouflaged by a layer of leaves and dirt. The sticks were also notched so that they snapped off when stepped on, leaving only the points inside the wound, which then proved almost impossible to extract, thereby increasing the likelihood of infection. As they would soon discover, these vicious little calling cards were common throughout the forest.

Though Stanley anticipated a counterattack from the villagers and posted sentries all around their camp, the first night passed uneventfully. Jephson noted in his diary that he slept well in a native hut on a bed of palm leaves. They were on the trail again at first light, but soon found themselves having to clamber over dozens of fallen trees that blocked their path, some as much as eight feet in diameter. They also encountered dozens of small streams, so the officers' boots were soon soaked. Then, as the day grew hotter, they encountered their first swamp, full of "thin, black, unwholesome smelling mud." The donkeys and donkey boys floundered badly in the ooze. Stanley stopped the column at noon, in keeping with his plan to begin the trek with shorter marches until the carriers got used to being on the trail again.

Happily, Stairs appeared to be improving steadily, though still too weak to walk. Unfortunately, both Parke and Jephson were running fevers, with Parke's spiking all the way up to 106 degrees. He dosed himself with an injection of pilocarpine, inducing a drenching sweat, after which he "felt considerably relieved." His larger concern was malaria. He called the forest "a conservatory of malaria, as the ground is thickly covered with the spongy debris of decomposing vegetable matter." Because the sun couldn't penetrate the dense canopy to dry out the forest floor, it was "very much like the atmosphere of a hot-house, or a Turkish bath."

Not surprisingly, a caravan of nearly four hundred men (not to mention half a dozen donkeys), especially one that communicated with bugles and trumpets, made a considerable amount of noise as it moved through the forest, noise that gave ample warning to any natives, human or animal, that might be in the vicinity. The result was a total absence of any game animals that might have provided meat for the expedition, as well as an absence of native people in the villages they encountered. The natives would simply abandon their villages before the caravan reached them, taking all of their goats and chickens with them, along with most of their other foodstuffs, leaving behind only their cooking utensils and a few other household items. As often as not, they would lurk in the forest, unseen but not necessarily unheard as they waited for the expedition to move out of their territory.

On their third night in the forest, with the expedition members camped in just such an abandoned village, the locals spent much of the night taunting them from the cover of darkness, performing a singsong call-and-response that described the fate awaiting their unwelcome guests. Stanley's translation went as follows: "Hey, strangers, where are you going? (Where are you going?) This country has no welcome for you. (No welcome for you.) All men will be against you. (Against you!) And you will be surely slain. (Surely slain!") It was not a restful night.

The next day, July 1, Stanley noticed that some of the trees along their path had already been "blazed," by a marking technique in which a section of bark about the width of a man's hand was peeled away from a tree trunk as an indicator of the direction to be followed. Since the natives didn't blaze, the markings could mean only one thing: bands of Arab ivory and slave hunters had already been there.

Stanley kept his own counsel, but it was a truly disheartening sign. He had had enough experience with these roving bands of marauders to know what their presence would mean for the expedition. First of all, whatever small chance there might have been that some of the natives they encountered would be friendly was now probably gone, because the Arabs were unspeakably savage in their encounters with local tribes. They slaughtered the men and enslaved the women and children. Word spread quickly through the jungle, so the Arabs' presence was no doubt already known throughout the area. That was bad enough, but from Stanley's point of view worse was the wholesale destruction the Arabs wreaked after raiding a village. They not only burned the huts and lodges; they destroyed any and all crops, cutting down banana and plantain trees and sugarcane and ruining the fields of manioc that provided the staple of the local diet. Wherever the Arabs had been, there would be nothing left behind to eat.

They were less than a week into the forest, but already the canopy overhead was so dense that little sunlight penetrated to the floor below. The tallest trees soared to a height of more than one hundred feet, with broad thick leaves at the very top, often festooned with orchids and ferns. The effect was that the floor below was plunged into a gloom of perpetual twilight. Jephson, who would soon learn better, at first found the atmosphere almost magical. In his diary, he wrote, "It reminded one of the forests one read about as a child, in which Kings sons used to get lost & have all sorts of adventures in robbers castles."

Although the pattern of abandoned villages continued, the expedition did occasionally encounter natives, whom they would immediately capture. Stanley would keep them as prisoners for a few days, hoping to learn as much as he could about the surrounding territory. He also hoped that the Zanzibaris might be able to pick up enough of the local dialects to facilitate communication.

They were already having trouble getting enough to eat. Every few days, Stanley would call a rest day, sending out large details in all directions to look for food. If they were lucky, they would find a field of manioc, but with so many mouths to feed, even a large tract would yield only enough to last a few days. Occasionally, they found wild fruit, but the diet was both monotonous and lacking in nutrition. Diarrhea became a common problem.

Stanley tried to impress on the Zanzibaris the dangers of wandering off alone into the jungle, telling them that they were to search for food in groups of at least ten men, but his warnings were repeatedly ignored. He wrote, "The reflection came into my mind that they had little or no reasoning faculties, and that not a half of the 389 people then in the camp would emerge out of Africa. . . . [T]hey will lose their lives for trifles which a little sense would avoid, and . . . I shall never be able thoroughly to impress on their minds that to lose life foolishly is a crime."

After more than a week on the trail, Stanley decided that the expedition would be better off by sticking close to the river, even if it entailed deviating from the most direct route. In the forest, the caravan could sometimes travel only a quarter mile in an hour, and the best they ever did was one mile per hour, so they rarely managed even five miles in a day. Stanley's minimum goal was six miles a day. On the river, they could once again use the *Advance*. That alone would free as many as one hundred carriers of their loads—the forty-four men needed to carry the boat itself plus fifty more whose loads could be carried in the boat. Another ten men who were too sick to march could ride in it. Also, Stanley reasoned that the natives tended to cluster near the river, which meant more villages to camp in and, possibly, more food.

It worked, at least for a while. Just as it had on the Congo, the expedition split in two columns, with the smaller group on the river and the larger contingent paralleling them as much as possible on land. The plan was to rendezvous the two groups each night.

At first, Jephson was in charge of the *Advance*, and he was delighted to be back on the water with his crew of boatmen. On their first day, they saw four native canoes, which they immediately fired on, hoping to scare their occupants into abandoning them. They managed to get only one, but it contained an unexpected bonus—a goat. It was the first meat any of them had had since well before leaving Yambuya.

The next day, after portaging around a rapid, they encountered another flotilla of native canoes pulled up on the bank, all of them laden with food. As they were appropriating the contents, Jephson heard shots. His scouts had been exploring the territory beyond the riverbank when they saw two men, presumably from the canoes, disappearing into the forest. The scouts shot them. Jephson, who had not seen the skirmish with the natives on their first day in the forest, was unnerved by the violence and its aftermath:

> One was shot in the side, the bullet entered at the top of the thigh & had come out through his stomach, the main artery was severed & he was fast bleeding to death—the other, an oldish man, had his leg bone broken & would probably recover. Poor old fellow he looked so emaciated & thin & wretched. Both looked at me with doglike eyes, like suffering animals, I felt sickenly sorry for them & awfully choky. It was such a cruel ruthless, unnecessary thing, for neither were armed & both were running away, & here they were lying all huddled up & bleeding to death, all we wanted was the food & that we could take—unjustly enough, though necessary—without shooting them. I left them there, for as soon as we left their people would find them & do the best they could for the poor fellows. I couldn't get the look in their eyes out of my mind.

Shaken or not, Jephson still had his men tow the captured canoes back across the river, an instant fleet for the expedition.

Stanley had been right about the greater prevalence of native villages along the river. Some of them were quite large and well laid out, with handsome conical huts arranged in rows on either side of a center street. Parke was impressed by the presence of primitive but effective sanitation arrangements. "They always make their beds at some height from the ground, and have special pits for collection of ash and refuse. . . . In some villages, indeed, they have rather well-made latrines—even [water] closets—to sit on; and upon the whole they are much cleaner and tidier than the inhabitants of our remote villages at home."

As they continued to move in twin columns, the officers' assignments rotated on a daily basis, though Stanley seemed to spend more and more time on the river, along with Stairs, who, while continuing to improve, still wasn't ready for overland duty. His own assessment: "I am gradually getting stronger going in the boat every day, but my legs and arms are still very thin and my face bones are sticking out almost through the skin."

The land contingent continued to encounter all sorts of problems, but there was the occasional unexpected delight. On more days than not, they had to hack their way through the jungle, because no path was apparent, but then there would be intervals when the forest yielded an almost unearthly beauty. Jephson seemed especially susceptible to these isolated treasures:

> The stream wound about, flowing over a bed of white sand, great moss grown trunks lay across it, whilest the roots of fallen trees upreared themselves to a great height & over hung the path, everything was covered with moss or ferns, there was a deep silence & in the half light one half expected to see some supernatural fairy sitting on a stone dangling her feet in the clear stream—it was so exactly like the pictures in the fairy tales.

They encountered enormous swarms of butterflies so thick that they would blanket the entire caravan. Then, in a clearing, they saw vast spiderwebs that hung like sheets between the trees, seemingly placed in anticipation of the butterflies, which were trapped in them by the thousands.

Not all the insect life proved so enchanting. The men were plagued by ticks, which attached themselves to the inside of their noses and could be removed only with forceps, a removal process that often tore the mucous membranes of the victim. One evening, when the land column was unable to find an abandoned village, and was forced to camp in the midst of the forest, a ferocious colony of flesh-eating ants attacked. Parke sounded almost impressed by their numbers and efficiency:

> They travel in army corps: with their commissariat, pioneers, intelligence, and other departments thoroughly organised. They frequently pass in a continuous stream for several hours by our tents, sometimes even through them. If not molested, they go along quietly; but once disturbed, and their line broken, they become vicious and revengeful. The majority are small and red, but a certain proportion of large black ones are to be seen among the crowd. We are obliged to strap our

knickerbockers very tightly round the leg; petticoats would never do in this country.

For the most part, however, the expedition continued to stay in abandoned native villages. Stanley, for one, appreciated the convenience. On departing one such accommodation, he observed,

> As we were disappearing from view of Gwengwére, the population was seen scurrying from the right bank and islands back to their homes, which they had temporarily vacated for our convenience. It seemed to me to be an excellent arrangement. It saved trouble of speech, exerted possibly in useless effort for peace and tedious chaffer. They had only one night's inconvenience, and were there many caravans advancing as peaceably as we were, natural curiosity would in time induce them to come forward to be acquainted with the strangers.

It seemed, at times, as though Stanley occupied a universe parallel to that of the rest of the expedition. While his officers' diaries were filled with notes of continual fevers and headaches, sores and abrasions that would not heal, dysentery (severe diarrhea), and various other ailments that kept the men feeling "seedy" much of the time, Stanley wrote that Stairs seemed almost fully recovered from his bout of "bilious fever"* and that the other officers "enjoyed the best of health."

He also made virtually no mention of the violence that was becoming a near-constant in the expedition's interactions with the natives. In his diary entry for July 16, Jephson recorded a gruesome episode on the river. Too sick with fever to march, he was riding in the *Advance*. Stanley was also on the river, riding in one of the canoes. Throughout the morning, they saw natives crisscrossing the river ahead of them in canoes. Whenever he thought they might be in range, Stanley shot at them with his Winchester. Finally, he got close enough to a canoe with four men in it to hit one of them. The other three paddled to shore and fled, leaving their wounded comrade behind. Jephson wrote, "We towed the canoe to the other side of the river with the wounded native

---

*Probably malaria.

in it, but he bled to death before we reached the bank & the men threw him overboard. . . . The men then washed the canoe which was covered with blood & we manned & put loads into her." The episode doesn't even rate a mention in Stanley's account.

Perhaps he omitted references to the expedition's violence because of the criticism he'd received after his first Congo expedition, including the damaging memo to the Foreign Office from John Kirk, the British consul-general in Zanzibar. Either that, or as far as he was concerned, native bloodshed simply came with the territory. Rather than editing himself, he perhaps simply didn't think it was worth writing about.

They started getting more rain, rain that came in torrents, rain that lasted all day and sometimes all night—in one instance, nineteen hours at a single stretch. Every load got wet, every blanket, every article of clothing, and there was never enough time between storms for anything to dry. Parke's medical kits, which were made of unfinished wood, started to warp and split. He fretted that he no longer had enough dry surgical dressings to tend the men properly. When things got wet, they naturally also got heavier. The porters were carrying nearly eighty pounds to begin with—sixty-pound loads, a nine-pound rifle, and their personal gear. When all was soaking wet, it became a heavier burden than some of the men could handle, especially as their nourishment and strength continued to dwindle.

The rain also created new problems on both the river and the trail. Rivulets became streams, streams became rivers, small tributaries to the Aruwimi swelled into major obstacles. Jephson counted seventeen different streams and rivers that had to be negotiated in a single day's march. Bridges had to be thrown across side streams now too deep and swift-moving to be forded. Sometimes the only solution was to ferry the men and loads across in canoes, a time-consuming and dangerous process. The Aruwimi itself was becoming unnavigable in more and more places. As the rains increased the volume of water in the river, new rapids and cataracts were born, and existing ones became ferocious. The boat and canoes had to be taken out and portaged regularly, which could take hours or even an entire day.

Rain, however, wasn't their greatest problem; food was. There simply wasn't enough to eat, and there was almost no meat. What meat they got came from a few birds—doves, weaver birds, the occasional hornbill ("dry as parchment," said Parke) that the officers managed to shoot—and a few goats they were able to capture from the natives. With almost four hundred mouths to feed, even the goats didn't go very far.

The food issue caused another problem—it took time. Marches had to be halted early so that the men had time to forage. Once or twice a week, a rest day had to be taken, except "resting" usually meant "foraging." For the officers, manioc, boiled or roasted, weevily biscuits, half a cup of rice, and weak tea constituted a generous meal. It was considerably more than the Africans usually got. Even Stanley remarked that the men were beginning to look "jaded and seedy."

As if the rain and lack of food weren't bad enough, the expedition was beset by a series of calamities, large and small, that caused Parke to muse, "I wonder how Job would have got on here?" The land column was attacked by hornets; Jephson fell into an elephant pit (much to the amusement of his men); so did three of their donkeys, much to Parke's dismay, because his came out lame. In fact, the donkeys were finding so little to eat that they were too weak to be ridden. Parke said they were suffering with fever as much as the men. On two different occasions, they managed to flip several canoes while negotiating rapids on the river, dumping their contents, including more than twenty rifles and several boxes of ammunition, into the torrent. Remarkably, on both occasions, one of the Somalis, tethered with a rope tied around his waist, managed to dive into the swift current and retrieve most of the lost goods.

The Zanzibaris kept going out alone or in twos or threes to look for food, and they kept getting attacked by the natives and coming back with various arrow and spear wounds, some of which Parke could treat, a few of which proved fatal. Not even the threat of cannibals could prevent the Zanzibaris from wandering—and they were now clearly in cannibal country. Not only did many of the natives they encountered file their teeth to points; several of the officers couldn't help noticing a change in their expressions as they regarded the passing expedition. Jephson wrote that "the way they look at you as if you were meat is very creepy, & they have a peculiar smell about them which is also suggestive of man eating." Finally, they spent a night in an abandoned village where their suspicions were incontrovertibly confirmed. Jephson's diary: "Opposite my hut is a large dead bough stuck in the ground & garnished with skulls & bones, some of them are not picked clean, the natives have not eaten all the meat off them—it is not a pleasant idea."

In his account of their travails, Stanley chose this juncture to deliver himself of an extraordinary paean to his young officers, especially Jephson:

> During these days Jephson exhibited a marvellous vigour. He was in many things an exact duplicate of myself in my younger days, before years and hundreds of fevers had cooled my burning blood. He is exactly of my own height, build and weight and temperament.* He is sanguine, confident, and loves hard work. He is simply indefatigable, and whether it is slushy mire or a muddy creek, in he enters, without hesitation, up to his knees, waist, neck or overhead it is all the same. A sybarite, dainty and fastidious in civilization, a traveller and labourer in Africa, he requires to be restrained and counselled for his own sake. Now these young men, Stairs, Nelson and Parke, are very much in the same way. Stairs is the military officer, alert, intelligent, who understands a hint, a curt intimation, grasps an idea firmly and realises it to perfection. Nelson is a centurion as of old Roman times, he can execute because it is the will of his chief; he does not stay to ask the reason why; he only understands it to be a necessity, and his great vigour, strength, resolution, plain, good sense is at my disposal, to act, suffer or die; and Parke, noble, gentle soul, so tender and devoted, so patient, so sweet in mood and brave in temper, always enduring and effusing comfort as he moves through our atmosphere of suffering and pain. No four men ever entered Africa with such qualities as these. No leader ever had cause to bless his stars as I.

It was quite a contrast to "the G——d d——n son of a sea cook" characterization of only six months earlier.

---

*Stanley generously described himself as 5' 6"; newspaper articles put his height variously at 5' 3", or 5' 4"; Jephson was closer to 6'. Stanley was built like a fireplug; Jephson was slender and lithe.

On August 1, one of Jephson's carriers died, the first casualty not directly related to confrontations with the natives since leaving Yambuya. Jephson ordered the body buried, over the strenuous objections of the Zanzibaris, who argued that the natives would dig it up and eat it. They wanted to dump the body in the river but Jephson said, "For my part I do not see that it matters whether one is eaten by men or crocodiles." Stanley commented that this first death in the advance column, coming as it did on the thirty-sixth day after departure from Yambuya, represented "a most extraordinary immunity."

On August 4, the expedition reached Panga Falls, the largest waterfall they had yet encountered. At a large settlement on an island below the falls, which had been abandoned, Stanley captured a dozen goats. It was their first substantial ration of meat in several weeks. Like everyone else, Stairs was ecstatic.

> Just fancy how pleased we must have been, gentle stranger, after marching along rough marches for thirty days without one mouthful of meat to at last sit down to a chop and some soup. Ah, those who have not been without meat for a month on hard work cannot know what its absence means. Today we are all smiles and full of hope. Yesterday we were grumpy, surly, and despondent—this all on account of the gentle goat.

Their good fortune didn't last long. Within a few days, Parke wrote, "Our men are greatly reduced in condition, and are growing very weak for want of food. If this way of living continues much longer, we shall have to throw away some of the loads."

Ironically, they were constantly confronted with evidence of the one animal that could have filled their bellies all by itself. Jephson noted, "The country must be swarming with elephants one passes their tracks all day long, in fact since we have left Yambuya we have never marched a day without coming on their tracks." Yet in more than six weeks on the trail, they had seen only a single pachyderm, which Stanley had taken several shots at but failed to bring down.

In the midst of so much misery, it wasn't surprising that the young officers' thoughts began to drift homeward. Stairs, in particular, wrote long diary entries about his native Canada:

I wonder what they are doing at home now. Playing tennis, drinking gallons of tea, and eating cakes by the score as usual, I should say. . . . Now is the season for the wily sea trout in the streams of Nova Scotia and New Brunswick. Many a fisherman will now be driving out to some farmer's house, away by the side of a sparkling stream as happy as the day is long. . . . Oh those are the times one feels oneself . . . with a good chap beside you of kindred spirit, yarning of old times and the different places you have fished together. Why they are the best days of one's life. . . .

When he brought his thoughts back to the expedition, Stairs reckoned they were perhaps a third of the way through the forest,* and already well behind schedule, yet they had already marched more than 270 miles. At that rate, they would march more than 800 miles before reaching the far side of the forest. One look at the men told him they would never make it.

It was only a matter of time before the lack of food started taking a heavier toll. The weaker they all became, the more susceptible to fevers, dysentery, anemia, and other debilitating conditions they became. A Zanzibari named Hassani, who Parke said was probably dying, was simply abandoned. He was too weak to walk, and there was no one to carry him. When a foraging expedition turned up virtually nothing to eat, a quarrel between carriers got out of hand and one of them was fatally shot, though it was unclear who the perpetrator was. On the same day, one of the Sudanese simply disappeared into the bush. Parke noted that "such an accident may occur to any person here, for if one walks 100 yards way from camp into the bush, and turns round two or three times, he does not know where he is, or in what direction to move." An all-day foraging expedition, with ninety men led by Parke and Stairs, yielded only enough bananas for one meal. And all of this was before the disaster at Avisibba,† when the expedition had almost disintegrated.

---

*While they were in the deepest part of the Ituri, accurate estimates were virtually impossible, but Stairs based his estimates on a combination of compass and pedometer readings. Unfortunately, he was using Stanley's erroneous estimate that the forest was 320 miles across.

†See the prologue.

DURING THE FRIGHTENING separation of the land and river columns that followed the attack at Avisibba, Parke became deeply apprehensive about all the wounded men with Stanley on the river. He had reason to be. Stairs, remarkably, turned out to be the one bright spot; his rapid recovery from what Parke had feared would be a fatal wound was beyond explanation, but there were plenty of others to worry about. In addition to the two men with tetanus-like symptoms who had died from their wounds, another man had succumbed to dysentery, and twenty-eight others were "prostrate in the camp."* Stanley counted sixty more who were "fitter for hospital then to continue our wandering life." The leader was moved to confide to his diary, "The dearest passion of my life has been, I think, to succeed in my undertaking; but the last few days have begun to fill me with a doubt of success in the present one."

Nevertheless, Stanley figured their chances weren't improved by staying in one place, so on they went. They found a brief reprieve from their troubles when they reached the confluence of the Aruwimi and the Nepoko rivers, where a village of more than five thousand inhabitants (Stanley's figure) had emptied ahead of their arrival. In a welcome break from the usual pattern, the natives hadn't taken all their food with them. The men feasted on chicken, bananas, vegetables, and manioc, with corn pudding for dessert—"quite the best dinner we have had since leaving Yambuya," wrote Jephson. They also captured an enormous canoe, nearly sixty feet long, which, on days when the river was navigable, would carry dozens of loads and many of the sick.

But for every tiny stroke of good fortune, there always seemed to be a price to pay. A shooting accident on the trail shattered a Zanzibari's foot. Parke had no choice but to amputate, with Nelson serving as anesthesiologist (using chloroform) and Stanley assisting. Parke worried that other amputations might become necessary because so many men were suffering from deep ulcers on their legs, some caused by the punji sticks left by the natives, some simply by the harshness of the trail. The

*Parke managed to take a sample of the arrow poison back to England for analysis. It was found to have two components, *Erythrophleum*, which caused muscular paralysis, and a form of strychnine derived from plants, which caused the tetanus-like muscular convulsions.

sores never seemed to heal, with infections often eating into the flesh all the way to the bone. Gangrene became a distinct possibility.*

By the end of August, the entire expedition was on most days subsisting solely on bananas. "One eats eight or nine for a meal and then feels very much like a football afterwards," wrote Stairs.

On the morning of August 31 ("the evil date," Stanley called it), Stanley was supervising the cutting of a trail through the bush wide enough that the *Advance* could be carried without disassembly when his valet, William Hoffmann, "came running at a mad pace, crying out as he ran: 'Sir, oh, sir, Emin Pasha has arrived.'"

"Emin Pasha!" replied Stanley.

"Yes, sir. I have seen him in a canoe. His red flag, like ours (the Egyptian), is hoisted up at the stern. It is quite true, sir!"

Except that it wasn't. Stanley raced back to the river's edge, only to find that the red-flagged canoe was full of Manyuemas, slaves who worked for an Arab ivory hunter whose real name was Uledi Balyuz, but who was known to the natives as Ugarrowa. The Manyuemas were his scouts, sent by Ugarrowa to confirm the rumor that a large expedition had entered his territory. The Manyuemas said that they were camped about six miles up the river and that Ugarrowa was about eight days beyond that in a permanent camp with several hundred armed men. They invited Stanley to visit them the next day, when they could give him a proper reception.

Stanley had called it an "evil day" because he knew what was coming—desertions. Though they'd already seen evidence of the Arab presence in the forest, this was their first direct contact. The appearance of Ugarrowa's advance party caused an immediate stir among the men, especially the Zanzibaris, because the Manyuemas spoke some Swahili. Much more important, even though they were slaves, they were clearly getting plenty to eat. Sure enough, that night a man named Juma disappeared, taking with him a box of biscuits.

---

*Most of the Africans on the expedition went barefoot or wore only sandals, increasing their susceptibility to hookworm, which entered through the soles of their feet. They also suffered from anemia, as a result of the chronic protein deficiency caused by their meager, starchy diet. Consequently, abrasions and small cuts on their feet and legs routinely developed into the tropical ulcers that plagued the expedition from beginning to end.

The following morning, their expected rendezvous with the Manyuemas turned into a horror show. Ugarrowa's men had decided not to wait for Stanley's arrival, abandoning the native village where they had camped instead, but they left behind several calling cards. Stanley's report: "At the gate there was a dead male child, literally hacked to pieces; within the palisades was a dead woman, who had been speared." Jephson told of many more casualties scattered about the compound, including a young boy who was still alive though "his entrails were protruding through a spear wound." Unlike the expedition, whose arrival seemed known to every village they approached long before they got there, the Arabs came unannounced and undetected. By the time the natives knew they were there, it was too late.

At first, Stanley thought the grisly scene left by the Manyuemas might dampen the Zanzibaris' enthusiasm for desertion, but that night two more of them disappeared, taking four loads of ammunition and one of salt. Evidently, they thought they could use the loot to buy their way into the Arabs' good graces. It was a risky gamble because it was rumored that the Arabs paid their Manyuema henchmen with a percentage of the people they captured—forest natives or others. They were said to keep a few as their own slaves, but most of them were eaten. Whether a box of bullets or a carton of salt would be bounty enough to change their appetites remained to be seen. On the other hand, perhaps the Zanzibaris reasoned that they were already so skinny that they weren't worth the firewood it would take to cook them.

Seven more men disappeared in the next two days. "At this rate," wrote Stanley, "in sixty days the Expedition would be ended." In retaliation, discipline was increased. If a man threw down his load without permission on the trail, he was put in chains. When Stanley caught a man trying to desert, he wanted him immediately hanged. The Zanzibari chiefs managed to talk him out of it, but the man was placed in irons for a month. Infractions that had earlier brought only warnings now brought floggings. Stanley had the breech blocks removed from dozens of the Zanzibaris' rifles, rendering them useless. Under the circumstances, however, it was hard to know whether the stricter discipline deterred potential deserters or encouraged them.

The entire expedition was now back on land, since the river was so full of rapids and waterfalls that the river contingent was spending more time portaging than paddling. The jungle was equally daunting, so dense that they every day required endless work by the pioneers to clear a path. The rain, which had never left entirely, was now back with a vengeance, rarely letting up for more than a few hours. They often had to camp wherever they found themselves at the end of the day's march, because villages had become scarce in this part of the forest. Such bivouacs were especially hard on the men. Stairs wrote, "One wet cold night in the bush takes it out of the men far more than a heavy day's march." The soggy conditions often made it hard to get a fire started, so the men could never get warm, and cooking was impossible.

Foraging expeditions became more desperate, if no more productive. Stanley reported the results of one: "Foragers returned after a visit into the interior . . . with four goats and a few bananas, numbers of roast rats, cooked beetles, and slugs." Stanley, however, didn't need to partake of these delicacies; he had his own provisions, a fact that did not go unnoticed by his subordinates, especially Lieutenant Stairs. "The way in which we are fed and looked after in this expedition is simply disgraceful. Stanley does not care a jot about our food as long as he is well fed. He never interests himself in his officers' behalf in any way." According to Stairs, Stanley even kept all the candles for himself, so on the rare occasions when the officers had time and energy to read or write, they could do so only by the fire.

Occasionally, foraging expeditions, which were really nothing more or less than scavenger hunts in abandoned villages, would yield unexpected prizes in addition to manioc, bananas, and plantains. The natives used tobacco, but they cured it in a way that made it quite harsh by the officers' standards. Still, they were grateful to have something to smoke, since all of their own supplies were long since depleted. And on one occasion, the foragers came back with a large quantity of *bhang* (Indian hemp), another native indulgence. Parke promptly had it confiscated, noting that the effects—"exhilaration of spirits, a kind of inebriation; then a mirthful delirium; then confusion of intellect; and, finally, sleep"—would be deleterious for the men. The Zanzibaris, not surprisingly, were less than grateful.

By September 12, they didn't have enough healthy men to carry all the loads. Jephson wrote, "I started from Yambuya with a company of eighty-eight strong. This morning I had forty-nine men capable of carrying loads. Nine men have died or been lost. The other companies have suffered equally." If there weren't enough healthy men to carry the loads, there certainly weren't enough to carry the sick. When men became too weak to march, they were simply left behind, sometimes with a bit of food and water, sometimes with nothing at all. In just three weeks, they had lost thirty men to death and desertion, bringing the total to almost fifty since they had left Yambuya. Oddly enough, Parke thought the desertions actually supported Stanley's initial arguments in favor of the Congo route. "What would have happened if Mr. Stanley had taken advice and gone from the East Coast? Simply this: we would not have a man left by this time." Not all of the missing men could even be accounted for. Some of those who were thought to have deserted might simply have been swallowed by the jungle. As Stanley put it, "Like the waves divided by a ship's prow uniting at the stern, so the forest enfolds past finding within its deep shades whatsoever enters, and reveals nothing."

Finally, on September 16, they reached Ugarrowa's headquarters, making camp about a mile below the Arab's village. Within an hour of their arrival, a flotilla of canoes, announced by drums and horns, came downstream, bringing Ugarrowa and his considerable retinue. Jephson described the scene:

> Ugarrowa landed first & took his seat in silence, on a mat . . . opposite Stanley, whilest his inferior officers took seats on one side of him in the tent. Behind him in four rows were seated his guard of honour & on the other side six or seven very fat, but rather nice looking, women, whose faces were smeared with white paint. . . . When the people were all seated, all being done in perfect silence, the presents, three goats, 8 chickens, 40 lbs of rice & ripe plantains were brought to Stanley, Ugarrowa's snuff box was handed to him & he took a big pinch of snuff & the women struck up a song accompanied by two men & drums. . . .

Parke, the physician, couldn't help noticing how healthy the Arabs looked. "What a contrast the sleek, fat, and burly Arabs made with our lank and sickly skeletons, reduced as they are by the hardships of the forest and the march! The latter have all an ashy-grey colour, terribly suggestive of decomposition; the Arabs look sleek and prosperous."

Stanley was particularly taken by the presence of a young pygmy woman, or "dwarf," as he called her, who was part of Ugarrowa's group.

> She measured thirty-three inches in height, and was a perfectly formed young woman of about seventeen, of a glistening and smooth sleekness of body. Her figure was that of a miniature coloured lady, not wanting in a certain grace, and her face was very prepossessing. Her complexion was that of a quadroon, or of the colour of yellow ivory. Her eyes were magnificent, but absurdly large for such a small creature—almost as large as that of a young gazelle; full, protruding, and extremely lustrous. Absolutely nude, the little demoiselle was quite possessed, as though she were accustomed to be admired, and really enjoyed inspection. . . .

When the welcoming ceremonies—and inspections—were over, Stanley and his men retired to their camp.

The next day, after their camp had been flooded by a violent rainstorm during the night, the expedition moved up the river to establish itself directly across from Ugarrowa's well-fortified village. Before long, Ugarrowa came calling again, and the entire ceremony from the day before was repeated. This time, however, Stanley got himself gussied up as though preparing for a formal state occasion. He put on his best suit, doused himself in wood violet ("which," he wrote, "especially adds to one's importance amongst these people"), and strapped on a ceremonial sword given to him by Sultan Barghash of Zanzibar, to whom, he hoped, Ugarrowa might still have some sense of fealty.

After the formalities were gone through again and pleasantries exchanged, Stanley and Ugarrowa got down to business. An agreement was quickly struck to leave fifty-six of Stanley's sickest men at the Arab's camp. In exchange for feeding and, hopefully, taking care of them, Ugarrowa would be paid five dollars per man per month until such time as Barttelot or another officer showed up to claim them. In addition, Ugarrowa was low on gunpowder; since Barttelot would have more than two tons of this commodity when all the loads came

up from Leopoldville and Bolobo, Stanley made another deal. If Ugarrowa would send a messenger back to Yambuya to inform the rear
guard of Stanley's position and circumstances, Stanley would see to it
that Ugarrowa would get three hundredweight of gunpowder.*

While this "palaver" went on, Ugarrowa's men crossed over to the
expedition's camp, eager to trade. According to Stanley, "the sellers of
bananas, potatoes, sugar-cane, rice, flour of manioc, and fowls clam-
oured for customers, and cloths and beads exchanged hands rapidly."
According to Jephson, "The Arabs men came over with plantains ripe
& green to sell & very nice flour made of dried plantains pounded up
fine; they also brought chickens & Indian corn. We had no cloth &
were unable to buy anything." Luckily, that night, Ugarrowa sent Stanley a feast of curried chicken and rice; because it was a dish he was
"not fond of," Stanley gave it to his men. "It was very good," said Jephson, "& moreover, it had salt in it, which was a great treat."

After only two days at Ugarrowa's camp, Stanley was ready to move
on. He would leave behind forty-five Zanzibaris, five Somalis (all who
remained of the original thirteen), and five Sudanese. Stairs, who was
capable of great sentiment for his native Canada, delivered a singularly
*un*sentimental comment about the men being left behind. "What a
great relief this getting rid of the sick will be to us. All the old crawlers
with rotten limbs who took six hours to do a two hour march are gone
. . . perhaps the column will make better marches to the promised
land, 'the grass country.'"

On leaving Ugarrowa's, Stanley had planned to keep his entire column on land, but Ugarrowa talked him into returning to the river,
insisting that it would be "much more navigable above for many days
than below." He also told him that there was another Arab village,
under a chieftain named Kilonga-longa, farther up the river.

Once again, this was not good news. Stanley had been hoping that
once they were clear of Ugarrowa's sphere of influence, they would be
done with the Arabs for good, and with the devastation they wreaked

*As it happened, about six weeks later Ugarrowa did dispatch a contingent of forty men
down the river to Yambuya, but they turned back after suffering too many losses from
hostile natives. Barttelot never got Stanley's message, and Ugarrowa never got his
gunpowder.

on land and people alike. Kilonga-longa was evidently not affiliated with Ugarrowa, which meant that passing from Ugarrowa's territory would merely mean entering another piece of Arab hell. Stanley began to think that the only way to be free of the Arabs was to be free of the forest itself.

On September 19, the Emin Pasha Relief Expedition was back on the trail and the river. The men found tough going immediately. "The road was full of elephant holes &, as there had been heavy rain last night, the mud was frightful," wrote Jephson. That night in camp, a canoe arrived from Ugarrowa containing three men who had attempted to desert to him that morning. He'd had them flogged, put in chains, and sent back to Stanley. Parke noted that "the Arabs were cordially thanked, and received a present for what they had done." Stanley then ordered the three prisoners tied to trees for the night, to be dealt with in the morning.

At the muster the following morning, Stanley announced to the assembled companies that the three men were to be hanged, one each day for the next three days. He then ordered the prisoners to draw straws; the unlucky holder of the short straw was to be strung up immediately. A noosed rope was produced and slung over a tree limb and snugged around the condemned man's neck. His fellow deserters were made to haul their comrade into the air. Parke reported that the first tree limb proved too flimsy and broke, but a stronger one was promptly found, and the execution proceeded. Jephson wrote that the man, whose name was Mabruki, "died very easily & was left hanging as a warning to other deserters."

The following morning, it was discovered that one of the two remaining prisoners had escaped. Two chickens were also missing and Parke noted drily that "the latter was looked upon by many as the much more serious tribulation." Still, the companies were ordered to fall in to witness the execution of the remaining prisoner. The noose was put around his neck, and Stanley asked whether he had anything to say. He did not. Then, just as Stanley was about to give the order to haul him up, an extraordinary thing happened. The Zanzibari chiefs suddenly rushed forward, threw themselves at Stanley's feet, and begged him to spare the man's life, pleading that the first hanging was example enough to discourage any further desertions. Stanley was so moved by their heartfelt pleas that he relented. The hanging was stopped. He also delivered "a fiery oration" about his determination to complete his mission, no matter the obstacles, saying, among other things, "Don't think I'm afraid to go on even if you desert me." When he finished, he wrote, the men rose up as one in support of their commander.

> Then such a manifestation of feeling occurred that I was amazed—real big tears rolled down many a face, while every eye was suffused and enlarged with his passionate emotions. Caps and turbans were tossed into the air. Rifles were lifted, and every right arm was up as they exclaimed "Until the white cap is buried none shall leave him!* Death to him who leaves Bula Matari! Show the way to the Nyanza [lake]! Lead on now—now we will follow!" . . .
>
> Merrily the trumpet blared once more, and at once rose every voice, "By the help of God! By the help of God!" The detail for the day sprang to their posts, received their heavy load for the day, and marched away rejoicing as to a feast. Even the officers smiled their approval. Never was there such a number of warmed hearts in the forest of the Congo as on that day.

In fact, the entire melodrama had been staged, or at least the part involving the "spontaneous" pleadings by the chiefs to spare the deserter's life and Stanley's magnanimous clemency. That piece of theater was Stanley's idea, arranged with the head chief of the Zanzibaris, Rashid bin Omar. According to Stanley's version of the episode, he actually had to talk Rashid into going along with his plan, because the chief was initially adamant that the second execution proceed. As for the effusive protestations of loyalty the incident provoked from the men, they were not mentioned in any of the other officers' accounts.

All three of them did mention that, by the third day back on the trail, there was nothing to eat for either the officers or the men, though

---

*Stanley wore a cap of his own design that featured a ring of brass eyelets and a canvas flap that covered his neck.

Stanley, as Jephson noted, was not similarly deprived. "Left camp this morning with no food . . . the men are perfectly spiritless & dejected from want of food & we do not go along with any elan. We got no food in the middle of the day either & one felt in reality the gnawing pain of hunger. . . . [M]eanwhile the seven chickens [a parting gift from Ugarrowa] continue to go one by one into Stanley's tent & we have seen nothing of them." Stairs wrote, "Probably never since we have left Yambuya have the men been so hungry and in such low spirits. . . . All along the road came the same cry 'Njaa' (I am hungry), or 'apana chakula' (no food). Not a shout to be heard, just the slop-slop of the men's feet. . . ."

A week later, things had not improved. Jephson wrote, "The people are daily getting weaker & weaker from hunger, for the one day on which they got a full stomach they starve for three or four, & the consequence is they are going down hill very fast." He also noted that Nelson had developed a vicious case of psoriasis,* principally on his feet, that left him unable to march. Stairs was beginning to wonder whether they were the victims of some cosmic malevolence. "Some fate seems to be against our getting on; obstacle after obstacle comes in our way. . . . What is it that is acting against us? People in England no doubt are now supposing that we have long since arrived at the lake, relieved Emin Pasha perhaps, and started to take him out to the east coast." (This latter comment reinforces the notion that Stanley's officers believed that the objective of the expedition had always been the rescue, rather than relief, of Emin Pasha.) Even Stanley admitted that his people "were so reduced by hunger, that over a third could no more than crawl."

Once again the land column was taunted by continual evidence of abundant game in the forest; it even managed the occasional shot, but never a kill. Jephson wrote, "We marched on till 1:00 p.m., seeing fresh signs of elephant, hippo, deer, pigs, and buffalo but did not get a shot at anything else, though we heard buffalo crashing through the bush close at hand. . . ."

On one occasion, Stairs wounded a large elephant, but then, as he related, the tables were quickly turned:

---

*Most likely tropical foot ulcers.

I again sneaked up to this spot to get another shot at him, but could not see him properly and was just moving to one side to get a better view when he gave out a fiendish yell and charged straight at me. I ran like a shot behind a big tree and had my rifle ready, but he stopped on his side, and I on mine quite still. He did not seem to know where I was ... it was a deuced near shave as he could have very easily put his trunk around the tree and squashed me flat.

Their luck was only slightly better when they turned their guns on the natives. In a startling passage, Stairs described the scene as they prepared to attack a small village on an island in the river:

It was most interesting, lying in the bush and watching the natives quietly at their day's work. Some women were pounding the bark of trees preparatory to making the coarse native cloth used all along this part of the river. Others were making banana flour by pounding up sun-dried bananas. Men we could see building huts and engaged at other such work. Boys and girls [were] running about, singing, crying; others playing on a small instrument (thumb piano). All was as it was every day until our discharge of bullets, when the usual uproar and screaming of women took place.

Their bullets killed at least three men and wounded several more before the natives fled in terror, but when Stairs and his cohorts searched the village, they found nothing except a few spears, some dried bananas, and a few pieces of smoked elephant meat.

It was hard to say which column, land or river, was having the tougher time. The river had narrowed and was now so full of rapids and rocks that it was becoming almost impossible to navigate. The surrounding terrain was punctuated by steep ravines and littered with enormous boulders and rock debris, so the men were often reduced to crawling on their hands and knees.

On October 4, Stanley ordered the canoes sunk and the *Advance* disassembled. He was abandoning the river. That night, Jephson wrote, "What we shall do now for food I've no idea for we are without food almost & are in the middle of a wilderness & don't even know how far ahead the Arabs may be." Parke's response was to break out a bottle of brandy.

The next morning, Stanley called a *shauri*, a gathering of the officers and chiefs, to consider their options. For all the difficulties the expedition had already encountered, the men were now facing arguably their greatest crisis. For days, they'd had nothing to eat but fungi and a bitter paste made from bean pods that fell from the trees. Jephson noted that of the eighty-eight men in his company when he'd left Yambuya, fewer than half, forty-two, were still fit enough to carry a load, and not a full load at that. Nelson had been unable to walk for more than a week, and his feet were getting worse instead of better. Stanley's longtime coxswain, Uledi, one of the ablest of all the Zanzibaris, suggested that the five senior chiefs be sent ahead to try to find the Arab camp and perhaps bring back food. Stanley and the officers reluctantly agreed. Then Stanley proposed a truly drastic step. They would leave Nelson, along with fifty-six of the weakest men and several dozen loads for which there were no longer carriers. It was, in all likelihood, a death sentence, and everyone, including Nelson, knew it.

In truth, it wasn't a proposal at all, because Stanley had already made up his mind. His expedition was on the verge of total disintegration. There was a real possibility that they would all starve to death in "the horrible, lonely, uninhabited wilderness" (Stanley's phrase) that was the Ituri forest.

Typically, Stanley wasted no time in implementing his decision. They were camped at the base of a thundering cataract, a not unattractive location under other circumstances, but all the other officers could think about was the relentless noise of the waterfall that would be inescapable for Nelson and his men, the kind of noise that could drive men insane. Nelson was to be given a tent and two days' rations from the dwindling European provisions for himself and his camp boys. There would be nothing for the other men. They would have to exist on fungi, roots, and anything else they could scavenge. There was the scant possibility that a few fish might be caught, but of the men they were leaving, no more than five or six were even capable of looking for food.

Their departure that morning moved Parke, usually a master of understatement, to write, "It was altogether the most heartrending good-bye I have ever experienced or witnessed. I cannot fancy a more trying position than that of abandoning, in this wilderness of hunger and desolation, our white companion and so many faithful men; every one of whom has risked his life dozens of times for the relief of our hypothetical friend, Emin Pasha."

As he often did, Stanley left without saying good-bye.

WITH THEIR NUMBERS reduced, and now having to haul the disassembled *Advance* over very difficult terrain, the column's progress became excruciatingly slow. At camp the night after leaving Nelson, the officers asked Stanley whether he'd ever been in so much difficulty on any of his previous expeditions. Stanley said nothing for a moment. Then, rising to take his leave of them, he said, "No."

The next day, Stanley's fox terrier, Randy, somehow managed to find and kill a wild guinea fowl, much to the delight of the officers. Stanley noted that the dog was duly given "his lawful share." The meal served as Jephson's birthday dinner. He was twenty-nine years old.

The day was also marked by another encounter with a small native village, populated by pygmies. Once again, the expedition members shot and killed several men, but this time they also captured several of the women. The raid yielded a few ears of Indian corn and some black beans. As usual, Stanley made no mention of the violence. Rather, his account made the episode sound like a pleasant intercultural exchange: The natives asked, " 'What would you, unruly men?' 'We would have meat! Two hundred stagger in these woods and reel with faintness.' The natives did not stand for further question, but vanished kindly, and left their treasures of food."

The next day brought more violence. Three men were dispatched to a small island in the middle of the river where a patch of grass had been spied—forage for the donkeys. As they were cutting the grass, a native attacked them with a knife, leaving one of them, a Zanzibari named Feruzi Ali, who was one of Parke's favorites, with a critical head wound. Stanley immediately sent a retaliatory strike. The attacker was killed, and a dozen women and children were captured. Jephson noted, "The women were full of information but as nobody understood a word of what they said it was not of much use." Whether the donkeys ever got their grass wasn't noted.

The officers were beginning to fantasize, if not hallucinate, about food. Stanley said they spent the better part of an afternoon "drawing fanciful menus, where such things figured as: Filet de boeuf en Chartreuse, Petites bouchées aux huîtres de Ostende, Bécassines rôties à la Londres." Little wonder, given that for dinner that night "grubs were gathered, also slugs from the trees, caterpillars, and white ants—these served for meat."

The porters began disappearing, figuring, no doubt, that their chances on their own couldn't be any worse than with the Expedition. According to Stanley, the following occurred in a single day:

> A man of No. 3 Company dropped his box of ammunition into a deep affluent and lost it. Kajeli stole a box of Winchester ammunition and absconded. Salim stole a case containing Emin Pasha's new boots and two pairs of mine, and deserted. Wadi Adam vanished with Surgeon Parke's entire kit. Swadi, of No. 1 Company left his box on the road, and departed himself to parts unknown. Bull-necked Uchungu followed suit with a box of Remington cartridges.

A week after leaving Nelson, they had still found no signs to indicate that they were anywhere near the next Arab settlement, nor had the advance party of five Zanzibari chiefs returned. It was clear, however, that word of their presence had preceded them among the natives. Even in their weakened condition, their guns still made them objects of fear.

By mid-October, they were back on the river as well as the land. Jephson, in the *Advance*, recorded this heartbreaking scene in his diary:

> All day long we were fighting our way up over the rapids & in the afternoon got amongst a network of islands with rapid channels rushing amongst them. Here we came upon a most extraordinary sight, some 50 natives, men, women & children were in the rapid clinging to rocks & the boughs of trees—they evidently thought the boat would

come up the other side of the island & had thought they would hide themselves from us in this way. They were ducking & dodging behind the rocks with just heads above water trying to hide; their terror was great as we approached, women abandoned their children & made for the shore, it was piteous to see small children & babies swept past us in the rapid, one saw tiny hands & feet appearing for an instant above the rushing water & then disappearing for ever over the cataracts below.

On October 15, Stanley ordered one of the two remaining donkeys shot and butchered. What followed could only be described as a feeding frenzy. Men were seen licking the animal's blood off the ground before it could soak into the soil. Fights broke out over the entrails and even the hooves. The officers got a hind leg, out of which they made a soup and a stew. Stanley estimated that the men had each gotten about half a pound of meat from the feast, the first time any of them had had anything close to a full belly in weeks.

The next morning, at last, they found trees marked by Arab blazes. Jephson wondered whether it was too late. He and Parke had been suffering with fevers for days, Jephson admitting, "Every bone in my body is racked with pain." Men were now literally dying of hunger, dropping dead on the trail. Their bodies were left where they fell.

Their woes were becoming almost biblical: trying to pick fruit hanging high up in a tree, three men fell to their deaths; they were once again attacked by hornets; a terrifying thunderstorm forced them to camp on the trail, with no hope of getting a fire lit or a tent put up or finding any other shelter from the storm; the men had begun stealing from each other and from the officers. Everyone was starving. Finally, on October 18, they saw what must have seemed a mirage—"great open fields of rice & Indian corn at the far end of which rather more than a mile off we could see the Arab village." Parke noted, "This one clearing must be at least 700 acres in extent and one can see another stretching further away still." As the expedition got closer, however, they saw that the fields were surrounded by armed sentries. Though the Arabs clearly had plenty of food, their willingness to share it appeared to be very much in doubt.

Their initial reception was promising. The village, called Ipoto, was indeed the fiefdom of a runaway slave named Kilonga-longa. There were 150 rectangular huts, housing about five hundred people. Kilonga-longa, as it turned out, wasn't at home, but his three sub-chiefs, Ismaili, Khamisi, and Sangarameni, greeted the expedition in a friendly enough manner. The officers were presented with three fat goats, along with twenty-seven heads of corn for each of them. The men were given four heads of corn each. The officers were also told they could have huts to live in. So far, so good.

The expedition's luck wasn't to last. The subchiefs, all Manyue-mas, quickly proved to be extremely stingy. They were willing to trade for food, but the only thing they would take in exchange was cloth, of which the expedition had not a shred. They had only a few *matokos*, which were of no interest. Their cowrie shells and beads had all been either left behind or lost when the canoes overturned in the river. The officers were reduced to selling articles of clothing. Parke, whose personal kit had been stolen by a deserter, had virtually nothing to offer. He sold a scarlet mess jacket and waistcoat, which he "brought to wear on state occasions," for fifty-six ears of corn and a chicken.

The men were in even worse shape because they had absolutely nothing to offer in trade, except their rifles. These began disappearing quickly, along with ammunition. Stanley was furious, meting out severe floggings to any man who couldn't account for his weapon. One man who had stolen two rifles and sold them in addition to his own was hanged. The only solution was to confiscate all the rifles and ammunition, which left the men with no alternative but to try to steal corn from the fields. Predictably, the Manyuemas caught them more often than not. Rather than returning them to Stanley and the officers for punishment, the Manyuemas did it themselves and their beatings were savage, commonly including cuts and stab wounds in addition to the sting of the rod. It was a nightmare. Jephson wrote that they were all in danger of becoming "slaves of slaves."

Stanley tried to get the Manyuemas to provide a rescue party to retrieve Nelson and the men left with him. The Manyuemas agreed but then kept finding excuses to avoid supplying the needed men. Finally, after a week in Ipoto, they offered thirty men for the rescue mission (Stanley had asked for eighty to help with the loads left behind). Stanley filled out the contingent with his own men, though most of them were in no better shape than they had been on reaching the village. Jephson was appointed to head the mission to "Starvation Camp," as the officers called it. He left on October 26, with thirty Manyuemas, several of them women and children, and forty Zanzibaris. Nelson had already been stranded for three weeks.

Jephson was a man obsessed. He was desperately afraid that Nelson wouldn't be where they had left him or that, if he was, he was already dead. Accordingly, he drove the men at a furious pace. When the Manyuemas balked, he went ahead without them, sometimes covering as much ground in a day as the column had covered in three. As they marched, they saw the corpses of their former comrades who had collapsed on the trail, many of the bodies already picked clean by birds and ants.

Before sunrise on the morning of the twenty-ninth, in what he called "a feverish anxiety" to know Nelson's fate, Jephson took only one man with him and set off at a virtual sprint, determined to reach his man before day's end. He made it by early afternoon.

"As I came down the hill into Nelson's camp, not a sound was heard but the groans of two dying men in a hut close by, the whole place had a deserted and woe-begone look. I came quietly round the tent and found Nelson sitting there; we clasped hands, and then, poor fellow! He turned away and sobbed. . . ."

Of the fifty-six men who had been left with him, only five remained, and two of them were dying. The rest had deserted—thirty-five in the first week alone—or died.

Though he was incredibly weak, Nelson's feet were actually better, and he insisted that he could walk. Jephson felt considerable urgency about getting back to Ipoto because he wanted to start after Stanley, who would already have left with the advance column, as soon as possible. Since Stanley had announced that he would be leaving more men behind at Ipoto, and would therefore be moving on with a smaller, faster caravan, Jephson was afraid that if Stanley had too much of a head start, he would be hard to catch.

With only four Starvation Camp survivors, including Nelson, and with all the women and children among the contingent of Manyuemas (not to mention the recalcitrance of the Manyuema men), Jephson didn't have enough carriers for the loads. He decided to bury thirteen boxes of ammunition and seven other loads at Starvation Camp, even though he was sure it would infuriate Stanley. He couldn't see any other way. The following morning, he was back on the trail with sixty loads and a gimpy, but game, Nelson in tow.

Stanley had indeed left Ipoto, the day after Jephson went to retrieve Nelson. With him were a disgruntled Stairs and 145 men. They left behind an even more disgruntled, or at least disheartened, Parke, because Stanley had initially indicated that he would leave Jephson and Nelson at Ipoto, assuming that Nelson was still alive and that Jephson could get him and any other Starvation Camp survivors back to Ipoto. Then, much to everyone's surprise, the night before Jephson departed, Stanley changed his mind and decided that Parke would stay instead of Jephson. Though he said nothing, Jephson was delighted, even though he felt bad for Parke. Stairs, on the other hand, was disappointed because, while he liked both of his colleagues, he preferred Parke's company, not to mention his medical skills. Stanley's explanation was that the sick men at Ipoto would be better off with Parke to attend them. When Parke asked how long he might expect to be at Ipoto, Stanley was vague, "perhaps three months, perhaps longer, he couldn't say" (Jephson). Stairs reckoned it couldn't be less than four or five months and perhaps as much as a year. When Parke asked what arrangements had been made with the subchiefs regarding food, Stanley said he'd arranged with Ismaili for Parke and Nelson to be taken care of, although he admitted that they were unlikely to see much meat. He also told Parke that he must "make love" to Ismaili, as a great deal could be got "by smiles," adding, "Why, I smile a dozen times a day!" Stairs and Jephson both found this suggestion especially patronizing.

Since their arrival at Ipoto, relations between Stanley and his offi-cers, already strained, had reached a new nadir, with words such as "cur" and "cad" showing up regularly in the officers' diary entries about their commander. Even the relentlessly diplomatic Parke wrote, "Our leader certainly seems rather hard," but he quickly added, "I must confess that I do not see how else he could have dealt with these barbarous people." Still, Jephson may have spoken for all of them when he wrote, "I think it is a mistake his [Stanley's] having European officers under him, he should merely have Zanzibari chiefs & see to all the work himself."

The officers' particular grievance was that Stanley had done little or nothing to provide food for them at Ipoto, though, as Parke noted, "We were, according to our contract, to have our food provided by the Expedition." To make matters worse, Stanley always seemed to have plenty for himself, not that that was really anything new. The humiliation of having to sell their clothes and other personal belongings to the leering Manyuemas for a few ears of corn was particularly galling, especially since Stanley seemed to find nothing terribly upsetting about the arrangement. When Parke had the temerity to ask him for additional rations, Stanley asked in return whether Parke "had nothing to sell for food." At the rate he was going, Parke cracked, he would soon be wearing "bark-cloth and an ivory bangle!"

When Stanley, Stairs, and what remained of the advance column marched out of Ipoto on October 27, they left Parke with twenty-nine men who were still too sick or weak to march or carry, soon to be joined by Nelson and whatever survivors there were from Starvation Camp. Stanley later swore not only that he had arranged with the Manyuemas to feed and care for the men he was leaving behind, but that the agreement had been drawn up in both Arabic and English and witnessed by three men. That may have been true, but, if so, none of the witnesses came from the expedition. After Stanley left, when Parke and Nelson asked repeatedly to see a copy of the agreement, the sub-chiefs not only vehemently denied its existence; they denied that Stanley had made any arrangements about food at all, except to agree that only those Zanzibaris who were willing to work in the Manyuemas' fields were to receive any rations. Those too weak or lazy to work would have to depend on the generosity of their colleagues. Clearly, someone was lying, but, in the end, it didn't really matter whether it was the Manyuemas or Stanley. The result was the same; the expedition's men continued to starve.

With the advance column's departure, the Emin Pasha Relief Expedition had become utterly fragmented, scattered across the Congo like so many refugees. The largest single group was actually the rear guard back at Yambuya, presumably joined by the men from Leopoldville and Bolobo. Then there was the contingent left at Ugarrowa's camp and now the one left at Ipoto, and there would soon be yet another contingent under Jephson, trying to catch up with Stanley and the advance column. What had begun as a veritable army of more than 800 men in Zanzibar was now reduced to a starving caravan of 150, inching its way through the hell of the Ituri forest. No matter what sorts of problems Emin Pasha may have been facing, he must have been better off than the men who were trying to save him.

Chapter Eight

THE LAKE

STANLEY AND STAIRS divided the advance column into two companies, each with about seventy men, though Stairs complained that Stanley took almost all the good men and left him with "the scum." They were accompanied by a number of Manyuema guides. With only two officers for the caravan, Stanley took the lead and Stairs brought up the rear. They left behind the *Advance*, the Maxim gun, and a significant amount of the ammunition intended for Emin Pasha. There simply weren't enough porters.

Shortly after plunging back into the forest, they began gaining elevation, soon reaching a plateau that Stairs estimated to be more than 3,200 feet above sea level. Though they suffered the usual shortage of rations and, with it, the predictable desertions, there were a few hopeful signs. The elevated terrain was slightly more forgiving than the impenetrable bush they had come through; they were sometimes making as much as ten miles in a day. The Manyuemas also seemed to have a talent for finding food—bananas and sweet potatoes, mostly—but the bananas were getting bigger and sweeter than the stunted ones found lower down in the forest gloom. They were not sweet enough, however, to prevent Stairs from fantasizing once again about the comforts of home: "Fancy sitting down to a breakfast of bacon and eggs, coffee, toast, and good butter with honey or marmalade. Or a good chop to finish off with. Oh ye Gods."

On November 6, nine days after Stanley and Stairs had left, Jephson departed Ipoto with forty-five men, including eight of those left behind by Stanley who had recovered sufficient strength to resume marching. The Manyuemas denied that Stanley had made any arrangement for provisions for Jephson's group, either, so he was reduced to bartering his shirts, blankets, sewing kit, and bullets for a few chickens, some flour, and a few ears of corn to take on the trail. His men would, as usual, have to fend for themselves.

Jephson's contingent took along relatively few loads—only one for every two men—so it could do double marches in order to catch up to Stanley. Once they were on the trail, however, the men refused to do more than a regular day's march. Jephson tried every inducement he could think of, ranging from threatened (and sometimes delivered) floggings to promises of enough food to stuff every man twice over once they reached Stanley, but without a strong Zanzibari chief with him to translate and reinforce his pleas, they fell on deaf ears. Frustrated and fearing that Stanley might not wait for him, he bolted ahead, virtually on his own, setting a blistering pace that the men could try to match or not. Jephson no longer cared.

Just two days after Jephson left Ipoto, the advance column, with eleven days' head start, reached what must have felt like the Promised Land. As they came to a series of villages known collectively as Ibwiri, their Manyuema guides told them they had passed into territory that was no longer under Arab control.

The guides needn't have said a word; the change in the countryside was all the evidence they needed. Suddenly, the villages were intact, and though most of the natives fled before they arrived, a few stayed behind and were cautiously friendly. Most important, there was food. Entire huts were filled with corn, enough for Stanley to distribute fifty ears to each of his men; there were chickens, goats, sweet potatoes, and sorghum. There were even rumors that, just a few days ahead, they would find natives who kept cattle. It was a cornucopia such as they had not seen since their arrival in the Congo. Stanley announced that they would rest at Ibwiri. They would wait for Jephson, and, while they waited, they would eat!

Jephson, unencumbered by his slow-footed porters, reached them only a week later, sprinting over twenty miles on the last day. When he saw the advance column, he could scarcely believe his eyes. He called the amount of food "simply bewildering . . . such abundance [he'd] never dreamed of." The men looked remarkably different after only a few days of decent rations. Not only had they gained weight, but their skin tone had recovered its former luster (Stanley said they were "glossy like oiled bronze"), and their spirits had revived. They were chanting and singing again, making jokes and carrying on the way they had when Jephson first met them in Zanzibar nearly a year before. The only sour note of the reunion came when Jephson presented Stanley with strongly worded letters from Nelson and Parke, both witnessed by Jephson, criticizing Stanley for leaving them in such a precarious position at Ipoto and imploring Stanley to write a letter to the Manyuema chiefs, promising them that they would receive two additional bolts of cloth if they would provide proper rations for Nelson, Parke, and their boys. Stanley was furious, berating Jephson for witnessing the letters, swearing that he had made proper arrangements before leaving Ipoto, and fuming about the ingratitude of all of his officers. Jephson stood his ground, telling Stanley, "If Nelson asked me to do the same tomorrow, (witness his letter) I should do." It worked. When he had calmed down, Stanley wrote the letter.

Stanley sent Stairs on a reconnaissance mission to see how far they were from the edge of the forest and the open country they so yearned for. He returned without having found it but reported that the track ahead was good and the food plentiful. The natives assured Stanley that the grasslands were only a few days away, and Stanley's own calculations, though he was no longer sure of the accuracy of his instruments, put Lake Albert less than one hundred miles from their current position. Finally, on November 24, after more than two weeks at

Ibwiri, Stanley mustered the troops for the final push to the lake. He reckoned that, of the 389 men who had left Yambuya nearly four months before, he had lost 111. (This would prove incorrect, because it didn't take into account the losses still to be discovered at Ugarrowa's and Ipoto.) Still, he wrote, "We filed out of the village, a column of the happiest fellows alive. The accursed Manyuema were behind us, and in our front rose in our imaginations vivid pictures of pastoral lands, and a great lake on whose shores we were to be greeted by a grateful Pasha, and a no less grateful army of men."

For nearly a week, the expedition continued to pass through small native villages* that were abandoned in advance of their arrival; unlike the villages of the interior, however, these had not been stripped of everything edible. Rather, the men continued to find corn, sweet potatoes, chickens, goats, and even sugarcane. In the absence of the pestilential Arabs and their henchmen, the villages contained so much bounty that there was no need to hoard it.

On their sixth day out of Ibwiri, several men came running back to Stanley from the front of the column. The caravan had been marching along a forested ridgeline across a series of hills, culminating in a rocky outcropping that Stanley later measured at more than 4,600 feet above sea level. From this bony promontory, the men pointed to the east, and Stanley saw "the long promised view and the long expected exit out of gloom." Below them, at last, were the open grasslands that marked the end of the Ituri forest. Stanley named the promontory Mount Pisgah, after the mountain from which Moses first glimpsed the Promised Land.

The men exulted. After more than five months, they were finally out of hell. According to Stanley, they turned and shook their fists at the forest, cursing it for the horrors it had visited upon them and for "the murder of one hundred of their comrades," but then, as though acknowledging a worthy opponent, Stanley wrote, "The great forest which lay vast as a continent before them, and drowsy, like a great

---

*In *In Darkest Africa*, Stanley writes that all of these villages, beginning with Ibwiri, were inhabited by pygmies, but neither Stairs nor Jephson makes any mention of diminutive natives in his diary.

beast, with monstrous fur thinly veiled by vaporous exhalations, answered not a word, but rested in its infinite sullenness, remorseless and implacable as ever."

IT TOOK THE advance column four hours to descend from Mount Pisgah to the lush valley below. They spent the night in a native village where they found clear evidence that they had entered cattle country, including vests made of cow and buffalo hide that were thick enough to resist not only arrows and spears, but might even have been bulletproof. They also found shields made of cowhide and bows and arrows of considerably greater size and power than those they'd seen in the forest. That night, the Zanzibaris sang and danced for many hours in celebration.

The next morning, Stanley reckoned that the lake was no more than fifty miles away, though he didn't trust his instruments, which had taken a dreadful beating on the march through the forest. Nevertheless, even if he was off by half, they would still reach the lake in under a week.

Like the Africans, Stairs and Jephson are ecstatic to be in open country. Both of them saw England in the lush countryside. Stairs wrote,

> The whole country to the south of us today was one huge English scene: rolling hills divided by patches of bush in the gullies; every shade of green that one could imagine is to be seen. . . . In back of us to the NW is the dark green bush graveyard we have passed through and left so many men's bones in. I only wish Parke and Nelson were here to enjoy the pleasure of being out of prison, in fact, [I wish] the whole expedition [were here].

In addition to all the chickens and goats they found, they were also beginning to see game—the actual animals rather than just their hoofprints. Stanley got a shot at an eland, and they saw herds of buffalo and springbok. After so many months of deprivation, the men are almost giddy with the abundance all around them. They marched with vigor and enthusiasm, no longer arguing about their loads or complaining of exhaustion after only an hour or two on the trail. It was, perhaps, the expedition they had all envisioned as they sailed around the Cape of Good Hope on the *Madura* so many months ago.

As they moved through the hills and valleys of the open country, they were persistently shadowed by native warriors, watching them and sometimes creeping close enough to yell angrily at them and let fly an arrow or two. Whenever they were fired upon, the column immediately fired answering shots, which usually succeeded in driving their attackers away—for a while. Then, on the night of December 5, one of Stairs's men took an arrow in the thigh. The next morning, they found that several more arrows had been fired into their camp during the night. As they broke camp that morning, more natives than ever were moving in parallel with them, watching their progress.

After a few hours march, they came to a river that was deep, wide, and swift enough to require a boat to cross. They found only one small native canoe, so it took most of the day to get the entire column across. By the time they finished, the number of natives visible on the nearby hillsides had grown significantly. That night, Stanley ordered a strong perimeter built around their camp and posted double sentries. He was sure an attack was coming.

To their surprise, the night passed uneventfully, but the next morning, as they passed through a series of villages in a long valley, native archers fired repeatedly at their rear guard. Once again, as soon as they returned fire, the attackers fled, but the harassment continued throughout the day, heavier than before. Hour after hour, the valley echoed with the staccato crack of their rifles as they fended off their pursuers.

The pattern continued for two more days. At one point, Stanley dropped a native bowman at a distance of 350 yards, so impressive a shot that the natives kept their distance for a while. Finally, as they neared an extensive wheat field, where the grain was high enough to hide a good-sized force, Stanley decided to make a stand. He was sure it was only a matter of time before the natives would mount an all-out assault, so rather than letting the enemy pick the time and place, he decided to make a strong camp and force the issue or, as Jephson put it, to wait "until either the natives made friends with us or we gave them a good licking." Jephson allowed that these new adversaries "have a much better idea of warfare than the bush niggers we have been accustomed to hitherto. They understand manoeuvering & taking advantage of positions & the lay of the land. . . . These people . . . have some courage about them." He also worried about a night attack because he feared that the Zanzibaris, not the most disciplined marksmen, would end up shooting each other instead of the enemy—"their shooting in the day time is wild enough."

On December 9, the natives gathered in force, shouting and jeering at the encamped expedition. One of the porters, a native of Unyoro, understood some of what was being said and engaged in a long-distance dialogue. The natives wanted to make friends, he said, and wanted the expedition to take away their "tubes which threw out fire and smoke at them." Stanley responded that he, too, wanted peace. He sent Jephson out with the interpreter, giving him a piece of red flannel and some *matokos* to present as examples of the gifts the natives would receive. He also instructed Jephson to volunteer to make blood brotherhood with one of the native chiefs. The native spokesman came down from the hilltop, took the flannel and *matokos*, and disappeared. Because it was already almost dark, Jephson returned to the camp, and everyone waited.

After a tense but quiet night, the expedition awoke to find, as Jephson wrote, that "hundreds of natives were gathered on the hills all round, all were armed with immensely long spears, bows & arrows & had on their war feathers they began shouting across the valley & were apparently shouting to each other to signal to begin for they were evidently bent on war."

Stanley made his move. Three rifle companies were dispatched, with Stairs commanding the largest contingent (fifty guns), while Jephson took thirty men and Uledi, Stanley's most trusted Zanzibari, took twenty. They moved out swiftly, Stairs in the center, Jephson and Uledi on the flanks, shooting as they went and setting every native hut, corral, and granary on fire as they passed. By noon, the entire valley was ablaze, and the enemy had fled to the hills, leaving behind many casualties and carrying with them dozens of wounded. Only one expedition rifleman had been wounded. In his account of the skirmish,

Stanley noted, "It should be observed that up to the moment of firing the villages, the fury of the natives seemed to be increasing, but the instant the flames were seen devouring their homes the fury ceased, by which we learned that fire had a remarkable sedative influence on their nerves." Who but Stanley would label arson a sedative?

In the afternoon, a few of the natives crept back, and small skirmishes continued for a few hours, but the message had been delivered. The natives' bows, arrows, and spears were no match for the "tubes which threw out fire." In Stanley's view, there had been "no alternative but to inflict an exemplary lesson upon them." For an exclamation point, when the expedition broke camp the next morning, the severed head of one of the enemy dead was left hanging in a tree "as a warning to the natives to behave themselves when we return this way" (Jephson).

Despite the sound beating they'd taken, the natives refused to go away, continuing to dog the expedition as it continued east toward the lake, but they had become a minor annoyance, rather than a genuine threat. The expedition turned its focus to the lake.

On December 13, marching across a high plateau, they finally saw what they had dreamed of for so long. There in the distance, some 2,500 feet below them, "glittering like silver in the sun" (Jephson) was Lake Albert.

> Cheer after cheer burst from the men ahead & several of them rushed madly up & down shouting out "Nyanza, Nyanza, cheer for Bula Matari." . . . To say one experienced a feeling of relief or even of joy on at last seeing the Lake would hardly describe what one felt. The Lake had ever been the goal held up before one's eyes since we had left Yambuya, nearly 6 months ago. In our first dark days we had always looked to it as the haven where all our troubles would end. . . . [A]t last we suddenly came on the Lake lying below us & one felt a warm glow, almost a feeling of triumph & mixed up with it a feeling of thankfulness & gratitude, it was as if one had wakened out of a bad dream—& the waking was very pleasant.

On a more somber note, Jephson added, "We had left Yambuya with 389 men & arrived on the shores of the Albert Nyanza with 169 only, the difference between the two numbers speaks for itself. . . ."

Somehow, through all the horrors of the forest, Stanley had still managed to lead the expedition to almost the exact spot he'd been aiming for, a native settlement called Kavalli's after its chief, located near the lake's southwestern corner. It was a remarkable piece of orienteering through unknown and uncharted territory, a reminder that, for all his character flaws, there was perhaps no other man alive who could have brought them to this spot.

Strangely, Stanley seemed reluctant to share in the celebration. He was too busy scanning the horizon through his telescope, looking at the lakeshore for signs of a steamer that would signal the presence of Emin Pasha or his representatives or, failing that, a suitable boat or even a large canoe in which they might go and look for him. He saw nothing. There weren't even any trees large enough to be made into a canoe. The *Advance*, of course, would have been perfectly suited to the task, but the *Advance* was back at Ipoto, and there was no telling what the Manyuemas might have done with it. While he certainly must have felt some sense of relief in arriving at the lake, Stanley knew that his task was far from over.

He had an even more immediate problem; he was afraid that the natives would take advantage of the steep terrain between the plateau and the lake to mount a final attack on the column. He was right. "After a short stop to feast our eyes," wrote Stairs, commanding the rear guard, "we commenced the descent and then began our worst piece of fighting ever since we landed in Africa. Every inch down this desperately steep hill the natives pushed us. . . . Again and again I took back the rear guard and pasted [*sic*] them, but still on they came. . . ." Luckily, only one man was wounded, and, when they reached the open ground at the base of the plateau, their tormenters, with no cover to hide them, finally retreated. Exhausted, the column officers decided to make camp on the spot and defer their final march to the lake until the next day. They pitched their tents within a mile of the lakeshore.

The following day, Stanley sent Stairs to make contact with the natives to try to obtain some kind of boat or canoe. He returned frustrated, the natives having told him that no one could talk to him until the afternoon. Stanley decided to send Jephson instead. After he had marched up the lakeshore for several hours without making contact with the natives, several canoes emerged from behind an island half a mile from the shore, paddling toward him. The boatmen refused to come closer than a few hundred yards from shore, insisting on a long-distance conversation. Jephson told them that he wanted to buy a big canoe to take to the other side of the lake and that he would pay well for it. If no big canoes could be had, he would buy some small ones. The boatmen laughed. They had no big canoes, they said, and they wouldn't sell him any small ones. They were afraid of the expedition's guns, afraid that they would do to them what they had done to the people on the grasslands and the plateaus, the people they traded with and depended on for much of their food. They wanted the expedition to go away. Jephson protested that they had come in peace, but the natives clearly already had too much evidence to the contrary. Jephson switched tactics, asking whether anyone knew of a "big white man at the North of the lake." One of the men said he had seen such a man when he was a little boy. He had come to Kavalli's in a "smoke boat," shot a hippopotamus, and given the meat to the natives. Then he had gone away. After a few more questions, Jephson figured out that he must have been talking about an American named Mason, who had served in Equatoria under Gordon, principally as a surveyor. Then Jephson asked whether he knew of a man called Emin Pasha. The native called back, "Emin who?" He had never heard the name before.

HENRY STANLEY had no way of knowing whether the letters he had dispatched to Emin Pasha from Zanzibar had ever reached him and, therefore, whether he knew that the expedition was coming. The fact that the pasha was not waiting for them when they reached Lake Albert, *and* that no one seemed to know anything about him or his whereabouts, indicated to Stanley (a) that Emin had not gotten his letters or otherwise learned that they were coming, (b) that he had not been there to meet them, because he had already left Equatoria, or (c) that he was already dead. (Stanley seemed to overlook the possibility that his letters *had* reached Emin, but since he had written that he expected to arrive at the lake in August and it was now mid-December, Emin might have given up on him.) The last intelligence he had received before leaving Zanzibar was that, in the event that Emin was not waiting for him at the lake and in the absence of word from him, the most reliable source of information would be Signore Gaetano Casati, an Italian traveler who had been marooned with Emin in Wadelai for several months and had then made his way to Unyoro. At last report, Casati was supposedly in the Unyoran village of Kibiro, on the opposite shore of the lake from Kavalli's, about thirty-five miles away. If Emin was still alive and in Equatoria, Casati would be the most likely to know, and also best able to get word to him so that arrangements could be made for a rendezvous.

At this point Stanley made a truly startling decision. He chose not to try to contact Casati. After almost a year of hellish trekking in the bush, after the loss of several hundred lives and the fragmentation of his expedition into so many contingents that it was hard to keep track of their locations and numbers, after getting within 125 miles of Wadelai, Emin's last known headquarters, and within 35 miles of Kibiro, where Casati was supposed to be, Henry Stanley seemingly aborted his mission. Over the strenuous objections of his junior officers, and to the bewilderment of the Zanzibaris, he decided to retreat. They would leave the lake and go back to the jungle.

Chapter Nine

THE FORT OF
PEACE

WHAT ON EARTH had happened? Stanley, of course, had his reasons for the abrupt about-face. His rationale began with the lack of a suitable boat with which to navigate the lake. Even if they could persuade the natives to sell them a small canoe or two (or, more likely, if they simply took them), Stanley said, setting out for either Wadelai or Kibiro in such a flimsy craft on the unpredictable waters of Lake Albert was "too risky." He also ruled out marching to Wadelai or Kibiro, because he was sure they would have to fight their way through hostile natives to reach either destination, and he feared that they had neither sufficient numbers nor enough ammunition to get through. Even if they could make it to Wadelai, he said, there was the distinct possibility that they would no longer have enough ammunition to provide adequate relief to Emin Pasha. (He chose to ignore the fact that the reason they were so low on ammunition in the first place was that he had left most of it behind in order to reach the lake as quickly as possible.) In Stanley's judgment, they simply did not have the means to continue their search for Emin at that point. What was more, he announced, because of the shortage of food near the lake, they could not afford to remain there while they implemented plan B, whatever it might turn out to be. Ergo, there was nothing to be done but to go back to Ibwiri, where food was plentiful. There they would build a permanent fort from which parties would be sent to retrieve the men and supplies left at Ipoto and Ugarrowa's, and (perhaps) even at Yambuya, and then, with their numbers and supplies replenished, they would come back to the lake for another attempted rendezvous with the elusive Emin Pasha.

As Stanley told it in *In Darkest Africa*, this momentous decision was reached only after holding another exhaustive *shauri*, in which everyone was given a chance to speak, all options were considered, and a consensus was reached. Once again, however, the accounts of his subordinates, not to mention common sense, contradicted Stanley's version of reality. There was indeed a *shauri*, but, as always, Stanley's mind was made up before anyone said a word.

The decision was so startling, and had such far-reaching consequences for the expedition, that it demands closer examination, starting with the lack of a suitable boat. Stanley spent more time bemoaning the fact that the *Advance* had been left behind than considering possible alternatives, but did it need to be the *Advance* or nothing? After all, by this time Jephson had spent literally hundreds of hours on the water, navigating the Congo, the Aruwimi, and their tributaries, not only in the *Advance* but in all sorts and sizes of canoes. He had proven himself an able and resourceful mariner, and he had also trained a crack crew of Zanzibari boatmen who were proud of their skills and devoted to Jephson. They would have done anything he asked of them, and no doubt would have welcomed the challenge of the lake. In addition, both Jephson and Stairs had proven themselves to be very creative improvisers, both on and off the river. They could build, jury-rig, and fix just about anything. If the expedition had managed to coax its unlikely flotilla of steamers, lighters, whaleboats, and barges all the way up the Congo, surely they could have fashioned a worthy craft out of one or more canoes to navigate the lake. Perhaps most important, both Jephson and Stairs desperately wanted to try.

Stairs, in particular, couldn't believe that Stanley was proposing to turn back at the very moment when they seemed to be so close to achieving everything for which they had worked and sacrificed.

> Are we to return again to the bush from the goal without having a try at communicating with Casati after five months of starving, fighting men and rapids, after fevers, ulcers and rebuffs of every sort, [and] after passing the Manyuemas, the destroyers? By George, no! I say let us have some sort of a shot at it by all means, let us fight and starve here a bit longer if we shall then be masters of the question. Is Emin Pasha still alive and at Wadelai? [It is] a question that all Europe must be bursting to know by this time. No, Stanley must have more men and the boat, he says. . . . Now is the time for a short bold dash for [Kibiro], win or lose. If this flood is not taken, ten months may elapse before we can get our entire force within striking distance of the lake shore and Emin Pasha [may] be a dead man.

The ever eager Jephson, the man who so reminded Stanley of his younger self, was ready, as well. "I suggested that as a last resource we should . . . march North till we were opposite Kibero, strike the Lake at that point, try & seize a canoe from the natives & I would go across the lake in it & take my chance of reaching Kassati. Stanley said, No, it would not do. I said let us try anything rather than turn back when we were on the eve of success."*

As for the argument that the advance column couldn't stay near the lake for lack of food, it, too, crumbles under closer scrutiny. Jephson wrote, "The game is all so tame & has evidently been little hunted by the natives, it would be easy to supply the whole expedition with meat here. On my way back to camp a large flock of guinea fowl ran along ahead of us for some distance . . . this place is a perfect paradise for hunters."

---

*In a footnote inserted sometime later, Jephson added, "Had my advice been followed we should have reached M'swa Emin Pasha's most southerly station, for M'swa is exactly opposite Kibero & we should have saved 4 months."

It could be argued that a marksman of Stanley's expertise could probably have supplied the expedition with enough meat all by himself. There was also a Zanzibari named Saat Tato, a veteran of two previous Stanley expeditions, who had been recruited specifically because of his hunting skills—"a better shot than I am," said Stanley. Then there was the lake itself and all the fish therein. For a caravan that had subsisted on bugs and fungi for weeks at a time, the lake and its environs would seem to have held the prospect of at least enough food to sustain them for a while, if not a smorgasbord.

Finally, Stanley argued against attempting to march to either Wadelai or Kibiro because he feared more fighting with the natives, which would cost them in both manpower and ammunition, neither of which they could afford. Stairs was almost contemptuous in his rebuttal of this argument, pointing out that the slash-and-burn tactics they had used in crossing the plains from the edge of the Ituri to the lake made the objection moot. "We are already enemies of nine-tenths of the natives of Kavalli, or of that part we have marched through." In fact, Stairs, who wasn't a professional soldier for nothing, wanted to up the ante.

> My plan was to at once seize the biggest canoe we could find close at hand, send a strong force—seventy men, say—back up the hill to collect food for ten days and then start the canoe south to [the] end of [the] lake and up to the Unyoro shore to Casati. When the canoe was dispatched, retire the whole column to [the] plateau, build [a] strong *boma,* collect plenty of food, and then set to burn all the natives' huts [the sedative effect, again] destroy—where it would not hurt ourselves—their property, raid their goats and cattle, endeavour to draw them into some position advantageous to ourselves and then kill as many of them as possible.

Alternatively, he suggested they might "send the canoe up the west side of the lake for two days or so and from the natives perhaps learn something." In short, either exterminate the brutes or have a chat, but at least try *something.*

In the end, none of their objections or ideas mattered. Stanley was the commander in chief, and he said they were going back to Ibwiri.

But why? His arguments were flimsy at best, transparently wrong at worst. So what was really behind the decision to retreat? What was Stanley afraid of?

The simplest answer, and perhaps the best, is that he was afraid of being humiliated, not that he ever would have admitted it or was probably even aware of it. Nevertheless, instead of arriving at Lake Albert with flags flying and bugles blaring, his forces intact, his porters laden with rifles and ammunition, trade goods and tools, even champagne and caviar from Fortnum and Mason, to bestow upon Emin Pasha and his beleaguered followers, he had arrived with only a fraction of the expedition he'd started with—less than a quarter of it, in fact. And the men of the advance column who stood on the shores of Lake Albert could more accurately be termed survivors than saviors. Their ammunition was buried across half of Africa, their uniforms were in tatters, they had bartered most of their belongings for a few ears of corn, and from Yambuya to the lake, they'd lost more than half of their number to disease, desertion, and death. Of all the men in Equatoria on December 15, 1887, it could be argued that the ones who truly needed relief were the remnants of the Emin Pasha Relief Expedition. And Stanley must have known it.

Though he had an enormous capacity for both exaggeration and self-delusion, he wasn't blind. Regardless of what he wrote after the fact, in that moment, he had to see what his once mighty expedition had become. Henry Stanley, the greatest explorer in the world, was in no position to relieve anyone, so from his point of view it was, perhaps, just as well that he did not find Emin Pasha, not just then. Humiliation was a diet that had once been all too familiar to the boy John Rowlands. Half a century later and half a world away, it was a ration that Henry Stanley did not need to taste again.

IT TOOK TWO WEEKS to get back to Ibwiri, and it was a dispirited journey. As they set out, Jephson confided his disappointment to his diary: "Four days ago we had been standing there looking down on the Lake with feelings of triumph & relief, now we were looking on the Lake which we should lose sight of in a few minutes with feelings of utter dejection & bitter disappointment. We marched along feeling as if we were going to an execution or a funeral." As they passed Mount Pisgah again, Stairs wrote, "We got our last sight of the lake from the top of the hill and with sad hearts turned our faces westward, perhaps not to see Albert Nyanza again for ten or twelve months. . . . I think a greater mistake was never made."

Christmas, which came a week into the retreat, naturally brought thoughts of home. "No doubt our people are thinking of us," Stairs wrote, "and wondering where we are and what we are doing as they go to church or drink our health at dinner. . . . Our stay now in Africa cannot be much under three years." Jephson remembered that he had spent the preceding Christmas with his cousin, the countess, discussing whether or not he should join the expedition. Remarkably, given the circumstances, he gave no hint of regret about his decision.

The retreat brought more skirmishes with the natives, which provoked particularly brutal retaliation from the expedition, a reflection, perhaps, of their frustration. When Stanley, demonstrating his remarkable marksmanship yet again, shot a would-be attacker in the head from several hundred yards away, he ordered the Zanzibaris to mutilate the body and leave it displayed where all would see it. Jephson wrote, "He said it was the only way to put fear into the natives so that they would cease to attack us & was the most merciful way for otherwise we should have to kill a great many before they would see it was best to let us alone." Presumably, this strategy was necessary because the arson-as-sedative approach had already been used.

Four days after Christmas, they were back in the forest, their gloom matching that of their hated surroundings. Stairs pointed out that if Emin had already decamped from Equatoria, "then we are here slaving our lives out in the bush to get ammunition up to the lake absolutely for no purpose." Stairs and Jephson continued to be so angry with Stanley that even when the leader was felled by a serious fever and unable to leave his bed, their only comment was "one's feelings of anxiety when Stanley falls ill are greatly relieved on seeing the large plates of food which go into his hut & the empty plates which come out of it" (Jephson quoting Stairs).

As they marched, they were startled to discover that almost every native village they passed that they had not torched on their way to the lake had subsequently been burned to the ground by its inhabitants. Jephson reasoned, "The natives doubtless feared we were going to settle as the Manyema have done & thought thus to deter us from doing so." Much to their dismay, when they arrived at Ibwiri, the village where they had found such bounty on their emergence from Arab territory and where Stanley had decided to build a second permanent camp, they found that it, too, had been burned. Luckily, a foraging expedition uncovered some five hundred pounds of corn hidden in the bushes, as well as a stash of good lumber, so all was not lost.

On reaching Ibwiri, Stanley came up with a startling analogy to describe recent developments: "I felt precisely like a 'city man' returning from his holiday to Switzerland or the sea-side, in whose absence piles of business letters have gathered, which require urgent attention and despatch. . . ." He then swiftly turned his vacation analogy into a thinly veiled indictment of the man they had come to rescue:

> Our holiday trip had been the direct and earnest march to the Albert Lake, to serve the Governor who had cried to the world, "Help us quickly, or we perish." For the sake of this, Major Barttelot had been allowed to bring up the rear column, the sick had been housed at Ugarrowwa's and Kilonga-Longa's stations, the extra goods had been buried in a sandy cache at Nelson's starvation camp or stored at Ipoto, the boat *Advance* had been disconnected and hidden in the bush, Nelson and Surgeon Parke had been boarded with the Manyuema, and everything that had threatened to impede, delay, or thwart the march had been thrust aside, or eluded in some way.
>
> But now that the Governor, who had been the cynosure of our imaginations and the subject of our daily arguments, had either departed homeward, or could, or would not assist in his own relief, the various matters thrust aside for his sake required immediate attention.

In short, if the expedition had failed to relieve or rescue Emin Pasha, that fault lay with the rescuee, not the rescuer.

Having thus shifted the responsibility for his decision to retreat from the lake onto Emin Pasha's shoulders, Stanley turned his attention to building the expedition's second permanent encampment, an installation that he had already decided, without a trace of irony, would be called Fort Bodo—the Fort of Peace.

Fort Bodo would be a formidable installation, built to be not only arrow proof but nearly bulletproof as well (Stanley feared that the Manyuemas might try to expand their territory and attack the fort). Inside the stockade, towers were built for sentries and riflemen, elevated granaries were constructed to protect their food supplies from rats, which proved to be constant problem, and several mud buildings were constructed to house Stanley, the officers, and several of the more important Zanzibari chiefs. In addition, more then four acres were cleared and planted with corn, rice, beans, and tobacco. Immediately adjacent to the fort were large groves of plantains and bananas, and there was ample water nearby. In less than two weeks, the men had created a remarkably complete and secure village in the middle of the forest.

Stanley desperately wanted to reunite the disparate elements of the expedition. To that end, as the building of the fort neared completion, he called for volunteers for a mission to return to Ipoto to retrieve Captain Nelson, Surgeon Parke, and the men and supplies left there. The response was tepid at best. It seemed no one was particularly eager to return to the Manyuema hellhole, so Stanley had to offer bonuses—one pound to those who brought loads back from Ipoto, two pounds to those who carried the *Advance*. Eventually, eighty-eight men were persuaded. They were then asked whether they preferred to march under Stairs or under Jephson. They picked Stairs. He was pleased not so much because the men had chosen him but because it meant he could get out of camp and away from Stanley.

The relief party left on January 19. Stanley's orders to Stairs were to avoid any unnecessary confrontations with the Manyuemas at Ipoto unless he found that "blood has been shed by violence, and any white or black man has been a victim, or if the boat has been destroyed, then . . . let the results be what they ought to be, full and final retaliation." In contrast to the initial trip from Ipoto to Ibwiri, the relief party's journey started out with ample supplies of food. As Ipoto was "only" 79 miles away, making a round-trip of 158 miles, Stanley told Stairs he expected him back in twenty days.

They made excellent time, in part because, like Stanley, they were anxious to see Parke and Nelson and the comrades who had been left behind. They reached Ipoto in only a week. When they arrived, "Stairs . . . leading a column of the finest-looking, fat, muscular, glossy-skinned men I ever saw," wrote Parke, "we could scarcely speak for joy."

The scene that greeted the relief party was grim. For three months, the Manyuemas had systematically starved their "guests," officers and men alike, and had mercilessly exploited and brutalized the Zanzibaris. Nelson and Parke, both perilously malnourished, had been forced to sleep on top of the expedition's rifles and ammunition boxes, because the Manyuemas and their slaves tried to steal them almost every night. Luckily, however, Kilonga-longa, the Arab headman who had been away when the advance column had first been in Ipoto, had returned. He proved to be considerably easier to deal with than the subchiefs—Ismaili, Khamisi, and Sangarameni—who had been Parke and Nelson's primary tormenters. He agreed to let the men of the relief column take all the loads they could carry, extracting only a small additional payment in exchange for "safeguarding" sixteen loads that would have to be left behind. They would also have to leave behind ten Zanzibaris who had been conscripted into a Manyuema ivory-hunting expedition. Kilonga-longa promised they would be free to rejoin the expedition when they returned.

After spending only one night at Ipoto, the relief column, along with Parke, Nelson, and thirteen survivors, headed back to Fort Bodo. They carried with them the rifles and ammunition, the Maxim gun, and, most important, the *Advance.*

While Stairs was rescuing the Ipoto contingent, work continued at Fort Bodo, as Stanley and Jephson supervised additional planting, brush clearance, and road building. They also discovered that their new home was in danger of being overrun by all manner of pests—rats, fleas, tiny mosquitoes, and armies of voracious red ants. In an uncharacteristic digression, Stanley wrote at considerable length not only about the pests that attacked them but the enormous variety of plants and animals with which they shared their forest home. Written after the expedition was over, this zoological treatise contained another dig at Emin Pasha, whose seemingly unquenchable passion for collecting zoological specimens, even while on the march, would drive Stanley

wild. "None of us had the leisure, and probably but little taste, for collection of insects, butterflies, and birds (the latter being Emin's particular specialty). To us an animal or a bird was something to eat. . . ."

On February 8, Parke and Nelson arrived at the fort, along with
most of the loads. Stairs was several days behind them, struggling with
the *Advance* through the difficult terrain. Stanley commented that
Parke looked "wonderfully well," a characterization with which Parke
probably would not have agreed. Nelson, on the other hand, "was pre-
maturely old, with pinched and drawn features, with the bent back
and feeble legs befitting an octogenarian."

A few days later, when Parke provided Stanley with an "official
report" on their ordeal at Ipoto, the commander, who was usually so
dismissive of the hardships of others, wrote, "The stay of these officers
at the Manyema village required greater strength of mind and a moral
courage greater than was needed by us during our stormy advance
across the grass-land." From Stanley, it was high praise, indeed.

Stairs arrived with the *Advance* four days later. Though he had
taken five more days than Stanley had allotted, even his effort won
praise: "His mission had been performed with a sacred regard to his
instructions and without a single flaw." With the first of his far-flung
contingents now returned to him, Stanley decided it was time for
another *shauri*.

The question was whether to send another contingent (most likely
to be commanded by Stanley) to retrieve the rear column, as well as
the men at Ugarrowa's, or to march again to Lake Albert, this time
bringing the *Advance*, and make a concerted effort to find Emin
Pasha. The officers and men left no doubt as to their preference—the
lake—but Stanley was too worried about the rear column to turn his
back on it yet again. A compromise was reached. Stairs would go
back for the men at Ugarrowa's; then a small contingent under
Abdullah, one of the most reliable Zanzibari headmen, would continue on toward Yambuya (or wherever they might find Barttelot and
company on the trail), with instructions from Stanley to come on as fast
as possible. Stairs would bring the Ugarrowa contingent back to Fort
Bodo, in time, they hoped, to join the advance column on its second
march to Lake Albert.

Once again, Stanley had to offer a bonus to get enough volunteers for the mission to Ugarrowa's and beyond; a two-pound "gratuity" did the trick. On February 16, only four days after he'd returned from Ipoto, the indestructible Stairs led a company of twenty-five men back into the forest. Stanley told him that he would wait for him until March 25. If he had not returned by then, Stanley would leave for the lake without him. He was asking Stairs to cover 366 miles in thirty-four days—almost 11 miles a day. Even Stanley admitted that "this would be magnificent traveling, especially through the forest." It would, in fact, be almost twice as fast as their first trip over the same terrain.

William Stairs had already proved himself to be an outstanding officer, disciplined, brave, and resourceful, so it is doubtful that it ever occurred to him to refuse the mission; but he was not pleased. The schedule was insane; he was sure that he was doomed to miss his required return date, and that Stanley would leave without him, relegating him to "plantation life" (Stairs's words) with Nelson and the invalids at Fort Bodo, while the others completed the expedition's real mission. To make matters worse, he was sure he would find only a handful of healthy men at Ugarrowa's, too few, in his judgment, to justify the trip. Stanley predicted fifty. Considering that only fifty-six had been left there in the first place, that expectation verged on the delusional. Nevertheless, good soldier that he was, Stairs pressed on.

No sooner had Stairs left Fort Bodo than Stanley became seriously ill. He was suffering from acute gastritis, an ailment that had plagued him on previous expeditions, as well as other complications, most notably a painfully swollen arm. He was in such excruciating pain that Parke had to give him morphine injections morning and night.

For almost two weeks, Parke sat up all night with his patient, Jephson spelling him occasionally lest the doctor become a patient himself. Genuinely alarmed at Stanley's condition, Parke confided to Jephson that he wasn't sure their leader would survive. The Zanzibaris were deeply concerned, the headmen beseeching Parke to let them see Bula Matari, but the doctor kept them away. Jephson reported that, just as Stanley seemed to be recovering, in a sudden fit of temper, he struck his servant, Hoffmann, with his stick. The blow seemed to re-aggravate his inflamed arm, and he took a severe turn for the worse. Hoffmann, evidently, was uninjured.

Jephson also reported a long conversation he had one night while sitting up with Stanley in which the commander, seemingly unprovoked, delivered a detailed and singularly unflattering assessment of Jephson's character. He said he was full of "overweening pride—pride of birth & pride of self," and that Jephson "had only seen the soft side of life."

> He said that at the age of eighteen had I been sent out for three years into a very tough life, say, three years before the mast in a coasting vessel . . . it would have improved my character to a very great extent . . . He then gave me a sketch of his own character, he told me he had been just as impetuous & rash as I am when he was my age but that time etc had taught him to curb himself & a whole lot more rubbish. He made himself out to be a St John for gentleness, a Solomon for wisdom, a Job for patience & a model of truth. Whereas I do not suppose a more impatient, a more ungentle, a more untruthful man than Stanley could exist.

Maybe it was the pain, or the morphine, or his frustration with his own debility, but Stanley's criticisms served only to further alienate the one man who, because of his skill with the *Advance,* was about to become the most important member of the entire expedition.

After almost three weeks, Stanley finally began to rally, though he was still terribly weak. Parke contrived a carrier for him—he called it an "ambulance"—in which he could sit or lie for a few hours each day in the open air, but another week passed before Parke became confident that Stanley would recover fully.

As Stanley's strength came back, so did his impatience (his self-assessment for Jephson's benefit notwithstanding). With more than a week remaining before the return date Stanley had imposed on Stairs, he began wondering aloud how much longer they could afford to wait. He ordered Parke to consolidate all the loads of ammunition in anticipation of the march to the lake, and he ordered the officers to take target practice.

During Stanley's illness, the Africans had been occupied with road building, though Parke observed, "It is hard to see the future utility of this piece of engineering." He did admit, however, that the activity kept the men in trim and out of mischief. Jephson, meanwhile, had focused on getting the *Advance* ready for the lake. He fashioned five new oars and a new tiller and checked all the seals, bolts, and connectors. He pronounced the boat almost as good as new.

March 25 was Stairs's due date, but the day came and went with no sign of him, or any word of his whereabouts. As it turned out, Stairs had also gotten sick, having suffered an acute attack of fever and diarrhea at Ugarrowa's camp, after a month of hard traveling.

The situation at Ugarrowa's was even worse than Stairs had feared. Of the fifty-six men left at the camp six months before, twenty-nine were dead. To complicate matters further, more than half of the survivors were away on an ivory expedition with Ugarrowa's men, leaving only a dozen survivors still in camp.

Stairs decided he had to wait for the ivory hunters. For one thing, he was too sick to march; for another, he knew Stanley would be furious if he left more men behind than he brought back. He sent Abdullah and a contingent of twenty men on to Yambuya, with instructions from Stanley for Barttelot, telling him how to prioritize the loads if he didn't have enough porters to bring everything, the route he should follow, and the places where food was likely to be scarcest. Then, alone except for his camp boys, Stairs waited for the rest of the expedition's men to return, knowing that whatever slim chance he might have had to march with Stanley, or even to catch up to him after he left Fort Bodo, was gone.

Chapter Ten

"EMIN PASHA,
I PRESUME."

SURPRISINGLY, STANLEY WAITED An entire week beyond Stairs's due date before giving up on him. Then, on April 2, he led 119 men out of Fort Bodo on the return trip to Lake Albert. Left behind were poor Nelson, still far from recovered from his twin ordeals at Starvation Camp and Ipoto, and 45 "invalids," as Stanley called them. Parke noted that of the men left with Nelson, "hardly one of them weighs 100 lbs. at present." Stanley had originally intended to leave Parke at the fort as well, but the major lobbied so strenuously to go with the lake party that Stanley relented. Stairs would take his place at the fort when he returned.

The marching went well, despite the extra burden of the *Advance* and the onset of the rainy season, which brought downpours almost every afternoon. When they approached the end of the forest again, Stanley put Parke at the front of the column, realizing it would be the doctor's first glimpse of open country in almost a year. The gift was not lost on Parke. "It *did* feel a deliverance: I fancied that I could realise the feelings of Bonnivard when, after his six years of dungeon life in the Castle of Chillon, he was again able in freedom to look over his beautiful and beloved Lake of Geneva." That night, Parke and Jephson gorged themselves on goat, chicken, and beans. Unfortunately, the native tobacco they smoked to top off the meal was so strong that it made both of them sick.

For the first ten days of the march, the advance column redux was relatively untroubled by the hostile natives who had plagued the first trek to the lake, but on April 12 the native warriors reappeared. Once again, they began shadowing the expedition and firing the occasional arrow at the rear guard. As before, the arrows provoked immediate retaliation, with the expedition usually wounding or killing an enemy or two.

After two days of increasing tension, there was an unexpected development. The natives continued to shadow the caravan, but they did so quietly. The hostile gestures, bellowed imprecations, and occasional fusillade of arrows stopped. Stanley thought perhaps the time had come for a peace overture. He sent out a small contingent of unarmed men, including one who spoke and understood some of the local dialect. His hunch was right. The peace party returned to camp with a quartet of natives who told Stanley that all the people in the surrounding territory wished for peace. Stanley assured them that the expedition wanted nothing from the natives except safe passage to the lake. It was then that the native spokesman mentioned another white man who had come down the lake's western shore "in a big iron canoe & told them he was looking for his brother who was coming to him with a large number of people" (Jephson). It could only have been Emin Pasha. He had missed them by a month. The sighting meant not only that Emin Pasha was alive and still in Equatoria but also that he knew about the expedition. Fifteen months of struggle and sacrifice had not, after all, been in vain.

The next day, the most important of the local chiefs, a handsome man named Mazamboni, came to the expedition's camp to cement the peace treaty. He explained that the natives had attacked them on their previous trip to the lake because they thought they were a contingent of Kabba Rega's dreaded raiders from Unyoro, who regularly crossed the lake to terrorize and plunder their villages. He asked Stanley's forgiveness and said he wanted to make blood brotherhood as a demonstration of his good faith. Stanley gave the job to Jephson. It was "a most uncomfortable performance," Jephson wrote, one that involved sitting on the ground with Mazamboni with their legs wrapped around each other. Double incisions were made by a shaman on the inside of their legs and, as in the blood brotherhood Barttelot had made with the chief at Yambuya, salt was rubbed in the cuts before the blood was mixed.

Unpleasant as the ritual may have been, the peace brought bounty. At each village they came to, the natives welcomed them with cattle, goats, chickens, and even sheep—the first sheep they'd seen in months. Wherever they camped, the entire village would gather to stare at the white men and then follow them when they marched out in the morning, sometimes trailing them for several miles and even carrying their loads for them.

On April 17, two natives arrived from Kavalli's, the lakeside village where the expedition planned to wait for Emin Pasha. They brought with them a parcel. Carefully wrapped in an outer layer of oilcloth and an inner layer made from a yellowed page* from of *The Times* was a letter from Emin Pasha. Dated March 25, 1888, and sent from his station at Tunguru, at the northern end of the lake, it said, in part,

> Be pleased, if this reaches you, to rest where you are, and to inform me by letter, or one of your people, of your wishes. I could easily come to Chief Mpigwa [another settlement near Kavalli's], and my steamer and boats would bring you here. At the arrival of your letter or man, I shall at once start for Nyamsassi, and from there we could concert our further designs.
>
> Beware of Kabba Rega's men! He has expelled Captain Casati.
> Believe me, dear Sir, to be, yours very faithfully, Dr. Emin.

*Parke was so thrilled with this scrap of newspaper that he actually saved it and took it back to England with him. "It . . . contained a description of the 'Newmarket' first Spring meeting (Tuesday, April 27th, 1886), with the winning of the Two Thousand Guineas trial plate by Mr. Manton's 'Prinstead,' ridden by F. Barrett. What delight the reading of this scrap of civilized intelligence gave us! We were all in ecstasies!"

Stanley immediately wrote a response. Since he still did not know whether Emin had ever received his letter from Zanzibar, he first summarized for him its contents:

> The instructions of the Egyptian Government was to guide you out of Africa, if you were willing to leave Africa; if not, then I was to leave such ammunition as we had brought with us for you, and you and your people were then to consider yourselves as out of the service of Egypt, and your pay was to cease upon such notification being given by you. If you were willing to leave Africa, then the pay of yourself, officers and men, was to continue until you had landed in Egypt.

He also informed him that the same government that had, in essence, just cast him adrift had promoted him from bey to pasha.

Stanley then wrote that he would, as Emin suggested, await his arrival at the south end of the lake, adding, "If this letter reaches you before you leave your place, I should advise you to bring in your steamer and boats, rations sufficient to subsist us while we await your removal, say about 12,000 or 15,000 lbs. of grain, millet, or Indian corn, &c., which, if your steamer is of any capacity, you can easily bring." Never bashful, Stanley went on, "I hear you have abundance of cattle with you; three or four milk cows would be very grateful to us if you can bring them in your steamer and boats."

The next day, April 20, Stanley sent Jephson, Parke, and sixty men to the lake with the *Advance*. Jephson was allowed to handpick his boat crew. He chose Stanley's longtime coxswain, Uledi, and a dozen of his best men from the arduous days on the Congo and Aruwimi. Jephson was thrilled with his assignment, knowing that he would be the first man actually to meet Emin Pasha (Parke would return with most of the men after delivering the *Advance* to the lake). He carried with him Stanley's letter to the governor.

Their route to the lake differed slightly from the one taken on the first trek, enough so that they saw a range of mountains in the distance that they hadn't seen before. At first, they thought they were seeing some kind of optical illusion because on top of a trio of soaring peaks was what appeared to be snow. The Africans said the white stuff was actually salt but a closer inspection convinced the officers that the covering was indeed snow. They were less than twenty-five miles from the equator. Though they didn't know it at the time, they had made a significant geographical discovery—certainly as important as any made by the expedition. The mountains in questions were the Ruwenzoris, whose summits were almost perpetually shrouded in fog. Though other Europeans had passed within sight of them, Jephson and Parke may well have been the first to actually see their snow-clad summits. The sighting eventually led to a serious disagreement with Stanley, who claimed the discovery for himself, knowing there was little the junior officers could say to refute him.*

They spent the night in a native village where "the plague of mosquitoes was too terrible for the language of even a poet to describe with justice," wrote Parke. The surgeon, an Irishman and proud of it, went on to note that "the smell of the huts was unbearable; for the natives keep all their goats in the huts, reminding one of the brotherly kindness with which the Irishman treats his pig."

They reached the lake the next day around noon. The *Advance* was bolted together, and, amid much cheering and good wishes, Jephson and his crew rowed away. Their destination was M'swa, Emin's southernmost station, some fifty miles to the north.

They rowed for two days, the men strong at their oars, one of them singing a cadence to set their pace. His song recounted their struggles through the Ituri forest and their difficulties with the natives. The chorus, which everyone joined in on, blended the names of Emin Pasha and Bula Matari, and the men sang it with great gusto. They camped the first night at a native village on the lakeshore, where the entire population came to Jephson's tent to watch him eat with a knife and fork. None of the natives had ever seen such things before.

The next day's voyage brought the crew within twenty miles of its destination, close enough that Jephson could see M'swa in the twilight from his lakeside campsite. He wrote in his diary, "I sat down in the bright moonlight with the waves lapping up at my feet. It was so peaceful sitting there smoking my pipe with the cool breeze of the Nyanza playing round me & the voices & laughter of my men reaching

*See below, p. 187.

one faintly across the water. Here I was within sight of success after toiling for it for over 15 months, I alone had been sent forward & would be the first to see Emin Pasha & bring him our news." He ends the entry with a quotation from the poet Tom Moore: "Joy joy for ever my task is done, The gates are past & heaven is won."

Jephson had his crew back on the lake at sunrise. He had the Egyptian flag hoisted, and the men pulled for all they were worth, reaching M'swa by midmorning. Jephson wasn't sure what kind of reception awaited him at the station, but it is doubtful he expected anything as elaborate as what he got:

A guard of honor was drawn up to receive me on the beach. They gave me a grand salute & then with bugles sounding & flags flying they conducted me up to the station which stood on top of a low flat hill about a quarter of a mile from the Lake. The station is made entirely of grass & bamboo & is exquisitely neat & clean & the houses are all cool & airy. I was shown into a large "barrazan" or receiving room, in the East there is always one of these rooms to receive deputations in. There was a couch with a Persian carpet on it & pillow for me to recline on & chairs were placed near it, whilest my Zanzibaris were accommodated with a mat to sit upon behind me. Gourds of m'tamah beer were brought in for them & a large vessel full of snowy curds & whey were brought in for me of which I drank most gratefully. . . . Presently Shookri Aga, the chief of the station came in; a tall Nubian in a smart Egyptian uniform. . . . I was dressed in a torn and patched suit, which I had made out of an old checked flannel set of pyjamas, an old flannel shirt—the only I possessed—and my feet were shod in a pair of shoes, also manufactured by myself, out of the raw skin of a black-and-white-spotted cow with the hair left on. After talking a bit [Shukri Aga] told me that Emin Pasha was not here but was at Tunguru, an island higher up the lake, with his steamer . . . & he said that Emin Pasha would arrive here tomorrow at midday.

Jephson was escorted to his quarters, a "large lofty hut."

My luggage consists of a few old tattered clothes in a tent cover, a basket containing two or three very black looking cooking pots, my plates etc, some potatoes & a goat skin containing beans, in short it would be hard to describe more disreputable looking luggage. This baggage was brought in by two smart looking Turkish servants in snowy white clothes & deposited reverentially as if it contained the most valuable jewels. What a contrast we are, I & all my men are in rags & are a dirty looking lot whilest the people we have come to relieve are all beautifully clean looking & neat.

It was just what Stanley had feared—that the rescuers needed more relief than those they came to save.

After a hearty lunch ("an enormous omellette & some delicious bread") and a nap, Jephson awoke to find a bathtub full of steaming hot water waiting for him.

> I had not ordered the bath so they must have thought I looked dirty. How delightful the bath was: how I soaped—(I had been without soap for five months) & scrubbed myself with the Loofah till my skin was almost worn into holes & for the first time since we started from Yambuya I felt really clean. One quite hated putting on one's old patched & worn out clothes, they had been patched & washed & worn til they were quite thread bare.

In conversation with Shukri Aga ("Shookri" was yet another of Jephson's phonetic attempts to spell African and Arab names), he learned that Emin had, in fact, never received Stanley's letter from Zanzibar, but had received a letter from the British consul, Frederick Holmwood, telling him that the expedition was coming. Shukri Aga said, "The Governor won't sleep tonight when he hears you are here." It was then time for dinner, a feast so elaborate, wrote Jephson, "one wished one had ten mouths to feed & ten stomachs to fill, it was so good after not having had a decent meal served in a civilized manner for so long."

Emin Pasha did not arrive the next day, much to Jephson's disappointment. Nor did he come the following day, though he did send a note apologizing for the delay. Jephson sent a note to Stanley, updating him on the situation, dispatching two men in a canoe to deliver it. There was nothing else to do but wait, so he occupied himself by making the rounds of the station with Shukri Aga (another spelling attempt came up with "Shookriaga") and his second in command, Suleiman. The station was indeed impressive.

> They have some hundred of cattle, sheep & goats & abundance of vegetables such as onions, brinjales [a variant spelling of an Anglo-Indian word for eggplants] etc, whilest the natives supply them with corn & fish so that they live in plenty here. There are large fields of cotton & one sees numbers of people going about with little distaffs making the raw cotton into thread. . . . Emin Pasha has instructed his people how to weave & they make large quantities of loose strong cotton cloth. . . . It is wonderful with what love and affection his people speak of him & how they all look up to & revere him—what a difference from our leader with whom things are done by sheer brute force only.

The next day, when Emin still hadn't arrived, Jephson decided he'd waited long enough. He announced that he was taking the *Advance* to Tunguru, but Suleiman, Shukri Aga's number two man, pleaded with him not to leave. He promised that Emin would arrive the next day "& begged [Jephson] to cut his throat if he didn't!"

The Arab's throat was safe. At five o'clock the next afternoon, the steamer was sighted. Emin's officers and men immediately changed into their best uniforms and prepared a small cannon to fire a welcoming salute. They marched in formation to the shore, two large Turkish flags flying,* with Jephson and his Zanzibaris in formation behind them, carrying their Egyptian flag. The Zanzibaris begged Jephson to be allowed to fire their rifles in greeting. It was nearly dark as the steamer dropped anchor and a small launch made its way to the shore. In the bow was a short, slender man in a tailored uniform, his darkly bearded face dominated by thick eyeglasses. Emin Pasha. Jephson wrote, "As the boat touched the sand Emin Pasha leaped out & welcomed me with both hands, he kept repeating expressions of welcome & cordial greeting as he held both my hands in his; one really felt that the welcome was from the bottom of his heart."

---

*Egypt was still part of the Ottoman Empire, so on important occasions the Turkish flag was flown.

Not surprisingly, perhaps, Emin was a smaller man than Jephson had expected him to be. He spoke perfect English, albeit with a heavy accent, introducing Jephson to Casati, his friend and sometime envoy, and to Vita Hassan, a Tunisian apothecary who had been in his service for several years. Then he led Jephson to his quarters, where the young officer and the long-marooned governor sat in the moonlight and talked long into the night.

Emin wanted to know everything about the expedition,

> how it was got up & about all the officers & their names & how I became connected with the expedition, I told him all about it & could not help telling him when speaking of myself, how Madame de Noailles had said, "If I had a son I would send him on this expedition," the tears started in his eyes & for a moment he turned away, & then he took my hand & said "[I]f I lived for a hundred years I could not thank the English people enough for their disinterested kindness in sending me help when I have been abandoned by my own government for so many years."

The talk continued the next morning, over a cup of "delicious strong sweet coffee served in a very pretty dainty little cup." Emin insisted that Jephson give him a list of personal items he needed. Not wanting to seem greedy, Jephson asked only for soap, salt, and a notebook. Emin wasn't satisfied. He had already had some fresh clothes brought for Jephson, but now he summoned a tailor and a shoemaker to take measurements and make up properly fitting outfits and footwear. He also had cloth given to all the Zanzibaris so that they could fashion replacements for their rapidly disintegrating outfits. He furthermore gave Jephson a cigar left behind by Dr. Junker that he'd been saving for a special occasion, and got Casati to add a couple of cigarettes. Like the proper Victorian gentleman he was, Jephson promptly "sat and puffed [him]self into Paradise."

While Jephson was enjoying Emin's hospitality, Stanley was growing increasingly frustrated waiting to hear from him, moving between various campsites, from the high ground that afforded a commanding view of the lake (and perhaps Emin's steamer) to the flatlands nearer the lakeshore. On the morning of April 29, Jephson's note arrived. In less than three hours, the expedition members were waiting expectantly on the shores of Lake Albert. As the afternoon dragged on, their eyes grew tired from squinting at the horizon. Finally, at four-thirty in the afternoon, looking through his binoculars, Stanley spotted a plume of smoke. It was the *Khedive*, the larger of Emin's two steamers, slowly making its way south in the fading light. The Zanzibaris immediately lit huge bonfires to signal their location. The *Khedive*, its hold laden with grain, its decks crowded with milk cows, cattle, sheep, and chickens, not to mention several dozen soldiers, moved slowly, its ancient boilers capable of no more than six knots per hour.

Two hours later, the steamer dropped anchor in a cove a couple of miles north of Stanley's camp. Predictably, Stanley stayed put, dispatching Parke to bring the pasha to him. Parke marched out with a contingent of wildly enthusiastic Zanzibaris. As they neared the *Khedive*, the Zanzibaris started firing their rifles in the air by way of greeting. Emin's Sudanese soldiers promptly fired back at them, not in greeting, but in earnest, thinking they might be Kabba Rega's men (it was almost dark; visibility was limited). Luckily, no one was hit before the crew of the *Advance*, recognizing the voices of Parke's men, persuaded Emin's soldiers to cease firing. The *Advance*, which was on board the *Khedive*, was then launched, and a few moments later Emin, Jephson, Casati, and Shukri Aga came ashore. Parke described what followed:

> Emin Pasha then took Jephson's arm and Casati mine. . . . I had a most animated conversation with Casati; nothing deterred, apparently, by the fact that neither of us could speak two words in a common language. Jephson's attention was fully occupied in keeping the Pasha from stumbling into swamps and holes, as he is extremely short-sighted. He is very slightly built, and rather short in stature (about five feet seven inches in height). He wore a clean white shirt, with a spotless coat and trousers. His bronze skin and black hair were shown out in strong contrast by these garments. He looked cheerful, and was excessively polite.

At 8:00 p.m. on April 29, 1888, one year, three months, and eight days after he left London, Henry Stanley stepped out of his tent to meet the man who had brought him back to Africa. He didn't recognize him.

I shook hands with all, and asked which was Emin Pasha? Then one rather small, slight figure, wearing glasses, arrested my attention by saying in excellent English, "I owe you a thousand thanks, Mr. Stanley; I really do not know how to express my thanks to you."

"Ah, you are Emin Pasha. Do not mention thanks, but come in and sit down. It is so dark out here we cannot see one another."

Chapter Eleven

GETTING TO KNOW
YOU

SOMEHOW, STANLEY still had champagne. He had shepherded three half-bottles acquired from the station chief in Stanley Pool in anticipation of this specific occasion, secreting them inside a pair of trousers in his personal kit. They were promptly opened, and a round of heartfelt toasts commenced between Emin, Casati, Stanley, Jephson, and Parke. Emin continued to express his "immeasurable" gratitude, and, it seemed, the long-awaited rendezvous was as genuinely warm as anyone could have hoped for.

Like Jephson, Stanley was surprised by the physical appearance of the esteemed governor.

> I expected to see a tall thin military-looking figure, in faded Egyptian uniform, but instead of it I saw a small spare figure in a well-kept fez and a clean suit of snowy cotton drilling, well-ironed and of perfect fit.

A dark grizzled beard bordered a face of a Magyar cast, though a pair of spectacles lent it somewhat an Italian or Spanish appearance. There was not a trace on it of ill-health or anxiety; it rather indicated good condition of body and peace of mind.

They talked for several hours, mostly of Europe and the travails of the expedition, and life in Africa. Before they retired, they agreed that a new campground large enough to accommodate both Emin's men and the expedition would be selected in the morning, and then they would begin making plans in earnest.

It seemed like an excellent beginning, but there was one disquieting note, observed by both Parke and Stanley. "The Pasha said that he could scarcely express his thanks to the English for sending him relief at the expense of so much trouble and cost; but he added that he did not know whether he would care to come out, after doing so much work in the province, and having everything now in perfect order" (Parke). Stanley, blunt as ever, wrote, "This evening Emin Pasha came ashore, and we had a lengthy conversation, but after all I am unable to gather in the least what his intentions may be." Stanley wasn't too worried, though. After all, he hadn't begun to bring his considerable powers of persuasion to bear on the governor as yet. Give me ten days, he thought, and all will be arranged.

The next morning, Emin's men and the expedition's forces moved several miles north along the lakeshore to a beautiful grassy campsite called Nsabé. When they were situated, Stanley presented the "relief supplies" whose delivery had extracted such an enormous price from him and his men. The supplies consisted of thirty boxes of ammunition, which worked out to about twenty rounds for each of Emin's soldiers—enough for one short skirmish. There were also some maps, a few scientific journals from Germany, and packets of letters, one for Emin, another for Casati. Stanley had also had some trousers made for Emin while he was in Cairo, guessing at the correct size on the basis of his conversations with Junker and Schweinfurth. They turned out to be six inches too long. It didn't really matter, because the trousers, like everything else except the bullets, were badly mildewed.

For his part, Emin had brought a steamer full of provisions for the expedition, just as Stanley had requested. He immediately distributed enough corn to last every man at least ten days. In addition, he brought milk and beef cattle, goats, chickens, several tons of grain and flour, fruit, vegetables, and honey. He assured Stanley that his steamers could quickly retrieve anything else the expedition required.

In the shining light of their first morning together, the disparity between the condition of the rescuers and that of the people they had come to rescue was unavoidable. Even Stanley acknowledged it, but not without his typical spin: "Our Zanzibaris, by the side of these upright figures [Emin's Sudanese troops], seemed altogether a beggarly troop, and more naked than ever. But I was not ashamed of them. It was by their aid, mean as they appeared, that we had triumphed. . . ." Yet if the roles of "rescuer" and "rescued" were virtually reversed, Emin proved to be such a gracious host that the embarrassment was muted, if not erased. Stanley, of course, proceeded as though everything was as it should be.

His plan, initially, was to spend ten days to two weeks assessing the situation, considering options with Emin, and making preparations for what he was confident would be the evacuation of the governor and those of his people who chose to accompany them, either back to Egypt via Zanzibar (his official mission on behalf of the khedive) or to some intermediate destination near Lake Victoria (the Mackinnon/ IBEAC plan). His five and a half months of hell in the Ituri forest had already convinced him that a large-scale evacuation back through the Congo was out of the question. They would go home by going east.

The only major problem, from his point of view, was the rear column. In six weeks, it would be a year since he had left Yambuya with the advance column; he had expected to return in five months. As the weeks turned to months, and his worry and frustration continued to mount, there had been not a word from Barttelot, Jameson, or the others. Nor could he be sure that his communiqué sent with Stairs from Fort Bodo had reached them. Stanley felt he had no choice; he had to go back for the rear column himself. While he was gone, he reasoned, Emin could gather his people together and bring them to the south end of the lake, in preparation for the evacuation of the province. With eleven stations to deal with, the gathering of Emin's subjects might take almost as long as the mission to retrieve the rear column—Stanley reckoned eight months, minimum. Jephson suggested that the men and supplies at Fort Bodo might also be brought to the lake, so that when Stanley returned with the rear column, they could embark on their return journey almost immediately.

To be sure, there was always the chance that Barttelot was already en route; perhaps Tippu Tib had fulfilled his contract and provided the porters. Perhaps his second set of instructions, the ones he had sent with Stairs from Fort Bodo, had in fact gotten through, and the rear column was following the right trails and not having too much trouble finding food. If Barttelot was indeed already on the way, that would change everything. He would bring the rest of the supplies with him, the thousands of rounds of ammunition Stanley had been forced to leave behind, the cases of food, the bolts of cloth, the *matokos*, the full inventory they had brought from Zanzibar, not just a few boxes of bullets. Then he'd be able to show the beleaguered governor that "Emin Pasha *Relief* Expedition" wasn't a misnomer (though, in truth, the governor didn't seem all that beleaguered to Stanley). But he was getting ahead of himself; Barttelot might still be stuck in Yambuya; and even if he could bring genuine relief to Emin Pasha, the ultimate goal was still to get him out of Equatoria.

Stanley and Emin talked every day, often for hours. Mostly Stanley talked and Emin listened. It turned out that, even though Stanley's letter from Zanzibar had never reached him, Emin had known for some time of Egypt's intention to abandon Equatoria. The news had come in the same communiqué that told him of his promotion from bey to pasha. He also knew that he had a choice; the khedive and prime minister had not ordered him to leave his province. In fact, they had said that he was free to remain in Equatoria, but that he would have to do so on his own. Considering that he hadn't even been paid for the last eight years, and that he'd been cut off from almost all outside communication for almost three years, he didn't see Egypt's withdrawal as a very compelling reason to leave. It was more like an acknowledgment of the status quo, since, for more than a decade, virtually everything that he had done in Equatoria he had done on his own.

Emin had also known for some time that a relief expedition was coming. He had enthusiastically trumpeted its importance to his garrisons, telling them that, with the supplies and ammunition the expedition would bring, they would be able to remain where they were for a long time. Secretly, he hoped that the expedition would bring an offer of protection from England; failing that, he thought that adequate supplies, especially guns and ammunition, and perhaps a more secure line of communication to either coast, would allow him and his people to maintain themselves where they were. But then Stanley had showed up with his ragtag band of Zanzibaris and a paltry supply of bullets, which provided no real relief at all. How was he supposed to explain *that* to his garrisons?

Ironically, it was entirely possible that the expedition's arrival had actually complicated Emin's situation rather than simplified it. He suddenly had more to think about, more to worry about, and more decisions to make. And, as Stanley and his expedition were about to learn, for all his strengths, Emin Pasha was not very good at making decisions.

Stanley knew there was a problem right away: "The Pasha's manner is ominous. When I propose a return to the sea to him, he has the habit of tapping his knee, and smiling in a kind of 'We shall see' manner. It is evident he finds it difficult to renounce his position in a country where he has performed viceregal functions." Not to mention trusting his fate, and that of his people, to a man who had missed his estimated time of arrival at Lake Albert by approximately eight months, and then shown up with a band of starving, half-naked refugees.

A return to the sea wasn't the only option that Stanley proposed. He had two other scenarios to present to Emin, the ones that had been put into place before he left England. The first was King Leopold's proposal that Equatoria become part of the Congo Free State, with Emin remaining as governor-general. However, just as the calamity of the Ituri forest had changed Stanley's mind about his return route, it had also soured him on the feasibility of annexing Equatoria into Leopold's dominion. The logistics and obvious problems with communication were simply too daunting. Even as he made the proposal, he recommended that Emin turn it down. Emin concurred.

The second proposal, which Stanley and Mackinnon had agreed

to in principle back in England, called for Emin and his people to relocate to the northwest corner of Lake Victoria, near a placed called Kavirondo. Emin would then be in the employ of the IBEAC, overseeing development of a trade corridor from the lake district to the East African coast. The terms were a bit fuzzy; in truth, the idea for the Kavirondo location had come to Stanley after the expedition was underway. He admitted to Emin that the charter for the IBEAC had not actually been granted when he left Zanzibar, but he expressed great confidence that it had been subsequently, and that by the time they reached Lake Victoria, all the necessary arrangements would be in place. In fact, according to Emin, Stanley went so far as to say, "Four hundred thousand pounds have already been subscribed. They ask you to have confidence: all the rest will be seen to forthwith. A first caravan of supplies for you would immediately leave the coast."

Emin was intrigued. If he couldn't stay in Equatoria, at least he could stay in central Africa; he could be with his people; he could continue his scientific work. And if England was not ready to make a formal protectorate of Equatoria, at least he would be remaining under English auspices, which was the next-best thing. There was much to recommend the IBEAC idea, but he wasn't ready to commit.

The ten days that Stanley had planned to spend with Emin stretched to almost a month. In anticipation of his mission to retrieve the rear column, Stanley asked the governor to provide additional porters (the irony of who was providing relief to whom seems, once again, to have been lost on Stanley). If, as he feared, Tippu Tib had not come through with his promised carriers, and if there had been significant attrition in the rear column, whether from desertion, illness, or hostilities with the natives—all distinct possibilities—he would need additional carriers to bring the remaining relief supplies back to the lake. Emin said he could provide the needed men, but they would have to be ferried from one of his northern stations.

As they waited for the carriers, Stanley began to hear more and more information that was at odds with the preconceptions he (and most Europeans) had formed about Emin and his province. Those impressions had been created primarily through Emin's correspondence with people such as Felkin and Junker who, in turn, had publicized Emin's plight, principally by getting letters published in various newspapers, including *The Times*. Collectively, they painted a portrait of a man and his people that was, in retrospect, probably too good to be true. As Jephson described it, "We started from Europe believing that Emin ruled over a loyal, faithful, and obedient people, who were devoted to him, and into whom, to use Dr. Felkin's words, Emin had been able to instill some of his own great enthusiasm. All Europe thought that Emin's soldiers were loyal and united—had he not himself in his letters called them heroes!" So it must have given Stanley considerable pause when he learned from Shukri Aga that the governor's First Battalion, which occupied the northernmost stations along the Nile, had been in open revolt against his authority for more than three years. The First Battalion's officers and men hadn't gone over to the Mahdi; they hadn't even renounced the khedive's authority; they had simply stopped obeying Emin's orders.

Emin, of course, denied the revolt. He acknowledged that there had been difficulties—communications had been the bane of every Equatorian governor's administration from Sir Samuel Baker on down— but he had confidence in the northern stations. Had they not fought bravely and successfully when the Mahdist forces had attacked two years earlier?

Stanley also received a visit from two Egyptians from the station at Tunguru, one an officer, the other a clerk, who were also part of Emin's party. They came to lodge a complaint, saying that Emin had treated them badly, though the specific nature of their maltreatment was vague. Stanley told them there was nothing he could do for them, suggesting that they take their grievances to the proper authorities when they reached Cairo. As far as Stanley was concerned, they seemed to be nothing more than a pair of whining bureaucrats. Still, he found it disquieting that they would go behind their commander's back in the way they did, though he didn't mention the incident to the pasha.

After much consideration, Emin announced, he had decided what he wanted to do. He wanted Stanley to go with him on a tour of his stations to explain the situation to his officers and soldiers. Stanley could present the letters he had brought from the khedive and the prime minister and explain their meaning. Emin revealed that many of his men, perhaps a majority, especially in the northern stations, still did not believe what they had been told about the tragedy at Khartoum. Rather, they believed that Gordon was still alive and that he would send relief to them from the north. Emin said that if they could see Stanley in the flesh, and hear from his lips what had happened at Khartoum and what the expedition had done on their behalf, they would finally understand the reality of the situation. Then Emin would ask them what they wanted to do—stay in Equatoria or evacuate.

Stanley had two problems with Emin's proposal. The first was the rear column; he couldn't very well retrieve the men at Yambuya (or wherever) if he was making a tour of Equatoria with Emin. Second, why did Emin need someone else to convince his men of the truth? Was his authority really that tenuous? It was a disturbing thought. Nevertheless, Emin made it clear that he would not be willing to leave, whether for Egypt or Lake Victoria, until he had talked to his troops. And, he warned, if they chose to stay, he would not abandon them.

Stanley proposed a compromise. He would send Jephson as his representative, along with his three remaining Sudanese soldiers, presumably to bolster credibility. Jephson would read the letters, explain the realities, answer their questions. And while that was happening, Stanley would race back to Yambuya.

Jephson didn't want to do it. Though he liked Emin, he thought retrieving the rear column was the more important task, and he didn't want to be separated from the expedition. Stanley convinced him otherwise, telling him that he was the only man for the job and that if he could persuade the garrisons to leave, it would be the most important work he could possibly do. Reluctantly, Jephson agreed.

On May 22, the steamer *Khedive* arrived from Wadelai with 120 warriors of the Madi tribe (no connection to the Mahdi), who would serve as Stanley's additional porters. They were an impressive group, albeit all stark naked—handsome, well muscled, carrying large, powerful-looking bows and arrows. The next night, the Zanzibaris presented a lively farewell dance in Emin's honor. Stanley said of his faithful Zanzibaris, "Though they are quite well aware of the dangers and fatigue of the journey before them, which will commence to-morrow, there are no symptoms of misgiving in any of them. But it is certain that some of them will take their last look of the pasha to-morrow."

The next morning, after elaborate farewells and pledges to rendezvous again as soon as possible, Stanley, Parke, the Zanzibaris, and the 120 Madis moved out.

The Madis deserted before lunch.

About 20 of them were rounded up, but Parke had to scurry back to Emin's camp to see about getting replacements. Emin reasoned that the Madis were afraid of serving under strangers, and of being taken even farther away from their homes. There was also the possibility that the Zanzibaris had scared the hell out of them with stories of the horrors awaiting them in the Ituri forest. Luckily for Stanley (if not the Africans), another 80 Madis were still at M'swa, the closest of Emin's stations. The *Khedive* was immediately dispatched, and the additional men arrived the following day. They were then tied together in groups of ten before being marched off to the waiting Stanley. Jephson suspected, "He [Stanley] will keep them tied up until he has gone some days march & placed two or three hostile tribes between them & the Lake, return will then be impossible for them & they will be obliged to follow him or be cut to pieces by hostile natives."

Less then twenty-four hours later, word came back from Stanley: the new carriers had arrived, and he had some exciting news—he had just discovered the snow-capped peaks of the Ruwenzori Mountains! As Emin, always interested in anything geographical or scientific, sent back his congratulations on such a significant find, Jephson could do little more than stew in his diary: "He says nothing of Parke & I having seen it more than a month ago & having told him about it, but he makes it out to be his discovery." Rank ... privileges, etc.

Thankfully, for Jephson had been growing restless with inactivity, the next day he and Emin left to begin their tour. Poor Jephson. He would be leading a quintet consisting of himself, three Sudanese soldiers, and an interpreter; it would constitute all the evidence the soldiers of Equatoria would see of the vaunted Emin Pasha Relief Expedition.

The beginning of his tour with Emin also marked the end of the first volume of Jephson's journal. He closed it with the following: "We have now been just a year & four months out from England & what prospect have we of getting back for another year [or] two years & more?" He went on to say that, though the journal had been kept "in just a helter skelter kind of fashion . . . without much regard to grammar or spelling," he hoped it would nevertheless "answer it's purpose which is to tell a true & exact story of the expedition, of how we found & relieved Emin Pasha & of the trials & difficulties we met on the road & how through the strong determination of our leader & the hardiness of our Zanzibaris we over came them all. . . ." At this point, however, Jephson had neither his leader nor the Zanzibaris. And his trials and difficulties, great as they had already seemed, were just beginning.

Part

TWO

Chapter Twelve

A PROVINCIAL
TOUR

THE FIRST STOP was M'swa, and it turned out that Emin's first order of business was to form a war party. It had been almost five months since Gaetano Casati, the Italian traveler whom Emin had pressed into service as his envoy to Kabba Rega of Unyoro, had been abruptly expelled from his quarters in Kibiro, on the opposite shore of Lake Albert. Casati had not just been expelled; he had been arrested, stripped, and tied to a tree by the king's henchmen. Only by luck had a party of Emin's soldiers found and rescued him. He had pleaded with Emin to launch a punitive strike immediately afterward, but Emin had hesitated. Now, when the incident seemed almost forgotten, he was ready. He sent both of his steamers, and a substantial force, across the lake. The raid was swift, brutal, and successful. The village was burned to the ground, Kabba Rega's troops were routed, and many weapons were captured, along with a large quantity of salt, which was the village's principal trade commodity.

Although neither Jephson nor Emin accompanied the raiders, Jephson was impressed by the apparent efficiency of the operation, and by Emin's willingness to use decisive force when warranted. Casati, however, deemed the response too tardy to do much more than annoy the Unyoran king and perhaps provoke an escalation of hostilities.

When the raiders returned, the party moved on to Tunguru, even though Jephson had not had an opportunity to address the troops at M'swa. Emin said they could do it on their return. On reaching Tunguru, located near the northern end of Lake Albert on a long spit of land jutting out into the water, Jephson was laid low with a fever, a condition that seemed to be plaguing him with increasing frequency.

As he convalesced, he began to hear some disturbing rumors. Tunguru was the home station of Achmet Mahmoud and Abdul Wahab, the two Egyptians who had approached Stanley to complain about Emin Pasha's treatment of them. The pair had returned to Tunguru before Emin and Jephson arrived. As it turned out, the station chief, Suleiman Aga, a man whom Emin trusted fully, was away from the station, collecting grain taxes from the native tribes of the district, so the Egyptians took the opportunity to continue their treachery against Emin, telling the Tunguru garrison that Stanley wasn't really who he said he was. He wasn't a savior but an adventurer, "in league with the Pasha, who had formed a design with him to take the people out of the country and hand them over as slaves to the English" (Jephson). Moreover, they had sent letters containing these accusations to Emin's other stations.

The day after Emin and Jephson arrived at Tunguru, loyal Sudanese officers came to Emin and told him what had been going on. He immediately mustered the troops and had the two Egyptians arrested, along with two other Egyptian officers who were said to be in league with them. Achmet Emin's Mahmoud, the clerk, was literally sent down the river to the station at Dufilé, headquarters of the Second Battalion, where he was to be imprisoned. The other three, all officers, were reduced a grade in rank and placed under house arrest. However, as Jephson noted, "This . . . was not effected without a good deal of talking, which breach of discipline surprised me greatly." Jephson's observation echoed a comment made by Stanley as he observed Emin's interactions with his subordinates while they were camped at Nsabé. He found Emin's manner with his troops to be altogether too solicitous rather than commanding.

To his credit, Jephson told Emin what he thought (something Stanley had not done). His candor elicited a startling revelation: Emin told him the truth about the rebellion of First Battalion, something he had not done with Stanley. It had been the First Battalion, manning Emin's northern stations, that had successfully fought off repeated attacks by the Mahdi's troops some four years before. Despite these victories, however, Emin had been convinced that the best long-term strategy for the survival of the province was to abandon the northern stations and concentrate his resources in the south. His thinking was that if it became necessary to evacuate his people from Equatoria, their best chance would be to travel southeast through Unyoro and Uganda and then on to Zanzibar. It was in anticipation of that possibility that he had built the station at Wadelai and moved his headquarters there.

The men of the First Battalion had refused to leave their posts. One officer in particular, an Egyptian named Ali Aga Dgabor, who had taken part in the Arabi rebellion, said to the men, "Why should we be afraid to oppose Emin Pasha, when we in Egypt were not afraid to rebel against the Khedive himself?" (Jephson). In addition, as Emin had already mentioned, there were still many in the First Battalion who refused to believe that Khartoum had fallen. They remained convinced that if and when relief came, it would come from the north—all the more reason to remain where they were. "The result was that the soldiers declared they would no longer obey their Governor's orders, and openly rebelled against him" (Jephson). Emin also admitted that, just a few months earlier, on his last inspection of the northern stations, he had turned back before reaching Rejaf, the First Battalion's headquarters, because of rumors of a plan to take him prisoner.

It was the Egyptians, said Emin, who had always been his greatest problem. The Egyptian government had turned Equatoria into a dumping ground "to which all the scum of Egypt had been banished" or, to be more precise, fifty-six officers and clerks. Some had been sent as punishment for their participation in the Arabi rebellion, but the majority were simply common criminals who happened to be in the army. Emin also admitted that, even in the Second Battalion, which he swore was loyal and faithful to him, there were a few Egyptian officers who could not be trusted.

Jephson was stunned. "Though we all knew from what he had told us at Nsabe that things were somewhat difficult in his Province, we had no idea that rebellion had taken such a hold on his people." He was especially disappointed that Dr. Junker, who had been in the province when the rebellion of the First Battalion had taken place, had never said anything about it to Stanley or anyone else connected to the expedition. When Jephson spoke about the situation with Casati, the Italian confided that Emin "could not, or would not, see how serious the position of affairs in the country had become."

When Suleiman Aga, the station chief at Tunguru, finally returned from his tax collecting, Jephson immediately went to speak to him in private. Would he and his soldiers be loyal to Emin, even if it meant leaving the province, or would they throw in their lot with the First Battalion? Suleiman Aga formed his hands into a circle. "These are my soldiers & the Pasha goes in the middle, that is the way we will travel, by whatever road the Pasha wishes." The conversation eased Jephson's mind a little, but Emin's revelations about the First Battalion created serious misgivings about the outcome of his mission.

The next day, Emin mustered the Tunguru garrison so that Jephson could address them on behalf of the expedition. The troops were turned out in their best uniforms, with flags flying and bugles blowing. After the khedival hymn was played, Jephson made a few introductory remarks, which had to be translated by his interpreter, Binza. He then turned to a reading of the two official letters from Egypt, one from the khedive himself, Tewfik; the other from the prime minister, Nubar Pasha. These, too, had to be translated, in this case by one of the station's clerks, since they were written in Arabic. The whole process was somewhat cumbersome, but the audience seemed to be paying close attention.

The letters were very similar, both addressed "To His Excellency

Mehmed Emin." There were flowery opening passages praising the courage and steadfastness of the troops and expressing the government's gratitude for their dedicated service. Then came the heart of the matter, the announcement that an expedition was being sent for them, under Stanley's command, to bring them relief supplies and, if they chose, to bring them back to Egypt. The fact that they had a choice was very clear: "I [Tewfik] give to you, your officers and soldiers full liberty to rest where you are, or to do your best to come out with the Expedition which is now sent to you." If they came to Cairo, they would be paid in full through their arrival in Egypt. However, if they chose to stay, they "must not in future expect any assistance from this Government." Nubar Pasha's letter reiterated, almost paragraph by paragraph, the content of the khedive's letter.

In his journal, Jephson noted "that no direct order was given to Emin or his people to leave the Province, nor was any promise of employment given to them when they reached Egypt." In fact, the letters didn't even specify that they had to come to Egypt to collect their pay, but since none of them, including Emin, had been paid for so long, it was certainly a reasonable inference.

Jephson then read a third letter, this one from Stanley. It was a document quite different in both length (almost twice as long as the prime minister's) and tone from the official government correspondence. Though it was addressed to the "Soldiers of Emin Pasha," Stanley didn't begin with words of praise; he began with words of doom: "For you must know that the river el Abiad [the Nile] is closed, that Khartoum is in the hands of the followers of Mohammed Achmet [the Mahdi], that the great Pasha Gordon and all his people were killed over three years ago, and that the country and river between Wady Halfa and the Bahr Ghazal [to the north and west] are occupied by your enemies and by the rebels." He continued by pointing out that he was the only man who had been able to reach them, where four other attempts to bring them relief had failed.* He then stated his business:

---

*This was an extremely liberal accounting. There had been two early attempts to mount relief expeditions, but both had been quickly aborted. Stanley was also including Gordon's last stand at Khartoum and the failed British military mission to rescue him as attempts to relieve Emin Pasha.

"I have come . . . to lead you out of this country and show you the way to Egypt." He acknowledged that they had the option to stay in Equatoria, but did so in a way that was virtually a direct challenge to their manhood: "The Khedive says that if you think the road is too long, or are afraid of the journey, that you may stay here, but if you do so you are no longer his soldiers, and that your pay stops at once, and that if any trouble befall you hereafter you are not to expect any help from him." Then came the most important sentence in the letter: "Should you decide to *obey* [italics added] him [the khedive] and follow me to Egypt, I am to show you the way to Zanzibar, and there put you on board a steamer, and take you to Suez and thence to Cairo . . . [where] all rewards promised to you will be paid in full."

Of course, since there were no actual orders given in the letters from the khedive and the prime minister, there was nothing to *obey*, but that didn't stop Stanley. Soldiers are taught to obey orders, and Stanley needed these soldiers to believe that an order had been given to leave Equatoria, whether it had or not. He closed with a note of almost paternal assurance: "If you say, 'Let us go to Egypt,' I will then show you a safe road, and will accompany you and not leave you until you stand before the Khedive. . . ." He signed it "from your good friend, Stanley."

As soon as Jephson (or rather, the interpreter) finished the reading, several men stepped forward and made speeches swearing their loyalty and devotion to their pasha, but Jephson told them that they should talk over their choices among themselves. He would speak with them the next day to "receive their decisions."

As he expected, the next day, the answers were the same from everyone: "wherever the Pasha goes, we will follow." It occurred to Jephson that, to most of the Sudanese soldiers, the khedive wasn't even real. "They all spoke most respectfully of 'Effendina' [the khedive] but he was only to them a person in the clouds . . . a Mythical person who sends them fine words, but through all these years has neither helped them nor sent them their pay." No wonder they professed their undying loyalty to Emin—at least he was flesh and blood.

Jephson and Emin left Tunguru on June 25, headed overland to Emin's headquarters at Wadelai. It was beautiful country, full of wild animals, with prosperous-looking native villages spotted every few miles. Throughout the journey, Emin was absorbed in making scientific observations and in taking measurements needed for a network of roads he was hoping to build to connect his stations. Some of the villages they passed had obviously been told in advance of their coming, and the natives were waiting for them with fresh water and curdled milk (a treat, as far as Jephson was concerned). He was impressed, too, by the warm and respectful reception given to Emin by the natives.

A few days "in the field" also made Jephson realize that Emin's real passion was science, not governance. Nothing gave him greater pleasure than collecting flora and fauna, cataloging his finds, making detailed observations, and adding to his ever-expanding collections. Indeed, in the packet of letters the expedition had brought to him, he read most eagerly the correspondence from scientific colleagues in England and on the Continent.

Emin's headquarters at Wadelai were truly impressive. Built on a hill overlooking the Nile, Wadelai was home to some two thousand people, including Emin's beautiful little daughter, Farida. Jephson learned that Emin had been married to an Abyssinian woman who had borne him two children, a son who had died shortly after birth, and Farida, whom Jephson judged to be about four. In March 1887, about the time the expedition was leaving Zanzibar, Farida's mother died from an infection, leaving Emin and Farida alone together. Emin said he still grieved for his wife but found solace in his daughter's love. Their affection for each other was unmistakable.

Emin's quarters were comfortable and well furnished with "a very home-like air." Jephson was particularly impressed by two bulging bookcases filled with volumes in half a dozen languages. Jephson was installed in a hut just across the courtyard from Emin's house, fronted by a garden full of citrus, pomegranate, and apple trees. Dogs, cats, goats, guinea fowl, and even a tame eagle strolled the grounds.

When Emin opened the correspondence that had accumulated during his absence, he found a most unexpected letter. It was from Hamad Aga, a major in the rebellious First Battalion. Emin described Hamad Aga as a good man and a loyal officer who had simply been swept along by the rebellion, powerless to resist its momentum, but he still believed Hamad Aga was loyal in his heart. In his letter, Hamad

Aga said "that the officers of the 1st Battalion, hearing that the expedition had arrived at the south end of the lake, with ammunition from Egypt, to the people, were now convinced that their Governor had been right, and wished to apologize for what they had done, and make their submission to him." They were sending a delegation to Wadelai, "to ask his pardon, and to beg him to come down to Rejaf, bringing with him Mr. Stanley's representative, whom they were all desirous of seeing. Their Governor might dictate his own terms to them, and they would obey all that he commanded." It seemed too good to be true. After more than three years, the rebellion of the First Battalion was ended, the province reunited. Emin was thrilled; Jephson was skeptical.

Thrilled or not, Emin was not willing to forgive and forget without a show of displeasure. Jephson wrote, "Emin told me that when the envoys came, he did not wish to see them, but desired me to see them, and to try and show them the enormity of their crime in rebelling. He intended to forgive them in the end, if he felt sure of the sincerity of their expressions of regret for what they had done, but he did not wish to appear to forgive them too easily. . . . It was a farce, but as he wished it, I agreed to carry it out."

When the delegation from Rejaf arrived a week later, led by Hamad Aga himself, Emin's theatrics seemed to have the desired effect.* The more aloof Emin was, the more distraught the delegation became, and the more desperate to win back his favor. At one point, Hamad Aga ordered his troops to refrain from drinking alcohol, lest they offend their governor. (Jephson commented, "Poor simple man! If he only knew the enormous proportion of Christians that . . . get drunk!")

When they had been in Wadelai for almost two weeks, Jephson started to worry about time: at this rate, the tour would drag on forever. He asked Emin to muster the troops so that he could make his presentation, and Emin agreed. As had been the case at Tunguru, everyone seemed to listen attentively, and as soon as the reading of the letters was finished, there were immediate affirmations of loyalty to the pasha. Once again, however, Jephson told the soldiers to talk things

---

*In its way, the incident was reminiscent of Stanley's grandstand play when he arranged to have the Zanzibari chiefs plead for the life of a condemned man.

over among themselves and give him their decision the next day. As he expected, the answer came back unchanged: "We will follow our pasha."

A few days before Jephson's address to the troops, both Hamad Aga and the Wadelai station chief, a man named Kodi Aga, had approached him to ask about the possibility of leaving Equatoria for "some country nearer civilization, where they could settle down." In other words, the Kavirondo plan. Clearly, word of Stanley's discussions with Emin at Nsabé had gotten out, because Jephson had also been approached with similar inquiries by officers at Tunguru. Emin had already declared that the Kavirondo plan was his preferred option, so Jephson suggested that they make the plan public while at Wadelai. Emin said no. He felt it would be disloyal to the khedive, to whom he (and, perhaps more important, many of his troops) still felt considerable loyalty. He was also afraid that the troops might see the Kavirondo option as a last-minute change in plans that would only confuse them. Better to reveal the Kavirondo idea later, perhaps even after the evacuation had begun. For now, they would rely on the sincerity of the men when they promised to follow their pasha "wherever he would take them."

Jephson wasn't satisfied. He had a final parlay with the officers and noncommissioned officers, and while he didn't specify Kavirondo, he did say to them, "From what I have heard from certain officers, I understand that it is not your wish and that of the soldiers to go to Egypt, but to follow us with your Governor to a country somewhat nearer the sea, and there to settle down. Is this your wish? I was answered by a deafening 'Aywah' [yes] from all."

To both Emin and Jephson, Wadelai felt like a turning point, with two huge "wins" for their mission. Not only had the First Battalion apparently returned to the fold, but the Kavirondo plan was beginning to look more and more realistic. It was time to move on to Dufilé, the oldest and largest station in Equatoria, but before they departed, Kodi Aga and Emin showed Jephson several storehouses filled to the rafters with magnificent ivory tusks—Emin's fabled cache. Emin told him there were equal, if not greater, stores in Dufilé, and another thousand tusks stored in Monbuttu, a tribal area where the chiefs could be trusted to safeguard them. Emin said he estimated the total value of his cache at £75,000, but Jephson realized he was calculating the worth at an outdated price—eight shillings per pound. When he left London more than a year before, the price was up to twelve shillings a pound, which meant Emin's ivory was worth as much as £112,500, perhaps even more if the price had continued to rise. The question was how they could possibly move so much tonnage to the coast. Jephson ruefully concluded that much of it might have to be abandoned. Evidently Emin had reached the same conclusion some time ago; he'd stopped collecting ivory three years earlier.

THEY TOOK THE STEAMERS from Wadelai to Dufilé, a sixty-mile trip down the Nile that went slowly because the river was clogged with islands of matted vegetation not unlike the Sudd. Dufilé was, if anything, more impressive that Wadelai. The most developed station in the province, it had originally been built by Gordon. There was a wharf for the steamers, and a twelve-foot moat and substantial earthen walls surrounded the compound, "making it impregnable," in Jephson's opinion. Inside the walls were lovely, broad, tree-lined streets, buildings made of brick with proper wooden doors and windows, including a school and a mosque, and, in the very center of the station, a village square where, under a trio of enormous fig trees, "all the celebreties of the Equatorial provinces have sat & talked & had their coffee & cigarettes as they settled the affairs of the Province" (Jephson).

As usual, they arrived to a full military welcome, flags flying, bugles playing (including the now inevitable khedival hymn), and troops in formation. Unfortunately, at least from Jephson's point of view, there was also a local gesture reserved for first-time visitors. As they stepped from the steamer, a bullock was slaughtered right in front of them so that its blood would flow across their path as they walked. Welcome to Dufilé.

The station chief, who was also commander of the Second Battalion, was a wily Egyptian named Hawash Effendi who had been banished to Equatoria after he was caught selling government stores to the enemy during Egypt's war with Abyssinia. He freely described himself (and most of his countrymen) as "scoundrels" and, shortly after meeting Jephson, gave him this piece of advice: "If a Soudanese comes at you with a loaded gun & from the other side an Egyptian comes towards you with a carpet, go towards the Soudanese, he with his loaded gun will do you less harm than the Egyptian with his carpet & friendship."

Hawash Effendi was a controversial figure in the province. As chief of the largest station and battalion commander, he was arguably the second-most powerful man in Equatoria. But whereas Emin Pasha was regarded mostly with affection, Hawash Effendi was mostly feared and despised. He had made himself wealthy (by Equatorian standards) by abusing his power and position, extracting tribute from subordinates, stealing cattle, women, and other assets, and generally behaving in a high-handed manner. Still, he enjoyed Emin's trust and protection. The reason was simple: Hawash Effendi got things done, an uncommon attribute among the province's officers. Emin knew that Hawash Effendi was unpopular, and he knew why, but he needed him, so he turned a blind eye to his bad behavior.

They stayed in Dufilé only three days. The night before they left, Hawash Effendi hosted an elaborate banquet in their honor, eaten in the traditional manner with fingers rather than utensils. When they finished, Jephson and Hawash Effendi took their pipes to the veranda and had a long conversation. "He had a bad word to say for most people, but spoke well of the pasha, though he said he was not sufficiently firm with the people. . . ." When the talk turned to Hamad Aga and the apparent return of the First Battalion, Hawash Effendi was extremely skeptical. He warned Jephson that he and the pasha should be very careful as they moved to the stations of the First Battalion. Clearly, he was unmoved by their protestations of renewed loyalty. As far as he was concerned, they were not to be trusted.

The conversation rekindled Jephson's fears that had been briefly assuaged by the developments at Wadelai, but the following morning, as they prepared to leave Dufilé for the northern stations, when he told Emin what Hawash Effendi had said, the pasha made light of it. He continued to be optimistic about the outcome of their tour. Perhaps it was that optimism that led them to depart Dufilé without Jephson's doing "the presentation of the letters." As he had been at M'swa, Emin was confident enough to defer the presentation until their return journey.

Owing to rapids, the Nile was un-navigable north of Dufilé, so the rest of the tour was conducted on foot (or in Emin's and Jephson's case, on donkey). Spending only one night in each location, they quickly covered the four smaller stations at Chor Ayu, Laboré, Muggi, and Kirri. The countryside between the stations was beautiful, and Jephson felt as if he were on a nature walk, especially when he saw his first large elephant herd, with several hundred animals arrayed impressively across the plain.

When they reached Kirri, the next-to-last station before Rejaf, Emin called a halt. He had decided to deliver an ultimatum to test the sincerity of the allegedly repentant rebels at Rejaf. His messenger was Hamad Aga, the senior officer from the Rejaf delegation to Wadelai. Hamad Aga was to tell the commanders at Rejaf that they were to come to Kirri to make their submissions and apologies to their pasha; he would not come to them. He was also to tell them that, if they refused, Emin would close down all the stations between Rejaf and Dufilé in preparation for a withdrawl from the province. In short, if they did not apologize and beg his forgiveness, they would be abandoned.

Rejaf was only thirty miles from Kirri. Hamad Aga would reach it in two days, so Emin hoped for a quick response to his ultimatum. It didn't come. More than a week went by before a boatman brought a message he had smuggled out of Rejaf in the folds of his turban, a subterfuge made necessary because Hamad Aga had become a virtual prisoner at the station. The message was that the officers of Rejaf would not come to Kirri until they could consult with the battalion's senior commanders, Ali Aga Dgabor and Mahmoud Effendi el Adeini, who also happened to be the rebellion's ringleaders. The pair was no longer at Rejaf, having established themselves in a satellite station several days away in an area called Makaraka, where they operated without pretense of military purpose. Rather, they spent their time terrorizing the local tribes and stealing cattle, women, and anything else they fancied. According to Jephson, "these men were among the worst of the many scoundrels in Emin's province. . . ."

When Hamad Aga's message arrived, Hawash Effendi's warning rang in Jephson's ears. He told Emin it was pointless to stay at Kirri any longer—Rejaf wasn't coming back into the fold. They should immediately carry out the ultimatum, starting with the closure of Kirri. Emin, as often happened, wanted to wait.

Annoyed and frustrated, Jephson decided to address the troops, even though he was nervous about the reception he might receive, since the station had suffered significant desertions to the rebel side, and the loyalty of some of those who remained was suspect. He needn't have worried; the response was the same one he had heard everywhere else: "We will go where our Pasha goes." Some of the officers and soldiers wanted to know whether they would be allowed to take their women, children, and slaves with them if they followed the expedition out of Equatoria. When Jephson replied that as far as the expedition was concerned, "they might bring with them whom they pleased," the troops were greatly relieved and seemed ready to begin the evacuation of the station immediately.

Shortly after Jephson's presentation, another message arrived from Hamad Aga. Emin must not, under any circumstances, come to Rejaf. If he did, he would be captured and taken in chains to Khartoum, where the rebel officers still believed Gordon was alive and in power.

For Emin, it was déjà vu, the same scenario that had unfolded at Kirri nine months before. Once again, his optimism had been misplaced. Jephson was right—it was time to leave. Emin gave orders for the evacuation of Kirri, telling the soliders to start with the station's stores of ammunition, which were to be prepared for immediate shipment to the south. He and Jephson would go on ahead to initiate the evacuation of the other stations. He also told the troops that, when the last man left Kirri, he was to burn it to the ground—a final, dramatic statement to the rebels of Rejaf.

Emin and Jephson left Kirri early the next morning, heading south to the station at Muggi. They hadn't gone more than a mile when a breathless messenger caught up with them. The soldiers at Kirri refused to part with their ammunition; they suspected some kind of trick.

"Such an open act of insubordination was outrageous," wrote Jephson, "and I begged him [Emin] to return and see that his order was carried out himself. I knew that had Stanley given an order, and heard that his people had refused to carry it out, he would very soon have been on the spot to see it obeyed in person." But Emin didn't go back. He didn't even turn around. He merely sent another note, telling the garrison to obey his order. That night, at the station at Muggi, another message came. The garrison at Kirri had decided to join the rebels at Rejaf.

The news devastated Emin. He woke Jephson in the middle of the night, telling him he didn't know what to do and asking his advice. Jephson was still for going back to Kirri and confronting the renegades, but Emin wasn't sure. He thought perhaps they should concentrate on the remaining stations, reasoning that the farther south they went, the greater the loyalty of the troops. Despite the day's keen disappointment, he refused to believe that his other garrisons would not remain loyal.

Then, as if they didn't have enough problems already, a note came from Hawash Effendi in Dufilé. A large party of men, on foot and horseback, had been spotted north and east of the Nile, and there were reports of clashes with local tribesmen. Hawash Effendi wondered whether it could be another relief expedition, this one coming from the north, but Emin knew better. Though he couldn't be sure, he was afraid that the unknown party was the development he'd been dreading for more than three years—the return of the Mahdi.

Emin and Jephson were not averse to sharing the news. In fact, they used it to motivate the garrison at Muggi, consisting of only ninety men, to evacuate and head south for Dufilé. The process began at once and proceeded in a remarkably orderly fashion, the first groups of women and children leaving in less than a day. Emin also sent a small party of soldiers back to Kirri with a letter. It contained no orders or ultimatums, but stated that he would still be willing to take back those officers and men who wished to go with him to the south. Those who had joined the rebels were acting within the parameters of the khedive's letters, and he bore them no ill will. When his soldiers returned, they brought with them fifteen men, including several who had defected from Rejaf, but the vast majority of the Kirri garrison chose to stay there.

With the evacuation of Muggi well underway, Emin and Jephson moved to the next station, at Laboré. There the troops were assembled for Jephson to give the presentation of the letters. "Whilst I was speaking I noticed that the soldiers were not as attentive as was generally the case and that there was a good deal of whispering going on . . . there was an uneasy stir amongst them, as if something unusual was going to happen."

> After I had finished speaking, Emin, as was his custom, added a few words to what I had said. Whilst he was speaking, a big bull-headed, sullen-looking Soudanese stepped out of the ranks, and exclaimed, "All you have been telling us is a lie, and the letter you have read out is a forgery, for if it had come from Effendina [the khedive] he would have *commanded* us to come, and not have told us we might do as we pleased. You do not come from Egypt, we know of only one road to Egypt, and that is by Khartoum, we will either go by that road, or we'll live and die in this country."

It was the proverbial last straw. Emin, the soul of patience, finally snapped. In Jephson's words, he "instantly sprang forward and seized him, and trying to wrench his gun out of his hand, shouted to his four orderlies to arrest the man, and carry him off to prison. A struggle then ensued and the mutineer shouted to his companions to help him. Then arose a scene of confusion and uproar which is impossible to describe."

For Emin and Jephson alike, the Emin Pasha Relief Expedition very nearly ended in the next moment. They were suddenly surrounded by angry troops, screaming and yelling and pointing loaded weapons at them. Emin drew his sword and "dared them to come on." Jephson was sure he would never see Stanley or the others again. "At this moment, some one called out that my orderlies were going to seize the powder magazine . . . the soldiers wrenched their companion from the grasp of Emin's orderlies, and rushed off to the magazine, bearing their comrade with them with shouts of defiance and contempt. Emin and I were left standing almost alone. . . ."

With a remarkable show of bravery, Jephson followed the riotous troops to the powder magazine and confronted them, alternately scolding and reasoning with them until he managed to calm everyone down, telling them, "I have no fear of you because you are soldiers, not savages." It turned out that the soldier who had stepped from the ranks was the orderly of an Egyptian officer named Surore Aga, who was in league with the rebels at Rejaf. The whole episode had been his idea.

There would be no resolution to the matter before they left Laboré. The next day, some of the soldiers came to Jephson to apologize; others remained defiant, saying that Emin should never have seized their brother. Emin, badly shaken, refused to see anyone. Jephson thought it best to leave the station as quickly as possible. As they were preparing to depart, Binza, Jephson's interpreter, said to him, "Master, these are a rotten people, the good material in them is not sufficient to make a hut, but there is enough evil in them to build a palace." Jephson didn't disagree.

They stopped at the next station, Chor Ayu, short of Dufilé, in part because it was the beginning of a three-day Islamic holiday when there would be much feasting and drinking. Dufilé would be a madhouse, and they had had quite enough excitement for the moment. But there would be no relief at Chor Ayu. Another letter came from Hawash Effendi. Dufilé was in revolt; Hawash had been made a prisoner in his own house, and the Egyptian clerk Achmet Mahmoud, who had started this nightmare with his complaints to Stanley, had been released from prison.

They were trapped. "Rejaf at one end, Dufilé at the other and Laboré in between," wrote Jephson. What could they possibly do? For once, Emin knew the course he would take. They would go to Dufilé and confront their antagonists.

It had been only five weeks since they had first traveled from Dufilé to Chor Ayu, when Jephson had written, "The country is perfectly beautiful & of a wild park like description; small valleys run up into the mountains full of fine trees, whilest the little plain between the river & the hills is covered with short cropped grass & dotted about with large finely shaped trees, there is an air of quiet & peacefulness about it . . . which gives a feeling of security & retirement." On approaching Dufilé a second time, he wrote, "One was struck even more than on our journey down by the inexpressible loneliness & solitude of this huge rocky waste of uninhabited country."

They paused on a hill to look down at Dufilé.

There were Emin and myself, Vita Hassan, the apothecary, Rajab and Arif Effendis, who were Emin's clerks, Kismullah, Emin's collector and preparer of birds, our servants and orderlies, and some twenty Madi carriers. We stood gazing on the station, wondering what our reception would be like, whether we should be able to make any impression on the mutineers and get them to abandon their plot, or whether we should now take a long farewell to liberty and freedom. We changed our hats [!] and made ourselves tidy, drew the column together in an orderly line, and shaking out all our bravery, in the way of flags and pendants, we set our teeth and prepared to descend into the station.

On their first trip to Dufilé, they had been greeted with full military pomp and ceremony. On this day, Jephson wrote,

as we approached, there was a deep silence, everyone seemed holding his breath to see what would happen. We rode through the lines of silent people, and entered the station. No salutes had been fired, nor were the soldiers drawn up in line to salute the Governor. . . . As we passed through the postern gate, an order was given by an Egyptian officer, and sentries took their places in front of and behind us, thus cutting us off from our people. As the sentries took their places, a rush was made at Kismullah, the Pasha's collector, and his gun was torn form his hands, and he and some others were hurried off to prison. At this signal a perfect din of voices arose, the station seemed alive with people and every one, men women, and children pressed forward to witness their Governor's humiliation. . . . The only man who greeted us that day was a little Circassian tinker. Undismayed by the frowns and threatening looks of the crowd, he started forward and seized the Pasha's and my hands. He could not speak for weeping, but could only raise our hands to his lips, and look at us in speechless misery. We were then conducted into our compound, which was surrounded by a high thick boma or fence, and eight sentries were posted at the entrance, with strict orders to allow no one to have ingress or egress. Thus began our imprisonment.

Chapter Thirteen

THE REAR
COLUMN

WITH ONLY THEIR personal gear to carry, plenty of food (thanks to Emin), and only a few hostile natives to contend with, Stanley virtually sprinted to Fort Bodo, getting there in a little over a week. The fort had flourished under Stairs's command (or, as Stanley put it, "Of the condition of the garrison at Fort Bodo, there was but little to complain.") There had been minor problems with the neighboring tribes, principally the Wambutti pygmies, who continually raided the crops being raised in the fields surrounding the fort, and with the local elephant herds, which ravaged the banana groves. Still, the "invalids" were healthier, and Nelson, though still prone to fevers and crankiness, looked almost fit again. True to form, Stanley reported that the meeting with Emin Pasha had gone splendidly, the governor was grateful beyond words, the arrival of the expedition had saved him and his people from a dreadful fate, and he and his followers would be ready to leave the province as soon as Stanley returned from "rescuing" the rear column.

In fact, Stanley reported, they would soon hear all about it from Emin himself because he and Jephson would be coming to Fort Bodo as soon as they finished their tour of the province. Stanley estimated they should arrive in about two months. They would then lead the Fort Bodo contingent back to the plateau overlooking Lake Albert, where they would bivouac and await Stanley's return with the rear column. Then, the reunited expedition would escort Emin and his soldiers and subjects to Lake Victoria (the Kavirondo plan) and/or Zanzibar, depending on Emin's final decision. Stanley sounded so confident about this scenario that he made it sound almost like a fait accompli.

As for rescuing the rear column, Stanley had decided that he would be the only officer going.* He reasoned that taking any of the others meant more loads to be carried, and he wanted to travel as light as possible. Furthermore, there were still enough sickly Africans at Fort Bodo that Parke's services would be better utilized there (a very questionable call, given the relative tranquillity of the fort juxtaposed to the certain dangers and deprivations awaiting the rescue party in the Ituri forest). In addition, Nelson still wasn't in shape for the rigors of the trail, and Stairs had already gone above and beyond the call of duty so often that he deserved a rest. (For his part, Stairs was torn. Though he loathed Stanley and dreaded being alone on the trail with him again, he was bored and restless after "tending the garden" at Fort Bodo for so long. Frying pan or fire.)

Stairs had his own theory as to why Stanley wanted to go by himself: "afterwards in his book he can say [he] alone braved the terrors of famine and the bush, found [his] way down the river and by [his] skill and nerve, saved Major Barttelot. . . ." He also suspected that the inevitable scarcity of food in the forest influenced the decision. If Stan-

*Stanley was so determined to go it alone that he even left his faithful fox terrier, Randy, who had been with the expedition every step of the way, with Stairs. Unfortunately, as Stanley later wrote, "the poor dog misjudged my purpose and resolutely refused his food from the moment I left him, and on the third day after my departure he died of a broken heart."

ley didn't take any other officers with him, he wouldn't have to share his rations!*

Though he would take no other officers with him, Stanley was planning to take every able-bodied African available. His decision to go with such a large party reflected his mounting anxiety about what might have happened at Yambuya. He was convinced that Tippu Tib must have reneged on his agreement to provide porters; otherwise Barttelot would have been at Fort Bodo already, or at least he would have been somewhere on the trail between Yambuya and the fort and would have gotten word to them regarding his whereabouts and situation. But that hadn't happened. If Barttelot was stuck in Yambuya, it could only be because he didn't have enough carriers to move out. It was thus up to Stanley to provide them. Hence the decision to take all the men he could.

Stanley gave the men a week to prepare. They were to grind as much Indian corn and plantain flour as they could carry and still move at top speed. Stanley was aiming to make the round-trip to Yambuya and back in 200 days. Given that it had taken 160 days to cross the Ituri *one way* the first time, the goal was beyond ambitious. By the same token, they would have some distinct advantages over the first trip. For one thing, they knew the route. For another, they might be able to use some of their previous camps. The men would have to carry only their own food, at least on the first half of the trip—no cumbersome (and desertion-inducing) loads. And, during the river-borne portions of the journey, they would have the current with them instead of against them, a considerable blessing.

In his instructions to Stairs, Stanley laid out a precise calendar of destinations, distances, anticipated arrival dates, and so on. He told him they would be back at Fort Bodo on January 2 and at Lake Albert on January 16, 1889. He made it sound almost as if he were going for a hike in the Cotswolds, rather than a trek through a cannibal-infested jungle.

On June 16, Stanley marched out at the head of a caravan consist-

---

*Evidently, Stairs forgot that Stanley *never* shared his rations at any point on the expedition.

ing of himself, his servant Hoffmann, 113 Zanzibaris, and the 95 Madi tribesmen provided by Emin, along with 14 additional men (the healthiest of the invalids) under Major Parke who were going back to Ipoto to pick up the last few loads that had been left there. By the end of the third day, they were back in the gloom of the forest.

They did encounter many of the same villages they'd seen on their first crossing, but none were occupied or occupiable. The Manyue-mas had driven out the inhabitants and laid waste to all of them. What the Manyuemas hadn't destroyed, the jungle was already reclaiming. Stanley's party also saw several skeletons of fallen comrades, particularly disconcerting for the Madi.

At Ipoto, they dropped off Parke and his contingent of carriers. They retrieved about half of the rifles and only a fraction of the ammunition that had been left there. Kilonga-longa, the Arab chieftain who had been away during their first visit, was extremely apologetic for the behavior of his henchmen, though he wasn't interested in renegotiating any of his agreements about additional payments, including black powder and bolts of cloth from the supplies of the rear column. After only one night, Parke headed back for Fort Bodo. Stanley and the main column headed in the opposite direction.

On June 28, 1888, the first anniversary of his departure from Yambuya, Stanley found himself back at Nelson's Starvation Camp. Remarkably, the loads that Jephson had been forced to bury there for lack of porters were intact, and the ammunition was still usable.

They were making good time, but the Madi tribesmen were beginning to falter, being utterly unprepared for the ordeal of the forest. By the end of the third week, four of them had already deserted, no doubt to be captured and either enslaved or eaten by the locals. Many of those who remained had been jettisoning some of their food supplies in order to lighten their burdens, so their rations were already running low. They were also singularly unskilled in the arts of the trail, such as building makeshift shelters during the inevitable rainstorms and avoiding the little poisoned skewers that the local tribes were still planting along the pathways. They were also completely naked, so the chill of the forest nights was especially hard on them. They began to get sick—and then they began to die.

The Zanzibaris, on the other hand, were doing splendidly, grateful to be without loads, their hunger held at bay, if not completely satisfied. They maintained Stanley's breakneck pace with almost no complaints. They were utterly unsympathetic to the plight, and the pleas, of the Madis.

At the one-month mark, they reached their old camp opposite Ugarrowa's headquarters, but the Arab camp was deserted. Stanley was extremely disappointed, for two reasons. He had hoped Ugarrowa might have some news from Barttelot, since it was from Ugarrowa's that Stairs had sent the contingent of twenty Zanzibaris back to Yambuya seven months earlier. In addition, the entire rescue column was running low on food. From the looks of the abandoned camp, Ugarrowa and his people hadn't been gone long. If they were headed in the same direction as the column, there wouldn't be a speck of food to eat. With as many as six hundred people in his party, Ugarrowa would have picked the forest clean.

Stanley's fears were well founded. They were indeed following in Ugarrowa's footsteps, and the forest had been stripped bare of edibles. As he had on the first trip, Stanley split the column, putting their dwindling food supplies, along with those too weak to march, into canoes on the river, while the able-bodied paralleled them on the land. After almost three weeks of this, passing through Avisibba, where they had been attacked and Stairs had taken the poisoned arrow in the chest, and then Panga Falls, where so many canoes had overturned, they finally caught up with Ugarrowa.

The Arab chief was headed down the river to sell his cache of ivory, which amply filled fifty-seven canoes. With him at his camp were the survivors of the Zanzibari contingent sent by Stairs to find the rear column. As they had made their way down the river, they had been repeatedly attacked by native tribes, suffering such heavy casualties that they had been forced to turn back. (Either that, or many of them had simply deserted—there was no way of knowing which.) In either case, they hadn't reached Barttelot, so they hadn't delivered Stanley's letters, and they didn't know anything about the whereabouts or condition of the rear column. If Stanley had been worried before, he was now on the edge of panic. After gratefully accepting a gift of several goats, and a few bags of rice from Ugarrowa, the rescue column pushed on.

On August 17, Stanley was with the flotilla of canoes on the Aruwimi. "It was a sombre morning; a heavy greyness of sky painted the eternal forest tops of a sombrous mourning colour," he wrote. As they rounded a large curve in the river, the villages of Banalya came into view. Several of the villages were abandoned, having suffered the same Arab devastation that the column had been seeing for weeks. But at the far end of the curve, Stanley wrote,

we saw one village, a great way down through the light mist of the morning, still standing. . . . Presently, white dresses were seen, and quickly taking up my field glass, I discovered a red flag hoisted. A suspicion of the truth crept into my mind. A light puff of wind unrolled the flag for an instant, and the white crescent and star was revealed. I sprang to my feet and cried out, "The Major, boys! Pull away bravely." A vociferous shouting and hurrahing followed, and every canoe shot forward at racing speed.

About 200 yards from the village we stopped paddling, and I saw a great number of strangers on the shore. I asked, "Whose men are you?" "We are Stanley's men," was the answer delivered in mainland Swahili. But assured by this, and still more so as we recognised a European near the gate, we paddled ashore. The European on a nearer view turned out to be Mr. William Bonny, who had been engaged as doctor's assistant to the Expedition.

Pressing his hand, I said,

"Well, Bonny, how are you? Where is the Major? Sick, I suppose?"

"The Major is dead, sir."

STANLEY HAD ALWAYS had a vivid, and often paranoid, imagination. In the absence of concrete information, he was prone to conjuring dramatic scenarios with numerous permutations, almost none of them ever optimistic. He had indulged in this predilection at length as the rescue column made its way through the forest, but none of the dire possibilities he had conjured in his mind, none of the endless equations of disease, starvation, desertion, disloyalty, native attacks,

betrayal, malfeasance, insubordination, and incompetence came close
to the truth of what had really happened to the rear column. As he put
it in his hyperventilated prose, "If I were to record all that I saw at
Banalya in its deep intensity of unqualified misery, it would be like
stripping the bandages off a vast sloughing ulcer, striated with bleeding arteries, to the public gaze, with no earthly purpose than to shock
and disgust."

The statistics were startling enough. After Ward, Troup, and Bonny
had been moved up the river from Bolobo and Leopoldville with their
extra men and loads, there had been a total of 271 men and 660 loads
at Yambuya. As Stanley stood on the shore at Banalya, two-thirds of
both were gone. He found 98 men alive, of whom, in his judgment,
only 60 "seemed likely to survive," and fewer than 250 loads. Barttelot
was dead; so was Jameson (though no one at Banalya knew it yet).
Troup had been invalided home to England after months of desperate
illness. Herbert Ward, the savvy young veteran of African travel who
had thrown in his lot with the expedition in hopes of adventure, had
been dispatched on a suicidal journey all the way back to Banana
Point to send a telegram to the relief committee in London. Bonny, the
lowest-ranking European on the expedition, was the last man standing. What in God's name had happened?

In some respects, the answer began and ended with Stanley himself, though he eventually expended considerable energy avoiding any
and all responsibility for the fate of the rear column. To begin with, he
had left Barttelot, Jameson, et al. with the dregs of the expedition—the
sick, the lame, the lazy, and the crazy—so that even when Ward and
Bonny showed up with the 125 men who had been left at Bolobo,
there were still almost four times as many loads as there were fit men to
carry them. That was where Tippu Tib was supposed to have come
in. He was to have delivered 600 additional porters to Barttelot, supposedly (according to Stanley) within ten days of the departure of the
advance column. It didn't happen, as Stanley and everyone else had
feared. Without the additional carriers, the rear column was stuck.
There was no point in trying to follow Stanley's trail with only one
carrier for every four loads. The back-and-forth necessary to move all
the supplies would have been insane; even the hyperactive Barttelot

had recognized the folly of such a maneuver, at least at first. So there was nothing to do but wait and periodically try to cajole Tippu Tib into making good on his promise, which was exactly what Barttelot and the other officers had done—for a while.

Poor Barttelot. If ever a man had been miscast in a role, it was he in his capacity as commanding officer at Yambuya. A military man through and through, he was devoted to discipline and routine. In addition, as the weeks and months dragged on, the lack of meaningful work at the camp drove him mad—perhaps literally. Ward observed that the other officers learned to fend off boredom by chatting, reading, sketching, and collecting. Barttelot did none of these; he simply paced. In Ward's judgment, Barttelot exhibited "the contempt and disdain natural to the highly strung young officer who believed nothing was equal to the British soldier."

That contempt was especially apparent when it came to dealing with the Africans. Ward wrote, "[Barttelot] was a stranger to African manners and speech, with ever-present suspicion of everyone and everything which this disadvantage must always excite. . . ." Troup put it more plainly: "He had an intense hatred of anything in the shape of a black man, for he made no disguise of this, but frequently mentioned the fact. His hatred was so marked that I was seized with great misgivings concerning his future dealings with them. . . ."

When it came to his dealings with the Arabs, Barttelot provided his own assessment in a letter to his parents: "To deal with Arabs, you require an urbane disposition, a rare facility for lying, an impassible face, a suave and gentle manner, and a limitless purse. None of these I possess. . . ."

Barttelot's correspondence from Yambuya provided revealing and, in some cases, touching glimpses of the struggles of a proud man in an impossible situation. In an effort to maintain discipline, he devised a strict routine for the camp and expected it to be adhered to faithfully. "Our life is very simple—we rise at 5 a.m.; get the men to work at 5.45; breakfast at 6 a.m.; work till 11.30 a.m.; luncheon; work at 1.30 p.m. till 5.30; dinner at 6.30 p.m.; talk till 9 p.m.; go round the sentries and to bed. Alternative nights we visit the sentries four times during the night. Any man caught sleeping gets twenty-five lashes. . . ."

He wrote to his family frequently. Though formal to the point of rigidity in his dealings with the men, he revealed another side in his family correspondence. A letter to a young nephew was clearly designed both to shock gently and to amuse: "I am now living amongst bloodthirsty savages, who delight in eating the flesh of the white man and drinking his blood while yet warm. Their favourite dish is English boy roasted whole and stuffed with bananas." But then, in the same letter, a Christmas wish that contains more than a whiff of homesickness: "My dearest little boy, I must wish you a very merry Christmas. I hope I may spend the next one with you, when we will have the biggest turkey, plum pudding, and mince pies that can be got; we will have a rare merry time. Good-bye dear little Bobbie; grow your teeth, and don't forget your antique relative, who with many kisses and much love will always remain, your very affectionate uncle. . . ."

The diaries and journals kept by the officers at Yambuya made it clear that the situation there was difficult from the outset. Though Barttelot had gone through the distasteful blood brotherhood ceremony with the chief of the local tribe, relations between the rear column and the natives remained rocky at best, in part, no doubt, because the expedition had summarily evicted them from their village in the first place. Barttelot tried to use access to the extensive manioc fields surrounding the camp as a bargaining chip with the natives, requiring them to bring food, especially meat, fowl, or fish, in exchange for access to the fields. It didn't work very well, mostly because the natives didn't have all that much food to share. Then the soldiers took to kidnapping native women and children, trying to ransom them for food. That didn't work very well, either.

All the while, they were waiting for Tippu Tib to arrive with the extra carriers. About six weeks after Stanley left, a group of Manyuemas attacked the natives across the river. At first, Barttelot and Jameson thought they might be an advance party of Tippu Tib's carriers, engaging in the usual Manyuema sport of raping and pillaging before reporting for duty. Unfortunately, it turned out to be an independent band of raiders under an Arab subchief who was only loosely affiliated with Tippu Tib. They were simply moving into new territory, hoping, as always, to find slaves and ivory. When they learned that the rear guard's stockade was full of weapons, ammunition, and sundry other supplies, they decided to stick around. They set up their camp near the native village and settled into the business of making life miserable for everyone.

For the next several months, the Manyuemas put relentless pressure on Barttelot, contriving endless excuses to visit the stockade to reconnoiter, continually preying on the natives, at one point terrorizing them into refusing to trade with the rear guard at all. As conditions inside the stockade worsened, they also began tempting the Zanzibaris to desert, since they always seemed to have food, and the stockade often didn't.

It turned out that Tippu Tib had, in fact, sent a large contingent of porters north from Stanley Falls toward Yambuya not long after Stanley's departure. But they had been set upon by hostile natives and had sustained heavy casualties. In addition, the men, most of them slaves, were unfamiliar with paddling canoes on the river. Having to pull against the current, their hands were soon ripped and bleeding, and many of them simply gave up.

When Barttelot found out about this, he immediately dispatched Jameson and Ward to Stanley Falls, the first of a seemingly endless series of messengers to Tippu Tib. The messengers took turns begging, threatening, pleading, wheedling, and cajoling the wily Arab, trying to get him to fulfill his contract.

In his highly slanted account of what happened to the rear column (discussed at greater length in chapter 18), Stanley placed the heaviest blame for its tragic fate squarely at Tippu Tib's feet: "He contrives to delay performing the terms of his solemn contract, and months are wasted before he moves to take the necessary steps for accomplishing his duties. . . ." He added, "his natural love of power, his ignorance of geography,* his barbarous conceit, his growing indolence, and his quickened avarice proved insuperable obstacles to the realizing of Barttelot and Jameson's wishes, and were as fatally opposite to their interests and dearest desires as open war would have been."

---

*A remarkable assertion, since Tippu Tib probably knew the geography of his territory better than any other man alive.

It wasn't quite that simple. While there is little doubt that Tippu Tib was less than conscientious in attempting to fulfill his contract with Stanley, he wasn't completely derelict in his duties. He did recruit the initial contingent of six hundred porters and accompanied them himself on their trip north from Stanley Falls until they were turned back by the aforementioned problems. In addition, Tippu Tib had other significant responsibilities, official and unofficial. Officially, he was assuming his position as the newly appointed governor of the Stanley Falls district of the Congo Free State. Unofficially, as the uncrowned king of a vast territory covering thousands of square miles, from which he had been away for several months, he had some catching up to do. The twin foundations of his power and fortune, ivory and slave collecting, required his attention.

Nevertheless, when Jameson and Ward returned from that first visit to the falls, they reported that Tippu Tib had promised to round up another group of carriers, as close to six hundred as he could find, though he said that what had happened to the first group would make a second round of recruitment more difficult. He would then deliver the men himself within ten days. That didn't happen, either.

As the weeks and months dragged on, several patterns emerged at Yambuya, each more depressing than the next. For one thing, the officers seemed to take turns getting sick. Barttelot's journal is peppered with notations such as "Bonny and Troup both ill with fever," "Jameson and Troup not well," "I cannot eat much," "Jameson is yellow as a guinea* and very ill," and "Troup a wreck." At one point, Ward went down with fever for five weeks and nearly died. Troup became so ill that he had to be invalided back to England. After several months at Yambuya, Barttelot decided to measure himself: "Round the chest I measure 34 inches; I used to measure 36. I must have shrunk."

The officers, of course, had considerably better rations than the men, so while they took turns getting sick, the Africans took turns dying. By December 5, approximately six months into their ordeal, they had lost thirty-one men.

A second pattern was that of relentless physical discipline. Barttelot

---

*A classic symptom of *falciparum malaria*, the most deadly variety of the disease.

had never been one to spare the rod, but as the months wore on, he meted out punishment with increasing frequency. Floggings became a daily occurrence. The offenses ranged from falling asleep on sentry duty to stealing and desertion. Near the end of their confinement at Yambuya, Barttelot ordered three hundred lashes for a Zanzibari thief, enough to kill a healthy man, let alone one who had been starving for several months. The man died within twenty-four hours. A Sudanese deserter was summarily executed by firing squad. The more desperate the situation became, the more rigid Barttelot became. He was convinced that the column's survival, both mentally and physically, depended on strict enforcement of the rules. Morale, not good to begin with, plummeted.

A third, and perhaps most demoralizing, pattern was that of false hope followed by crushing disappointment. This, too, began and ended with Stanley. The first hope of the rear column derived from Stanley's contract with Tippu Tib. When Stanley left, they were buoyed by the belief that the porters would indeed arrive and that they would be able to follow Stanley to the lake. But as June gave way to July, then August, then September, with still no sign of the carriers, they were rapidly approaching a point at which it made less and less sense to leave, because they all firmly believed that Stanley would return in November. This growing sense of "now or never" prompted a second trip to Stanley Falls. This time, Barttelot went himself.

When Barttelot pressed him to deliver the promised carriers, Tippu Tib told him that he would have to go to Kasongo, his territorial headquarters, in order to find enough men. Kasongo was a month away. One month to get there, one month back, and at least a week or two to round up the men. By the time he got back, it would be November and Stanley would be back. What was the point?

Then, of course, Stanley didn't come back in November. There had been, however, a fairly steady stream of deserters from the advance column, mostly Zanzibaris, who came back hoping to ingratiate themselves with Tippu Tib, their goal being eventually to make their way back to Zanzibar. They told frightening tales of the difficulties Stanley and his men were encountering. Their progress had been so much slower than Stanley had predicted that Barttelot realized Stanley could not possibly return until well into the new year. Once again, it made sense to try to get Tippu Tib to obtain the porters. He sent another messenger to Stanley Falls, but Tippu Tib wasn't there. He was at Kasongo.

On January 29, Jameson recorded the temperature at Yambuya at 136 degrees. He wrote in his journal, "This waiting . . . is sickening, and the men are dying off like rotten sheep." If Jameson was bored and depressed, Barttelot was starting to lose his grip. He decided to send Jameson to Kasongo to tell Tippu Tib that in addition to six hundred porters, he needed four hundred "fighting men." His reasoning was that if Stanley was in trouble, he'd need more than porters to help him: "I consider it useless to try and relieve Mr. Stanley, if he be in a fix, with a force as small as he started with. . . ." But if Tippu Tib had already proven unwilling or unable to provide six hundred carriers, how did Barttelot expect him to come up with four hundred "fighting men"?

Sending Jameson to Kasongo also deprived Barttelot of his one true friend at Yambuya. Jameson was his pal, his confidant, his boon companion. In his letters and diaries, Barttelot continually sang his praises, writing at one point, "Such a man is met but once in a lifetime." With Jameson gone, Barttelot became more susceptible to the predations of William Bonny, the medic with a chip on his shoulder. Bonny was a sergeant, and the officers treated him like one, excluding him from decisions, from meals, from what little camaraderie had existed on the expedition. He bitterly resented what he perceived as their condescension, especially from Jephson and Jameson, who were civilians.* Bonny took particular pleasure in spreading gossip and rumors, usually at the expense of the officers, especially Herbert Ward (also a civilian). Barttelot was beginning to exhibit symptoms of paranoia, and Bonny's innuendos and self-serving tattletales did no good. Barttelot's journal

---

*In fact, they were all civilians. Technically, the Emin Pasha Relief Expedition was a private undertaking; the regular military officers, Barttelot, Nelson, Stairs, and Parke, all took leave from their military duties to participate. But Stanley ran it like a military expedition, calling his subordinates "officers," including references to Jephson and Jameson as "lieutenants," and he thought of himself as a military commander. Hence, Bonny's attitude.

became full of cryptic asides such as "The opportunity was taken to play me false" (March 24), "I find they have been playing the mischief since I was away" (March 26), "I am much upset by what I find" (March 27), and "More disclosures made to me" (March 30). Interestingly, the specific malfeasances, real or imagined, were not mentioned.

It was in this state of mind that Barttelot seized upon a bizarre plan to send Ward all the way back down the Congo to Banana Point—a journey of almost 1,500 miles—then by steamer to the nearest coastal location where he could send a cable to London, requesting instructions from Mackinnon and the committee. Clearly, this was not a rational decision. For one thing, there was ample reason to believe that Ward would never make it. The perils of the river and the jungle, already amply demonstrated to the expedition, would be even greater for a white man traveling virtually alone. In addition, the trip would take at least four months, and in all likelihood longer, so that in the unlikely event that Ward actually made it back to Yambuya, there would probably be no one to hear what he had learned, as the rear column would, in all likelihood, have moved on. Finally, what was the committee in London likely to say other than "Carry on"?

Still, on March 28, 1888, Ward departed, along with Troup, who was being sent downriver to buy goats, and thirty Zanzibaris who would accompany Ward as far as the Congo Free State station at Bangala. Barttelot was left at Yambuya with only Bonny and the Africans.

By the end of March, the death toll was up to sixty-six, with another twenty-five men having deserted. The loss of manpower gave Barttelot something new to worry about. He became convinced that the Manyuemas, still camped across the river, under the command of an Arab named Selim Muhammad, who had been sent by Tippu Tib, supposedly because he would be better able to control the Manyuemas, were planning to attack the stockade. His conviction wasn't completely irrational. The rear column had lost so many men that a concerted attack by a large force would have been difficult to repel, although there had been no changes in the Manyuema camp to indicate that any such plan was afoot. Still, Barttelot was sure they were in peril. He decided to make yet another trip to Stanley Falls, leaving Sergeant Bonny in charge.

Barttelot's objective was to get Tippu Tib's number two man (Tippu Tib still being in Kasongo), Bwana Nzige, to order Selim Muhammad to relocate his camp farther from the stockade or, better yet, recall him and replace him with a more cooperative commander. To Barttelot's immense satisfaction, Bwana Nzige agreed to recall Selim Muhammad.

April went by with no word from Stanley or from Tippu Tib, Jameson, or Ward, but in May it seemed that Barttelot and the rear column had finally caught a break. The steamer *AIA* arrived unexpectedly at Yambuya with Lieutenant Van Kerckhoven, the commander of the Congo Free State station at Bangala, on board. He brought with him the Africans who had gone downriver with Ward. The Belgian was headed for Stanley Falls; Tippu Tib and Jameson were rumored to be on their way there from Kasongo. Barttelot decided to go, too.

Jameson and Tippu Tib did indeed arrive almost simultaneously with Barttelot and Van Kerckhoven. They had good news and bad. The good news was that Tippu Tib was at last coming through with carriers. But there were only 400, not 600, and no fighting men. And, Tippu Tib announced, since the carriers were Manyuemas, not Zanzibaris, they couldn't be expected to carry as much as the more experienced porters. Of the 400, 300 could carry 40-pound loads; 100 could carry only 20 pounds (the average Zanzibari load was 60–65 pounds). Jameson protested that Tippu Tib had now promised him 800 porters, but he said 400 was all he could spare. Basically, it was take 'em or leave 'em. Barttelot took 'em.

They all went back to Yambuya—Barttelot, Jameson, Tippu Tib, and Muni Somai, the Arab headman who had been hired for an additional £1,000 (personally guaranteed by Barttelot and Jameson) to serve as commander of the Manyuema porters.

What followed was a welcome flurry of activity. With only four hundred porters, plus a handful of the expedition's original contingent who were still healthy enough to carry, there were decisions to be made about what to take and what to send downriver. In addition, Tippu Tib's weight limitations required that all the existing loads (principally ammunition) had to be repacked into smaller parcels.

Barttelot and Jameson attacked their tasks with relish, grateful finally to have something meaningful to do, and ecstatic at the prospect of getting back on the trail and out of Yambuya. The reconfiguring of the loads was an enormous amount of work, made even more difficult because Tippu Tib kept insisting that the heavier loads had to weigh precisely 40 pounds, not 41 or, God forbid, 45. More unpacking and repacking ensued until finally, on June 11, the rear column was ready to leave.

Tippu Tib's weight requirement created some very difficult choices for Barttelot. In May, there were just over 600 full (60–65 pounds) loads at Yambuya. It was determined that 140 loads, including a significant amount of ammunition, would have to be sent down to Bangala, where they would be stored at the Congo Free State station (the Belgians had generously sent the *AIA* and the *Stanley* for this purpose). But that still left upward of 450 loads—full loads—to be carried, and Tippu Tib's insistence on the 40- and 20-pound weight limits meant there was still much too much to carry. Tippu Tib proposed a solution: he and Muni Somai would take the extra matériel as down payments on their fees; thus another substantial amount of ammunition, powder, cloth, and trade beads was left behind. The relief supplies that had been the raison d'être of the expedition were dwindling by the hour.

In the days leading up to departure, Barttelot wrote literally tens of thousands of words—memos, instructions, letters, reports, and inventories. He was determined to document every decision and the reasons behind it, because he knew what was likely to happen if and when he caught up with Bula Matari with so much of the expedition's inventory missing: "Stanley, if he gets home, will no doubt twist events so as to make it appear that all the failure was due to me; but if I come back, too, I can show him up in his true light, for I have not been round these villages and all the Arab stations hereabouts for nothing. . . ."

In a letter to his parents just before leaving Yambuya, he wrote, "Stanley, when he left me here, knew what he was leaving me to . . . but in me he saw an excellent scapegoat, and gave me a work to perform which he knew perfectly to be well-nigh impossible. That we are going to perform it, with but scant material, is no thanks to him. . . ."

When they marched out of Yambuya on a blisteringly hot Monday morning, the rear column consisted of 3 officers, 115 Zanzibaris, 22 Sudanese, and 1 Somali (the original expedition members), plus 430 Manyuemas under Muni Somai (Barttelot had managed to cajole 30 more carriers out of Tippu Tib.) Left behind were Troup, Ward (still not heard from and presumed dead or in transit somewhere on the river), and 35 Africans who were too sick to go with them. Troup would be invalided home, along with one of the Sudanese and Assad Faran, an interpreter ("thoroughly useless," in Barttelot's judgment). The rest would remain at Stanley Falls with Tippu Tib, who said he would do his best to return them to Zanzibar.

Thrilled as he was to be leaving, Barttelot had few illusions about what lay ahead. On the night before departure, he wrote that they were headed for "abomination, desolation, and vexation, but I hope in the end success."

BARTTELOT WAS SO PLEASED finally to be out of Yambuya, which he had come to regard as his personal prison, so enthusiastic about actually *doing* something, so grateful to feel a part of the expedition again, that he didn't seem to notice the disaster that began unfolding around him almost as soon as the rear column hit the trail. His diary entries for the first few days were brief but positive. June 11: "We left camp at 7 a.m.; all glad to start—I hope never to return. . . ." June 12: "It rained in the early morning. We left camp at 10 a.m., and arrived at Sala's camp at sunset. I was rear-guard. The road was shocking; the men carried well." But then on June 14: "Muni Somai's men are all over the place, they won't be in till to-morrow, so I shall leave Jameson with him, and march myself with the Zanzibaris. Fine day but hot."

The next day brought fourteen desertions and twelve missing loads. The trail was virtually nonexistent, the column already spread out over miles of forest. In the days that followed, they sometimes spent hours going in the wrong direction; once they discovered that they'd been marching in a circle. The Manyuemas were out of control, with Muni Somai, the high-priced Arab headman, proving utterly useless. They marched when they wanted to and, worse, where they wanted to. When they got tired, they threw down their loads and refused to move. When no one was looking, they broke into their loads and stole anything that appealed to them. They seemed to fire their weapons whenever they felt like it, creating repeated false alarms, scaring and provoking the natives, and wasting precious ammunition. Then, to cap it all off, smallpox broke out in their ranks.

The Zanzibaris, on the other hand, were deserting in droves. Less than two weeks after leaving Yambuya, Barttelot had lost twenty-five out of the 115 he started with. In response, he first took away all their weapons and then made another of the peculiar decisions that gave credence to the notion that he was no longer in complete possession of his faculties. He decided that he would go all the way back to Stanley Falls to get chains from Tippu Tib to shackle the Zanzibaris together, again leaving Bonny in charge of the column (Jameson, bringing up the rear, was already several days behind). Bonny's orders were to continue on to the village of Banalya, where he was to halt and await Barttelot's return.

The major left with fourteen Zanzibaris and three Sudanese on the morning of June 24, covering the almost two hundred miles to Stanley Falls in only eight days. Tippu Tib, who thought he'd seen the last of the expedition for quite some time, if not forever, was so startled at Barttelot's unexpected appearance that he actually acceded to his requests with almost no delay. The chains were provided, as was a written order to the Arab chieftain at Banalya, a man named Abdullah Koroni, to supply Barttelot with sixty more men to serve as guards over the Manyuema porters, along with some additional food. Barttelot was pleased, noting in a quick letter to his father before leaving Stanley Falls, "I think now I have so arranged matters that I shall have no more stoppage." He then double-timed it back toward Banalya.

He arrived on July 17. As it turned out, Bonny had reached Banalya only two days earlier, and Jameson, still with the rear of the column, remained several days away. Barttelot immediately went to Abdullah Koroni to present his written orders from Tippu Tib, and Abdullah Koroni immediately told him he couldn't comply—he could spare neither the men nor the food.

According to Bonny's official report about the events of the next two days, when Barttelot reached Banalya, the Manyuemas were engaged in an ongoing celebration of unspecified cause that involved much singing, beating of drums, and indiscriminate firing of weapons. The noise, which went on day and night, drove Barttelot to distraction. He asked Muni Somai to intervene, but the Arab replied that he could do nothing. At one point, an errant round slammed into the roof of Barttelot and Bonny's hut, missing their heads by only a foot or two. Finally, in the early morning hours of July 19, in a tent near their hut, a Manyuema woman began beating a drum and singing loudly. Barttelot sent his tent boy to tell her to be quiet. Loud voices were heard and then two shots rang out, but the singing continued. Barttelot then summoned some of his Sudanese soldiers and told them to go find out who fired the shots. Shortly after they left, he got out of bed, grabbed his revolver, and followed them, telling Bonny he was going to shoot the first man he caught firing his weapon. When the Sudanese reported that they couldn't tell who was doing the firing, Barttelot shouldered them aside and confronted the Manyuema woman who was still singing and drumming. According to some, but not all, reports, he raised his revolver to strike her. As he did, a shot rang out from a nearby house. The bullet struck the major just below the heart, passed completely through his body, and lodged in a post behind him. He was dead before he hit the ground.

All hell broke loose. What followed was nothing short of a riot, as Manyuemas and Zanzibaris alike scattered in all directions, most taking loads with them, which they then ransacked, flinging the contents all over the bush. Bonny, who at one point was sure he was going to be killed, stayed remarkably cool under the circumstances. With the few men who remained in camp, he set about recovering the missing loads. He sent an urgent message back to Jameson, telling him to come as quickly as he could. Later he even managed to compose brief letters to Tippu Tib and Mackinnon, explaining what had happened. And, after sewing the body into a blanket, he buried Major Barttelot. "I dug a grave just within the forest, placing leaves at the bottom of the grave, and covered the body with the same: I then read the Church Service from our Prayer-book over the body." If anyone else was present, it was not noted.

Jameson didn't arrive for three days. He immediately took an inventory to determine what had been lost (48 loads), and then began repacking what remained (Bonny had recovered 300 loads). He wrote in his diary, "There is a sadness hanging over everything, which no amount of work will shake off."

Jameson also talked to several of the Manyuema headmen to find out where Barttelot's murderer might be. There was never any doubt about who did it; it was the husband of the singing woman. His name was Sanga, and he was said to be a hunter. Jameson determined that Sanga and Muni Somai, the useless Arab commander, had fled together, most likely headed back to Stanley Falls.

So many Manyuema and Zanzibaris had run away that there were no longer enough carriers to transport the remaining loads; Jameson thus decided there was nothing to do but go back to Stanley Falls. He had three objectives: to get the rear guard back on the trail, for which he needed more porters; to replace Muni Somai with someone whom the Manyuema respected or feared enough to do what was asked of them; and to find Sanga and see him brought to justice. For all three, he reckoned he needed Tippu Tib.

Like Barttelot before him, Jameson set a blistering pace and reached the falls in eight days. When he got there, he discovered another newly arrived European, a Belgian lieutenant named Baert, who was to be Tippu Tib's secretary. He had arrived via steamer the preceding day, and he had news of the long-lost Ward, whom he saw downriver at the CFS station at Bangala. It seemed that Ward had indeed managed to get all the way down to the coast and had sent Barttelot's cable to the committee in London requesting instructions. He had also received an answer and then headed immediately back upriver until he reached Bangala. There he'd gotten further orders from Barttelot (sent with Troup on his way home), telling him to remain at Bangala in order to keep an eye on the loads sent down from Yambuya. Under no circumstances, said Barttelot, was Ward to attempt to catch up with the rear column. Ward waited.

The one piece of information Jameson wanted most concerned the committee's reply to the cable Ward sent to London. What had it said? Baert didn't know. As Jameson put it, he was "in a most serious position, not knowing what reply the Committee have sent, and I can only judge that it is not a recall from the fact that Ward did not send it on, and that, according to the last news from Europe, nothing is known of Mr. Stanley." (Barttelot had thought it possible that Stanley had already rescued Emin Pasha and gone on to Zanzibar, simply neglecting to inform the rear guard. Hence the possibility, at least in Barttelot's mind, of recall orders from London.) Baert also told Jameson that Ward had packets of letters from home for all the officers. Jameson couldn't believe that Ward hadn't sent them upriver with the lieutenant, but Baert told him that Ward "was not very pleased with his position." Perhaps hoarding the letters and the reply from the committee was Ward's way of getting even.

Jameson next turned to Tippu Tib and the subject of a replacement for Muni Somai so that he could move on from Banalya. "Give me a man who was a sufficient representative of [your] power, to command them [the Manyuemas], that I might feel . . . some hope of success in the undertaking. . . ." Tippu Tib replied, "I am almost afraid to send you with these men; I think Major Barttelot's murder must have been a thing thought of by many." The clear implication was that Jameson might be next. Jameson said, "As regard[s] my own life, I said that [Tippu Tib] could not be held answerable for its safety, for there were a hundred ways in which I might die on such an Expedition, and that if I undertook it with my eyes open, I alone was answerable for anything that might happen to me. . . ."

He asked for Tippu Tib's nephew, Rachid, whom he considered the second-most powerful man in the territory. Tippu Tib countered by offering Selim Muhammad, the same man he'd sent to keep an eye on the Manyuemas at Yambuya, but Jameson wanted nothing further to do with Selim Muhammad. They went back and forth without a resolution.

Jameson turned to the topic of Sanga. As rumored, he had indeed returned to Stanley Falls, and Tippu Tib had immediately placed him in custody, though Sanga said he was innocent. They agreed that a trial should be held, after which Sanga would be shot.

For the next several days, Jameson continued "palavering" with

Tippu Tib, and then with Rachid, who had been away when Jameson arrived, trying to persuade him to join the expedition. Rachid didn't want to go, partly because the work sounded so unpleasant, but mostly because he was expecting a huge shipment of ivory to arrive any day, and he didn't trust anyone else to look after his interests. Then Tippu Tib made a startling proposition. "He jumped out of his chair," Jameson wrote, "and said 'Give me £20,000 and I and my people will go with you, find Mr. Stanley, and relieve Emin Bey.' "

Jameson was nonplussed. On the one hand, if Tippu Tib was sincere, his offer represented far and away the best opportunity to get the rear column through to the lake, or wherever Stanley might be. On the other hand, £20,000 was equal to the cost of the entire expedition! Jameson didn't know what to do. If he took up Tippu Tib's offer, he would be doing so on his own authority. What if the committee didn't agree with his decision? Might it hold him personally responsible for the entire amount? He would be ruined; his family would be ruined. He wanted time to think it over, but Tippu Tib was pressing for an immediate decision. "At last," Jameson wrote in his diary, "I sent back to say that I would agree to his terms, being driven to desperation and having thought of every other way out of it with a hope in it of our going on." It was an incredible personal gamble. But at least Jameson had gotten himself the ultimate headman.

That left Sanga. A court-martial was convened, consisting of Tippu Tib and three Belgian officers. What did Sanga have to say in his own defense? He launched into "a rambling tale" about the major's coming to his house and confronting him about the drumming and singing. He said the major kicked him, and then someone else shot the Major from behind, "the ball going in at his back." One of the Belgian officers asked why, if he was innocent, he had run away. Sanga said everyone thought he was guilty, even though he wasn't, so he ran away. Jameson then testified, "All the muniaparas of the Manyéma had assured me that Sanga had shot Major Barttelot."

The jury delivered a unanimous guilty verdict. The senior Belgian announced the verdict and told Sanga that he would be shot. He laughed. "Well, do it quick," he replied. They tried. A firing squad was immediately assembled; Sanga was marched to the riverbank. Just before the riflemen took aim, he said with another laugh, "It is all right; the white man is dead, I am going to die too."

The firing squad proved singularly (or collectively) inept. It fired twice, but Sanga was still alive. One of the Belgians had to finish the job with his pistol. "We then had lunch," wrote Jameson in his diary.

With a jungle version of justice done, he turned his attention back to the contract with Tippu Tib. The Arab began changing his conditions almost immediately: if they met Stanley anywhere on the trail, even at the beginning of their march, he would still be paid the full £20,000; if they were attacked by a stronger opposing force and he was in danger of losing too many men, he would turn back—but he would still get the full £20,000. And so it went, but the condition that caused the greatest problem for Jameson was Tippu Tib's insistence on changing the route to a more southerly path. Stanley had been adamant that if and when the rear column left Yambuya, they were to follow the trail he had blazed and only that trail. Jameson couldn't agree to the change without authorization. He decided he would go to Bangala to find out from Ward what the committee had said in reply to Barttelot's wire. "If I find the reply from the Committee to be 'go on at all hazards,' I will return at once and start with your men myself. If I find that it does not tell me to go on at all hazards, I will send Mr. Ward with a telegram to Banana stating my present position, your proposals, and asking for orders." Surprisingly, Tippu Tib agreed. Perhaps he didn't really want to go.

Jameson left on August 9, taking two canoes and a party of twenty-five men. They paddled day and night. His diary entry for August 10: "Reached the Lumami River at daybreak. I was frightfully seedy, having caught cold inside after a big dose of medicine."

The next night, a Sunday, again having paddled all day, Jameson described a

> very curious scene. Shot out of an open reach—fine clear night—into a dark narrow channel, not more than forty yards wide. All at once it became lit up with dozens of fires on both sides, throwing a bright light back into the forest and across the water. We glided on without a sound from us but the zip-zip of the paddles, drums beating, horns blowing,

ATTACK AT AVISSIBA, where Stairs was wounded.

EMIN PASHA at home in Equatoria.

JOHN ROWLANDS,
the future Henry M. Stanley,
at age fifteen.

MAJOR BARTTELOT'S CHRISTMAS CARD, 1887, drawn by Jameson.

"THE MOST PERFECTLY ORGANIZED EXPEDITION THAT HAS HITHERTO
ENTERED TROPICAL AFRICA."
—Frederick Holmwood, British Consul-General, Zanzibar.

HIRAM MAXIM'S GUN was fired in anger only once.

THE *ADVANCE*. Stanley's pride and joy, Jephson's refuge.

JEPHSON RESCUES NELSON from starvation camp.

THE LONG-AWAITED RENDEZVOUS.
The first meeting of Stanley and Emin Pasha.

JAMESON'S FINAL VOYAGE.

EMIN BETRAYED.

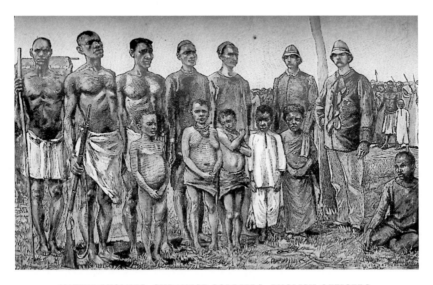

NATIVE PYGMIES, SUDANESE SOLDIERS, ENGLISH OFFICERS.

"ONE IS NOT ABLE TO RELAX ONE'S VIGILANCE FOR A MOMENT."
—Jephson.

shouts and cries on every side. . . . I don't think I ever heard such a noise before. We shot out away to our right, and soon left all the tumult behind. What they thought of us I should like to know.

It would be the last entry in his diary. The weather turned nasty, with rain and high winds, and Jameson's cold turned into hematuric (black water) fever.* By the time he reached Bangala a week later, he was dying. Ward wrote, "A boy came rushing into my room, saying in Kiswahili that a white man had just come down from the Falls in a canoe. I rushed to the beach, and there saw a deathlike figure lying back in the men's arms, insensible. I jumped into the canoe, and, great Heavens! It was poor Jameson."

He drifted in and out of consciousness for the next twenty-four hours. Ward never left his side:

> 1 p.m. I asked him just now if he was in any pain. "No, old chap, no pain, only tired—Oh! So tired. I think it's time to turn in; it's so dark—so tired," . . . —3 p.m. I have given him nourishment upon every occasion, but he does not rally, and only gets feebler.—6 p.m. Daruru and I put hot bricks round him, as his extremities have grown cold. He grows weaker and weaker. The drums just now sounded to knock off work in the Station, he opened his eyes and stared at me, clutching my hands, and said, with a husky voice, "Ward! Ward! They're coming; listen!" (and as the drums rumbled in the distance), "Yes! They're coming—now let's stand together." He was thinking of the drums calling the savages to fight him, while he drifted down the river past the villages.
>
> 7.20. His pulse grows weaker and weaker.—7.30. As I supported him to administer brandy, he drew a long breath, and his pulse stopped.
>
> *August 18th.*—I walked about until daylight quite beside myself with sadness. . . . My "Union Jack" covered the coffin, which was borne to the canoe by four Houssa soldiers, and we all proceeded across the

---

*Falciparum malaria often causes blood clots and infection of the kidneys. In such cases, broken-down red blood cells appear in the urine, turning it dark brown, hence the term "black water fever."

river in the early morning, without a sound but the splashing of the paddles. Upon arriving at the opposite shore, we bore the coffin to the grave, and I read a chapter from the Bible. His resting-place is at the foot of a giant cotton tree, on the island opposite Bangala, one thousand miles from the sea.

Ten hours before Jameson died, Stanley arrived at Banalya.

Chapter Fourteen
REBELLION AT THE
EQUATOR

WHEN STANLEY RECOVERED from his initial shock (he called the scene at Banalya "a charnel house"), he did two of the things he was really good at: he got mad, and then he got organized. Wanting to separate the smallpox-ridden Manyuemas from the rest of his men, he moved everyone upriver several miles to an island called Bungangeta where he could establish separate camps.

The move, which should have taken only one day, took three because of "the utter unruliness of this mob of slaves," as Stanley characterized the Manyuemas. As a result, Stanley decided he would take only as many Manyuemas as absolutely necessary when he headed back to Fort Bodo. To weed them out, he issued the most tepid of invitations: "If you decline the journey it is well, if you proceed with me it is well also. Exercise your own free will. I do not need you, but if you like to follow me I can make use of you, and will pay you according to the number of loads you carry." It worked. All but sixty-one of the Manyuemas declined to continue, and Stanley reckoned he could control those who remained.

To boost morale, and to help the men prepare for the march back through the forest, he distributed beads, cowries, and cloth to the Zanzibaris and Sudanese. It turned out that Ugarrowa and his people were camped on another island not far from the expedition, and the men found a ready market for their trade goods among the Arab's flock. In exchange for their trinkets, the Arabs ground flour and made manioc cakes for them.

Stanley also inspected all the remaining loads, taking inventory, reorganizing what remained, and having new loads made up. He focused on ammunition and trade goods, taking little else. It seemed that he still thought he could bring enough "relief" supplies to Emin to make an impression.

Less than two weeks after his arrival, he was ready to head back into the forest, but before he did, he wrote a series of letters and reports that revealed the strategy he had already devised to deal with the disaster of the rear column.

He refused to accept any responsibility whatsoever for what had happened. None of it was Stanley's fault. Had Barttelot et al. done as they were told, none of this would have happened. Stanley's orders had been disobeyed, and a horrible price had been paid. It was that simple.

On August 30, the day they moved out of Bungangeta, he wrote a letter to Jameson, who he thought was still alive at Stanley Falls. Petulant (Stanley was particularly upset that some of his personal effects had been shipped downriver), sarcastic, and characteristically indifferent to the suffering Jameson and his colleagues had endured, the letter was a blistering indictment of a dead man:

> I cannot make out why the Major, you, Troup, and Ward have been so *demented*—demented is the word. You understand English; an English letter of instructions was given you. You said it was intelligible— yet for some reason or another you have not followed one paragraph. You paid £1,000 to go on this Expedition; you have voluntarily thrown

your money away by leaving the Expedition. Ward is not a whit better; he has acted all through, as I hear, more like an idiot than a sane being. You have left me naked. I have no clothes, no medicine; I will say nothing of my soap and candles, photograph apparatus and chemicals, two silver watches, a cap, and a score of other trifles.

Then, after more petty venting, he described the route he intended to take back to Lake Albert and told Jameson he could try to catch him—"if you can bring my kit with you." He made only one concession, and it was conditional: "Though, as reported to me, you and all of you seem to have acted like madmen, your version may modify my opinion."

The letter, which was, of course, undeliverable to its intended recipient, eventually made its way to England, where it was published as part of Jameson's diaries and letters. Stanley, not surprisingly, omitted it from *In Darkest Africa*, but in that volume, in his self-serving and highly selective discussion of the Rear Column, he did write, "When he [Jameson] descended from Stanley Falls [to Bangala], he deliberately severed himself from the Expedition. . . ." In other words, he was a deserter. The fact that the trip had killed him didn't matter.

Stanley also wrote a letter to Tippu Tib, the man to whom he eventually assigned primary responsibility for the fate of the rear column. Inexplicably, the letter contained not a word of censure or remonstration. Rather, the tone was almost cordial. He reported on his meeting with Emin Pasha, characterized as triumphant, and said that, while he could not afford the time to come to Stanley Falls to see Tippu Tib in person, he would, owing to the condition of many of his men, be traveling slowly on his return to the lake, so Tippu Tib could easily catch up with him, if he chose to do so. He closed with the wish that the two of them would "be face to face before many days."*

He left the island camp leading a ragtag band of 465 souls back into the maw of the Ituri forest. Of them, only 283 were strong enough to carry a load (165 Zanzibaris, 57 Madis, 61 Manyuemas). The rest consisted of 21 Sudanese soldiers, a lone Somali (of the original 13

---

*In fact, the two men never saw each other again.

recruited by Barttelot in Egypt), 45 "invalids," 3 Europeans (Stanley, Bonny, and the inevitable Hoffmann, Stanley's valet), and 108 Manyuema camp followers, mostly women and children.

Ironically, he actually had more carriers than loads, though he knew that would change once they got into the forest. Of the original complement of 660 loads at Yambuya, only 275 remained. Thanks mostly to assistance from Ugarrowa, Stanley was able to assemble a fleet of canoes large enough to take not only all the loads but all the invalids as well. Everyone else walked.

The third trip through the Ituri forest proved as grueling as the first, perhaps even worse, because this time there was smallpox. As he had feared, the Manyuemas quickly infected the hapless Madis, whose numbers had already been reduced by half on the trip from Fort Bodo to Banalya.

Stanley took a more northerly route than before, thinking it would not only be a more direct approach to the lake but might avoid some of the areas of Arab devastation where food had been so hard to find. It didn't work. The natives along the new route proved even more hostile than those along the first route. They harassed the land column on a daily basis, killing and maiming men, women, and children with spears and poisoned arrows and, more often than not, dragging their victims into the forest to eat them.

Even the least debilitated survivors of Yambuya were still in such poor condition that they soon began succumbing to exhaustion, malnutrition, and general weakness. The caravan lost almost a man a day through the first seven weeks. By December, still deep in the forest, they had been without real food for days, surviving on a thin broth made of butter, milk, and water. Stanley had no choice but to call a halt. He sent every able-bodied man out to forage while he and Bonny stayed behind with a hundred men who were near death. When a week went by with no sign of the foraging party, Stanley thought they had all deserted and that his expedition had totally collapsed. Leaving Bonny behind, he went alone into the forest to search for the missing men. He later told Parke that he had taken with him his revolver and "a full dose of poison," intending to kill himself if he didn't find his men. In all his travels in Africa, he had never been so low.

Vain was it for me to seek for that sleep which is the "balm of hurt minds." Too many memories crowded about me; too many dying forms haunted me in the darkness; my lively fancies were too distorted by dread, which painted them with dismal colours; the stark forms lying in links along the path, which we had seen that afternoon in our tramp, were things too solemn for sudden oblivion. The stars could not be seen to seek comfort in the twinkling; the poor hearts around me were too heavy to utter naught but groans of despair; the fires were not lit, for there was no food to cook—my grief was great.... [A]nd the sough of the wind through the crowns of the thick-black bush seemed to sigh and moan "Lost! lost! lost! Thy labour and grief are in vain. Comfortless days upon days; brave lives are sobbing their last; man after man roll down to the death, to mildew and rot, and thou wilt be left alone!"

The next day, Stanley found the foragers. Five days later, having changed his course, he reached Fort Bodo. He had lost 106 men.

It was hard to say who was more shocked: Stanley, at finding Fort Bodo still occupied, or the occupants of Fort Bodo, at the condition of Stanley and the remnants of the rear column. Stanley's expectation was that the fort would long since have been abandoned. He came back only because he was in such desperate need of food for the rear column and thought there might still be stores there. But the men were supposed to be at the lake with Emin and Jephson, waiting for him, along with any of Emin's subjects who wished to leave Equatoria. What had gone wrong?

To his horror, Stanley learned that Emin and Jephson had never arrived. Even worse, there had been no communication from them. No one even knew where they were. After the shock of the rear column and yet another horrific trip through the Ituri, Stanley was at his wit's end. It was as though the universe were conspiring against him.*

The fact that, after more than a year and a half, he had finally gotten his entire expedition back together (albeit in considerably reduced

---

*In his discussion of the rear column in *In Darkest Africa*, Stanley wrote, "A conviction flashes upon my mind that there has been a supernatural malignant influence or agency at work to thwart every honest intention."

form) gave him no satisfaction. He was still missing his prize and, once more, didn't know where to find him.

The only good news was that Fort Bodo had again prospered under Stairs's command. There was ample food from the crops they had planted, including a successful rice harvest, and though they had lost eight men to illness and disease, the remaining fifty-one were hale and hearty. Even the fragile Nelson was doing better.

Stanley wasted no time. After only three days at the fort, he ordered the expedition to pack up as much food as could be carried, and began his third trip to Lake Albert.

Appropriately, perhaps, Captain Nelson was left behind one last time, but only temporarily. Parke noted in his diary on December 23,

> Nelson and Bonny remained behind for some hours with thirty men, to burn the Fort, bury a large glass bottle or demijohn (about three feet in height) at the eastern extremity of the enclosure, and then bring on some loads. The "demijohn" was buried about a couple of feet under ground, and contains a letter written by Nelson, and a few small things of European manufacture; which may teach the African antiquarian of a thousand years hence that a crude form of civilization, known as the "English," had penetrated into the heart of Africa, in the year of grace 1888.

Thus ended the short, unhappy life of the Fort of Peace.

THEY SPENT THEIR SECOND Christmas eating rice and beans, topped off with a cup of coffee and a little brandy. Parke, whose good humor almost never flagged, noted that the officers had now taken to dining alone: "In the first place, we can never all sit down at once, as duty always requires that one or more should be on the move. . . . A second reason . . . whenever we are fortunate enough to have a piece of goat, some like it underdone and some overdone. . . ."

Between the ravages of Yambuya and the losses on the final march through the Ituri forest, Stanley no longer had enough men to carry the loads, so he was once again forced to split the expedition in two. On January 10, at a village called Kandekoré, when the men were ordered to fall in for inspection, 136 were found unfit to continue. Stanley declared that they would be left with Stairs, Parke, and Nelson to recuperate while he and Bonny continued on to the lake (Parke immediately dubbed the new camp the Convalescent Home). That night, Stanley called Stairs and Parke into his tent. In a windy lecture, he repeated some of his favorite maxims, such as "the path of duty is the way to glory," and other wheezes that his officers had already heard too often. But he also told them that he had decided that he was not going to attempt to take Emin Pasha out of Equatoria! "Our object will be to give him ammunition as relief; . . . as we have so few men left we can barely drive through to Zanzibar by ourselves, without taking up the additional trouble and responsibility of looking after Emin and his people."

It was a stunning reversal. Gone was the grand scheme to establish a new colony at Kavirondo; gone was the plan to deliver Emin's beleaguered subjects to Cairo; and, perhaps most remarkably, gone was Stanley's dream of bringing Emin Pasha to England for a triumphal tour in which the grateful governor would sing the praises of the indomitable Bula Matari. It seemed that all of Stanley's grand schemes for the Emin Pasha Relief Expedition had been reduced to nothing more than the fervent wish to simply survive it.

The next morning, Stanley and Bonny marched out of the Convalescent Home with one hundred men. A day later, they met a group of natives who told them that "the Pasha was building big houses at Nyamsassi, and the rumour was that he and many followers intended to pass through the land . . . [T]his piece of good news was hailed with great satisfaction" (Stanley).

On January 14, they reached a village where the chief, an old man named Gavira, told them that Jephson was waiting for them at Kavalli's. Stanley wrote, "Old Gavira had reason to suppose that afternoon that 'Bula Matari' was a very amiable person." He continued, "But at 5 p.m. two Wahuma messengers came with letters from Kavalli's, and as I read them a creeping feeling came over me which was a complete mental paralysis for the time, and deadened all the sensations except that of unmitigated surprise."

The letters were from Emin and Jephson. Emin's was brief, referring Stanley to Jephson's more detailed communication. Jephson's letter, written in Dufilé and dated November 7, began, "I am writing to tell you of the position of affairs in this country, and I trust Shukri Aga will be able by some means to deliver this letter to Kavalli in time to warn you to be careful. On August 18th a rebellion broke out here, and the Pasha and I were made prisoners."

It was everything Stanley had feared and more. Not only had Emin's tenuous authority over his province finally been stripped away, but something even worse had happened. After an absence of almost three years, the Mahdi's army was back. Equatoria was in chaos.

JEPHSON'S LETTER (with two postscripts) was actually a remarkably compact, yet accurate, description of the events that had taken place during the disastrous tour of Emin's garrisons. After the announcement that he and the pasha had been made prisoners, he continued, "The rebellion has been got up by some half dozen officers and clerks, chiefly Egyptians, and gradually others have joined; some through inclination, but most through fear. . . ." He fingered the principal instigators as the two men who had approached Stanley at Nsabé to complain about Emin, saying that while he and Emin had been making their way north to Rejaf,

> these two . . . went about and told the people they had seen you, and that you were only an adventurer, and had not come from Egypt; that the letters you had brought from the Khedive and Nubar Pasha were forgeries; that it was untrue that Khartoum had fallen, and that the Pasha and you had made a plot to take them, their wives and children out of the country, and hand them over to [be] slaves to the English. Such words, in an ignorant and fanatical country like this, acted like fire amongst the people. . . .
>
> The rebels then collected officers from the different stations, and held a large meeting here to determine what measures they would take, and all those who did not join in the movement were so insulted and abused, that they were obliged for their own safety to acquiesce in what was done. The Pasha was deposed, and those officers who were suspected of being friendly to him were removed from their posts, and

those friendly to the rebels were put in their places. It was decided to take the Pasha away as a prisoner to Rejaf, and some of the worst rebels were even for putting him in irons, but the officers were afraid to put these plans into execution, as the soldiers said they would never permit anyone to lay a hand on him. Plans were also made to entrap you when you returned, and strip you of all you had.

Things were in this condition when we were startled by the news that the Mahdi's people had arrived at Lado with three steamers and nine sandals and nuggars,* and had established themselves on the site of the old station. Omar Sale, their general, sent down three peacock dervishes† with a letter to the Pasha demanding the instant surrender of the country. The rebel officers seized them and put them in prison, and decided on war. After a few days the Donagla attacked and captured Rejaf, killing five officers and numbers of soldiers, and taking many women and children prisoners, and all the stores and ammunition in the station were lost. The result of this was a general stampede of people from the stations of Bidden, Kirri, and Muggi, who fled with their women and children to Laboré, abandoning almost everything. At Kirri the ammunition was abandoned, and was at once seized by the natives. The Pasha reckons that the Donagla numbers about 1,500.

The officers and a large number of soldiers have returned to Muggi, and intend to make a stand against the Donagla. Our position here is extremely unpleasant, for since this rebellion all is chaos and confusion; there is no head, and half a dozen conflicting orders are given every day, and no one obeys; the rebels officers are wholly unable to control the soldiers. We are daily expecting some catastrophe to happen, for the Baris‡ have joined the Donagla, and if they come down here with a rush nothing can save us. . . .

The officers are all very much frightened at what has happened, and we are now anxiously awaiting your arrival, and desire to leave the

---

*Troop and cargo transport ships.

†"Peacock" referred to bits of brightly colored cloth that some of the Mahdi's soldiers pinned to their robes; "dervishes" was one of the many names Europeans used to refer to the Mahdists; another was "Donagla," which referred to the district in which the Mahdi was born and from which many of his original troops came. Jephson used the latter term exclusively in referring to the Mahdist army.

‡The Baris were the native tribe that lived near Rejaf and some of the other northern stations. They had been routinely abused by the soldiers of the First Battalion, so their affiliation with the Mahdi's forces gave them an opportunity to retaliate.

country with you, for they are now really persuaded that Khartoum has fallen, and that you have come from the Khedive. The greater part of the officers and all the soldiers wish to reinstate the Pasha in his place, but the Egyptians are afraid that if he is reinstated vengeance will fall on their head, so they have persuaded the Soudanese officers not to do so. The soldiers refuse to act with the officers, so everything is at a standstill, and nothing is being done for the safety of the station, either in the way of fortifying or provisioning it. We are like rats in a trap: they will neither let us act nor retire, and I fear unless you come very soon you will be too late, and our fate will be like that of the rest of the garrisons of the Soudan. . . .

In a postscript written November 24, Jephson added,

Shortly after I had written to you, the soldiers were led by their officers to attempt to retake Rejaf, but the Donagla defeated them, and killed six officers and a large number of soldiers: amongst the officers killed were some of the Pasha's worst enemies. The soldiers in all the stations were so panic-stricken and angry at what had happened that they declared they would not attempt to fight unless the Pasha was set a liberty; so the rebel officers were obliged to free him and sent us to Wadelai, where he is free to do as he pleases, but at present he has not resumed his authority in the country: he is, I believe, by no means anxious to do so. . . .

Our danger, as far as the Donagla are concerned, is, of course, increased by this last defeat, but our position is in one way better now, for we are further removed from them, and we have now the option of retiring if we please, which we had not before when we were prisoners. We hear that the Donagla have sent steamers down to Khartoum for reinforcements; if so, they cannot be up for another six weeks; meantime I hope that until the reinforcements arrive they will not care to come so far from their base as Wadelai or Tunguru. If they do, it will be all up with us. . . .

There was one more postscript, written on December 18. It said, in part,

We are now at Tunguru. On November 25th the Donagla surrounded Dufflé and besieged it for four days, but the soldiers, of whom there were some 500 in the station, managed at last to repulse them, and they retired to Rejaf, which is their headquarters. They have sent down to Khartoum for reinforcements, and doubtless will again attack and take the country when they are strengthened. In our flight from Wadelai I was asked by the officers to destroy our boat lest is should fall into the hands of the Donagla; I therefore broke it up, as we were unable to save it.

Dufflé is being evacuated as fast as possible, and it is the intention of the officers to collect at Wadelai, and to decide on what steps they shall next take. The Pasha is unable to move hand or foot, as there is still a very strong party against him, and the officers are no longer in immediate fear of the Mahdi's people.

Do not on any account come down to Nsabé, but make your camp at Kavalli's: send a letter directly you arrive, and as soon as we hear of your arrival I will come down to you. I will not disguise the fact from you that you will have a difficult and dangerous task before you in dealing with the Pasha's people. I trust you will arrive before the Donagla return, or our case will be desperate.

With typical Victorian understatement (unless the Victorian was Stanley), Jephson neglected to mention any of the sordid details of the rebellion, or his own bravery in dealing with it. For weeks on end, he had had legitimate reason to fear for his life and for Emin's, as the rebel officers threatened, postured, and bullied, dividing their time between endless "council meetings" and kangaroo court sessions, and getting drunk, which they did on a daily basis. In his diary, Jephson confessed to a fear that "in their drunken state they may . . . commit some deed of violence & plunge the whole station into wholesale riot & bloodshed." In addition, he only hinted at the level of chaos and absurdity that accompanied the rebellion, perhaps because the truth of it would have strained credulity. The lunatics were, indeed, running the asylum.

Some of their shenanigans had been almost comical in their ineptness; others, ugly and frightening. At one point, to prove that the expedition had not been sent by the khedive and was, in fact, a fraud, they had summoned the three Sudanese soldiers sent with Jephson by Stanley, assuming that they were imposters. The rebels ordered them to perform the standard military drills taught to all Egyptian troops. Much to their surprise and chagrin, the Sudanese performed them flawlessly (a belated payoff from Stairs's work with them aboard the *Madura?*), at which point the rebels decided it was time to begin drinking again.

The rebels' activities weren't always so harmless. One of their primary targets was Hawash Effendi, whom they labeled, with some justification, "a seducer, a robber, and a scoundrel." Having abused his authority for years by extorting tributes and payoffs ranging from animals to slaves and money, it wasn't surprising that many of his fellow officers hated Hawash, whom they felt the pasha had favored unfairly. He had therefore been arrested and put on trial, but the rebels were at least as interested in stripping him of his wealth as in taking away his power. When a search of his house failed to uncover the bounty the rebels were sure would be there, his wives and household servants were beaten and tortured in an attempt to find out where his money and other valuables were hidden. The brutality went on for hours, the screams of the innocent victims "making our blood boil" (Jephson).

Jephson also chose to omit details about the humiliation that was heaped upon Emin. Throughout his imprisonment, Emin had no contact with or knowleddge of his young daughter, Farida; he was not allowed a single book to read, or even any writing materials. Confined to a small compound inside Dufilé, he wasn't even able to see the surrounding countryside. In his diary, Jephson wrote, "Emin longed for a glimpse of trees and green grass once more. I discovered that by standing on a chair, we could just see a small patch of green grass with five or six Borassus palms growing on it, some mile and a half from the station. We used, therefore, frequently to mount on our chairs, and stand gazing at this small picture."

Emin was not permitted to attend his own trial, let alone testify in his own defense. Though the rebel council combed through his reports, correspondence, and meticulous accounting records, looking for evidence of malfeasance, they found nothing. They ransacked his house in Wadelai, allegedly searching for misappropriated government property. Again they found nothing. The truth was that Emin Pasha, like Gordon before him, had been scrupulously honest throughout his service in Equatoria. His integrity was unassailable. Nevertheless, the rebel council brought a 37-count indictment against him, accusing him of betraying the khedive in a conspiracy with Stanley. Though not a shred of legitimate evidence was produced against him, after a two-day sham of a trial, he was formally deposed and forced to sign a document stripping him of all authority and recognizing the rebel officers who were taking over for him.

Having overthrown him, the rebels couldn't decide what to do with their former governor. Some wanted to keep him imprisoned in Dufilé; other others wanted to send him to First Battalion headquarters at Rejaf; a few even wanted to execute him. Not surprisingly, Emin plunged into a deep depression. When he heard that he might be sent to Rejaf, he threatened suicide and wrote a will, naming Jephson executor and asking him to see that Farida was cared for.

There was another aspect of the rebellion against Emin that Jephson failed to note, not out of his sense of decorum or tact, but because he simply didn't recognize it: in several key respects, the spark that had set the rebellion ablaze was the expedition itself. The Egyptian clerks, who were the prime movers of the rebellion, along with most of the Egyptian officers and some of the Sudanese officers, had no interest in leaving Equatoria. The clerks, especially, were mostly convicted felons who had been exiled to Equatoria from Egypt. Once they were there, however, their ability to read and write, while many of the officers, especially the Sudanese, could not, gave them power and influence far beyond their stations. Life might not have been grand in the garrisons of Equatoria, but for the clerks it was considerably better than anything they might have expected to return to in Cairo. The same was true for many of the officers. Through the years, they had accumulated large households with wives, children, and slaves and, by African standards, a reasonable standard of living. Even among the officers of the Second Battalion (with one or two notable exceptions), who had professed their loyalty to Emin, that loyalty was as much a matter of practicality as true allegiance. Though they loudly swore that they would "go where their Pasha led," the truth was that they had no wish to leave Equatoria—at least as long as the Mahdi's forces stayed away. As Hawash had explained to Jephson, "with the exception of a very few people, no-one really wished to leave the country; they were much too comfortable where they were."

So when Stanley (and then his proxy Jephson) showed up with his khedival letters and pronouncements and ultimatums, the salvation he thought he was offering to the beleaguered people of Equatoria was perceived as something very different. From the Equatorian point of view, Henry Stanley wasn't the solution; he became the problem.

It was little wonder, then, that the clerks started plotting and spreading rumors among a gullible population of officers, soldiers, and subjects. They had everything to lose if Stanley succeeded in selling his plan for evacuation, so they did everything in their power to scuttle it. As far as the rebellion was concerned, Emin may have been the victim, but Stanley was the catalyst.

As it turned out, the expedition's arrival also stimulated the return of the Mahdist forces. When reports of Stanley's arrival reached Khartoum, reports that characterized the expedition as a large force under European leadership, Khalifa Abdullah, the Mahdi's successor, became alarmed, fearing a possible attack from the south. He therefore ordered a second invasion of Equatoria, in hopes of eliminating the last major pocket of resistance to the jihad in Sudan *before* Stanley's force could do anything. He specifically ordered his general Omar Saleh to capture Emin Pasha, if possible, or to kill him, if necessary. Ironically, however, the arrival of the khalifa's troops at Lado in mid-October was the event that set Emin Pasha free.

When the three "peacock dervishes" delivered Omar Saleh's letter demanding the province's surrender, the rebel leaders went into a full-bore panic. Some were ready to capitulate immediately, others wanted to fight, and still others wanted to flee. In desperation, they turned to Emin. They didn't offer to reinstate him, but they did ask his advice.

At first he refused to cooperate, but his lingering affection for his rank-and-file troops, and his seemingly inexhaustible willingness to believe the Egyptians' pleas for forgiveness and protestations of loyalty, overcame his anger. He suggested a plan of action: they should ignore the general's letter, withdraw from all the stations north of Dufilé, and seriously consider concentrating all of their forces at Tunguru, the station that could best be defended. The rebel leaders agreed, but then did nothing to put the plan into action.

Less than a week after the dervishes appeared,* word came that Rejaf had fallen to the Mahdi's army. Somewhat surprisingly, given their inability to agree about almost anything after Emin had been deposed, the rebel council decided to send a force north to try to retake the station. Disaster ensued. Not only did their counteroffensive fail; many of their officers and soldiers were slaughtered, including several key members of the rebellion. In addition, horror stories came back to Dufilé about the cruelty of both the Mahdi's forces and the Bari tribesmen who had joined with them.

One consequence of the debacle, however, was the elevation of Selim Bey as commander (temporarily, it turned out) at Dufilé. He had been the station commander at Laboré and was, at heart, an Emin loyalist, so he promptly granted Emin's request to be allowed to return to Wadelai and his daughter, Farida. Emin left at once, taking Jephson, Casati, and Vita Hassan with him.

They hadn't been long in Wadelai before rumors arrived that all the northern stations had fallen, and that the Mahdi's army was on its way to Dufilé. If Dufilé fell, the invaders could be in Wadelai in a day. The decision was made to abandon the station and move south to Tunguru, on Lake Albert. Since the steamers were both still in Dufilé, they would have to march.

The evacuation of Wadelai was a heartbreaking—and deadly— fiasco. For Emin, it meant leaving virtually his entire life in Africa behind. "His books, clothes, papers, beads, brass bracelets, and all the useful things he had saved and collected for our people with so much care and forethought, all had to be cast away" (Jephson). Most painfully, all of his specimens, including four boxes of stuffed birds that were ready to be shipped to the British Museum, also had to be left.

For his part, Jephson had to leave a considerable cache of items he had been collecting to take to his fellow officers—boots, clothing, cotton cloth, tobacco, beautiful carrying bags made of animal skins. He

---

*The dervishes were imprisoned, tortured, and eventually beaten to death by the rebels. According to Jephson, throughout their ordeal, none of them ever uttered a sound.

also abandoned his own African souvenirs—ivory trinkets, bows, arrows, spears, knives, shields, and body adornments.

When the time came to move out, most of the soldiers and officers, who had begged Emin to reassume command and lead them from danger, changed their minds, so the evacuees consisted mostly of women and children. They were utterly unprepared for what lay before them.

In his diary, Jephson painted a pathetic, albeit moving, picture.

> We got off by seven o'clock, and as we left the station we could see a confused straggling line of women and children, goats, cattle and sheep, donkeys, and baggage stretching ahead for three miles. All was utter confusion and noise. Some women might be seen hurrying along with their goods, and dragging little children or goats after them. Others were seated mournfully in small groups with their loads before them, trying to soothe the crying of their children, while they waited for their fathers or husbands to join them. There were sick people who implored us to help them to get along, and wept and wrung their hands in an agony of despair at being left. The shouting of the people and crying of the children, the lowing and bleating of cattle and goats, rose in a deafening uproar.
>
> Here and there a woman might be seen toiling bravely along with a huge load on her head, a baby slung across her back, and dragging a small child along. It was a pitiful sight. The whole road was strewn with things of all sorts, which they had started with and found too heavy to carry. We passed several small children, too, abandoned by the road-side.

People took absurd items with them—heavy carved bedsteads, a bouquet of ostrich feathers, a sledgehammer, a crosscut saw, grinding stones, baking irons. Several people brought their parrots; one man brought his cat.

> At one place we had to cross a broad shallow river, with steep sloping banks on either side. Here a scene of utmost confusion prevailed. The high bank was soon churned into a black slippery mud, in which the women and children sank up to their knees, and were continually falling. The press on the further bank was terrible, and when some

unfortunate child or woman fell, the dense mass of donkeys and people behind swept over them and trampled them under foot. . . .

At the end of the first day, Jephson wrote, "After one of the most trying and painful marches I have ever made, we camped at three o'clock, having done only ten miles." Considering all he had been through in the preceding two years, it was a remarkable statement.

The next morning, the column spotted one of the steamers speeding in their direction. Concluding that it was the Mahdi's men, Jephson later wrote that he thought "it was all up with us," but it turned out to be refugees from Dufilé, headed for Wadelai. Even though they had repulsed the Mahdi's army, the rebel officers had decided to abandon Dufilé and retreat to Wadelai. Many of the evacuees with Emin and Jephson decided to go back to join them, but Jephson, Emin, and a few loyal followers pressed on to Tunguru, to await Stanley's return. That is where they were when Stanley read Jephson's letter.

STANLEY BEING STANLEY, the letter made him furious. After the disaster of the rear column, he could not conceive that any greater debacle could befall his expedition, and yet it had. He took his anger out on Jephson.

January 17th/89

My dear Jephson,

Your letter of Nov 7th/88 with 2 postscripts one dated Nov. 24th the other dated Dec. 18th is to hand and its contents noted.

I will not criticise your letter nor discuss any of its contents. I wish to be brief & promptly act. With that view I present you with a precis of events connected with our journey.

We separated from the Pasha on the 23rd of May last with the understanding that in about two months—you with or without the Pasha would start for Fort Bodo with sufficient porters to take the goods at the fort, & convey them to Nyanza. The Pasha expressed himself anxious to see Mt. Pisgah, & if words may be relied on he was anxious to assist us in his own relief. We somewhat doubted whether his affairs would per-

mit the Pasha's absence, but we were assured you would not remain
inactive. It was also understood that the Pasha would erect a small station, on Nyamsassie Island as a provision depot, in order that our expedition might find means of subsistence on our arrival at the Lake.

Eight months have elapsed & not one single promise has been
performed. . . .

For someone who wished "to be brief and promptly act," Stanley
then launched into a detailed description of what he found at Banalya,
including a listing of his personal items that had been shipped downriver. Regarding his return to Fort Bodo, he wrote, "Your non arrival
. . . had left us with a larger number of goods than our own force could
carry at one time. . . ."

He continued in this accusatory tone, going so far as to lump Jephson in with the officers of the rear column:

> The difficulties I met at Banalya, are repeated today near the Albert
> Lake & nothing can save us now from being overwhelmed by them but
> a calm and clear decision. If I had hesitated at Banalya—very likely I
> should still be there waiting for Jameson & Ward with my own men
> dying by dozens from sheer inanition. And when I should have started
> at all I should have found my strength, stores & men exhausted. But
> the officers were plunged in their own follies, the rear column was
> wrecked by indecision. Barttelot, Jameson & Ward reaped only what
> they had sown.
>
> Are the Pasha, Casati & yourself to share the same fate? If you are
> still victims of indecision—then a long good night to you all—but while
> I retain my sense—I must save my expedition. You may be saved also if
> you are wise.

He then quoted (not quite accurately) several passages from the
khedive's letter to Emin, including the following:

> "Try to understand the contents well & make them well known to
> all the officers & men that they may be fully aware of what they are
> going to do."
>
> It is precisely what the Khedive says, that I wish to say to you. Try &

understand all this thoroughly that you may be saved from the effects of indiscretion, which will be fatal to you all if unheeded.

The first installment of relief was handed to Emin Pasha on or about May 1st/88. The second final installment of relief is at this camp with us ready for delivery at any place the Pasha designates or to any person charged by the Pasha to receive it. If the Pasha fails to receive it or to decide what shall be done with it—I must then decide briefly what I must do.

Our second object in coming here was to receive such at our own camp as were disposed to leave Africa—our Expedition has no further business in these regions & will at once retire. Try & understand what all this means. Try & see the utter & final abandonment of all further relief, & the bitter end & fate of those obstinate & misguided people who decline assistance when tendered to them. From May 1st/88 to January/89 are nine months—so long a time to consider a simple proposition of leaving Africa or staying here!

Therefore in the official & formal letter accompanying this explanatory note to you I designate Kavalli's village as the rendezvous where I am willing to receive those who are desirous of leaving Africa. . . .

And now I address myself to you personally. *If you consider yourself still a member of this expedition subject to my orders* [italics added]—then upon receipt of this letter you will at once leave for Kavalli's with such of my men, Binza, & the three Soudanese as are willing to obey you & bring to me the final decision of Emin Pasha, Signor Casati respecting their personal intentions. . . .

You will understand that it will be a severe strain on Kavalli's resources to maintain us with provisions for longer than 6 days & if you are longer than this period we must retire to Mazamboni's & finally to our camp on the Ituri Ferry. Otherwise we must seize provisions by force & any act of violence would cut off & close native communication, this difficulty might have been avoided had the Pasha followed my suggestion of making a depot at Nyamsassie. The fact that there are provisions at M'swa [mentioned by Jephson in his letter] does not help us at all. There are provisions in Europe also, but unfortunately they are as inaccessible as those of M'swa. We have no boat now to communicate by Lake—& you do not mention what has become of the steamers, the Khedive & Nyanza.

Stanley kept up his harangue for several more paragraphs, with such pointed jibes at Jephson as "You have been pleased to destroy the boat & have injured us irreparably by doing so. I presume the two cases of Winchester ammunition left with the Pasha are lost also." (They weren't.)

Remarkably, Stanley wasn't through. He added a postscript labeled "strictly personal" that was little more than a continuation of the abuse dished out in the body of the letter. "I read your letters half a dozen times & my opinion of you varys with each reading. Sometimes I fancy you are half Mahdist, or Arabist, then Eminist. . . ."

He then delivered a final swipe at both Jephson and the officers of the rear column:

> Jameson paid a thousand pounds to accompany us. Well you see he disobeyed orders & we left him to ponder on the things he had done.* Ward, you know was very eager to accompany us, but he disobeyed orders & he was left at Bangala a victim to his craving for novel adventures, Barttelot poor fellow, was mad for Kudos, but he has lost his life & all a victim to perverseness.
>
> Now do'nt you be perverse, but obey—& set my order to you as a frontlet between the eyes, & all with God's gracious help will end well.

He closed with a series of sneers at Emin:

> I want to help the Pasha somehow, but he must help me & credit me. If he wishes to get out of this trouble I am his most devoted servant & friend, but if he hesitates—something rises within me which causes me excessive wonder & perplexity. I could save a dozen Pasha's if they were willing to be saved. . . .
>
> . . . I am ready to lend all my strength & wit to assist him. But this time there must be no hesitation—but positive Yea or Nay—& home we go.

Even for Stanley, the letter was extraordinary, exceeding his usual standards for vitriol, self-pity, and myopia. That he had sent Jephson on a

---

*Stanley still didn't know that Jameson was dead; he wouldn't find out for seven more months.

mission in his stead that had little, if any, real chance of succeeding; that said mission had resulted in life-threatening peril and imprisonment during which Jephson had managed to maintain both his wits and his courage when all around him had lost theirs; and that Jephson was still endeavoring to inform and advise his commander about developments as best he could—all that was of no interest to Stanley. As far as he was concerned, Jephson, like the officers at Yambuya, had disobeyed orders, thereby causing him great inconvenience. Nothing else mattered.

Jephson's response to Stanley's letter, recorded in his diary, was remarkably muted, focusing primarily on the slights to the men of the rear column:

> His letter to me is in many ways greatly wanting in common sense & I think the way he speaks about the officers of the rear guard is not very pleasant. He seems to forget he told them he would be away at the outside 6 months & in point of fact was gone 14 months, meanwhile these people were left encumbered with loads, unable to move, & the men, from his description, dying like flies. . . .

Nevertheless, as soon as Stanley's poisonous missive arrived, Jephson made arrangements to leave Tunguru by canoe to rejoin the expedition as quickly as possible.

Stanley also wrote to Emin. The tone was more formal, but the anger and resentment were just as apparent.

> Sir,
>
> I have the honour to inform you that the second instalment of relief which this expedition was ordered to convey to you is now in this camp ready for delivery to any person charged to receive it by you. . . . This second installment of relief consists of sixty-three cases of Remington Cartridges, twenty-six cases of gunpowder, each 45 lbs weight; four cases of percussion caps, four bales of goods, one bale of goods for Signor Casati—a gift from myself; two pieces of blue serge, writing paper, envelopes, blank books, etc.
>
> Having after great difficulty, greater than was anticipated, brought relief to you, I am constrained to officially demand from you receipts

for the above goods and relief brought to you, and also a definite answer to the question if you propose to accept our escort and assistance to reach Zanzibar—of if Signor Casati proposes to do so, or whether there are any officers or men disposed to accept our safe conduct to the sea.* In the latter event I would be obliged to you if you would kindly state how those persons desirous of leaving Africa can be communicated with.

He went on to detail "an approximate statement of our movements," which was a list of his expected locations for the next twenty days, and then added, "If at the end of 20 days no news has been heard from you or Mr. Jephson, I cannot hold myself responsible for what may happen. . . ."

Emin sent back a typically polite, but ambiguous, response, which infuriated Stanley still more. After promising to send one of his officers to collect the second installment of relief supplies and to supply an itemized receipt for them, Emin wrote,

> Concerning your question if Signor Casati and myself propose to accept your escort and assistance to reach Zanzibar, and if there are any officers and men disposed to accept your safe-conduct to the sea, I have to state that not only Signor Casati and myself would gladly avail us of your help, but that there are lots of people desirous of going out from the far Egypt, as well as for any other convenient place.† As these people have been delayed by the deplorable events which have happened during your absence, and as only from a few days they begin to come in, I should entreat you to kindly assist them. I propose to send them to Nyamsassi, and a first party start to-day with Mr. Jephson. Every one of them has provisions enough to last for a month.

Emin then explained, ever so diplomatically, that the twenty-day deadline given by Stanley was simply not enough time for all of the people who might wish to join the march out of Equatoria to reach the staging area at Kavalli's with their households and possessions. He

---

*Interestingly, Stanley makes no mention of Kavirondo or any other intermediate destination.

†Evidently, Emin had *not* given up on Kavirondo.

asked for at least ten more days, but even as he did, he acknowleged that Stanley might not be able to grant it. He then closed with a heart-felt appreciation of Jephson and, unexpectedly, a farewell:

> As Mr. Jephson starts by this steamer, and has kindly promised to hand you this note, I avail myself of the occasion to bear witness to the great help and assistance his presence had afforded to me. Under the most trying circumstances he has shown so splendid courage, such unfaltering kindness and patience, that I cannot but wish him every success in life, and thank him for all his forbearance. As probably I shall not see you any more, you will be pleased to inform his relations of my thanks to him and them.
>
> Before concluding, I beg to be permitted to tender anew my most heartfelt thanks to you and to your officers and men, and to ask you to transmit my everlasting gratitude to the kind people who sent you to help us. May God protect you and your party, and give you a happy and speedy homeward march.*

When Stanley had first arrived at Lake Albert, in December 1888, Emin Pasha was the governor of a province that included a total of ten stations, not counting the disaffected First Battalion at Rejaf and its satellite settlements. The Mahdi's forces had not been seen or heard from in nearly three years. Relations with Kabba Rega, the increasingly unpredictable king of Unyoro, were fragile, but the king was preoccupied with his endless war against Uganda, so he posed no immediate threat. Emin's garrisons were strong, his fields, gardens, and orchards were bountiful, his people were fed and clothed, and, thanks to a style of governance that utilized an ever-shifting repertoire of adaptation, persuasion, accommodation, guile, benign neglect, and strategic denial, Emin and his province were managing to survive.

A year later, Emin Pasha was no longer the governor of Equatoria, though it was far from clear that any single leader had emerged from among the rebels to replace him. The province consisted of only three stations: Wadelai, where the endlessly bickering officers of the rebel

---

*Emin did not permit Jephson to see his letter, so Jephson was unaware that it contained Emin's farewell to the expedition.

council had taken residence; Tunguru, where Emin was ensconced, though the station seemed more aligned with the rebels than with Emin; and M'swa, the smallest (and newest) station in the province, and the only one that could still clearly be labeled loyal to Emin. Everyone agreed that it was only a matter of time before the Mahdist hordes, strengthened by reinforcements from Khartoum, would swoop down again to finish what they had started, and, thanks to the punitive raid against Kabiro at the beginning of Jephson and Emin's provincial tour, Kabba Rega's Unyoran forces were said to be preparing to wage war on two fronts. In short, Equatoria, owing in no small measure to the arrival and intervention of the Emin Pasha Relief Expedition, had collapsed. The irony was completely lost on Henry Morton Stanley.

Chapter Fifteen

OIL AND WATER

WHEN STANLEY SENT JEPHSON to tour the province with Emin, he told him to do everything in his power to convince Emin that he should abandon the province, with or without the majority of his people. After the rebellion, Jephson thought, the matter should have been beyond discussion. When Emin was released from Dufilé by Selim Bey, and the two of them went to Wadelai, Jephson wrote in his diary, "He can, without the slightest blame being attached to him, leave the country as a private man, leaving the people who have thrown him over, and taking with him only such people as have been faithful to him throughout. When once people have said they don't want him, his duty to them entirely ceased." As they waited anxiously at Tunguru for word of Stanley's return, Jephson assumed that Emin would be ready to go as soon as Stanley appeared. He was wrong. As he prepared to leave Tunguru to rejoin the expedition, Jephson realized that Emin was still waffling. The pasha continued to fear that if he went with the expedition, it might be said that he had abandoned his people. Jephson couldn't believe it. He took one of the steamers and headed south for M'swa, not knowing whether he would ever see Emin again.

When he got to M'swa, the steamer crew deserted, so he took canoes to reach the southern end of the lake. He then went inland, climbing the escarpment that rose nearly 2,500 feet from the lakeshore to the plateau. There, at Kavalli's village, Stanley had made his camp. Jephson arrived on February 6, 1889, and immediately reported to Stanley that Emin still couldn't make up his mind.

Despite what he had said to Parke and Stairs only a few weeks before about leaving Equatoria without Emin or his people, the truth was that Stanley couldn't afford to go home without his trophy. It was the only way to salvage what had otherwise been an unmitigated disaster of an expedition. Though he accepted none of the responsibility for the expedition's failures, Stanley was no fool; he knew what people would say if he came home empty-handed, especially with the Mahdi's army back in Equatoria. Emin knew it, too. He wrote of Stanley, "For him, everything depends on whether he is able to take me along, for only then, when people could actually see me, would his expedition be regarded as totally successful. To Stanley's chagrin, when he went on the expedition to find Livingstone, he experienced what it meant to leave behind in Africa the main object of his expedition. This time, he would rather perish than leave without me!"

Stanley's problems, however, had multiplied: in addition to Emin's endless vacillation and the return of the Mahdi's army, he had to deal with the uncertain intentions of the rebel council. Would it allow Emin to leave? Would it allow anyone else to leave? Would it try to stop the expedition's withdrawal, with or without Emin?

Typically, Stanley's solution was to confront the problem head-on. If he had to, he was prepared to take Emin by force. He would dispatch Stairs with three hundred riflemen, along with two thousand native "auxiliaries," to rescue Emin from Tunguru (Stanley had already sent for Stairs, Parke, Nelson, and the invalids camped at Kandekoré). He wrote another letter to Emin (actually he wrote two letters; Jephson deemed the first one so condescending that he persuaded Stanley to redraft it), telling him that he was prepared to use force to rescue him if necessary, but urging him to first try to appropriate one of the steamers and come to M'swa with those of his followers who remained loyal. If he couldn't get a steamer, he should *march* to M'swa. If he couldn't march, Stanley would send the rescue force. Stanley was adamant that Emin make a decision. No more of the "lachrymose and melancholic" disposition demonstrated in his previous letter—"it was absolutely necessary that I should be clearly told what the Pasha wished."

As it turned out, Emin would deliver his answer in person. Unbeknownst to Stanley, the rebel officers, now headquartered at Wadelai, and still as fractious as ever, had heard that Stanley had returned to the lake leading a large, well-armed force—several hundred Zanzibaris with repeating rifles, augmented by machine guns. The report was greatly exaggerated, but it produced the predictable panic among the rebels. They feared that Stanley had assembled the large force to attack them for what they had done to Emin. After considerable bickering, a delegation under Selim Bey (the officer who had freed Emin at Dufilé) was dispatched to Tunguru to plead with Emin to intervene on the rebels' behalf with Stanley. To his credit, Emin refused—at first. The rebels then asked whether he would at least accompany them to Stanley's camp to serve as their interpreter. Again he refused. So they asked him to be their governor again! Emin suspected it was a ploy, but after more feverish protestations of remorse and renewed fidelity, he gave in and agreed to go with them. Both steamers were requisitioned, and, along with Casati, Vita Hassan, and the rest of his entourage, Emin headed south. He stopped in at M'swa to pick up more passengers and provisions, and then, a week after Jephson had appeared, a note arrived for Stanley from Emin; he was camped at the base of the plateau. "I arrived here with my two steamers, carrying a first lot of people desirous to leave this country, under your escort." He went on to say, "The wave of insanity which overran the country has subsided, and of such people as are now coming with me we may be sure."

Stanley dispatched Jephson and fifty Zanzibaris to escort Emin and his party up to Kavalli's. It turned out that Emin, Casati, Vita Hassan, and several others who were part of the group had brought with them their entire households in anticipation of their departure from the province. The sheer volume of matériel was overwhelming, and the inventories were ridiculous: Emin's possessions, despite his hasty evacuation from Wadelai little more than two months before, now came to two hundred loads.* Casati had brought nothing of use to anyone but himself, and he still had enough for eighty loads. Vita Hassan had forty, and a Greek merchant named Marcos, who, like Casati, had been marooned in Equatoria for some time, had the equivalent of sixty loads. Some of the Egyptian and Sudanese officers with Emin had brought comparable piles of detritus, and the steamers had already gone back to M'swa and Tunguru to collect more refugees and loads.

The Zanzibaris, augmented by additional native porters dragooned by Stanley, began hauling this inventory up to the expedition's camp. The Egyptians and Sudanese who were with Emin, and for whom sloth seemed to be a sign of status, refused to lift a finger, nor would they let their household servants or slaves assist in the carrying. To make matters worse, they treated the Zanzibaris like slaves, ordering them about and, on occasion, physically abusing them. The Zanzibaris were not happy. Not only was the work arduous, but they knew from experience that much of the stuff they were dragging up the hill would inevitably be left behind. They were obliged to haul heavy, unwieldy items such as beds, tables, chairs, beer-making jars, and oversized grinding stones that weighed well over one hundred pounds, not to mention nonsense like parrots and their cages. The list was as endless as it was idiotic, and the whole endeavor struck the Zanzibaris as a waste of time. Why couldn't everything be sorted at the lake, with only the essentials being designated for the eighteen-mile trek (including the 2,500-foot climb up) to Kavalli's?

While the Zanzibaris sweated up and down the hill, Jephson, Emin, and the rebel delegation arrived at Stanley's camp. They were followed almost immediately by Stairs, Parke, et al., arriving from Kan-

---

*In fairness, he had also brought substantial supplies of sesame, millet, and salt, as well as sixty tusks of ivory requested by Stanley to pay his Manyuema carriers. In addition, to Jephson's shock and delight, Emin brought the rescued and rehabilitated *Advance*.

dekoré, so that on February 18, 1889, for the first time in almost twenty months, the entire Emin Pasha Relief Expedition, or at least what was left of it, was together again.

Selim Bey presented Stanley with a letter, signed by all thirty-six officers of the rebel council, acknowledging that Stanley's expedition had indeed been sent by the khedive (thereby admitting that one of the rebellion's major justifications had been erroneous) and stating, somewhat cryptically, that all of them hoped "to be very soon with you," though no time frame was specified. Stanley smelled a rat.

In *In Darkest Africa*, he wrote at some length of his suspicions that the rebel officers were still conspiring against the expedition. Their intention, he suggested, was to deliver the expedition into the hands of the Mahdi. "They will curry favour with the Khalif [Khalifa Abdullah, the Mahdi's successor] by betraying their would-be rescuers and their former Pasha and his white companions into his hands, and win honour and glory by so doing." He went on to suggest that, even if the rebels couldn't make a deal with the khalifa, they might have an alternate plan. Assuming the voice of a rebel, he wrote, "We can fall back on the camp of the white men, and by apparent obedience disarm all suspicion, make use of them to find us a land of plenty, and suddenly possess ourselves of their arms and ammunition, and either send them adrift as beggars, or slay the whites and make their followers our slaves."

Given his history, these imagined scenarios seemed to fit squarely with Stanley's amply demonstrated tendency toward paranoia. On the other hand, given the rebels' capacity for deception and duplicity, perhaps not.

Nevertheless, Stanley wrote a reply to the rebels (referring to them as "the revolted officers at Wadelai"), assuring them that his offer of safe conduct out of the province still stood and telling them that he would wait "a reasonable time" for those who wanted to join him. His failure to specify what "a reasonable time" might be was, in all probability, deliberate; if the expedition set out for the coast before the mutineers at Wadelai managed to join them, Stanley must have reckoned, he would be avoiding all sorts of potential problems. In fact, if he could round up another sixty reliable fighting men out of Emin's forces, he would have been perfectly happy to leave the whole lot behind, as long as he had Emin.

Days turned into weeks; the steamers kept bringing more and more refugees from M'swa and Tunguru, all of whom seemed to be bringing all of their worldly possessions. Parke commented that even the household servants were bringing "three, four, or five loads, and we officers of the E.P.R. Expedition have had only three to cross Africa with." As the disgruntled Zanzibaris continued their backbreaking hill climbs, Parke and the other officers began openly to question the logic of so much wasted effort. Stanley's response was bland, only nominally plausible, and completely out of character: "I am aware of what is going on. But what can we do? These people are our guests. We are bound to help them as much as possible. We indeed came here for that purpose."

The refugees coming to Kavalli's were mainly women and children. Indeed, of the first 500 people to reach camp, only 125 were men, with few, if any soliders among them. Rather, the males were mostly slaves, servants, and a few low-level functionaries. Stanley was starting to worry about having enough guns for the trek to the coast.

By mid-March, Stanley had set their departure date as April 10. Emin immediately began angling for more time, fearing that the loyal officers and troops at Wadelai (if, indeed, there were any), as well as those at M'swa and Tunguru, might not all be able to reach Kavalli's in the allotted time. In his heart, Emin still wanted, perhaps needed, to believe that his people remained loyal, that the rebellion was an aberration, and that the majority of his "children," as he thought of them, would never desert him, nor he them. Though the rationalist in him knew that leaving the province was the only realistic option open to him, the emotional side of him longed to remain, somehow, in the truest home he had ever known. He had made a life for himself in Equatoria, and, as both his actions and inertia made more and more apparent, he couldn't imagine re-creating it anywhere else.

Another aspect of Emin's character became increasingly clear during the wait at Kavalli's; in his heart, he was a scientist. He filled his days at the camp not with administrative duties or strategic consultations with Stanley but with collecting. He chased butterflies; he sent his best hunters out in search of birds to add to his collections; he showed his daughter, Farida, how to capture beetles; he spent hours making notations and preparing specimens for shipment back to Europe. This was his passion. It seemed obvious that he would have been a happier man had he spent his thirteen years in Equatoria as a scientist who dabbled in governance rather than the other way around.

Stanley used Emin's scientific bent as the basis for a self-congratulatory comparison of himself and the Pasha:

> His love of science borders on fanaticism. I have attempted to discover during our daily chats whether he was Christian or Moslem, Jew or Pagan, and I rather suspect that he is nothing more than a Materialist. Who can say why votaries of science, though eminently kindly in their social relations, are so angular of character? In my analysis of the scientific nature I am constrained to associate with it, as compared with that of men who are more Christians than scientists, a certain hardness, or rather indelicacy of feeling. They strike me as being somewhat unsympathetic, and capable of only cold friendship, coolly indifferent to the warmer human feelings. I may best express what I mean by saying that I think they are more apt to feel an affection for one's bleached skull and frame of unsightly bones, than for what is divine within a man. . . . They seem to wish you to infer that they have explored the body through and through, and that it is a waste of time to discuss what only exists in the imagination.

With nearly a thousand people in camp, Stanley found himself facing a logistical problem that had been blessedly absent for a while—how to feed everyone. With his officers in charge, he sent out raiding parties to scour the countryside looking for cattle, goats, sheep, chicken, and grain. The raids were startlingly productive, quickly building the camp's herd of cattle to more than three hundred head. Stanley then hit upon an ingenious scheme to bolster his beleaguered Zanzibaris in their ongoing efforts to bring all the loads from the lakeside camp to Kavalli's. He sent word to the chiefs whose cattle had been "appropriated" that they could get them back in exchange for providing carriers for the loads. The exchange rate would be one cow for every five loads brought into camp. The tactic yielded several dozen additional carriers, though many of them deserted before getting any loads to camp. Of those who completed the long climb, Jephson observed, "until now they have never been payed for labour & did not know it had any market value." That they were being paid with goods that belonged to them in the first place didn't seem to occur to him.

On March 26, a letter arrived from Selim Bey, saying that he was having considerable difficulties at Wadelai and requesting more time for himself and Shukri Aga at M'swa to reach Kavalli's. Stanley used the letter as an excuse for one of his favorite exercises, a *shauri*. Like virtually every other *shauri* during the expedition, the outcome of this supposedly open forum was never in doubt.

Stanley called his officers and Emin Pasha to his tent, ostensibly to discuss whether or not to grant Selim Bey's request. The discussion quickly became a lecture in which Stanley provided a highly selective review of the events of the past year, rendered in a manner that was distinctly unflattering to Emin's officers and soldiers and, by extension, to Emin himself. An example: "Remembering the three revolts which these same officers have inspired, their pronounced intentions against this Expedition, their plots and counterplots, the life of conspiracy and smiling treachery they have led, we may well pause to consider what object principally animates them now. . . ."

Stanley continued in this vein for several minutes. Then, at the end of his rant, he polled his officers. As he knew they would, they voted unanimously to stick to the stated departure date. Letters to Selim Bey and Shukri Aga were duly dispatched, informing them of the decision. Everyone in the tent knew what the decision meant: in all probability, only a few of Emin's officers and troops would be leaving Equatoria with him. Emin could no longer delude himself or anyone else. He acknowledged as much when he asked the assembled officers whether, in Stanley's words, they could in "conscience acquit [Emin] of having abandoned his people" if they had not arrived by April 10. They all quickly assured him that they could.

The *shauri* charade was the first step in a rapidly escalating campaign on Stanley's part to assert his absolute authority over the upcoming march. His next step was to revisit the conspiracy theories he had voiced shortly after reaching Kavalli's. On March 31, he reported that he was visited by one of Emin's officers, Osman Latif Effendi, whom he labeled "the Lieut.-Governor of the Equatorial Province," even though no such position existed in Emin's chain of command. Osman Latif told him that Fadl-el-Mulla, the leader of the rebellion, along with his clerk, were not just rebels; they were out-and-out Mahdists. "They hoped to get great honour from the Khalifa for delivering the Pasha up to them. They have had an idea of getting you to visit them, and by sweet words and promising everything, to catch you and send you to Khartoum. If Fadl-el-Mulla Bey comes here with his party, all I can say is that you must be very careful." It was a variant on the plot Stanley had already imagined, now (allegedly) corroborated by an insider.

The day after Osman Latif's disclosure, Stanley dispatched Stairs with sixty riflemen and one hundred carriers, the latter mostly assembled from local tribes, to set up an advance camp at Mazamboni's. They took 140 loads with them. Stanley called it the "first move homeward," and it was clearly meant as a signal to everyone that the march to Zanzibar would be leaving as scheduled.*

Stanley's next step was to relocate his suspicion of a conspiracy from the rebels at Wadelai to Emin's own officers inside the camp. He cited one of his servants as his principal source of intelligence: "Sali, my boy, is the cleverest spy in the camp. How he obtains his information I do not know. But he appears to know a great deal more than Osman Latif or Hawash Effendi, or any of the young Egyptians. He is in the counsels of the captains. . . . Of course he has many subordinate informers to assist." What Sali told Stanley was that someone was trying to steal the Zanzibaris' rifles. Luckily, according to Stanley,

on each occasion the attempt was thwarted by the prompt wakefulness of the people. I was glad to hear that at last the Zanzibaris had learned the importance of securing their rifles close by them at night. There is

---

*For some reason, before Stairs left, Stanley had all of his officers weighed. Not surprisingly, all weighed less than they had when the expedition reached Banana Point, more than two years earlier. Stanley was down from 168 to 145, Jephson from 168 to 150, the endlessly convalescent Nelson from 176 to 146. Then there was Parke. Somehow, the good doctor had not only managed to maintain himself; he had actually fattened up from 162 to 170. Stanley listed Emin Pasha at 130 pounds.

a general feeling in the camp that something is about to happen. The whispering circles observed each day, the care they [the presumed conspirators] take that no outsiders approach too near them, the discovery that the Pasha's servants had actually informed the Pasha plainly that they would not accompany him, the huge packets of letters that were despatched by the Egyptians to the ever-dilatory Egyptians at Wadelai, the heavy mails that came from Wadelai in return, the insidious warnings of others not to trust in the Egyptians, coupled with . . . these bold attempts to steal a few more rifles, all conspired to prove conclusively that between this date [April 5] and the 10th of April some daring scheme is about to be tried.

How a few alleged attempts to steal rifles constituted a full-blown conspiracy within his own camp, Stanley did not feel the need to explain. Nor did he feel the need for greater specificity other than "a general feeling in camp" that "some daring scheme" was afoot. As far as he was concerned, the time for action had come. He went to see the pasha.

There are three accounts of what happened next: one from Stanley; one from Casati, who was only reporting what Emin had told him; and one from Parke, who was also only a reporter, not a witness. No matter whose account is the most accurate, what emerges is the story of a performance, whether calculated or spontaneous, that ended any and all questions of authority for the duration of the expedition.

In Stanley's version, presented in *In Darkest Africa*, his objective was to enlist Emin in a preemptive strategy to foil the "conspiracy" and avoid bloodshed. To this end, he told Emin,

"There was an attempt made last night to appropriate our arms. Three separate times they entered the Zanzibari huts and tried to abstract the rifles; but . . . the Zanzibaris . . . were wakened, and the intending thieves decamped. While you have been engaged with your collections and studies, I have been observing.

"They have yet five nights before our departure on the 10th inst. The attempt to rob us of our arms of defence failed last night. They will try again. . . . Of course, if they succeed in appropriating even one rifle, the punishment will be summary. . . . [T]his is what I wish to avoid. I should be loth to shed their blood, and create scenes of violence, when a better way of safeguarding our arms and ammunition, and effecting a quiet and peaceable departure from here, can be found.

"I propose to you one of two things. Sound the signal to muster all the Arabs and Soudanese with you, and then find out gently who is willing to leave with you. Those who are not willing, I shall order to leave the camp. If they do not obey, then it will be for me to employ compulsion. But as these people despise our Zanzibaris, they may very probably attempt resistance. Well, in a land where there is no appeal but to our fire-arms, it will certainly end violently, and we shall both regret it afterwards.

"The other proposal is much more effective and more bloodless. Do you order your baggage to be packed up quietly, and at dawn my people shall all be ready to escort you to a camp about three miles from here. From that camp we shall issue a request that those who intend following you shall come in and be welcome, but no other person shall approach without permission on pain of death."

"Hum! May I inform Casati of this?" demanded the Pasha.

"No, sir, Casati is in no danger; they will not hurt him, because he is not their governor or officer.* He is only a traveller. He can come the next day, or whenever he is inclined. If he is detained, I will attack the rebel camp and rescue Casati quickly enough."

The Pasha, while I spoke, shook his head in that melancholy, resigned manner peculiar to him, which has always seemed to me to betray pitiable irresolution.

"You do not like either plan, Pasha, I see. Will you, then, suggest some plan by which I can avoid coming into conflict with these wretched, misguided people, for as certain as daylight, it is impending? In my camp indiscipline and unruliness shall not prevail."

The Pasha, after a while, replied, "Your plan is not bad, but there is not sufficient time."

"Why, Pasha, you have told me you have been packing up for the last fifteen days. Do you mean to say that between now and to-morrow morning you cannot finish packing your baggage? In thirty minutes our Expedition can start. If you cannot be awakened to the danger of bloodshed, and you will not accept my plan, or suggest anything that

---

*Stanley suspected, not without justification, that Casati wielded undue influence over Emin, and that the Italian was urging Emin to stall for more time at Kavalli's so that Selim Bey, Shukri Aga, et al. could join them.

will relieve us of the necessity of destroying one another, I must at once take measures for the general safety; and should a single drop of blood be spilled, it must be upon your head that the guilt of it will lie. Adieu."

In Casati's account, Stanley was confrontational to the point of being abusive:

"Do not let us evade the question, Pasha; that is not my habit. I have two proposals to make to you; it is for you to choose, and that without delay. To-morrow morning I mean to make the round of my Zanzibaris and to tell them of our immediate departure. In case of any resistance or attempt at refusal, I am prepared to use force, and then start with you and the few who remain faithful to you. Should these strong measures not suit you, then I propose that you should start with a trustworthy escort at once, unknown to every one; I would soon rejoin you. Chose, Pasha; decide"

"I cannot accede to your proposals. The first I will not discuss; as for the second, you will understand that I cannot abandon Casati, Vita, and Marco."

"Do not think of them. . . . I shall come and take them (by force if necessary) from the hands of the Egyptians."

"But I do not think there will be any necessity for employing such means. We shall depart on the 10th."

Stanley's anger rose to its highest pitch. He stamped his foot upon the ground and said in a convulsed voice:

". . . ! I leave you to God, and the blood which will now flow must fall upon your own head."

He rushed out and whistled the signal of alarm, and entered his tent, leaving it again almost immediately, gun in hand and his cartridge pouch on his belt. . . .

I went to see the Pasha; he was pale with rage and indignation.

"We are going," said he to me with a trembling voice. "To-day, for the first time in my life, I have been covered with insults. Stanley has passed every limit of courtesy, but I have promised not to speak, so can say no more."

When Stanley left Emin's tent, he immediately sounded the alarm for a general muster at arms—all expedition hands to the camp square on the double with their weapons. The companies fell in promptly, lining three sides of the square. Stanley then told Emin to summon his own troops.

"We waited ten minutes in silence," wrote Stanley. "Then, perceiving that not much attention was paid to the signal, I requested Mr. Jephson to take No. 1 company, arm the men with clubs and sticks, and drive every Arab, Egyptian, and Soudanese into the square, without regard to rank, to search every house, and drag out every male found within."

The Zanzibaris set to their task with special zeal, unleasing all the pent-up resentment that two months of harsh labor and ill-treatment by the Egyptians had engendered. They laid into the Egyptian, Arab, and Sudanese tents, flailing furiously as they literally drove their occupants to the square like so many cattle.

Emin's men were sufficiently intimidated that, according to Stanley, "for the first time the Egyptians and Soudanese formed a decent line." Stanley again took center stage. In Casati's account, he raged at Emin's men,

> "If you have the courage, point your guns at my breast. I am here alone and unarmed."
>
> Blind fury made him forget that he held a Winchester rifle in his hand, and that there was wall of about a hundred armed Zanzibaris behind him.
>
> "My orders alone are to be obeyed here, and whoever resists I will kill him with this gun, and trample him under my feet. Whoever intends to start and follow me, let him pass to this side."
>
> In a moment everyone moved, and all was changed; the terrible conspirators became as quiet as lambs. The reputed chiefs of the opposition, being called in Stanley's presence, were ordered to be disarmed and cast into prison.
>
> "Will you start with me?" he said.
>
> "Yes," they all answered.
>
> "Will you obey my orders implicitly?"
>
> "Yes, we promise," they hastened to say, simultaneously.
>
> "I will conduct you to safety and will supply your needs during the journey. You have my promise; but I warn you that, as sure as my name

is Stanley, I shall not tolerate any renewal of the disturbances of Dufilé or Wadelai. Bear in mind that the departure is irrevocably fixed for the 10th."

Stanley's account, which was recalled in almost second-by-second detail, dripped with saracasm, much of it directed toward Emin. ("Why, Pasha, you have been misinformed, surely? These people vow they are all faithful. There is not a traitor here.") It ends with an openly dismissive view of Emin's decline: "After a patient and scrupulous analysis of the why and wherefore of these events, the result is manifest, and we see the utter unfitness of the scientific student and the man of unsuspecting heart to oppose these fawning, crafty rogues, who have made fraud and perfidy their profession."

It was left to Parke to render what was, no doubt, the most accurate characterization of the day's events:

> Looking at the performance as an uninterested observer, I should say that it was a most pitiful display of vacillation, and want of determination and initiative action on the part of the Pasha; while the violent display of temper assumed by Mr. Stanley, which would have been very unbecoming indeed among respectable or reasonable people, had become absolutely necessary, in order to make these wretches seriously think, and decide what they were going to do. The whole demonstration may be described as an effective dramatically arranged farce. . . .

What the rebels had started at Dufilé, Stanley finished that April morning at Kavalli's. In as public and humiliating a manner as possible, he stripped the pasha of the last shred of his authority, forcing the entire camp to witness and acknowledge his emasculation of a man he had clearly come to despise. Brutal, efficient, and summoned from the depths of his seemingly inexhaustible well of rage and distrust, the entire performance was vintage Stanley. Just as he had ordained, five days later, on April 10, 1889, the Emin Pasha Relief Expedition, under the sole command of Henry Morton Stanely, began its journey home.

Chapter Sixteen

THE LONG MARCH

THE DAY AFTER Stanley's humiliation of Emin, he ordered a census taken of Emin's followers to determine how many people and loads would be traveling. For Jephson, there was more than a whiff of déjà vu; he remembered that pathetic flight with Emin from Wadelai in December when hundreds of desperate, terrified people, utterly unprepared for the trail, tried to drag their households with them as they were forced, in effect, to leave their lives behind. He anticipated more of the same: "There will be some awful scenes on the way, just as there were in our flight from Wadelai, only that this will be such a long journey that the women & children will fall like flies on the road."

The count came to approximately 570 people (Jephson, Parke, and Stanley all gave slightly different figures). Some 380 of them were women and children and 190 men. For its part, the expedition had 230 of its original members, augmented by 130 Manyuemas. In addition, some 500 natives from Kavalli's and the surrounding territory had been pressed into service ("enslaved" might be a better word) as carriers, plus the assorted camp followers who always seemed to attach themselves to the expedition. Altogether, the caravan would number just over 1,500 souls.

As their departure date neared, the Africans, as was their custom, began to celebrate with dances and other festivities. Parke provided this singularly Victorian description of one performance staged for Stanley's benefit:

> Yesterday about twenty of the Wahuma women collected from the neighbouring districts, and danced in front of Mr. Stanley's tent. This was a great compliment to our chief. . . . The performance was somewhat like the *nautch*,* with a peculiar and characteristic voluptuous wriggle of the buttocks. The great object to be attained in the movement was to be able to shake the green banana leaves which each had stuck in her belt, "fore and aft." One branch was adjusted posteriorly in the gluteal fissure; another (smaller) one hung down in the median plane of the body in front. In the saltatory movements, these decorative appendages are shaken: both antero-posteriorly, and from side to side.

Various athletic competitions were also held prior to departure, and Parke wrote, "It is a fact worth noting, that the white man (Jephson) could run away from any of his black competitors." This would explain Jephson's African nickname, Boubarika—the cheetah.

Much to the Englishmen's surprise, the caravan's launch was virtually problem free. The line, including several hundred head of livestock, stretched out over three miles (Parke later complained that the cattle "are not good travelers"). As was the custom on such auspicious occasions, bugles were blown, flags were flown, and a festive air prevailed. Jephson's diary entry: "Raschid my head chief said it was like the story of the flight from Egypt under Moschi (Moses) as they read in the Khoran. Children, donkeys, goats, women, Zanzibaris, Egyp-

---

*According to the *Oxford English Dictionary*, the nautch is an East Indian exhibition of dancing, performed by professional dancing girls.

tians, Circassians, Greeks, Jews & Nubians all mixed up together formed a regular motley crowd."

Their route actually began with a bit of a backtrack, heading to the west before turning south to skirt the Ruwenzori Mountains.* On the first night, they camped in the open fields near a native village called M'pinga's, after the local chief. Parke noted wryly, "We formed two separate camps, adjoining each other: the 'Relief Expedition' in one, and the 'Relieved' in the other." Both camps were buffeted by a nasty rainstorm, which blew down several of the officers' tents. Many of Emin's people were either too lazy or simply unable to build their own shelters, so they spent a miserable night in the elements. Predictably, the morning revealed the caravan's first desertions, and the ensuing day saw the discarding of several loads that Emin's people had initially insisted on bringing from Kavalli's. The second day's march brought them to Mazamboni's, where Stairs, Hawash, and an additional 140 carriers were waiting. That night, Stanley fell ill.

"Sub-acute gastritis," the inflammation of the stomach that had nearly killed Stanley at Fort Bodo, was Parke's rueful diagnosis. In great pain, and under the influence of morphine, Stanley wrote in his diary that he feared the delay caused by his condition might give some of Emin's straggling officers, including, perhaps, a few of the rebels from Wadelai, a chance to catch up with the caravan.

Sure enough, Shukri Aga showed up the very next day, but he had only two soldiers and three women with him. Parke noted that Shukri Aga and his troops at M'swa had been thought to be the most loyal of Emin's garrisons, yet in the final reckoning only five of them had actually chosen to follow their leader. Shukri Aga reported that the situation at Wadelai was as chaotic as ever, with the officers drinking and squabbling all day and the soldiers firing their weapons randomly in the air, wasting their dwindling supply of ammunition. It seemed doubtful that any of them would be joining the expedition soon, if ever.

Stanley got worse, then better, then worse, necessitating round-the-

---

*The route also took them within sight of the Ituri forest, prompting Stairs to write, "It reminds one of a great big devil with outstretched claws, ever on the watch to catch passersby and draw them into its fathomless bosom, never afterwards to be heard of by man."

clock vigils and constant treatment by the ever conscientious Parke, assisted by Emin. Stanley never acknowledged Emin's participation, but Parke was most appreciative. "The Pasha has been very kind, and comes over regularly every day to see us. . . . He is really very well up in his work as a medical man, considering what he must have forgotten during the past thirteen years of African life. I feel even his presence a great support to me. . . ." Unfortunately, even with Emin's support, the lack of sleep got to Parke, and by the end of the first week he went down with a debilitating fever. Jephson, too, went down with fever, and Nelson with bronchitis, leaving Emin (and Bonny) trying to take care of all of them. Stairs busied himself by leading raiding parties on nearby villages to bring in more food and carriers. Stanley's justification for the raids was that they were directed only at those tribes that had refused to join with Mazamboni and most of the other chiefs in the area in making peace with the expedition, and had, in fact, continued to harass them with periodic attacks. Ergo, they had to be punished. The truth was that the raids were nothing more or less than slave taking and food appropriation.

The raids actually marked only a variation on the tactics the expedition had used at various times throughout its trek across the continent. In the forest and elsewhere, it had routinely captured natives, either to be ransomed for food, to get information, or simply to be used as guides for a few days. But the practice had always been used to meet immediate needs, not to impress people into long-term involuntary servitude. And their captives had not, for the most part, been ill-treated. As Jephson put it, "When we were by ourselves . . . such few natives as the Zanzibaris caught were kindly treated & looked after & soon became content to follow the caravan without any restraint being put upon them."

The presence of Emin's Egyptians and Sudanese changed all that. They were accustomed to having servants and slaves; it was a way of life for them. Therefore, when the English officers returned from a raid with a catch of natives, often including as many women and children as men, the Egyptians and Sudanese not only expected to share in the human bounty but proceeded to treat their new possessions as they treated their other slaves, which meant any way they wanted to. The situation became ugly very quickly. Jephson noted on April 20,

"This morning Stanley told us to count over the slaves, . . . whom our people had caught & hand half of them over to the Pasha to give to his people. This Stairs & I did & handed him over 20. We brought them over to the Pasha's house, upon my word it was a most shameful scene & was as bad every bit as the open slave markets that existed in the East. . . ."*

A few days later, another entry in Jephson's diary was more explicit:

> Today we heard a gun fired in camp & on Stairs' running out to find what it was he found that one of Osman Effendi Latif's servants—one of these brutal Nubians—had just shot one of the slaves we had caught in one of these raids, through the head, he was one out of three slaves we had handed over to him for helping him to carry his loads, & the servant had shot him because he had not instantly done what he was told—perhaps the poor fellow did not understand. The other two slaves were tied to him with raw cowhide & were trembling & shaking with fear. Osman Effendi himself was quietly eating his dinner apparently undisturbed by the sight of the bloody remains of the unfortunate slave, (his head was split to pieces & his brains splashed over the other two slaves) lying within two yards of him. . . . The scenes in camp now, the constant brutal illtreatment of the slaves by the Pasha's people, is getting beyond anything, & is enough to bring the judgement of destruction & utter annihilation on the expedition.

Jephson held Emin at least partially responsible:

> Now that Emin Pasha, who has been represented as one of the champions of Anti Slavery, who is supposed to have kept slavery far from him & his people, has come into our camp, scenes of the most disgraceful cruelty, constant beatings, constant shrieking of women and constant desertions are a daily occurrence, while ones heart gets sick & a strong indignation rises in one when one thinks how the sympathies of Europe have been tricked & played with. . . .†

---

*The Egyptians were soon engaging in their own slave raids; Jephson estimated at one point that they had captured more than 150 people.

†Later, after the abuse by the Egyptians had continued and even worsened, Jephson wrote, "And it is we, Stairs and I, who have in a wickedly weak manner carried out the orders given us & captured these unfortunates, why did we not stand up before we did & say 'we will not do this foul wrong,' it is a thing I shall always feel remorse for."

That Stanley had become ill so early in the march meant that the caravan was halted after only a few days' march from Kavalli's, and a few days' more from the lake. Not surprisingly, as the forced halt dragged into a second and third week, desertions from Emin's camp became rampant. One might have suspected that Stanley wouldn't have been all that upset to see the numbers in Emin's camp dwindle, but it wasn't that simple. The deserters took food, weapons, ammunition, and other supplies with them, and these were disappearing at such a rapid rate that the continuing safety and even viability of the expedition were potentially threatened. The desertions had to be stopped or at least slowed, which meant parties had to be sent out to find those who had fled and bring them to heel.

It was Shukri Aga who requested thirty Zanzibaris from Stanley and led a search that retraced their route since their departure. After a five-day roundup that took him as far back as the lake, he returned with more than a dozen people in tow, including an African named Rehan, who was considered the ringleader. Rehan was of particular interest to Stanley because he had been with him on the trip to retrieve the rear column (in fact, he had been "loaned" to Stanley by Emin). It turned out that Rehan was inciting potential deserters by telling them horror stories about the rear guard trek, with its hellish pace and lack of food, and the death camp scenes they had found at Banalya.

As soon as Shukri Aga returned him to camp, a tribunal was convened, consisting of Parke, Nelson, Stairs, and Jephson. They took about two hours to find Rehan guilty of inciting others to desert, as well as stealing a gun that belonged to the expedition. Stanley, who had to climb out of his sickbed, took about ten minutes to hang him.* He left the body swinging in the wind for the rest of the day and through the night as a warning to anyone else who was thinking about leaving.

Finally, after almost a month, Stanley was sufficiently recovered for the trail, though he had to be carried in a sling chair fashioned by Jephson out of cowhide and bamboo. The day after the march resumed, a small party of Selim Bey's men caught up with the caravan,

---

*Since the first rope broke, the execution may have taken more than ten minutes.

bringing with them a letter from their leader. He and his followers had finally made their way to M'swa, and the letter implored Stanley to wait for them. In his book, Stanley wrote that he politely replied to Selim's entreaty, telling him that he would wait for him for a few days at the northern end of the Ruwenzori Mountains, and that if he applied himself earnestly, he and his people could catch up. Jephson's diary told a different, and probably more accurate, story: "He answered that they had had more than a year now to get ready, they had refused his help, had ruined the country, imprisoned & deposed their governor, had ill treated his officer whom he had sent to help them, they had disobeyed orders . . . they had behaved like savages & madmen & now he would not give them a cartridge or wait an hour for them..."

Stanley and his officers had plainly had it with the Egyptians; they were tired of their scheming, their lies, their obsequiousness, laziness, and arrogance. Even the endlessly tolerant Parke had written of Emin's officers, "Some of them can be impartially described as licentious, indolent, over-fed, bloated, congested masses of human flesh. I never saw a more loathsome set of wretches in my life. . . ." After Selim Bey's men had been sent back to their leader, Jephson made a prediction about their fate and that of the other Egyptians still in Equatoria: "They will never move, but will just stay where they are till the ammunition is exhausted, the soldiers will then desert to their own countries & the officers, clerks, etc., will be killed by the natives, the same story will apply to Fadl el Mulla & his party; they could not have a better punishment than being left to themselves." None of his fellow officers would have disagreed with him.

The route Stanley had chosen took the caravan into territory never before seen by Europeans and led, some would later argue, to the only achievements of lasting significance the expedition could claim. In the course of the next month, they marched the length of the Ruwenzori Mountains, the fabled Mountains of the Moon. Though Parke and Jephson had first glimpsed their summits, only to have Stanley take credit for their discovery, it was Stairs who attempted to climb to one of the snow-clad peaks, reaching an altitude of almost twelve thousand feet before fog and freezing temperatures forced him to turn back. He managed to gather almost forty different plant specimens, at least two of which he believed were "new to science." He presented them for study and classification to a delighted Emin Pasha.*

Stanley and company were also the first Europeans to cross the Semliki River, the significance of which was that it connected Lake Albert and a smaller lake, also never before seen by Europeans, which Stanley dubbed Lake Albert Edward (later shortened to Lake Edward). To the south of Lake Albert Edward was a still-smaller lake that Stanley named Lake George. The two lakes were joined by a stream that he called the Kazinga Channel. Collectively, these newly discovered water sources filled in the last pieces of the puzzle that had animated African exploration for centuries and been a virtual obsession in Britain throughout the nineteenth century—the search for the sources of the Nile. The expedition's discoveries established that the Nile's origins began farther south than previously understood—that the drainage of the Ruwenzoris, via the two new lakes and their connecting channel, was an important source of the mighty river. The quest that had brought the likes of Burton, Grant, Speke, Baker, and Livingstone to Africa was finally finished.

The irony was that the Emin Pasha Relief Expedition was not a geographical expedition. Even the traverses of the Ituri forest had been a matter of expedience (so Stanley thought), not exploration. Unlike so many other expeditions of the preceding half century, including Stanley's first trip down the Congo, geographical discovery wasn't the primary, or even secondary, agenda of the search for Emin Pasha.

Stanley being Stanley, when the Nile-related discoveries were made, he couldn't simply say, "I (not we) found it"; he also had to say, in effect, "Everyone else missed it," including Emin Pasha. In *In Darkest Africa*, Stanley took the opportunity to pronounce himself "staggered" by the fact the Emin had never even bothered to visit the southern shore of Lake Albert during his tenure in Equatoria, which meant, of course, that he had failed to find the Semliki, the Ruwen-

---

*Emin named the two new specimens *Disa stairsii (Orchidaccae)* and *Viola eminii (Violaccae)*—Stairs's orchid and Emin's violet.

zoris, the lakes, and so on. "He had never visited the southern end of the Lake, examined the affluent at the south side, sounded the Lake from north to south and east to west; never visited the Ituri River, which was only two days' good marching from Mswa. Had he done so he would probably have seen the snowy range and left very little for us to discover in that district."

In fact, Emin had visited the southern shore of Lake Albert—several times—and he knew that a river of some consequence flowed into it from the Ruwenzoris, which he called the Usongoros. He also knew the native names by which the river was called, Kabiki and Duéru. He mentioned all this in a letter to his friend Robert Felkin in 1886. But evidently he said nothing about any of this to Stanley, a man who had never been reticent about taking credit for his achievements, whether or not they were actually his.

As the expedition moved deeper into new territory, it became increasingly clear that Emin Pasha saw himself as no more than a passenger in Stanley's caravan. Since his melodramatic humiliation at Kavalli's, he had made very few attempts to assert any sort of real authority, or even to take responsibility for his people. On the march, his attention seemed to be focused primarily on his daughter, Farida, who was carried in a hammock, with Emin riding immediately behind her on a donkey. Whenever the caravan halted, he busied himself with collecting, delighted with the opportunity to study the flora and fauna of territories that were new to him. While he continued to have some interaction with the expedition's officers, he seemed to have less and less with his own. And his relationships with Casati and Vita Hassan had apparently deteriorated almost as badly as his relationship with Stanley. Defeated and undoubtedly depressed, he withdrew into the haven of his beloved birds and beetles, virtually disappearing in plain sight.

IN *IN DARKEST AFRICA*, Stanley's account of the trek from Kavalli's to the coast is, to a remarkable degree, a pure travelogue.* He concerned

---

*Adam Hochschild, author of *King Leopold's Ghost*, has called Stanley "the most successful travel writer of modern times."

himself with geography, geology, topography, ethnography, anthropology, history (supplying an entire chapter on the evolution of knowledge about the sources of the Nile, including a dozen historical maps), botany, and zoology. He gave a name to everything, sometimes to the point that it seemed he had to be making them up: "Those semi-Ethiopic people who were known to us at Kavalli, as the Wahuma, Waima, Wawitu, Wachwezi, were now called Waiyana, Wanyavingi, Wasongora, and Wanyankori." Who was there to contradict him?

At times, his descriptions of the caravan's progress made it sound almost like a safari, with friendly natives doing their utmost to ease their way: "From the Albert Nyanza to this first important district in Ihangiro, nearly 600 miles, the Expedition had been supplied gratuitously and abundantly."

He also indulged in several long digressions, including a chapter disingenuously titled "Emin Pasha—A Study." It was, in fact, a highly slanted review of Emin's character and of his career in Africa; here Stanley took the opportunity to deliver several windy pronouncements on Emin's successes and failures. He even managed a slightly snide commentary on the sainted Gordon:

> The story of Gordon's trouble in the Soudan has never been written, and it never will be. Gordon is a name that English people do not care to examine and define too closely. Otherwise, I should like to know why there were so few English officers with him. I should be curious to discover why such as had an opportunity of working with him did not care to protract their stay in the Soudan.

He answered his own inquiry in a way that suggested that he saw himself, at the minimum, as the great Gordon's peer:

> I am inclined to believe by my own troubles on the Congo that his must have been great—perhaps greater; that not one of the least of his troubles must have been the difficulty of finding good, fit, serviceable, and willing men. In Emin Pasha he meets with a man who, though a German and a doctor of medicine,* is industrious, civil, ready, and obliging. Had I met Emin on the Congo, those qualities would have

---

*Traits Stanley evidently considered liabilities rather than assets!

endeared him to me, as they must have been appreciated by Gordon. . . . Out of three hundred officers on the Congo, I can only count ten who possessed them. . . .

Stanley's chapter on Emin, though predictably self-serving, ultimately made it clear that he didn't despise or even dislike him, even if he didn't begin to understand him. Rather, he found much in Emin that he admired. He did not admire, however, what he saw as Emin's vanity and gullibility. Here Stanley was at pains to make himself understood:

> Even the crafty Egyptians had become penetrated with a high sense of their power by the facility with which they gained pardon for offences by ostentatious and obsequious penitence. Is this too harshly worded? Then let me say in plain Anglo-Saxon, that I think his good nature was too prone to forgive, whenever his inordinate self-esteem was gratified. The cunning people knew they had but to express sorrow and grief to make him relent, and to kiss his hands to cause him to forget every wrong. There was therefore too little punishing and too much forgiving.

While Stanley was making it sound as though he was breezing across eastern Africa, the rest of the expedition seemed to be having a hell of a time. To begin with, the men were constantly getting sick. At times, Parke's journal was reminiscent of the days in the Ituri when everyone appeared to be afflicted with something. The worst culprit was fever. At first, Parke pronounced himself not all that worried, because, as he put it, he had "seen every officer now here *do a day's march with a temperature over* 105°F." But the fevers didn't go away, and after less than two months on the trail, Parke had apportioned out the last of his quinine. Jephson, in particular, was in such bad shape that on more than one occasion Parke was afraid he would lose him. "Jephson . . . feels that he is losing his senses; indeed, he is bordering on delirium from excessive fever." Another diary entry: "Jephson's temperature was 102°F. this morning; in the evening it was 104°. Bonny is also in high fever to-day. Jephson will surely die if this attack is prolonged much further. . . ."

Jephson (along with Parke) was the expedition's most conscientious diarist, yet there were no entries in his journal for more than two weeks in May; he was simply too ill to write. When, at last, his fever broke, he described what he could remember: "I have been carried from camp to camp more dead than alive, ever since the 10th day after day & night after night I have been lying half senseless wasting with fever which has only just left me, for days & nights my temperature never went down below 105° & I have become a shadow of my former self & am only able to totter along with the help of a stick."

A look in the mirror proved disconcerting: "I was startled to see what a ghost I had become, my hands are mere claws, hollow eyed, with hollows in my temples & cheek bones prominent, my cheeks fallen in like a toothless old man's & my neck in the last stage of scragginess: I am a most repulsive object."

He had lost twenty pounds and, at one point, been so sick that he hadn't cared whether he recovered. "After the first horrified feeling of dying in this miserable country was over, death seemed so easy, it seemed such an easy solution to many difficulties which troubled ones mind about the future, I was neither glad nor sorry but felt perfectly content to die, I made my will, wrote a few short letters, & felt quite ready. . . ."

In addition to fevers, many suffered from foot and leg ulcers, with Emin's people being hit the hardest. As in the Ituri, the ulcers quickly became infected, so they not only caused pain but also sapped their victims' strength and ability to resist other afflictions.

Then there were constant problems finding enough potable water. For long stretches of the march, the only water that was available came from stagnant pools, ponds, and small, slow-moving rivers. Parke was convinced that much of the sickness that plagued the caravan was due to the "malarial" qualities of the water.*

*Poor water quality also contributed to widespread infestation with worms, such as the aforementioned hookworms, as well as several other species, including *Ascaris lumbricoides*, or round worms. In his medical notes, Parke mentioned that one of the porters "voided a specimen of *ascaris lumbricoïdes*, about a foot in length, of a pinkish color." Another species common to central Africa, *Drancunculus medinensis*, the Guinea worm, can grow to a length of four feet or more inside the body.

During one of these bad stretches, all in the expedition rejoiced when they came upon a series of hot springs, halting for several days to indulge in the healing warmth of the gurgling pools, which were known to Stanley from previous expeditions and had evidently been frequented for centuries by native tribes from all over the region.

If the heat of the springs was a balm, the heat of the relentless sun was not, especially not for a contingent of pygmies who lived in the vicinity of Fort Bodo and had attached themselves in various capacities to the expedition. These forest dwellers were ill equipped to deal with the endless heat of the grasslands. One by one, they became sick, their skin turning the telltale dusky gray color that was a sign of systemic deterioration, their customary energy and good humor deserting them. (Ironically, the same change in skin color had afflicted the Zanzibaris when they were *deprived* of sunlight in the Ituri forest.)

One of the pygmies was a young woman whose freedom Major Parke had purchased from Kilonga-longa in June of 1888 "for a handful of beans, twelve cups of rice, and six cups of corn." Originally, he had planned to train her to be his valet but she had proved to be much more valuable than that. He wrote,

> I have to thank her for the comparatively good health which I enjoyed in the forest, especially during the starvation period; when she collected for me the roots, leaves, fungi, insects, &c., &c., which were good to eat, and which were, of course, known only to the natives. I might have starved, or might have been poisoned, had it not been for her ministering care.* She was always devoted and faithful to me, and, unlike some other ladies of the Dark Continent, her morals were entirely above suspicion. . . . She nursed me though many and many a fever with characteristic gentleness and modesty. . . .

The woman, to whom Parke referred often in his journals, but never by name, had eventually become an invaluable assistant, preparing his meals, guarding his tent, carrying his medical kit on the trail, and, occasionally, assisting him in his medical duties.* He had become very

---

*Perhaps "her ministering care" accounted, in part, for the fact that Parke was the only officer who not only maintained but actually gained weight during the expedition.

fond of her, as had the entire caravan—even Stanley mentioned her favorably. Like the other pygmies traveling with the caravan, though, she eventually found that the heat was too much for her, and after four months on the trail, she was too weak to continue. Parke arranged to leave her with a friendly native tribe in hopes that she could regain her health and eventually return to her homeland. It was a sorrowful parting. "She is a very great loss to me indeed. . . . She was a universal favourite in the caravan, and our parting with her was a very pathetic one. . . . [H]er last act . . . was to give me the ivory bangles which she wore in the forest. . . ."

Illness was one problem; hostile natives were another. Actually, it wasn't the locals who caused problems; it was Kabba Rega's mercenary force, the Warrasura. These roving bands of marauders had been making life miserable for the tribes who occupied the territories adjacent to Unyoro, operating not unlike the Arab ivory and slave hunters in Tippu Tib's territory, terrorizing the locals with violent raids on their villages in which those who weren't killed were often taken for slaves, and everything of value, especially livestock, was stolen.

Parke supplied a succinct description of the Warrasura's evolution (or Wara-Sura, as he wrote it—each officer seemed to have his own spelling): "This name of Wara-sura was originally applied, it appears, to Kabba Rega's body-guard; as he increased in power, and became more aggressive, his guard gradually swelled to so large proportions, that he is now able to send detachments of it all over the districts of Toro, Unyampaka, Usongora, &c. &c., to attack the natives, and loot their villages."

The Warrasura never attacked the caravan in force; they never sought an all-out confrontation. Instead, they hid in the tall grass and fired sniper rounds at stragglers. Thankfully, they weren't very good shots, but on the rare occasions when they hit someone, Parke discovered that they were using all sorts of odd materials for ammunition—rocks, scraps of brass, iron, or copper—anything that would fit into the

---

*Her nursing skills were evidently compromised somewhat by certain deficiencies in personal hygiene. Parke wrote in his journal, "My little pygmy is one of the best of nurses, and would be invaluable as attendant to anyone who had no optic or olfactory organs. . . ."

barrels of their old, muzzle-loading muskets. These makeshift bullets resulted in particularly nasty wounds.

The expedition also had a few run-ins with the local tribes. When its members reached the Semliki and tried to "appropriate" some canoes from the locals to make the crossing, they were met with fierce resistance that resulted in a severe arrow wound to the faithful Saat Tato, the expedition's best hunter. They also had to settle for one canoe, which meant it took them three days to get everyone across the swift-moving river.

One of their encounters with the Warrasura actually turned out to be beneficial, both to the expedition and to a group of natives. Near Lake Albert Edward was a much smaller lake, called Katwe, a volcanic crater that was filled with salt deposits that had been the basis of a brisk trading business for the local inhabitants, but the Warrasura had driven them away and taken over the trade. When Stanley learned what had happened, he sent a force to drive out the Warrasura, burn their settlement, and restore the lake—and the trade—to the local tribes. Their gratitude was a major reason that the expedition was so well treated as it moved through the neighboring kingdoms of Ankori and Karagwe, territory where Stanley had anticipated a hostile reception.

No sooner had the Warrasura problem started to abate than they began to hear reports that their old friend Kilonga-longa had started sending slave and ivory raiders out of his home territory into the grasslands. Sure enough, they soon encountered the telltale signs of burned-out, deserted native villages.

On May 30, Stairs's company was on rearguard duty when it was attacked by a small force of Kilonga-longa's Manyuemas. Stairs's favorite camp boy was killed. Ironically, the attack turned out to be a case of mistaken identity—the Manyuemas thought Stairs's men were Warrasura. Luckily, some of the Manyuemas in his company recognized their fellow tribesmen and shouted at them to stop shooting, which they did. That evening, Kilonga-longa's men even brought presents of sheep and goats by way of apology.

The attacks by the Warrasura, and the occasional hostile tribe, were not enough to slow the caravan's progress significantly or cause major headaches, but they did create anxiety, especially among Emin's people, and they gave Surgeon Parke even more to worry about. In a rueful diary entry, he wrote, "Alas! The last leg of my last smart pair of pyjamas—which I was carefully keeping as a 'banderrah' (flag) for my company, so that we might be able to make a respectably triumphant entry into Bagamoyo—has to-day been consigned to Hari's care, as dressing for the wounded."

Still, as the summer months dragged on, the caravan was making slow yet steady progress, meandering in a southeasterly direction toward the coast, but Jephson reckoned the "Egyptians," as he called Emin's people, were slowing their pace by at least half. It was taking a month to cover the same distance the expedition would have covered in eleven or twelve days before.

When they finally came in sight of Lake Victoria, a major milestone, not only for its size but because it meant they were within striking distance of Alexander Mackay's missionary outpost, where they would have an extended rest and perhaps even get mail, Parke noted, "From this camp to Msalala, the site of Mackay's Missionary Station . . . , is but two days by boat—it is eight days distant by land; this, however, means fifteen days for our caravan, with its ornamental Egyptian tail."*

A few days earlier, Stairs had observed candidly, "From 2 July to 4 August the pasha has lost 141 of his people by desertion, death, stolen by natives, and sold to natives for food. This is a great loss in numbers, but in reality a great gain to the strength of the column." As they made their way around the southern shore of the enormous lake, Stanley put their numbers at approximately 800, little more than half the number that had left Kavalli's.

They reached Mackay's station at Usambiro (Parke was mistaken in calling it Msalala), some fifty miles south of Lake Victoria, on August 28, 1889. Thanks to his correspondence with Emin, and with friends in England and Scotland, the indefatigable Alexander Mackay had arguably had as much to do with launching the Emin Pasha Relief

---

*In a nearby diary entry, Parke noted wistfully that it was the beginning of grouse-hunting season in England.

Expedition as any man alive, yet when he and Emin shook hands in the manicured courtyard of the station, it was the first time the two men had met.

For the exhausted caravan, the three-week respite at Mackay's was a godsend. Stanley's officers had their first taste of civilization in more than two years. Stairs waxed almost rhapsodic in his description of the delights of Mackay's hospitality: "Mackay and Deakes [another missionary at the station] made us very comfortable—good food, books, chairs, papers, and English tobacco. How we did revel in these things ... there is coffee in the morning and chat, then a little work and breakfast: biscuits, coffee, sugar, pepper, good stews, etc. Why one hardly knows how to use all these things after such a long sojourn in the wilds...."

At least as welcome as the good food and amenities* was news from the outside world. Though the newspaper clippings at Mackay's were months out of date, they still contained news of Europe that was as nourishing to the Englishmen as the provisions from Zanzibar (the ones Stanley had arranged for before the expedition had started), which Mackay had been guarding for more than a year.

Remarkably, the first question these proper Victorian gentlemen asked, noted Parke, was "whether her Majesty the Queen was still alive; then H.R.H. the Prince of Wales; then the Princess of Wales. We heard of two dead Emperors of Germany; no campaigns; that the Panama Canal was still unfinished, &c. &c."

They were amused by all the speculation in the papers that their long silence had engendered. Jephson reported, "One paper says we are completely Anihilated & another sends us off with Emin Pasha to fight the Mahdi; a third sends us to found a state East of the Niger, a fourth to found a state in Masai land; a fifth marches us off to Ujiji; a sixth leaves us sticking in a morass somewhere in a forest, & so on

---

*The officers were also able to replace their tattered uniforms and restock their personal kits. Parke gleefully listed all the items he acquired in his diary, including shoes and socks, trousers, soap, stud collar, and a "pyjamas suit."

through dozen of reports, letters & leading articles all vieing with each other in the utter falseness & improbability of their conjectures."*

Mackay's most recent papers, however, had been published after Stanley's reports had reached England from Banalya about the fate of the rear column. Some of the reaction was highly critical, including that of a few commentators who wrote that Stanley could and should be held directly responsible for Barttelot's death.† It was at this point, no doubt, that Stanley began giving serious consideration to the strategy he would adopt concerning the rear column, both in his book and when he returned to England.

Unfortunately, there was very little mail at Mackay's. It seemed the dispatches containing their letters had been sent via Uganda, where they had been intercepted and destroyed by Arab traders. Only Stanley and Stairs had letters waiting for them.‡

The rest at Mackay's also gave them a chance to find out what had been going on in Africa while they had been lost in the forest. Since the expedition's departure, the rivalry between Germany and England for control of East Africa had heated up considerably. Mackinnon's charter for the IBEAC had been granted, and he had already launched several expeditions to the interior to sign agreements and treaties with local kings and chieftains, just as Stanley had done in the Congo Free State. The Germans were doing almost exactly the same thing, under the auspices of the *German* East Africa Company.

Perhaps the most startling news, however, was that Mackinnon had launched a *second* relief expedition to find Stanley. Commanded by an IBEAC agent named Frederick Jackson, the expedition had left Mombasa, traveled through Masai country, and then been thought to be somewhere north of Lake Victoria. Both Mackay and Emin found this

---

*Jephson, who had never completely shaken his fever, was on the brink of nervous exhaution when he reached Mackay's. He confessed to his diary, "When we came in here, there was a musical box playing Auld lang Syne, I couldn't listen to it & had to leave the room; to hear that tune of all others was more than I could bear."

†Stanley's handling of the rear column controversy is discussed at length in chapter 18.

‡Stairs's letters brought sad news: his father had died while traveling in France, and his sister, who lived in Burma, had lost her house in a fire. It was also at Mackay's that the expedition finally got the news of Jameson's death.

a most intriguing possibility, because of yet another development of recent months involving upheavals in Uganda.

Mackay was at Usambiro only because he had been forced to flee Uganda for his life when Muslim elements at the royal court had managed to engineer the overthrow of the young king, Mwanga, replacing him with his bother Kalema. A reign of terror against Ugandan Christians ensued; both Mackay's Protestant mission and the French Catholic mission left abruptly. Remarkably, Mwanga hadn't been killed; he was living in exile on the Sese Islands, in Lake Victoria, hoping to gather his strength for a countercoup.*

Mackay thought that if Stanley's expedition and the Jackson expedition joined forces, they could restore Mwanga to the throne in Uganda (which would mean that he could go back to his original mission). He was confident that if they helped Mwanga, he would, in turn, grant exclusive concessions in his kingdom to the IBEAC. The pièce de résistance was that Emin could then be installed as the company's permanent agent in Uganda. Everybody would win!†

Not surprisingly, Stanley was having none of it. To begin with, he was furious with Mackinnon for having sent a second expedition to relieve *him*. Second, as far as he was concerned, Emin wasn't fit to administer anything except, perhaps, a box full of stuffed birds. Installing him in Uganda would be a disaster. Third, and most important, Stanley was not about to leave his prize anywhere. After all he and his men had been through, Emin was going to only one place—Zanzibar.

On September 17, after Mackay had helped secure some additional carriers, the expedition began the last leg of its journey. Their days of trailblazing were behind them, as they would be moving along the relatively well-established trading route from Lake Victoria to Bagamoyo on the coast, and they hoped to make relatively good time. It helped that Stanley had secured fourteen pack donkeys at Mackay's, all of

---

*Stanley already knew about these developments, having been approached by Mwanga's representatives while the expedition was in Ankori. They had asked him then to help restore Mwanga to his throne, but Stanley told them he didn't have time to get embroiled in Uganda's troubles.

†Mackay's scheme was, with slight variations, a reiteration of the Kavirondo scheme Stanley had proposed to Emin when they first met at Lake Albert.

which, he said, were given to "the Pasha's followers," along with three "riding asses" for himself, Emin, and Casati. They also "recruited" additional carriers from local tribes as they marched, though it is not clear whether they used the same extreme techniques of impressment they had used when they left Mazamboni's.

The extra carriers were needed because the expedition had so many people who had to be carried. Depsite the three-week respite at Mackay's, where there was ample food and virtually no work to do, nearly a hundred people, almost all in Emin's group, were still either unable or unwilling to walk.

The layover at Mackay's caused Jephson to ruminate on the viability of the missionary effort in Africa, and he expounded on the subject at length in his diary, along with several other observations on Euro-African relations that would have done Stanley proud. For example: "One cannot but say that Missionaries do a good work in Africa, but their work is not lasting & if their backs were turned tomorrow, every-thing would relapse into the old state of things in a very short time.... It seems to me such an absurd thing for missionaries to be teaching ignorant natives the mysteries of the Holy Trinity when the poor natives do'nt even know how to count three." In another passage, he opined, "Anything more painfully ludicrous than a native dressed in European clothes & aping European manners & phrases ... is diffi-cult to imagine. Better to have a good negro than a bad European."

He also compared his writing about Africa with Stanley's, conclud-ing his best-selling commander's penchant for hyperbole was a dis-service to his readers:

> I simply see things as they are & speak of them as they are, he writes flowery descriptions of King's palaces, court pages, etc, of colonels, generals & regiments, of pomp & show, & gives people at home a most false idea. . . . I think people like Stanley who write in that absurdly exaggerated style do a great deal of harm in Africa, people who do not know their style come out expecting to find all these fine things & go away disappointed.

As the caravan headed southeast from Mackay's mission station, it wasn't long before its members began to experience an eerie repetition of the difficulties that had beset them on their first trek to Lake Albert, when Mazamboni's warriors had stalked and harassed them for several days. They had moved into the territory of the Wasukuma, a tribe that was notorious for demanding outrageous *hongo*, or tribute, from any travelers who wanted to pass through their territory. When the Wasukuma confronted the expedition, they demanded most of their livestock and trading goods. Stanley was dismissive. His wasn't a trading expedition, he said; it was a relief expedition, so the usual rules shouldn't apply. A confrontation ensued in which several Wasukuma warriors directly threatened Stanley with their spears. The Zanzibaris opened fire and all hell broke loose, with the Wasukuma scattering in all directions and the Zanzibaris in hot pursuit.

After that, the Wasukuma began following the caravan, harassing its flanks with occasional sorties, shooting arrows and firing their muskets, rarely hitting anyone, but "ready to take advantage of the least carelessness, so that one is not able to relax one's vigilance for a moment & the noise they make, shouting & blowing horns & beating drums, is very confusing, & the whole thing is fatiguing to the last degree" (Jephson). The expedition responded with punitive sallies, picking off a few of its antagonists, driving them back temporarily, only to see them return in greater numbers. Before long, Stanley estimated there were more than two thousand of them.

The caravan took to traveling with all of Emin's people concentrated into a scrum, packed as tightly as possible, surrounded by the expedition's soldiers and officers, weapons at the ready. It was a slow-moving, awkward arrangement, but it kept the natives at bay. Still, Stanley was afraid that if the Wasukuma mounted an all-out attack, the caravan could be overwhelmed.

After three days of this harassment, Stanley was convinced that a major attack was coming. In the camp that night, he posted pickets at close intervals around the perimeter. Luckily, there was a lightning storm that night, and the flashes exposed "stray natives . . . creeping towards the camp" (Jephson), and they were promptly shot. The Wasukuma kept coming all night, but the large attack Stanley feared didn't materialize.

Nevertheless, the next day, Stanley decided it was time to strike. He ordered Stairs and Jephson to take their companies on a raid to destroy the natives' villages and capture as much livestock as they could herd back to camp. "One regretted having to burn the villages because they were so pretty & fresh looking," wrote Jephson, but he also observed matter-of-factly, "Nothing seems to terrify a native so much as the sight of his villages burning. . . ."

Still, the natives kept dogging them, and the next evening, they began massing for what seemed to be an all-out attack. For the first and last time during the entire expedition, Stanley ordered the Maxim gun fired in anger. Though it killed only one man, the noise it made terrified the natives, and they fled. The Zanzibaris took off after them, "so infuriated . . . that they cut the dead man up & slung pieces of him on their guns" (Jephson).

Finally, after the pattern had persisted for two more days, the natives sent a small delegation to the expedition's camp under a sign of peace. Stanley permitted the delegates to enter, but as he began talking to them, a large native force attacked. One expedition man was killed and two wounded before Stanley's men could respond, "but then with one howl the Zanzibaris were after them & there were a great many left dead on the field, the Zanzibaris cut off all their heads & made a pile of them in camp" (Jephson).

Despite the carnage, the natives were still shadowing them the next day, but then, as suddenly as they had come, they disappeared. It seemed that the caravan had passed out of Wasukuma territory into the territory of the neighboring Usongo tribe. As luck would have it, the Usongos were friendly.

With the danger of a hostile attack apparently behind them, the realization began to dawn on the officers that their long ordeal might indeed be ending soon. One by one, their diaries began to peter out, the meticulous, near-daily entries giving way to headlines and summary statements, collapsing a week's travel into a paragraph. They were horses heading for the barn, looking neither left nor right, focused only on the remembered comforts of home.

As the officers stopped writing, a new chronicler appeared on the scene, a French missionary named Père Schynse, who, along with a colleague, Père Girault, had visited Mackay's while the expedition rested there. Like Emin, Père Girault suffered from cataracts and was considering a return to Europe to have surgery. Emin strongly urged him to do so, and the two priests decided to attach themselves to the expedition as a means of escort to the coast.

Fluent in German, Père Schynse spent considerable time with Emin, as well as with the expedition's officers. His conversations led him to make a prediction about how the expedition would be judged. "Outwardly, it was a success, of course, and it will be acclaimed in Europe accordingly; but at heart the officers of the expedition are grievously disappointed with the result and quite admit it." Evidently, Jephson spoke for all of them when he wrote in his diary,

> Look at the lives we have lost, Major Barttelot & some 450 of our own people, to speak nothing of some hundreds of Manuyema & many hundreds of natives we have killed & whose villages we have destroyed in forcing our way here. Look again at the numbers we shall lose between here & Zanzibar & the natives we shall probably kill. On the other hand what have we done in return for all this? We have Emin Pasha—not alas the Emin Pasha we all imagined him to be—& some 50 Egyptian employés with their wives, concubines, families & slaves, the off scouring & dregs of Cairo & Alexandria. Is what we have got an equivalent to what we have lost? Ten thousand times, no.

Père Schynse also reported on a conversation with Emin about the expedition's true motives. "He makes no secret whatever of the real objects of the expedition. Why should a shrewd Scottish merchant [Mackinnon] be suddenly smitten with the idea of spending enormous sums in extricating an Egyptian official whom until that moment he did not even know by name?" Emin had come to believe that the expedition had been, from the outset, a purely commercial enterprise conveniently able to cloak itself in the guise of a mission of mercy.

It seemed there were no illusions left for anyone.

ON THE LAST DAY of October, the expedition met a caravan headed in the opposite direction whose native porters greeted them with "Guten morgen" and offered cheery parodies of a German army salute. It had entered the German sphere of East Africa. The caravan leader also had a letter for Emin from Herr von Wissmann, the "Imperial German Commissioner" for East Africa, welcoming him as a "distinguished son" of Germany and telling him that Kaiser Wilhelm II himself had asked to be kept advised of his progress.

Ten days later, they reached Mpwapwa, the westernmost military outpost in German territory. There, Lieutenant Rochas Schmidt and his soldiers welcomed Emin as a returning hero. There was champagne and brandy and cigars and much toasting. Given that he had long ago ceased to think of himself as a German, and that the Germans had apparently begun to think of him at all only in the last few months, Emin might have greeted all this attention with a bit of skepticism, but he didn't. After two years of disappointment, humiliation, betrayal, and imprisonment at the hands of his own soldiers, and another year of humiliation, belittlement, and dismissal from Stanley, the Germans' attention was a balm to him. He reveled in their interest and flattery, not caring to question its motives, at least for the moment.

They remained at Mpwapwa for several days, during which dispatches were sent to Bagamoyo and Zanzibar announcing their whereabouts and (relatively) imminent arrival. In addition, Stanley and Emin both wrote numerous letters. In Emin's, repeated references began to appear to "us Germans" and "my countrymen." He also noticed, with apparent satisfaction, the effect that the Germans' attention had on Stanley and his officers. "The gentlemen of the expedition see me for the first time acknowledged by my countrymen and are now most eager to be polite."

Polite because they were nervous. Stanley was clearly worried about the threat posed to his prize by the Germans' increased presence in the region. In a conversation with Emin about what should be done with the Madi carriers he had supplied to the expedition many months before, some of whom were still with them, Stanley suggested that it would be appropriate to hand them over to the IBEAC (rather than to the German East Africa Company), since it had been an English expedition, underwritten by English funds, that had fed them for so many months, while the Germans had done nothing for Emin until the eleventh hour. Stairs picked up the thread with the opinion that when the time came to be transported from Bagamoyo to Zanzibar, they should use only English steamers, not German ones, since this was an English expedition. Emin found their chauvanism amusing, but he also made it clear that he retained the right to put his loyalty in a place of his choosing, not theirs.

As they made their way from Mpwapwa to the coast, "escorted" by Lieutenant Schmidt, the news of their impending arrival touched off a flurry of activity. Herr von Wissmann sent them European provisions —German hams, more champagne, wine, cigars, and several head of cattle. Shortly thereafter, they were met by a contingent of European (mostly German) and American travelers, including two newspaper correspondents. One of them, Edmund Vizetelly, was from Stanley's old paper, the New York *Herald*, while the other, Thomas Stevens, was from the rival New York *World*. It seemed that Stanley's former employer, the *Herald* publisher James Gordon Bennett, was as determined as ever to scoop the British press. He had offered a reward for the first news of Stanley's return to civilization. Stanley, who still considered himself (justifiably) a working journalist, was only too happy to give the scoop to his old paper. Not surprisingly, perhaps, he had already written up his own dispatch, which he now gave to Vizetelly. The *World*'s Stevens had to content himself with interviews with the other officers and with Emin. Bennett also sent along a few amenities like toothbrushes, "Florida water,"* and soap.

Finally, on December 3, the caravan was camped on a riverbank, eight miles out of Bagamoyo, when it heard an unfamiliar sound in the distance. In the last entry in his diary, Stairs described the scene:

> About eight o'clock in the evening, while the men were leaning over the camp-fires cooking their evening meal, all of a sudden came the long low "boom" of the Sultan of Zanzibar's evening gun from the island far across the sea . . . Like some long lost and forgotten chord being again heard it reminded the Zanzibaris that their homes were near. With a roar of cheering that I still can hear, the men bounded

* A popular type of toilet water.

through the camp. Again and again, the volley of cheers rang out in the still night air. The men left their fires and surrounded the tents of the officers.

"*Tumefika pwani.*" (*"We have reached the coast."*)

"*Tumefika Mwisho.*" (*"We have come to an end."*)

Chapter Seventeen

BANQUET OF SORROW

THEY HAD INDEED reached the coast, but, as it turned out, they had not come to the end. The final day of their march started off well enough. Wissmann met them at their riverside camp to join Stanley and Emin for the final steps of the journey. Stanley put Stairs in charge of the caravan, and then he and Emin were ferried across the river, where Wissmann had horses waiting for them so that they could make a properly triumphant entrance into town.

All of Bagamoyo was waiting for them, Africans and Europeans alike, waving flags and cheering the returning heroes. The streets were decorated with palm branches, a band played, and in the harbor two British and two German warships flew all of their pennants and flags in salute. Stanley later wrote, "Presently rounding a corner of the street we came in view of the battery square in front of Wissman's headquarters, and on our left, close at hand was the softly undulating

Indian Sea, one great expanse of purified blue. 'There, Pasha,' I said, 'We are at home!' "

They were immediately taken to Wissmann's headquarters, where "a sumptuous luncheon" had been prepared, though Stanley said he took the precaution of diluting his champagne with "Sauerbrunn" water, lest he overindulge. "The Pasha," he wrote, "was never gayer than on this afternoon, when surrounded by his friends and country-men he replied to their thousand eager questions. . . ."

The caravan arrived at four o'clock that afternoon, to the accompa-niment of "the glorious tune" of "God Save the Queen" (Jephson), with the "refugees" being taken to quarters that had been constructed for them along the beach. There "the carriers dropped their loads and the long train of hammocks deposited their grievous burdens of sick men and women, and poor children for the last time on the ground . . ." (Stanley).

According to Stanley, Emin lingered so long at the luncheon that he had to rush to his quarters to change for dinner. The banquet was set for seven-thirty, and, at least by Bagamoyo standards, it was a lush affair. The guest list of more than thirty included the local vice-consuls (English, German, and Italian), Wissmann's cadre, the captains of the English and German warships, Père Schynse and Père Girault, offi-cials of the Imperial British East Africa Company and its rival, the German East Africa Company, Stanley and his officers, and Emin and Casati (no mention was made of Vita Hassan).

"Dinner was a triumph," wrote Stanley, "the wines were choice and well selected, and iced." There was even music, courtesy of the band from the German warship, the *Schwalbe*. While the officers supped, the Zanzibaris were having their own party on the street below, or, as Stanley put it, these "tireless creatures were celebrating the close of a troublous period . . . with animal energy vented in active dance and hearty chorus."

By all reports, Emin was having the time of his life. Jephson wrote, "He told us how he had never again expected to see such a scene as this, surrounded as he was by people each vieing with the other to do him honour. He seemed to have grown younger, and to be trans-formed by happiness and content."

Wissmann read a personal greeting to Emin from Kaiser Wilhelm II and then presented him with a medal. The citation read, "I, Kaiser Wilhelm, Emperor of Germany, award this medal, second class of the Order of the Crown with a Star, to Dr. Eduard Schnitzer, otherwise known as Dr. Mehemet Emin Pasha, for his exceptional achievements as a scientist and gifted administrator of the Egyptian province of Equatoria, and as an outstanding son of Germany." Emin was moved to tears.

Wissmann also gave an eloquent and moving speech of his own, saluting Emin, Stanley, and his officers. When he concluded his remarks, the entire party sprang to its feet in a spontaneous ovation.

Then it was Stanley's turn. For some reason, he began his remarks by noting, "I was unaware that Emin Pasha was a German when I offered my services to carry relief to him. . . ." It was unclear whether or not the implication was that if he'd known, he wouldn't have offered. He went on with platitudes about how he and his men "had devoted ungrudgingly every fibre, and all our strength, morally and physically, to accomplish the purpose for which we set out," and that "as the world educated men to become indifferent to its praise or censure . . . the safest plan was to seek the approval of one's conscience."

Finally, it came to Emin. He spoke "in the kindest and most graceful manner" (Jephson), giving thanks to "the generous English people who had thought of him, and to his German countrymen for their kind reception of him, and to His Imperial Majesty Wilhelm II for his gracious message of welcome and congratulation" (Stanley).

After Emin's remarks, Stanley said, "an effusive gladness pervaded the company," and the pasha seemed "supremely gay and happy." The pasha made a point of speaking to each of the expedition's officers to express his thanks, pausing especially with his medical colleague, Parke.

As the party continued, Emin wandered alone into an adjacent room, perhaps to get a breath of fresh air, or simply to reflect privately on this momentous evening. No one seemed to see him leave, nor (evidently) did he tell anyone he was going. He simply left.

It was Parke who pointed out that Emin probably had not been in a two-story building for almost fourteen years and that he was effectively blind in one eye and extremely shortsighted in the other, owing to cataracts. He surmised that these two factors combined to create the disaster that happened next. Stanley opined that it happened when Emin leaned out of a window to get a closer look at the celebrating Zanzibaris below; Parke thought he simply mistook a door for a window. Whatever the case, Emin Pasha fell out of a second-story window, plummeting headfirst onto the cobblestone street some eighteen to twenty feet below (Parke's estimate). Luckily, his fall was partially broken by a sloping roof beneath the window; otherwise, said Parke, he would have been killed. The German lieutenant, Rochus Schmidt, was the first to reach the motionless body. He unceremoniously doused Emin with a bucket of water, but the pasha remained unconscious, blood trickling from both ears.

Up in the banquet room, Stanley didn't understand the news right away. When his servant, Sali, told him that "the Pasha had fallen down," Stanley thought he meant he'd "stumbled over a chair." By the time he realized what had happened and rushed to the street, all he found were "two little pools of blood." Emin had already been moved to the German hospital. He remained in a coma through the night.

At first, both Parke and the attending German physician, Dr. Brehme, thought it was "an extensive fracture of the base of the skull," a potentially fatal injury.* There were also broken ribs, severe facial bruises, and subcutaneous bleeding, including badly swollen eyes (Parke inferred that Emin had landed face first).

In the early hours of the morning, however, Emin began to come around. When he opened his eyes, his first word was "Parke," which Parke found very touching ("I was, naturally, a good deal affected by this indication of . . . my poor patient's feeling, and felt myself bound to him by a new tie of friendship"). The "poor patient" was in a great deal of pain, and bloody fluid continued to seep from his ears, but he remained conscious and began complaining, which Parke saw as good

---

*Parke would eventually change his diagnosis, deciding that Emin had suffered a concussion, but not a fracture. The Germans, however, held to the more drastic diagnosis and insisted that in such cases only 20 percent of the patients recovered.

signs. He told Stanley that, "though the accident was undoubtedly a serious one, it need not be considered dangerous . . ." (Stanley).

For the next two days, Emin continued to improve, but then he came down with bronchopneumonia and continued "dangerously ill" (Parke) for several days. He also grew very upset when he was informed that his personal cases had been opened by the Germans. "Did they think I was going do die?" he asked Parke angrily. He then requested that Parke have all of his things brought to his hospital room and stored under his bed.

Gradually, Emin began to improve, though the disturbing fluid discharge from his ears persisted. Parke remained with him throughout his ordeal, but then, just as Emin was moving out of danger, Parke became desperately sick with an attack of hematuric (malarial) fever. He was taken to the French hospital in Zanzibar, where he very nearly died. In fact, on one particularly desparate night, his doctor summoned Stanley and the other officers "to see me breathe my last," as Parke later wrote in his diary. He had only one clear memory of his illness: "I practically lived upon iced champagne; and my sense of taste was never so completely benumbed as to prevent me from appreciating it."

Ironically, Parke's illness may have changed the course of both Emin Pasha's life and the way in which the Emin Pasha Relief Expedition would come to be judged. Parke wrote,

> When I was parting with Emin Pasha, he said that he would certainly follow in the next steamer (about a week later) to Cairo; and I feel quite convinced that he then intended to do so. He was quite well able to travel; and I feel certain that if I had not sickened at the time he would have come with us then. He was anxious to have the cataracts removed from his eyes, as his left eye was almost blind; and it was arranged that I was to assist at the operation. But all that was changed. . . ."

When Parke was stricken, the Germans closed ranks around Emin. When Stanley tried to have Emin moved to Zanzibar, where he and his officers were then billeted, he was told it would be too dangerous to move the patient. Thereafter, no one from the expedition was permitted to see Emin. When some members petitioned Wissmann and Emin's doctors for a visit, they were told that he had suffered a relapse.

When Stairs was detailed to take Emin's people by steamer to Mombasa* from Zanzibar, he was given a brief audience to say good-bye to the pasha. Stairs begged him to come with his people on the trip from Mombasa to Cairo, but Emin told him, somewhat cryptically, that while he wanted to, he could not. He didn't cite medical problems or give any other explanation; he simply said he could not.

Finally, at the end of December, Jephson was permitted a visit. He stayed with Emin for an entire day and night. Like Stairs, he implored him to come to Cairo, telling him that Parke thought that if Emin went on the voyage, "he would be well before we got to Suez." As with Stairs, Emin replied sadly, "I know it, and I wish I could go with you, but I cannot."

He asked Jephson to give him all of the officers' addresses so that he could send them souvenirs "to keep as a remembrance of the days we passed through together." When the time came for Jephson to leave, Emin seemed reluctant to let him go.

> In parting he held my hand in both his, and told me how deeply grateful he was for what we had done for him. He said, "You I shall never forget, for you have been my companion and friend through those months of our imprisonment together, those months which were the worst months of my life." I once more urged him to come with us. Again he shook his head and said it was impossible, so I sadly bade him good-bye and returned to Zanzibar.

He would never see or hear from Emin again.

As for any fond farewells between Emin Pasha and the man who had "saved" him, there would be none. Stanley remained in Bagamoyo for only one more day after the accident. The following morning, before embarking for Zanzibar, he went to see Emin at the hospital.

---

*After a few days in Zanzibar, "complaints of drunkenness and rioting on the part of the refugees came to the ears of the Consul-General" (Jephson), so they were moved to Mombasa to wait for an Egyptian steamer Stanley had ordered to take them home.

For a writer so fond of drama, his description of their parting scene is striking for its utter lack of emotion and perhaps credibility:

> He was in great trouble and pain. "Well, Pasha" I said, "I hope you don't mean to admit the possibility that you are to die here, do you?" "Oh! No. I am not so bad as that," and he shook his head.
>
> "By what I have seen, Pasha, I am entirely of the same opinion. A person with a fractured head could not move his head after that manner. Good-bye. Dr. Parke will remain with you until dismissed by you, and I hope to hear good news from him daily." We shook hands and I withdrew.

That was it, except for a footnote: "The Pasha arrived in Zanzibar about the beginning of March, 1890, perfectly recovered." Since Stanley was long gone by then, and the Germans were still keeping him sequestered, it's hard to know what evidence he used to reach this conclusion, beyond his own wishful thinking. In fact, Emin never fully recovered from his injuries and spent the rest of his life in deteriorating physical and mental health.

Jephson wrote that when he and Emin said their last good-bye, he was "profoundly touched by the sadness in [Emin's] tone. His simple words of friendship and touching manner were, I am convinced, sincere. But a will stronger than his own must have compelled him to act against his better nature. . . ."

The Englishmen were certain that the Germans had turned Emin against them, using a combination of flattery and propaganda to persuade him to remain with them, and there may have been some basis for their suspicions. On the other hand, as his correspondence with friends and colleagues in Europe would make clear, Emin harbored deep and lingering resentments toward Stanley for the repeated humiliations he had caused him, and though Emin could not be called a vindictive man, it is easy to imagine him deriving more than a little satisfaction in denying the imperious Stanley the one trophy he had so desparately hoped to bring back from Africa.

With the coming of the New Year, it was time for everyone to go home. The stalwart Zanzibaris were, of course, already home. Stanley arranged for them to receive bonuses, ranging from forty to sixty

rupees per man.* An additional ten thousand rupees was to be distributed among the survivors of those who had perished on the trip.

As it turned out, some of the faithful Zanzibaris were actually slaves
who were, in effect, on loan to the expedition, so for them, returning
home meant being returned to their masters. Stanley's young officers
were appalled by this revelation and petitioned Euan-Smith, the
British consul-general in Zanzibar, to intervene, but he declined on the
grounds that "existing customs" had to be maintained (even though
the importation of slaves to Zanzibar had been outlawed for years).†

In the course of three years together, the relationship between the
officers and the Zanzibaris had undergone a wholesale transformation.
In the beginning, the officers had routinely vilified the Africans, char-
acterizing them in their diaries (and to each other) as mischievous
"niggers" who were lazy, unreliable, prone to thievery, and utterly
immoral. It didn't help that Stanley repeatedly took the word of the
Africans against theirs, but by the end of their shared ordeal, the officers had come to think of their long-suffering companions as brothers
in arms. They had grown to trust them with their very lives, to admire
them for their loyalty, stamina, and perserverance, and to regard them
not only with profound respect but with genuine affection. It was perhaps no accident that the last paragraph in Lieutenant Stairs's diary,
his final salute, as it were, was a farewell not to his fellow officers but to
the Zanzibaris:

> Goodbye boys! Each and every one of you have passed through the
> fire and proved himself true as steel. Through the forests and across
> the plains of Africa, you have stuck to us like the men you are. Over
> 5,000 miles have some of you marched step by step.... Backwards and
> forwards through that forest which seemed unending, through fevers,
> starvation, and scenes of death have you marched like Trojans. We
> white men who have served with you for three long years, who have
> fought and starved, haved marched and camped with you, now go to

*The rupee was worth a shilling, more or less, so the bonuses were between two and
three pounds per man, or ten to fifteen dollars.
†An anti-slavery treaty had been signed by Barghash, the sultan of Zanzibar, in 1873, and
was strengthened by a second treaty in 1876. See Daniel Liebowitz, *The Physician and
the Slave Trade* (New York: W. H. Freeman, 1999).

our homes far across the sea. But deep down in our hearts has sunk the remembrance of your deeds, and in the home of the white men [*sic*] who knows you, will your names be kept bright . . . never are we likely to see again such splendid fortitude during dark and trying days as had been shown by you, the Zanzibaris of the Emin Pasha Relief Expedition. "Mekwisha Temepata." (It is finished; we have won.)

The end of the expedition brought another tribute to the Zanzibaris, this one from a somewhat unexpected source—none other than Queen Victoria. In her congratulatory telegram to Stanley, she wrote, in part, "Once more I heartily congratulate all, including the survivors of the gallant Zanzibaris who displayed such devotion and fortitude during your marvellous Expedition." It was one of literally hundreds of telegrams sent to Stanley in Zanzibar (a hefty selection of which he printed as "Appendix A" of *In Darkest Africa*), including messages from virtually every European head of state (Kaiser Wilhelm took the opportunity to remind Stanley, "Your way home led you through territories placed under my flag . . ."), as well as all of Europe's major geographical societies. Henry Morton Stanley was, at that moment, arguably the greatest hero in all of Europe.

Once it became apparent that Stanley was not going to be able to pry Emin away from his German protectors, he was ready to head for Cairo to complete the final task of his mission—the delivery of the refugees. There were only 260 of them, out of almost 600 who had started from Kavalli's, a frightening but perhaps predictable outcome, given that the majority of them were women and children who were utterly unprepared for the rigors of the African bush.

Stanley also wanted to get to Cairo to begin writing his account of the expedition, which he had already decided would be called "In Darkest Africa." It was easy to forget that, for all his fame and honors, Stanley still made his living as a journalist and lecturer, and his eagerly awaited tome (tomes, actually, for the work would stretch to nearly 1,100 pages and require two volumes) would not merely add to the historical record but bring him a paycheck, something the Emin Pasha Relief Expedition had not done.

Before he departed for Egypt, however, there was a final piece of

business to attend to. Shortly after arriving in Zanzibar, Stanley
learned that an Indian merchant and banker named Jaffar Tarya, who
served as an agent for Arab and Zanzibari caravan operators, including
Tippu Tib, was holding £10,000 in gold from the Belgians for Tippu
Tib, a payment for a delivery of ivory. Stanley decided that the sum
could be better used to compensate the Emin Pasha Relief Committee
for its initial outlay of funds for the expedition, which, conveniently,
was also £10,000. Since Stanley was already planning to make Tippu
Tib a focal point of his alibi for the disaster of the rear column, it made
perfect sense to sue the Arab for breach of contract. He sought and
received an injunction from the Consular Court in Zanzibar, prevent-
ing Tippu Tib from collecting his £10,000 from Jaffa Tarya until evidence could be heard regarding Stanley's allegations. His plan, he
said, was to use the money to pay each officer a bonus of £1,000 and
each surviving Zanzibari an additional 300 rupees. It was a nifty piece
of public relations (or so Stanley thought), so with this parting shot at
his old friend turned nemesis, he departed for Cairo.*

The officers all went together, with the still-recuperating Parke carried aboard their steamer from his hospital bed. They arrived in Cairo
on January 16, 1890. With a notable lack of fanfare, the refugees were
dropped on the khedive's doorstep, most of them as unhappy to be
there as the khedive was to receive them.†

Stanley immediately set about finding a suitable location in which to
write his book (along with some four hundred letters and one hundred
telegrams.) After a few days at Shepherd's Hotel, he moved to a new,
ultraluxurious small hotel called the Villa Victoria, where he took a suite
of rooms. He summoned his editor, Edward Marston, from London,
and settled in to begin writing. After a brief initial bout of writer's block,
his productivity was nothing short of astonishing. He produced 903

---

*When Tippu Tib learned of the lawsuit, he was so outraged that he left for Zanzibar
immediately to rebut the charges. On Stanley's return to Europe, both Mackinnon and
King Leopold urged him to drop his claim, which, eventually, he did.

†Unhappy because the Sudanese were almost as far from their homes as they had been in
Equatoria; many of the Egyptians were convicted criminals who were distinctly unwel-
come in their native land; and many of their wives, children, servants, and slaves were
Equatorians who would no doubt have preferred to stay where they were in the first place.

pages of "foolscap manuscript" in only fifty days. He wrote as much as sixteen hours a day, often lying on the floor, propped up on one elbow. When Marston suggested going out for a walk or out to dinner, Stanley showed no interest. On the rare occasions when he consented, he seemed so uncomfortable that Marston eventually quit trying.

While Stanley wrote, Parke remained in Cairo recuperating, and the other officers enjoyed a life of leisure at Shepherd's Hotel. On April 7, they all boarded a ship bound for Italy. As they left the dock at Alexandria, Parke wrote, "We waved, as we moved away from land, a farewell salute to the shores of the continent, from the unexplored interior of which each one of us had, I believe, at some period of the Expedition, lost all hope of returning."

LIKE PARKE'S RECOVERY, Emin Pasha's convalescence proceeded slowly. He remained in the hospital in Bagamoyo for almost two months. Then, as he continued his recuperation, he examined his options for the future. It quickly became apparent that he was not going to be able to come to an arrangement that would allow him to remain in the service of the khedive, so, at the end of February, he resigned his commission. Not surprisingly, the Germans immediately offered him one in their army, with the rank of colonel. Also not surprisingly, Emin couldn't decide whether or not to accept it.

Part of his hesitation, aside from his well-established inability to make up his mind, had to do with the fact that he still entertained some hope of working out an arrangement with Mackinnon's Imperial British East Africa Company, thinking it might afford the most expeditious means of returning to the interior. Mackinnon indeed toyed with the idea of offering him a position, but when Stanley found out about it, he was adamantly opposed, as was Euan-Smith, the British consul-general at Zanzibar. In truth, there was no longer much to recommend Emin. He had proven to be, at best, a mediocre administrator, and since he no longer commanded a fighting force that would be useful in facilitating colonial development, the only reason to give him a job was to keep him from working for the Germans. Ultimately, it wasn't enough.

In the end, the Germans got Emin almost by default, though they wooed him as though he had many eligible suitors. The German Geographic Society had given him not one but two gold medals; his old university at Königsberg had given him an honorary degree; he had been inundated with correspondence and congratulations from old friends and new admirers in Germany; and he had been reconnected with his family, with which, aside from his sister, with whom he had corresponded periodically, he had had little contact for almost fifteen years.

Still, after accepting his German commission, Emin seemed less than thrilled. Perhaps it was simply the accumulation of so many disappointments, not to mention the mental and physical toll exacted by the stresses of the last several years in Equatoria. At forty-nine, he was already, in many ways, an old man. His eyesight was so poor that anything more than three or four inches from his face was a blur, his hearing and balance continued to be impaired since his fall, and his once remarkable energy and stamina were sadly diminished. Nevertheless, he accepted an assignment from Wissmann to lead an expedition back into the interior.

Wissmann's orders made it plain that the expedition's purpose was purely imperialistic. Emin's charge was to "secure on behalf of Germany the territories situated south of and along Lake Victoria, from Kavirondo Bay, and the countries between Lakes Victoria and Tanganyika up to Lake Edward and Lake Albert." Wissmann also left no doubt as to the expedition's secondary goal: "to frustrate England's attempts at gaining an influence in those [same] territories," so Emin, the benevolent pasha, the scientist and scholar, the khedive's faithful servant, had become Emin the kaiser's imperialist. Interestingly enough, however, the first assistant he chose for the expedition was neither a military man nor a colonialist like Carl Peters; it was a scientist. He chose Franz Stuhlmann, a German zoologist.

On April 26, 1890, in a coincidence of which neither man was aware, Henry Stanley arrived in London to a hero's welcome, and Emin Pasha left Bagamoyo to go back to central Africa. It had taken three years, tens of thousands of dollars, and the lives of several hundred, if not several thousand people, to extract him from Equatoria, but less than five months after that agonizing ordeal had ended, Mehemet Emin Pasha, now called Colonel Eduard Schnitzer, was headed right back where he had come from.

Chapter Eighteen

AFTERMATH

TO JUDGE BY THE reception accorded Stanley and his officers on their return to England, the Emin Pasha Relief Expedition was an unalloyed triumph. The tributes began as soon as they arrived, and they didn't stop for months. It quickly became apparent that the royal family was as smitten with the expedition's exploits as everyone else. As soon as he arrived in London, Stanley was summoned to give an after-dinner talk to members of the royal family at Sandringham, and shortly thereafter, he was summoned for a private audience with Queen Victoria herself, who was rumored to be considering a knighthood for him.* The royal family was also in attendance at the gala

---

*Stanley's old friend de Winton advised the queen to wait until *In Darkest Africa* was published, lest it prove too controversial, which it did. As it happened, Stanley wasn't knighted until 1899, when he was given the Grand Cross of the Bath, a somewhat lesser order. Even that, it was rumored, came only after strenuous lobbying by his wife.

reception and banquet given by the Royal Geographical Society at the Royal Albert Hall. On that occasion, after the presentation of a special gold medal honoring his achievements, Stanley spoke to an audience of more than ten thousand that included the social, political, and scientific elite of England. For a man as sensitive to slights, real and imagined, as the self-made Stanley, the tribute must have been especially sweet because, some eighteen years earlier, on his return from the Livingstone expedition, the same Royal Geographical Society had flatly disbelieved his claims, and the entire London establishment had snubbed him as a poseur. The poseur had become the most celebrated explorer in the world.

The other officers were in almost as much demand as Stanley, feted by dozens of clubs, societies, and communities, all eager to bask in their reflected glory, and offer them memberships, medals, and honorariums in exchange for a few after-dinner remarks. As May gave way to June, the pace intensified. While Stanley was accepting honorary degrees from both Oxford and Edinburgh (Cambridge and Durham would have to wait until he could accommodate them on his schedule), music hall comedians were cracking jokes like "Why did Stanley have so much trouble finding Emin Pasha? Because there's no 'm' in 'pasha.'" And the wags in *Punch* and other humor magazines took to calling Stanley the "Emin-ent explorer."

Across the ocean, Stanley's old paper, the New York *Herald*, offered a $100 prize for the best poem about the explorer. In Scotland, the legendary master of doggeral William McGonagall (Punch called him "the best Bad Verse writer of his age") was moved to pen "A Tribute to Henry M. Stanley," of which only a verse or two is needed to suggest the eloquence of the entire work:

A TRIBUTE TO HENRY M. STANLEY
by William McGonagall

Welcome, thrice welcome, to the City of Dundee
The great African explorer, Henry M. Stanley
Who went out to Africa its wild regions to explore
And traveled o'er wild and lonely deserts, fatigued and footsore

And what he and his little band suffered will never be forgot
Especially one in particular, Major Edmund Barttelot,
Alas! the brave heroic officer by a savage was shot,
The commandant of the rear column—O hard has been his lot!

Remarkably, much of this Stanley mania occurred *before* the publication of *In Darkest Africa*, which appeared in bookstores on June 28, 1890. It was an immediate sensation, selling more than 150,000 copies in England and America,* and appearing almost simultaneously in ten translations.† The book spawned its own cottage industry of other books and articles about the expedition, ranging from a memoir by an engineer who had served briefly on one of the steamers that transported the men up the Congo, to a book by Stanley's editor, Edward Marston, entitled *How Stanley Wrote "In Darkest Africa."* Several of Stanley's previous books had also been best sellers, but nothing on the list approached the success of the story of "the quest, rescue, and retreat of Emin, Governor of Equatoria," as the subtitle of *In Darkest Africa* had it.

The book's enormous success brought with it intense scrutiny. Before long, praise for Stanley and the expedition was undercut by rumblings of criticism and controversy about both the book and the expedition itself. There arose questions about the cost, which had far exceeded the originally publicized figure of £20,000. Granted, the money had come from the Egyptian government and a few wealthy individuals, but the outlay struck some as excessive. What struck many more as excessive was the loss of life. The numbers spoke for themselves (though the numbers shifted slightly depending on who was doing the reporting). It was clear, however, that Stanley had left Zanzibar with more than 700 men. Of those, barely 200 returned. Of the original 60 Sudanese soldiers, only 12 survived; of the 13 Somalis, only 1. Of Emin's people only 260, well

---

*The American rights to the book were determined in a sealed bid auction between Scribner's and Harper's, with Scribner's winning with an advance of £40,000, or $200,000, an astonishing figure for the time.

†Danish, Dutch, French, German, Hungarian, Italian, Norwegian, Portuguese, Swedish, and Spanish.

under half of those who started from Kavalli's, were delivered to
Cairo. These numbers reflected only the losses to the expedition
itself. There were also the losses inflicted *by* the expedition as it
shot, burned, and looted its way across Africa. Some likened Stanley's militaristic approach to that of a latter-day conquistador, treat-
ing the native people he encountered as so many impediments to be
brushed aside and/or exploited with whatever force was necessary.
There was no way to determine exactly how many natives had been
killed by the expedition; clearly, though, there were several hundred,
if not several thousand. Victorian sensibilities were offended by such
violence, especially when other explorers, most notably the sainted
Livingstone, had traveled in Africa for years in relative peace.

In addition, more than a few members of the powerful antislavery
lobby in England were indignant at Stanley's willingness not only to
do business with Tippu Tib, the most notorious slaver in Africa, but
to offer him an official government position, albeit in service to King
Leopold, from which to conduct his operations. There were also accusations that Stanley's route through the Ituri forest had actually blazed
new trails, down which the Arab slavers had immediately followed to
practice their heinous trade. Stanley could rebut the criticism about
Tippu Tib by citing the clause in his Congo Free State contract that
the Arab was to work actively to stamp out the slave trade in his district, but it was a thin excuse. As far as the critics were concerned,
Stanley had not merely given the fox the keys to the henhouse; he'd
taken him to the door.

Then there were the critics who were convinced, with more than a
little justification, that the whole undertaking had never been anything
but a commercial enterprise masquerading as a humanitarian mission
(Emin's conclusion). Specifically, they believed that the expedition
had been about ivory. One newspaper wondered "whether the British
public had not originally been gulled into enthusiastic support for a
'rescue' attempt that was more concerned with retrieving elephants'
tusks than a short-sighted Prussian naturalist." That every ounce of
Emin's cache had either found its way to the bottom of the Nile or into
Arab hands made the whole enterprise seem that much more
pointless.

Not least, there was the question of exactly what had been accomplished. The bottom line was that all that money and all those lives had delivered to Cairo a mere 260 refugees, many of whom were less than thrilled to be there. More important, at least from the British point of view, they had *not* delivered Emin Pasha. To the contrary, he was now a colonel in the German colonial army, leading his own expedition right back where he had come from in order to deliver his former territory into the hands of the kaiser. Equatoria was in chaos; the Mahdi (or, more accurately, his successor), was still terrorizing the Sudan, and "Gordon's last lieutenant" was now working for the wrong side. The only winners in all of this seemed to be Egypt's khedive and his prime minister, who had managed to end their country's entanglement in the Sudan's most vexing province, for a mere £14,000, a remarkable bargain, by any reckoning.

Still, all these questions and grievances paled in comparison with the controversy that erupted over the fate of the rear column. Anyone who knew Stanley at all knew that he would not accept one scintilla of blame for what had happened at Yambuya. In this regard, he did not disappoint. In his book, he identified Tippu Tib as the biggest villain in the disaster; had he been content to leave the matter there, the rear column controversy might never have gained significant traction—but he didn't. He also took aim at Emin Pasha for his failure to be at Lake Albert when the expedition got there. This failure, wrote Stanley, "cost us the life of a gallant Englishman,* and the lives of over a hundred of our brave and faithful followers." The accusation conveniently ignored the fact that Emin had had no way of knowing when the expedition would reach the lake, not to mention the fact that Stanley had arrived several months later than he thought he would. Nevertheless, blaming Emin, like blaming Tippu Tib, was relatively safe, because by the time the book came out, Stanley and others had already painted him as a vacillating ingrate and, worse, a turncoat for shifting his allegiance to Germany.

But Stanley wasn't through. He went on to target his own officers,

---

*Presumably, this referred to Barttelot. It's hard to say whether Jameson was slighted because he wasn't a military man or because he wasn't English—he was Irish.

two of whom had died in his service. Indeed, he saved some of his most self-serving and sanctimonious prose for his indictment of Barttelot, Jameson, et al. His deconstruction of the debacle at Yambuya concluded that the rear column had been "wrecked by the irresolution of its officers, neglect of their promises and indifference to their written orders."

Among their many failings, said Stanley, one of the worst was that they had wasted so much time. Referring to Barttelot's and Jameson's repeated trips to Stanley Falls to see Tippu Tib and his lieutenants, he wrote, "These . . . visits to Stanley Falls which the Major and his friends have made amount in the aggregate to 1200 English miles of marching. . . . If only these 1200 miles had been travelled between Yambuya and the Albert. . . ." In perhaps the most sanctimonious passage in the entire 900 pages of *In Darkest Africa* (and there was lots of competition), Stanley wrote,

> How I wish that I had been there for just one hour only . . . when the five officers were assembled—adrift and away, finally from all touch with civilization—to discuss what they should do, to tell them that
> *"Joy's soul lies in the doing,*
> *And the rapture of pursuing*
> *Is the prize."*
>
> To remind them that
> *"The path of duty is the way to glory."**

If he was capable of an apology, this was it.

Clearly, Stanley hadn't reckoned that dead men could fight back, but they did. As soon as the six-month moratorium expired prohibiting anyone except Stanley from publishing anything about the expedition, both the Barttelot and the Jameson families published the diaries and letters of their fallen loved ones. Both made it clear that their only reason for doing so was to defend the reputations of men who could

---

*The poetry quoted by Stanley appears to be a compilation from several sources. Line one is from Shakespeare's *Troilus and Cressida*, act I, scene 2; line two is from Longfellow, ironically an abridgment of a line that reads in full, "And the rapture of pursuing is the prize of the vanquished"; the final line is from Tennyson's *Ode on the Death of the Duke of Wellington*.

no longer defend themselves against Stanley's slanders. Walter Barttelot, the major's brother, wrote in his introductory chapter, "Not a line of this book would ever have been written, not a word of its contents would have been published if justice, even partially, had been done, or any kindness shown by the leader of the Expedition for the relief of Emin Pasha to the officers left at Yambuya. . . ."

In her editor's note, Jameson's widow, Ethel, wrote, "These letters and diaries were not originally intended for publication; but it has been thought that they may be read with interest by many, and that, having regard to the accusations recently made against the leader of the Rear Column, it is desirable that they should be published in what is practically their original form, with only such alterations as their private nature required."

In his preface to the volume, Jameson's brother, Andrew, begins with a mocking repetition of Stanley's motto for *In Darkest Africa*, which was "Let there be light." He went on to quote Shakespeare's *Othello*:

Who steals my purse, steals trash: 'tis something, nothing; . . .
But he, that filches from me my good name,
Robs me of that which not enriches him,
And makes me poor indeed.

In their books, the Barttelots and the Jamesons provided detailed rebuttals to Stanley's highly slanted version of what had gone on at Yambuya. Walter Barttelot, for example, carefully broke down what would really have been involved had his brother attempted to follow Stanley into the Ituri with only 165 able-bodied porters for 660 loads. He concluded that such an undertaking would have involved traveling a total distance of 4,200 miles to reach Lake Albert. "Supposing they march 50 miles a week backwards and forwards through the forest (a great deal more than Stanley did), [the journey] would take them eighty-four weeks, or more than a year and a half, always supposing that there were no accidents or troubles—such as desertions, starvation, or attacks by Arabs or native—and fair roads." The latter list was, of course, an accurate description of all the calamities that had befallen Stanley's advance column.

Walter Barttelot, himself an army officer, went on to mock Stanley's exhortation in *In Darkest Africa* that "the path of duty is the way to glory." "Yes, Mr. Stanley," he wrote, "but the path of folly is the way to shame." He then stated unequivocally that, had the Emin Pasha Relief Expedition been a military expedition, Stanley would have been court-martialed for his unconscionable abandonment of the men of the rear column.*

Barttelot also published a letter, written by Stanley to Barttelot's father, also named Walter. The letter, Stanley's first communication with the family after the major's death, had been sent from the Villa Victoria in Cairo, while he was writing *In Darkest Africa*, so it had been almost two years since Barttelot's murder. Mackinnon and other members of the expedition committee, by contrast, had written and visited the family as soon as Barttelot's death became known, to express their sympathies. The other officers of the expedition had also called on the family as soon as they returned to England, but from Stanley the family had heard not a word. The letter that finally arrived was stunning in its insensitivity. While there were the obligatory protestations of grief and sympathy, Stanley's primary agenda was to review what he saw as the major's numerous shortcomings, including an eight-count indictment of specific failures. The unmistakable message to the grieving family was that, in Stanley's opinion, what had happened to Major Barttelot was his own fault. Walter Barttelot the Younger fired back a 4,000-word response, rebutting Stanley's accusations in detail. He then published both letters in the Barttelots' book.

It was strong stuff, and the public ate it up. Stanley, of course, was outraged, and the gloves quickly came off. In November, as he was

---

*Walter Barttelot also took Stanley to task for appropriating credit for discoveries that not only didn't belong to him but didn't belong to the expedition. Citing Schweinfurth's book *Emin Pasha in Central Africa*, published in 1888, as well as Emin's correspondence with Robert Felkin, he wrote, "Mr. Stanley's Mountains of the Moon are Emin Pasha's already discovered Usongora Mountains, and Mr. Stanley's Semliki River is Emin Pasha's already-discovered Kakibi or Duéru River. Surely Emin should not lose the credit for his discoveries, as well as his province and his wealth, as the result of the Expedition for his relief."

about to begin a lecture tour in America,* he gave an interview to the London correspondent of his old newpaper, the New York *Herald*, much of which was reprinted in *The Times*. In it, he hinted strongly that he had withheld much damaging information about the rear column, and particularly about Barttelot, out of deference to the family's feelings, but now that his discretion had been answered by vindictiveness, he had no choice but to defend his reputation by revealing the truth.

With that, he launched into a wide-ranging series of innuendoes and charges, all of which were couched in terms of "I have been told" and "reports have come to me." In other words, it was all hearsay, but that didn't stop Stanley. To the contrary, it made his accusations, in effect, irrefutable.

> I was told that Major Barttelot's life was twice saved by Mr. Bonny, once when Major Barttelot had suddenly seized a woman and fastened his teeth in her shoulder . . . I was told that with a steel-pointed cypress staff he had run about the camp prodding his people with it . . . and hitting about him indiscriminately, all this without apparent cause. . . . I am informed that Major Barttelot told Mr. Bonny that he had recommended his brother, Mr. Walter Barttelot, to look after Lieutenant Troup on the arrival of the latter in England [after Troup had been invalided home from Yambuya], in order that Troup might not be tempted to disclose what was going on at Yambuya with the rear column. I am further told that when the deserters from the advance column reached Yambuya, and told Major Barttelot about my having been killed, he exclaimed: "Thank God! I shall be made a colonel now."

This, however, was tame stuff compared with his most volatile insinuation. Without saying so explicitly, Stanley gave the unmistakable impression that Barttelot had been having an affair with the woman whose husband shot him. The clear implication was that the

---

*The tour, during which Stanley and his party (including Jephson) traveled in a private Pullman car named "The Henry M. Stanley," netted Stanley £12,000—$60,000—in six months. The only glitch was the cancellation of several dates in Texas when it was learned that Stanley had deserted from the Army of the Confederacy.

killing might not have been a murder at all, but a case of justifiable homicide.*

The innuendo was as brilliant as it was nasty. It played perfectly into the Victorian fascination with the deliciously taboo subject of the sexual behavior of white men on the Dark Continent. Speculating about the circumstances surrounding Barttelot's death and other dark doings at Yambuya turned into a ghoulish parlor game that engendered all sorts of absurd theories: the woman wasn't Barttelot's mistress; she was actually a plant, sent by Tippu Tib deliberately to provoke the major's attack, and the shooter, Sanga, was only following orders; Tippu Tib had sent to Yambuya a bevy of "houris," who used their sexual powers to bewitch the white officers, thereby delaying the rear column for weeks, if not months; Stanley had actually conspired with Tippu Tib to sabatoge, and perhaps murder, Bartellot. After all, had not Stanley declared, "Major Barttelot had no special aptitude for anything beyond being useful in case a fight should occur. In the meantime he could exist as a member of the Expedition, and as my nominal second-in-command, until he should develop meritorious qualities." So why not get rid of him, one way or another? This theory invited an obvious question: If Stanley had such a low opinion of Barttelot, why had he taken him on in the first place, let alone placed him in charge of the majority of the relief supplies that he deemed the raison d'etre of the expedition? But then, Stanley had never been one to worry excessively about consistency.

Throughout the autumn and early winter, the Barttelot-Stanley battle raged in the press, as well as the drawing rooms, clubs, pubs, and street corners of Britain. Stanley remained the lightning rod, even while he was on his lecture tour in America. The appearance of a memoir by John Rose Troup, which was highly critical of Stanley, seemed to tilt the balance toward the anti-Stanley faction, though Troup's book was also critical of Barttelot. Then Stanley fired back from New York with a lecture that renewed many of his existing

---

*The French American explorer Paul Du Chaillu sniffed at Stanley's "revelation" about the circumstances of Barttelot's shooting. He said African men would never be so upset about such a thing, because they shared their women freely, "No black would think of killing a white man for such a trifling offence in Africa."

charges, and added some new smears directed at Troup and Herbert Ward, the man who, at Barttelot's request, had undertaken the insane mission of canoeing all the way back to the coast to send a cable to Mackinnon in London requesting further instructions.* Stanley said that Troup and Ward had been derelict in their duty *because they had not relieved Barttelot of his command.* The charge was not only outrageous on the face of it; it ignored the fact that to have done so would have left them liable to a charge of mutiny, for which the penalty would have been death by firing squad. Even for Stanley, it was a moment of surpassing absurdity.

Sensing that the tide might be turning against him, Stanley brought out the heavy artillery in the person of William Bonny, the sole white man who had survived the entire ordeal of the rear column. Ironically, Major Barttelot was the only officer who had ever had any time for Bonny, whose problems with the other officers were well documented. After the expedition, or what was left of it, had finally been reunited at Kavalli's, and Bonny had begun relating the horror stories of the rear column to the others, Jephson wrote in his diary, "The officers are not pleased with Bonny's story of events which happened in the rear guard & do not give credence to a good deal of what he relates." Jephson and the others found it particularly offensive that Bonny had appropriated their fallen comrades' personal possessions for himself. "He has stocked his outfit with numbers of things belonging to the other officers such as European provisions, boots, clothes, books, boxes & even Jameson's ammunition & collecting gun, & seems to have been the residuary legatee of all the officers. . . . Even the Zanzibaris speak about it & say he came with only two small loads & now he has eight." Jephson went on to point out that Bonny wasn't really an officer, "only a hospital sergeant," and that he was actually being paid, as though that, too, were a mark against him. Finally, he wrote,

> The thing which is so bad is that Bonny seems to take such a pleasure in telling all the most dark & disreputable stories of the officers &

---

*To his credit, Ward remained above the fray until well after the controversy died down. Then he published his own memoir, *My Life with Stanley's Rear Guard*, in which he calmly refuted all of Stanley's criticisms and innuendoes.

he has certainly done his best to blacken their character as much as possible, for even were all the stories true—which we all of us doubt—still there is no necessity to repeat them with such pleasure. . . . He is a man none of us have ever liked or trusted, for he is simply dishonest.

After the debacle at Yambuya, Bonny had done nothing during the rest of the expedition to change anyone's opinion of him. When they reached Zanzibar, he had spent his time getting drunk and picking fights, including one with Dr. Charlesworth, the physician who had taken charge of Parke's care when he was stricken with fever while tending to Emin after his fall. That dustup landed Bonny in jail. He was released only on the proviso that he never return to Zanzibar. Then, when they reached Cairo, he had insisted on being put up at expedition expense for ten days at Shepherd's Hotel, the best in Cairo, before he finally got tired of waiting and headed back to England on his own. When he left, Stanley called him "a specious rogue."

Yet now, feeling the jackals nipping closer and closer to his flanks, William Bonny was the man Stanley turned to. In a series of interviews with the London press, Bonny, who was the only remaining eyewitness from the rear column, and therefore the most credible source, portrayed Barttelot as a madman who had gone so far out of control as to become a danger to himself and others. He not only revealed himself as the source of Stanley's "I have been told" stories; he proceeded to add more of his own. For example, he said that, in a rage, Barttelot had kicked one of his camp boys to death; that he had killed a man for a minor offense by giving him three hundred lashes with a rhinoceros hide whip; that he had been killed because he was kicking and beating Sanga's wife with a club when Sanga shot him. The list went on, grisly, incredible, and, for hundreds of thousands of readers, riveting. Then Bonny delivered the coup de grâce by reviving the Jameson cannibal story.

The story had first surfaced almost two years earlier, spread by an interpreter named Assad Faran who had been at Yambuya for several months before being invalided home along with Troup. He told a lurid tale asserting that Jameson had bought a young slave girl from Tippu Tib, for the express purpose of watching her be killed and eaten by Manyuema cannibals, and that he had actually made sketches of the scene as it took place. The story had caused something of a sensation at the time it surfaced, but because there had been so little news of the expedition, which was still deep in the African interior at the time, and because Faran was such a dubious source (for one thing, he wasn't a European but an "oriental" from Assyria), the furor had quickly died down. Then, under pressure from the relief committee, Faran had actually retracted his accusations. Now Bonny revived them.

The Jameson and Barttelot families were outraged. They once again attacked Faran's credibility (he was, by this time, long absent from London) and said that reviving such a baseless and horrific accusation against a dead man merely demonstrated how desperate Stanley had become. The only problem with their righteous indignation was that the Jameson story was, at least as far as the basic facts were concerned, true.* Remarkably, it was Ethel Jameson who provided the proof. Thinking that she would be clearing her husband's name, she published the letter he had sent her describing what had happened.

It seemed that, while he was traveling to Kasongo with Tippu Tib, the Arab had been telling him stories about cannibal practices in the region. Jameson wrote,

> I told him that people at home generally believed that these were only "travellers' tales," as they are called in our country, or, in other words, lies. He then said something to an Arab called Ali, seated next to him, who turned round to me and said, "Give me a bit of cloth, and see." I sent my boy for six handkerchiefs, thinking it was a all a joke, and that they were not in earnest, but presently a man appeared, leading a young girl of about ten years old by the hand, and I then witnessed the most horribly sickening sight I am ever likely to see in my life. He plunged a knife quickly into her breast twice, and she fell on her face, turning over on her side. Three men then ran forward, and began to cut up the body of the girl; finally her head was cut off, and

---

*Ironically, Stanley was at Mackay's mission when he first heard about Assad Faran's accusation of Jameson. He immediately sent a dispatch that stated unequivocally, "The horrible statement I have seen connected with Major Barttelot and Jamieson [*sic*] . . . is simply inconceivable nonsense—a sensational canard."

not a particle remained, each man taking his piece away down to the river to wash it. The most extraordinary thing was that the girl never uttered a sound, nor struggled, until she fell. Until the last moment I could not believe that they were in earnest. I have heard many stories of this kind since I have been in this country, but never could believe them, and I never would have been such a beast as to witness this, but I could not bring myself to believe that it was anything save a ruse to get money out of me, until the last moment.

Ethel Jameson thought that when the full explanation of what had happened was presented, the public would realize that her husband should be exonerated.* She was wrong. An English gentleman had watched savages kill, dismember, and eat another human being. It was monstrous—and unforgiveable. And because of it, Stanley won the battle of the rear column.

IT WAS A Pyrrhic victory. The charges and countercharges, the innuendoes, the lurid accusations and slurs leveled at dead men, and Stanley's absolute refusal to accept even the tiniest fraction of responsibility for the disaster of the rear column sullied the reputation of the expedition in general and Stanley in particular. In the *Saturday Review*, one pundit wrote of him, "If he ever induces another English gentleman to serve under him, the Englishman's relatives will have a good case for putting him under restraint as a lunatic." And Stanley's own paper, the New York *Herald*, concluded, "Whatever else these terrible charges and countercharges may have done or left undone, they have killed African exploration as a profession." It turned out to be an accurate assessment.

Lingering over the whole sordid business, like the acrid odor of smoldering rubbish, was the perception that Stanley's true colors had

---

*Ethel and Andrew Jameson eventually went to Zanzibar, hoping to find new evidence that might put the cannibal incident in a more favorable light. Andrew traveled inland as far as Mpwapwa, the German outpost, but turned back having learned nothing new. Eventually, they met in Zanzibar with Tippu Tib, who told them that the entire story was made up and that Stanley was a liar. Perhaps it made them feel better, but it changed nothing.

finally been shown. He was, after all, no gentleman, but a refugee from the basest possible origins. In Victoria's England, with its rigid social stratification and suffocating class consciousness, Stanley, no matter what accolades had been heaped upon him, could perhaps never truly be allowed to escape the shadow of St. Asaph's workhouse. At the loftier elevations from which London's social and political elite looked down on the world, Henry Stanley was still a scruffy little Welsh bastard, and his behavior in the aftermath of the Emin Pasha Relief Expedition only confirmed it. Far as he had come, much as he had done, Henry Stanley was never able to bury John Rowlands.

EPILOGUE

STANLEY NEVER LED another expedition. In fact, though he lived another fourteen years, he returned to Africa only once more, a purely ceremonial journey to observe the opening of the Bulawayo Railway in southern Rhodesia in 1897. He then toured several provinces in South Africa, after which, in a newspaper interview, he accurately predicted the coming conflict between the English and the Dutch, though the Boer War was more than two years away.

Bula Matari spent the rest of his life in relative tranquillity, a thoroughly domesticated man, devoted to his wife and adopted son, content to retire to a country home in Surrey, fussing over renovations and puttering in his garden. He did spend one term in Parliament, though it took him two tries to get elected, and the whole idea appeared to be his wife's, not his. He wasn't particularly effective, nor did he seem to enjoy himself. He continued to write, though not with the astonishing speed and productivity of his earlier years. Tellingly, perhaps, he was unable to finish his autobiography. He continued to give occasional speeches and make abbreviated lecture tours, but for all intents and purposes, the Emin Pasha Relief Expedition was Henry Stanley's final appearance on the world stage.

Sadly, given that he was as much as twenty years older than the expedition's junior officers, he outlived all of them except one, Jephson. Jephson and Lieutenant Stairs, who was promoted to captain shortly after returning to England, had talked of returning to Africa together, but it soon became apparent that Jephson's health would not permit it. He was dogged by chronic relapsing malaria. Stairs, on the other hand, seemed to have survived the expedition with his health intact (the arrow tip still lodged in his chest notwithstanding!), and in 1891 he headed back to Africa to lead his own expedition, in the employ of King Leopold of Belgium.

The expedition went from Mombasa to Katanga, retracing some of the territory Stairs had traversed with Stanley. He did well, accomplishing his mission, which included building a fort and signing treaties with a number of powerful chieftains in Katanga, in less time than expected. On his way back to the coast, he wrote a letter to Parke to tell him that he would soon be back in England. He mentioned in passing that he had "a dose of Typhomalia. Almost died—twelve days unconscious—well again now." But he wasn't. Three weeks later, he died of a malarial fever. His body was buried at Chinde, near the mouth of the Zambezi River in what is now Mozambique.

Nelson also made his way back to Africa, where, thanks to Mackinnon's IBEAC, he was placed in charge of the Kikuyu district in the territory that eventually became Kenya. Like Stairs, his first assignment was also his last; he died of dysentery in December 1892, six months after Stairs's death.

As for Surgeon Parke, the man of infinite patience and forgiveness, he returned to the Army Medical Service. He regularly kept in touch with Jephson, and in August 1893 they were trying to find a time when they could see each other, but a month later, while weekending with friends in Scotland, Parke died of a heart attack.

Parke's death left Jephson the expedition's only surviving officer, but there were other survivors. William Bonny, Parke's assistant, who became Stanley's unlikely ally in the battle against the Barttelots and Jamesons, disappeared into obscurity, dying shortly after the turn of the century in an English workhouse, his life ruined by drugs and alcohol. William Hoffmann, Stanley's valet, who managed the dubious distinction of enduring the entire ordeal of the expedition, including all three of Stanley's traverses of the Ituri forest, without rating even a single mention in *In Darkest Africa*, also returned to Africa. He worked in various capacities in the Congo Free State* and then returned briefly to his old job when he accompanied Stanley on his trip to Rhodesia and South Africa. In Stanley's twilight years, Hoffmann was a frequent visitor to his home, though he briefly fell out of favor with Mrs. Stanley when he asked his old employer for money. Nevertheless, Stanley remembered him in his will with a bequest of £300. Hoffmann died in the 1920s—the exact date seems to be unknown. A book, *With Stanley in Africa*, a highly unreliable account of the expedition, which he clearly wrote from memory many years afterward, was published posthumously in 1938.

The final expedition survivor was the intrepid Herbert Ward, who had arguably the most distinguished post-expedition career of all. He published two books about his African adventures, including one, *My Life with Stanley's Rear Guard*, written, in part, to rebut some of the uncomplimentary (and unjustified) comments Stanley made about him during the Barttelot controversy. He went on to become a very successful artist and sculptor, focusing on African themes and subjects, which he rendered with uncommon sensitivity. He died in 1919, having served valorously in the British Ambulance Corps and with the International Red Cross.

Surprisingly, perhaps, since they had clashed with him so often in the course of their trials together and been highly critical of him in their diaries (all subsequently published), the junior officers actually seemed to become closer to Stanley in the aftermath of the expedition. For one thing, after refusing to praise them during the expedition, Stanley became almost effusive in his compliments when they got

*He served for a brief time as postmaster at Yambuya.

home, often sharing the spotlight with them, seemingly without reservation. He asked them, along with Bonny, to be groomsmen at his wedding.* In fact, he invited Jephson to accompany him and his bride on their honeymoon in Switzerland.† With the deaths of Stairs, Nelson, and Parke, Stanley came to regard Jephson with special affection, the only other surviving officer from his last African adventure.

Like Stanley, Jephson lectured extensively about his experiences on the expedition, and while in San Francisco on an American tour, he met and fell in love with a young woman named Anna Head. When he asked her to marry him, however, her father refused to allow the engagement. A successful, hard-nosed businessman, he was unimpressed by Jephson's African exploits, seeing only a young man in questionable health with scant prospects for a career. Though she truly loved Jephson, Anna Head was a dutiful daughter and refused to disobey her father, thinking that, with time, he might change his mind. He did, but it took twelve years. Finally, on his deathbed, Addison Head gave his blessing to the marriage.

While Jephson waited faithfully for Anna Head, he had made repeated attempts to return to Africa, pursuing various governmental and commercial positions that would take him there. He had offers both from Mackinnon and the IBEAC and from King Leopold, but he could never stay healthy long enough to take advantage of them. He eventually spent six years as a queen's messenger, a relatively menial governmental appointment, but even this proved too taxing, so he accepted a largely ceremonial position as an usher at court. Luckily, Prime Minister Salisbury arranged for him to receive an annual pension of £400, which allowed him at least to maintain himself respectably.

After her father's death, Anna Head and her mother came to London, only to find Jephson in the hospital. He was very sick, and his

---

*Three months after his return to London, Stanley married Dorothy Tennant, a woman in her midthirties, from a wealthy and prominent family. He had proposed to her before the expedition and been turned down. After the expedition, she pursued him. She became his devoted champion and fiercest defender for the rest of his life and beyond.

†The newlyweds found themselves staying in the same hotel as Richard Burton and his wife. The two explorers spent many hours together, reminiscing and swapping African stories.

convalescence proceeded slowly. It took almost a year for him to recover sufficiently to be married. As a wedding present, Stanley and his wife gave them a soup tureen and ladle, with an inscription that read, in part, "To A. J. Mountenay Jephson (Boubarika). His loyalty and devotion, his unflagging zeal and courage—even in our darkest days—won my admiration and warm affection."

At Stanley's urging, Jephson wrote a book, *Emin Pasha and the Rebellion at the Equator*, detailing his disastrous provincial tour with Emin Pasha. Stanley wrote the introduction. The book filled an important gap of the record of the expedition; at the same time, Jephson painted a portrait of Emin Pasha that, while not devoid of admiration and even affection, reached harsh conclusions about his character and his conduct as governor.* In his closing paragraphs, Jephson wrote of Emin,

> A man with a kindly and generous mind, physically courageous, but morally a coward.
>
> A clever accomplished gentleman, enthusiastic for the science of natural history, but not of that firm temper required to lead men, or of that disposition to attract and sway them.
>
> A man whose natural kindness of heart is being constantly spoilt by his delicate susceptibility and childlike vanity.

Jephson and Anna Head's wedding finally took place in June 1904. After they had waited so long, it was a joyous occasion, but there was one sad note. While Jephson was recovering his health, Henry Stanley was battling what proved to be his final illness. Like Jephson, he suffered with recurrent malarial symptoms, as well as gastritis and other maladies, the legacy of four expeditions and more than fifteen years in the depths of Africa. At sixty-three, he was an old man whose prodigious strength had finally deserted him. He died on May 10, 1904, four weeks before Jephson's wedding.

In *In Darkest Africa*, Stanley had written, somewhat disingenu-

---

*Given the closeness that developed between Jephson and Stanley, it's likely that Stanley realized Jephson would judge Emin harshly in his account, which was no doubt one of the reasons he urged him to write it.

ously, about his disdain for honors, medals, and other forms of recognition:

> To one like me, what are banquets? A crust of bread, a chop, and a cup of tea, is a feast to one who, for the best part of twenty-three years, has not had the satisfaction of eating a shilling's worth of food a day. Receptions! They are the very honours I wish to fly from, as I profess myself slow of speech, and Nature has not fitted me with a disposition to enjoy them. Medals! I cannot wear them, the pleasure of looking at them is even denied me by my continual absence. What then? Nothing. No honour or reward, however great, can be equal to that subtle satisfaction that a man feels when he can point to his work and say, "See, now, the task I promised you to perform with all loyalty and honesty, and might and main, to the utmost of my ability, and God willing, is to-day finished."

There was one form of recognition, however, that he did covet. He let it be known that he would consider it his greatest honor to be buried in Westminster Abbey next to Livingstone, his hero. His widow, joined by Jephson, petitioned the dean, Joseph Robinson. To their dismay, the request was denied without comment, but in private correspondence, Robinson gave his reason: "the violence and even cruelty which marked some of his explorations, . . . contrasts with the peaceful successes of other explorers." The most peaceful of all was probably Livingstone.

Robinson did allow the funeral service to be held at Westminster ("secondary honors," he called it), but Henry Stanley was buried in a church cemetery near his home in Surrey. His widow commissioned a search on the plains of Dartmoor for a suitably impressive piece of granite to serve as his tombstone. The one she chose was a monolith more than twelve feet high and four feet across onto which she had carved a surprisingly simple inscription:

HENRY MORTON STANLEY
BULA MATARI
1841–1904
AFRICA

ON APRIL 26, 1890, as Henry Stanley was making his triumphant return to London, Emin Pasha was marching out of Bagamoyo at the head of an expedition almost as large as the one that had been sent for his relief some three and a half years before. His ultimate destination, at least according to his orders, was Uganda, but in retrospect it seems likely that his orders, as well as his itinerary, were of little importance to him. From the moment the expedition started, Emin was focused on collecting.

When he reached the German fort at Mpwapwa, he met Carl Peters speeding in the opposite direction. Peters was, in several key respects, Henry Stanley's German counterpart. Like Stanley, he was both an explorer and a colonizer. Since 1884, he had been working in East Africa to establish and extend German influence and pave the way for commercial development. In 1889, he had organized the German expedition to rescue Emin Pasha. Like Stanley's enterprise, Peters's effort was humanitarian on the face of it, but the humanitarianism concealed ambitious colonial and commercial agendas. Along with his search for Emin, Peters was particularly eager to try to extend the German sphere of influence into Uganda, Unyoro, and Equatoria, since none of those territories had been covered by the Anglo-German treaty of 1886. In this regard, Peters's agenda differed little from that of William Mackinnon, who, by sending Stanley to rescue Emin, had also hoped to gain the upper hand in the Equatoria sweepstakes.

Not long after he launched his expedition, Peters learned (by reading someone else's mail) that Stanley had already reached Emin and that Emin and Stanley were headed for the coast, having left Equatoria in chaos. With rescue no longer part of his mission, and Equatoria problematical at best, Peters headed for Uganda. When he and Emin met at Mpwapwa, he had in his possession a treaty signed by King Mwanga, who had been reinstalled on the throne, giving Germany suzerainty over Uganda. He was speeding back to Bagamoyo to announce his triumph.

Peters advised Emin to head for Tabora, an Arab stronghold to the south, which was not part of the itinerary Wissmann had given him. Peters reasoned that if Emin could establish German control there, he would then have a strong base of operations from which to move north into Uganda to reinforce the German presence there. Then, perhaps, he could move on to Equatoria, where he might even be able to hoist the German flag over his former province. What neither man (nor Wissmann) knew was that at that moment an addendum to the Anglo-German agreement was being negotiated in London and Berlin that would make all of their planning irrelevant.

Emin took Peters's advice and headed to Tabora, where the Arabs were surprisingly cooperative, agreeing to accept German authority if they could choose their own administrator. Emin promptly conveyed word back to Wissmann to send him fifty German flags. Wissmann's reply turned out to be a sharp reprimand, telling Emin he had no business being in Tabora and should get back to his mission at once. Emin headed north to Lake Victoria.

In the early fall, he reached the lake, where he learned that on July 1, 1890, the German and British governments had signed a second treaty, or "settlement," regarding East Africa, which extended the boundaries of the agreement of 1886 due west across Lake Victoria. With the stroke of a pen, Uganda, Unyoro, and Equatoria were all in the British sphere. In the blink of an eye, there was nothing left for Emin (or Peters or Wissmann) to claim—no flags to hoist, no treaties to sign—nothing. For all practical purposes, Emin's mission no longer existed. He should have turned back for Bagamoyo, but there was nothing for him to go back to. He didn't want to become an administrator, a shuffler of papers in a dreary German colonial outpost. For Emin, there was only one direction to go—farther.

After spending three months supervising the construction of a station at Bukoba, on the southwestern shore of Lake Victoria (just on the German side of the new border), he left half of the soldiers in his expedition, including their German lieutenant, and he and Stuhlmann took off with a caravan of almost five hundred people, more than half of them women and children. They were headed for Karagwe and then to Ruanda, or perhaps to Lake Edward and then Lake Albert and Emin's old stomping grounds—Emin wasn't sure. Perhaps they would eventually go to "the hinterlands of the Cameroons," whatever that meant.

It probably didn't matter that much to Emin, as long as there was collecting to be done and no one telling him what to do. What he seemed to want more than anything was to be left alone.

Emin decided to go to the lakes, a clear sign that he saw himself as a free agent, since the new Anglo-German agreement put the lakes squarely in the British sphere. While en route, a messenger arrived from Wissmann, with an order for Emin to return to Bagamoyo immediately. He ignored it.

Whether deliberately or not, Emin's route retraced some of the footsteps of Stanley's expedition, tracking along the Ruwenzori Mountains, then through the valley of the Semliki River. He encountered some Manyuema ivory hunters who told him about clashes they had recently had with soldiers to the north, in the area near Mazamboni's. From their description, Emin deduced that some of his former troops must have still been there, and, indeed, when he reached Mazamboni's, he found Selim Bey and the remnants of the M'swa garrison.

It was to be a bittersweet reunion. At first, Selim was overjoyed because he thought Emin and his caravan had been sent by the khedive to relieve him, the same persistent delusion that had caused so many problems for Emin (and Stanley and Jephson) before. When he learned that Emin no longer served the khedive and had, in fact, changed his allegiance to Germany, Selim was indignant. When Emin further suggested that Selim and his band join with him and march under the kaiser's flag (free agent or not, he still considered it better to march under the German flag than under no flag at all), Selim refused to have anything more to do with him.

In moving on toward Lake Albert, Emin deliberately chose a route that took him into the Ituri forest, where Stanley had suffered so much. Emin and Stuhlmann found the Ituri to be a collector's cornucopia, full of flora and fauna they had never seen, and they plunged into it like delighted schoolchildren. It wasn't long, however, before the forest began to take its inevitable toll. There wasn't enough to eat, and the perpetual gloom drove some in their caravan to desert. Then the forest dwellers began harassing them with poisoned skewers in the ground and poisoned arrows in the air. Just like Stanley's, Emin's expedition was soon falling apart in the forest. Emin decided to go back to Mazamboni's.

No sooner did they reach Mazamboni's than an epidemic of small-pox broke out. Emin now split the expedition, which at that point numbered between four and five hundred men, women, and children. He separated all those not yet infected and sent them with Stuhlmann to set up another camp several miles to the south. Their agreement was that if Emin didn't show up within a couple of months, Stuhlmann was to take his group back to Bukoba.*

For six months, Emin ministered to the sick as best he could, but dozens of them died anyway. By the time the disease had run its course, Emin no longer had an expedition; he had a few emaciated survivors and his personal baggage. Stuhlmann was long gone; so was Selim Bey, who had thrown his lot in with an expedition from Mackin-non's IBEAC, under the command of Frederick Lugard, which had shown up while Emin was tromping around in the Ituri. There was nothing to do but go on, so Emin and his tiny, ragged band of follow-ers went west—into the heart of Manyuema country.

Near Stanley's old Fort Bodo, they found an Arab settlement whose headman was none other than Ismaili, one of Kilonga-longa's subcom-manders who had made life so miserable for Parke, Nelson, et al. at Ipoto. Ismaili agreed to provide a few porters and personally to escort the caravan as it moved deeper into Arab territory. Emin's health and spirit were clearly failing by this point, as evidenced by an entry from his notebook: "30 June 1892. Ipoto. Feet very much swollen, right hand incapacitated for work, eyesight half or three parts gone; is life worth living?"

Three months later, they were still in Manyuema territory when they reached a settlement named Kinene, after its chief. Emin noted that Kinene was actually a slave who belonged to a major Arab trader and slaver named Said bin Abed, who was almost as rich and powerful as Tippu Tib. Kinene's immediate superior, however, was a man

---

*When Stuhlmann eventually made his way back to the coast, he brought with him the data and specimens he and Emin had collected. It was, at the time, arguably the most valuable field research ever done in central Africa.

called Kibonge, who operated out of a station on the Congo River, approximately a hundred miles away. If Emin wanted to continue through this territory, he would need Kibonge's permission. To that end, Ismaili and a man named Mamba were dispatched to obtain the necessary documents. Emin settled in to wait at Kinene—and, of course, do some collecting.

Several days later, when the two men returned, Mamba presented himself at Emin's hut and handed him a letter from Kibonge. Permission had been granted. Unbeknownst to Emin, however, Ismaili also had a letter, this one addressed to Kinene. In an account given to an interrogator after his arrest, almost two years later, Ismaili described what came next:

> On the verandah of the chief's house, Emin Pasha was seated, surrounded by a few of his soldiers. He was writing at his table, and many birds and bugs were scattered around. These he had caught coming from the Aruwimi. The first letter, which Mamba had brought, was in front of him; and he was laughing, and seemed in cheerful spirits at the thought of leaving next morning for Kibonge. Kinene came up with a few men who were carrying guns. Kinene had in his hand the letter which I had given him. He stopped near the Pasha and began reading to himself. When he had finished he said: "Pasha, as you are leaving tomorrow for a twelve days' march, don't you think you had better send your men into the plantations, and get bananas, manioc, and peanuts for the long march which you have before you? Tell your men to get all they wish; and I hope that you won't think of paying for them, as it is my present to you, and is in return for the many little things which you have given me and my women since you have been my guest." The Pasha looked up and thanked Kinene very much. He then told one of his orderlies to have the bugler call the men, which was done.
>
> When they arrived, Kinene said: "Tell the men to leave their arms on the side of the veranda, because if they go into the plantations carrying guns, the women working there will become frightened and run away." Thereupon Emin's men, numbering thirty or forty, placed their guns on the veranda and departed. The plantations were an hour's walk from the house. During the time it took to go to the plantations, Kinene talked to Emin, expressing his regret at his departure. Mamba

and I were standing next to the Pasha, and at a sign from the chief, we seized him by the arms as he was sitting in his chair. He turned, and asked what we meant. Kinene looked at him, and said, "Pasha, you have got to die." Emin turned, and exclaimed rather angrily: "What do you mean? Is this a joke? What do you mean by seizing me in this manner? What are you talking about my dying for? Who are you that you can give orders for a man to die?" Kinene replied: "I do not give the orders. I receive them from Kibonge, who is my chief; and when Kibonge gives an order, I obey it."

Three of Kinene's men came and assisted us in holding Emin, who was struggling to free himself and to get at his revolver lying on the table; but his efforts were fruitless, and we forced him back into his chair. Then Emin told Kinene that is was all a mistake, as he had just received a letter from Kibonge that morning saying that he should have safe-conduct to his village, and that the letter was on his table in front of him. Kinene replied, "Pasha, you read Arabic, don't you?"

"Yes."

"Then read this," holding the second letter close to Emin's eyes as the Pasha was nearly blind.

Emin read the letter, and saw that it was true. Drawing a long breath, he turned and said: "Well, you may kill me, but don't think that I am the only white man in this country. There are many others who will be willing to avenge my death: and let me tell you that in less than two years from now there won't be an Arab left in the entire country held by your people."

Emin showed no sign of fear but . . . when he spoke of having care taken of his daughter, two years of age, he trembled slightly. He said: "My child is not bad; she is good. Send her to Said bin Abed at Kibonge, and ask him to look out for her."*

At a sign from Kinene, the Pasha was lifted out of his chair, and thrown flat on his back. One man held each leg, and I held his head, while Mamba cut his throat. . . . Emin made no effort at resistance. His head was drawn back until the skin across his throat was tight, and

---

* Apparently, Emin had been involved with an African woman during his expedition. The child he referred to was theirs. When Emin left on his expedition, his other daughter, Farida, had been sent back to Germany, where she was cared for by Emin's sister, Melanie Schnitzer. Farida remained in Europe for the rest of her life, dying in 1923 in an influenza epidemic.

with one movement of the knife, Mamba cut the head half off. The
blood spurted over us and the Pasha was dead.

To prove that he had followed his orders, Kinene sent Emin's severed head to Kibonge. In the kind of ironic symmetry that history
sometimes provides, it was an exact duplication of the fate that had
befallen General Gordon at Khartoum. As the general had been taken,
so had his last lieutenant.

WHEN JOSEPH ROBINSON denied permission to bury Stanley in Westminster Abbey, it was, in its way, a kind of closure for an era that had
lasted almost exactly one hundred years. Throughout the nineteenth
century, the exploits of a succession of British explorers, including,
among others, Mungo Park, David Livingstone, James Grant, John
Speke, Richard Burton, Verney Cameron, John Kirk, Joseph Thom-
son, and Henry Stanley, fired the English imagination and gave a
veneer of nobility and even romance, whether justified or not, to the
English presence in Africa. Underneath the veneer, however, was a
shifting pattern of religious, commercial, political, and colonial agendas (for which Livingstone's "3 C's—Christianity, civilization, and
commerce"—provided a succinct motto), but that mattered little to
the people at home. England loved its heroes, and Africa provided a
steady supply of them.

Stanley was, arguably, the greatest explorer of them all. Only Livingstone spent more time in the bush, and no one could claim anything close to the number of "firsts" that belonged to him.
Remarkably, when he first went to Africa in 1868, the continent was
still more unknown than known, at least to Europeans. Most of the
interior had never been seen by white men. (In truth, much of it had
not been seen by Africans, either.) It was the Dark Continent not only
because of the skin color of many of its inhabitants but because so
much of it was an utter mystery to the outside world. Henry Stanley
did more to change that than any other man in history. Perhaps it was
appropriate, then, that at the end of the Emin Pasha Relief Expedition
there was almost nothing left to discover in Africa. In crossing the for-

bidding Ituri forest (three times!), Stanley had filled in the last great blank space on Europe's maps of Africa. True, there were still a few places that remained to be surveyed, measured, named, and claimed, but for all practical purposes, Africa was no longer a great unknown. In a span of only twenty years, it had evolved into a great opportunity.

In the decade that followed, during the so-called Scramble for Africa, that opportunity was ruthlessly exploited by a parade of nations, quasi-governmental enterprises, and individuals that continued well into the twentieth century, a parade whose malignant legacy haunts the continent to this day. Stanley was their point man and drum major. Bula Matari was more than a Breaker of Stones; he and his ilk broke Africa wide open, and no one has yet found a way to put it back together again.

Selected Bibliography

Barttelot, Walter George. *The Life of Edmund Musgrave Barttelot . . . from his Letters and Diary.* London: Richard Bentley, 1890.

Batchelor, John, and Julie Batchelor. *In Stanley's Footsteps*: *Across Africa from West to East.* London: Blandford, 1990.

Brode, Heinrich. *Tippoo Tib: The Story of His Career in Central Africa Narrated from His Own Accounts.* Translated by H. Havelock. London: Edward Arnold, 1907.

Caillou, Andre. *South from Khartoum:The Story of Emin Pasha.* New York: Hawthorne Books, 1974.

Casati, Gaetano. *Ten Years in Equatoria and the Return with Emin Pasha.* Translated by Mrs. J. R. Clay and I. W. Savage Landor. 2 vols. London: Warne, 1891.

Conrad, Joseph. *Heart of Darkness.* Edited by D. C. R. A. Goonetilleke. Peterborough, Ont.: Broadview Press, 1995.

Doyle, A. Conan. *The Crime of the Congo.* New York: Doubleday, Page, 1909.

Farwell, Byron. *The Man Who Presumed: A Biography of Henry M. Stanley.* New York: W. W. Norton, 1957.

———. *Prisoners of the Mahdi.* New York: Harper & Row, 1967. Reprint, New York: W. W. Norton, 1989.

Felkin, Robert W. "The Position of Emin Bey." *Scottish Geographical Magazine* 7 (1886): 705–19.

Hall, Richard. *Stanley: An Adventurer Explored.* Boston: Houghton Mifflin, 1975.

Hassan, Vita. *Die Wahrheit über Emin Pascha.* Berlin: Reimer, 1893.

Hochschild, Adam. *King Leopold's Ghost: A Story of Greed, Terror, and Heroism in Colonial Africa.* Boston: Houghton Mifflin, 1999.

Jameson, James S. *The Story of the Rear Column of the Emin Pasha Relief Expedition.* Edited by Mrs. James S. Jameson. New York: John W. Lovell, 1890. Reprint, New York: Negro Universities Press, 1969.

Jephson, A. J. Mounteney. *Emin Pasha and the Rebellion at the Equator.* London: Sampson Low, Marston, Searle and Rivington, 1890.

———. *The Diary of A. J. Mounteney Jephson: Emin Pasha Relief Expedition, 1887–1889.* Edited by Dorothy Middleton. Cambridge: Cambridge University Press, 1969.

Jones, Roger. *The Rescue of Emin Pasha: The Story of the Emin Pasha Relief Expedition, 1887–1889.* New York: St. Martin's Press, 1972.

Junker, Wilhelm. *Travels in Africa during the Years 1882–1886.* Translated by A. H. Keane. London: Chapman & Hall, 1892.

Lewis, David Levering. *The Race to Fashoda: European Colonialism and African Resistance in the Scramble for Africa.* New York: Weidenfeld and Nicholson, 1987.

Liebowitz, Daniel. *The Physician and the Slave Trade: John Kirk, the Livingstone Expeditions, and the Crusade against Slavery in East Africa.* New York: W. H. Freeman, 1999.

Manning, Olivia. *The Remarkable Expedition: The Story of Stanley's Rescue of Emin Pasha from Equatorial Africa.* New York: Atheneum, 1985.

McLynn, Frank. *Stanley: The Making of an African Explorer, 1841–1877.* London: Constable, 1989. Reprint, New York: Cooper Square Press, 2000.

———. *Stanley, Sorcerer's Apprentice.* London: Constable, 1991.

———. *Hearts of Darkness: The European Exploration of Africa.* New York: Carroll & Graf, 1993.

Moorehead, Alan. *The White Nile.* London: Hamish Hamilton, 1960.

———. *The Blue Nile.* New York: Harper & Row, 1962.

Officer, Laurence R. "Exchange rate between the United States dollar and the British pound, 1791–2000." *Economic History Services,* EH. Net, 2001. www.eh.net/hmit/exchangerates/pound.php.

Pakenham, Thomas. *The Scramble for Africa, 1876–1912.* London: George Weidenfeld & Nicholson, 1991.

Parke, Thomas Heazle. *My Personal Experiences in Equatorial Africa as Medical Officer of the Emin Pasha Relief Expedition.* London: Sampson Low, Marston, Searle and Rivington, 1891.

Peters, Carl. *New Light on Darkest Africa: Being the Narrative of the German Emin Pasha Expedition. . . .* Translated by H. W. Dulcken. London: Ward, Lock, 1891.

Quammen, David. "Megatransect I, II, & III." *National Geographic Magazine,* October 2000, March 2001, August 2001.

Richards, Charles, and James Place, eds. *East African Explorers.* Rev. ed., Nairobi: Oxford University Press, 1967.

Schweinfurth, George, et al., eds. *Emin Pasha in Central Africa: Being a Collection of His Letters and Journals.* Translated by Mrs. R. W. Felkin. London: George Philip, 1888.

Schweitzer, George. *Emin Pasha: His Life and Work.* Edited by R. W. Felkin. 2 vols. Westminster: Archibald Constable, 1898.

Smith, Iain R. *The Emin Pasha Relief Expedition, 1886–1890.* London: Oxford University Press, 1972.

Stairs, William G. *Victorian Explorer: The African Diaries of Captain William G. Stairs, 1887–1892.* Edited by Janina M. Konczacki. Halifax: Nimbus, 1994.

Stanley, Henry M. *In Darkest Africa; or, The Quest, Rescue, and Retreat of Emin, Governor of Equatoria.* 2 vols. London: Sampson Low, Marston, Searle and Rivington, 1890.

Stanley, Lady Dorothy, ed. *The Autobiography of Sir Henry Morton Stanley.* London: Sampson Low, Marston, Searle and Rivington, 1909.

Stanley, Richard, and Alan Neame, eds. *The Exploration Diaries of H. M. Stanley.* London: William Kimber, 1962.

Stuhlmann, Franz. *Mit Emin Pascha ins Herz von Afrika.* Berlin: Reimer, 1894.

———, ed. *Die Tagebücher von Dr. Emin Pascha.* 5 vols. Brunswick, Berlin, and Hamburg: Westermann, 1917–27.

Swann, Alfred J. *Fighting the Slave Hunters of Central Africa.* London: Frank Cass, 1910.

Symona, A. J. A. *Emin, Governor of Equatoria.* London: Falcon Press, 1950.

Troup, John Rose. *With Stanley's Rear Column.* London: Chapman and Hall, 1890.

Twain, Mark [Samuel Clemens]. *King Leopold's Soliloquy.* Boston: R. Warren, 1905. Reprint. New York and Berlin: Seven Seas Books, 1994.

Ward, Herbert. *My Life with Stanley's Rear Guard.* New York: Charles L. Webster, 1891.

Werner, J. R. *A Visit to Stanley's Rear Guard.* Edinburgh and London: William Blackwood, 1899.

White, Stanhope. *Lost Empire on the Nile: H. M. Stanley, Emin Pasha and the Imperialists.* New York: Roy Publishers, 1969.

Whitley, W. H., trans. "Maisha ya Hamed bin Mohammed el Murjebi yaani Tippu Tib." (Tippu Tib's autobiography: Swahili text with English translation.) Nairobi: East African Literature Bureau, 1959.

Illustration Credits

For information on sources, see the Selected Bibliography.

First Insert

Henry M. Stanley at age twenty: from Stanley, Lady Dorothy, ed., *The Autobiography of Sir Henry Morton Stanley.*

Stanley in 1895: from Stanley, Lady Dorothy, ed., *The Autobiography of Sir Henry Morton Stanley.*

Major Edmund Musgrave Barttelot: from Barttelot, *The Life of Edmund Musgrave Barttelot.*

James S. Jameson: from Jameson, *The Story of the Rear Column of the Emin Pasha Relief Expedition.*

Lieutenant William G. Stairs: from Stanley, Henry M., *In Darkest Africa.*

A. J. Mounteney Jephson: from Stanley, Henry M., *In Darkest Africa.*

Captain Robert H. Nelson: from Stanley, Henry M., *In Darkest Africa.*

Major Thomas Heazle Parke: from Stanley, Henry M., *In Darkest Africa.*

Hamed bin Muhammad: from Stanley, Henry M., *In Darkest Africa.*

William Bonny: from Stanley, Henry M., *In Darkest Africa.*

Herbert Ward: from Stanley, Henry M., *In Darkest Africa.*

John Rose Troup: from Stanley, Henry M., *In Darkest Africa.*

Emin Pasha in the uniform of a German officer: from Alan Moorehead, *The White Nile.*

The survivors at Zanzibar: from Stanley, Henry M., *In Darkest Africa.*

Second Insert

Attack at Avissiba: from Stanley, Henry M., *In Darkest Africa.*

Emin Pasha at home: from Mounteney, *Emin Pasha and the Rebellion at the Equator.*

John Rowlands: from Stanley, Lady Dorothy, ed., *The Autobiography of Sir Henry Morton Stanley.*

Major Barttelot's Christmas card: from Barttelot, *The Life of Edmund Musgrave Barttelot.*

"The most perfectly organized expedition . . .": from Stanley, Henry M., *In Darkest Africa.*

Hiram Maxim's gun: from Stanley, Henry M., *In Darkest Africa.*

The Advance: from Stanley, Henry M., *In Darkest Africa.*

Jephson rescues Nelson: from Stanley, Henry M., *In Darkest Africa.*

The long-awaited rendezvous: from Stanley, Henry M., *In Darkest Africa.*

Jameson's final voyage: from Jameson, *The Story of the Rear Column of the Emin Pasha Relief Expedition.*

Emin betrayed: from Jephson, *Emin Pasha and the Rebellion at the Equator.*

Native pygmies . . . : from Stanley, Henry M., *In Darkest Africa.*

"One is not able to relax . . .": from Stanley, Henry M., *In Darkest Africa.*

Acknowledgments

WE WOULD LIKE to thank David Kennard for bringing us together, and helping to shape the project, Michael Carlisle for believing in the project, and Michelle Tessler, who belies every canard ever uttered about agents. Our deepest appreciation goes to our editor, Star Lawrence, for sharing his wisdom and trusting us. Our thanks also to Roger Jones and Iain Smith, for treading this ground so ably before us, and to Thomas Pakenham and Alan Moorehead, for setting the standards for this kind of work. In addition, Dr. Liebowitz would also like to thank Dr. Stan Derezinski, Clinical Professor of Medicine, Stanford University, consultant in infectious diseases; Jacob Kyvungi of Bushcamps Safaris, Arusha, Tanzania, for guiding him to the pygmies of the Ituri Forest; and Debbie Lewis, for taking him to Bukoba.

Index